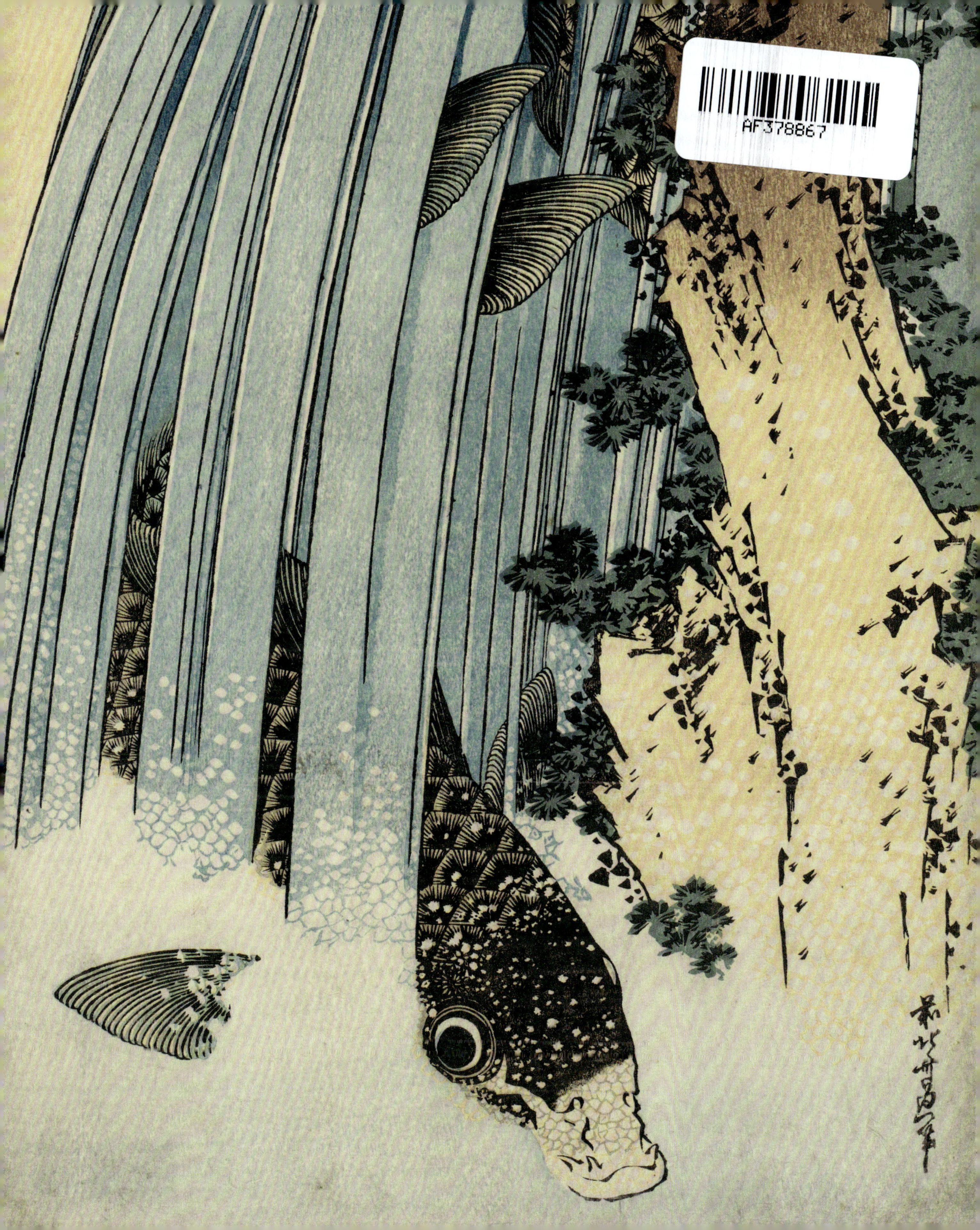

AF378867

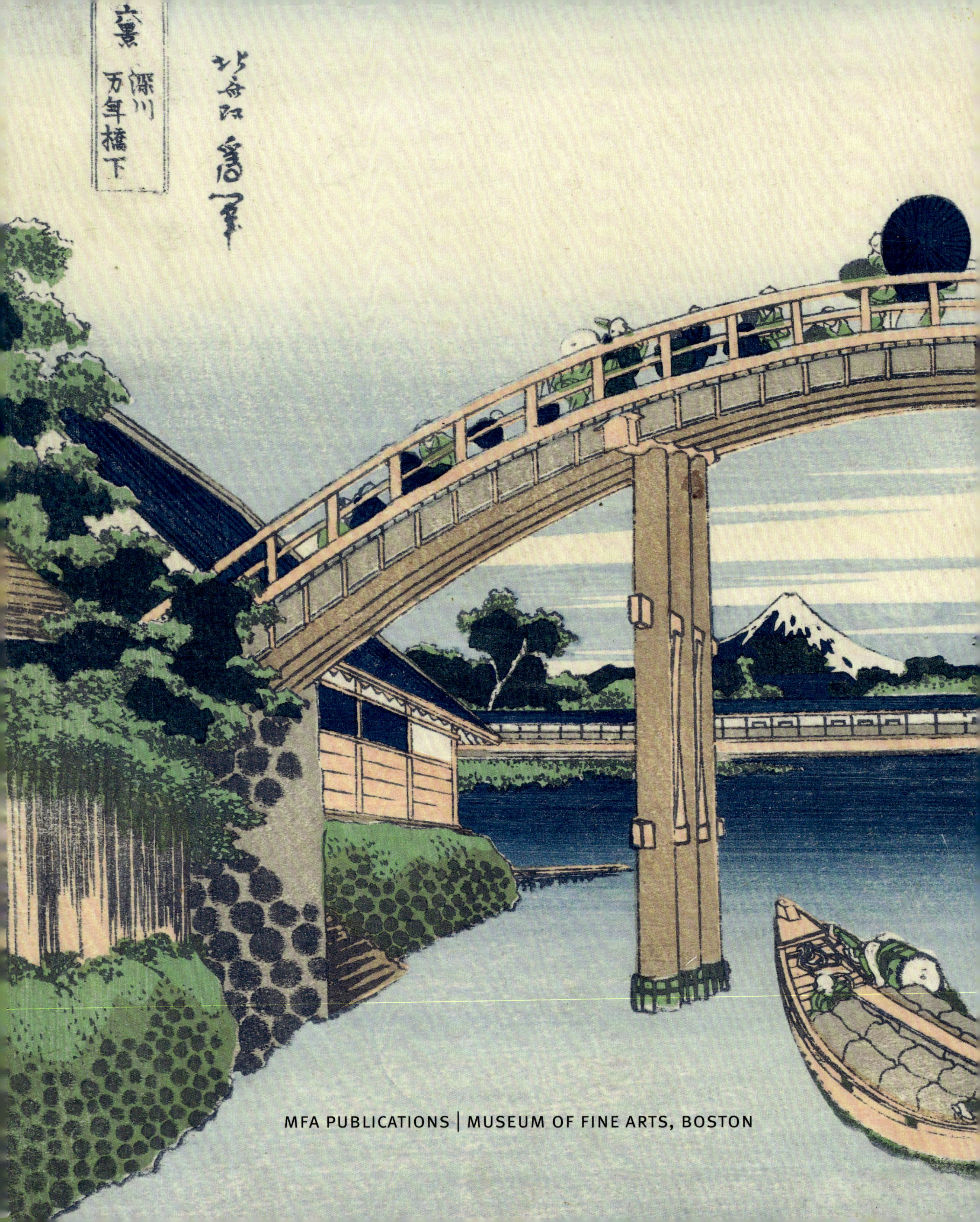
富嶽
深川
万年橋下
北斎画

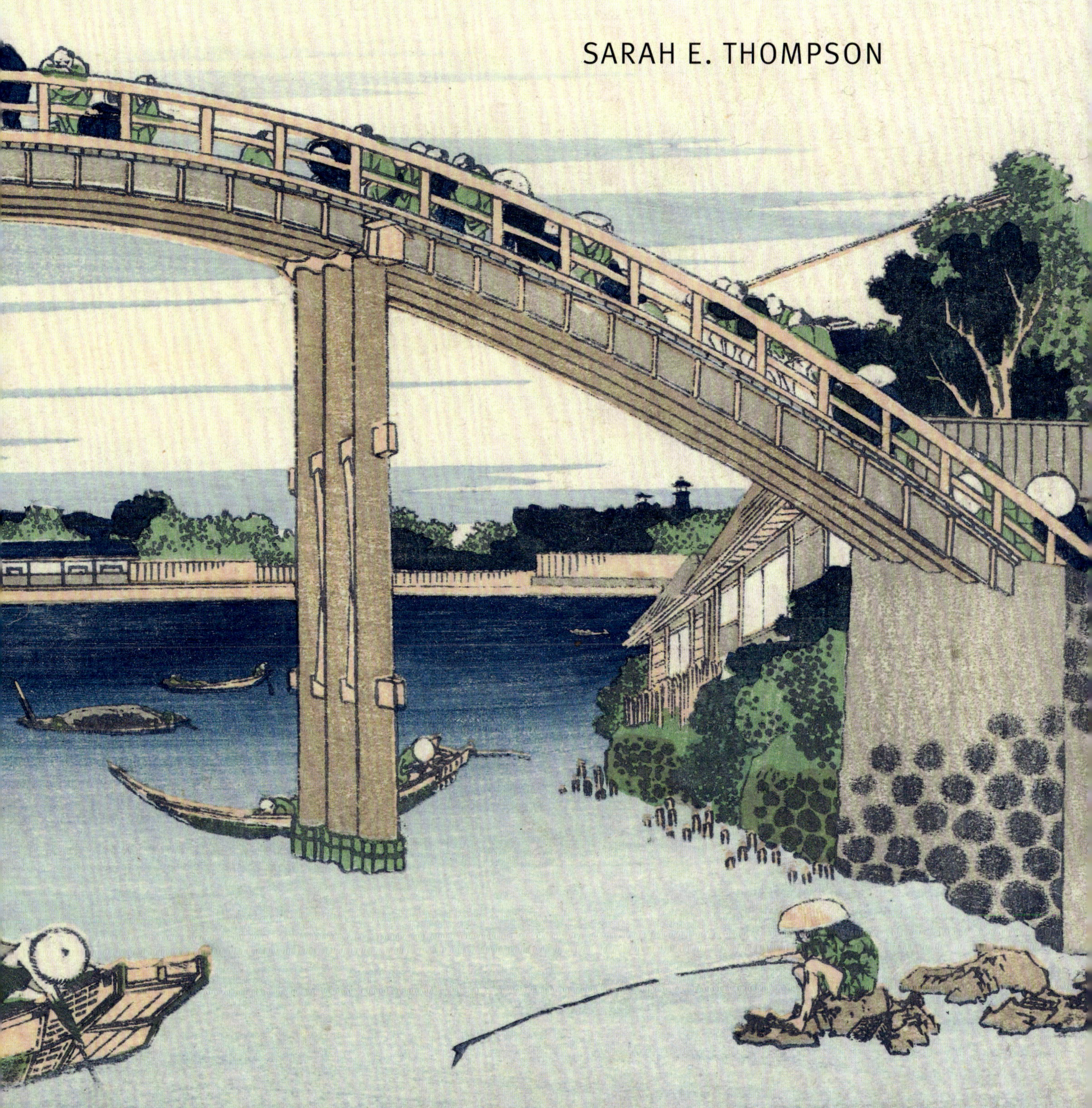

HOKUSAI

INSPIRATION AND INFLUENCE

SARAH E. THOMPSON

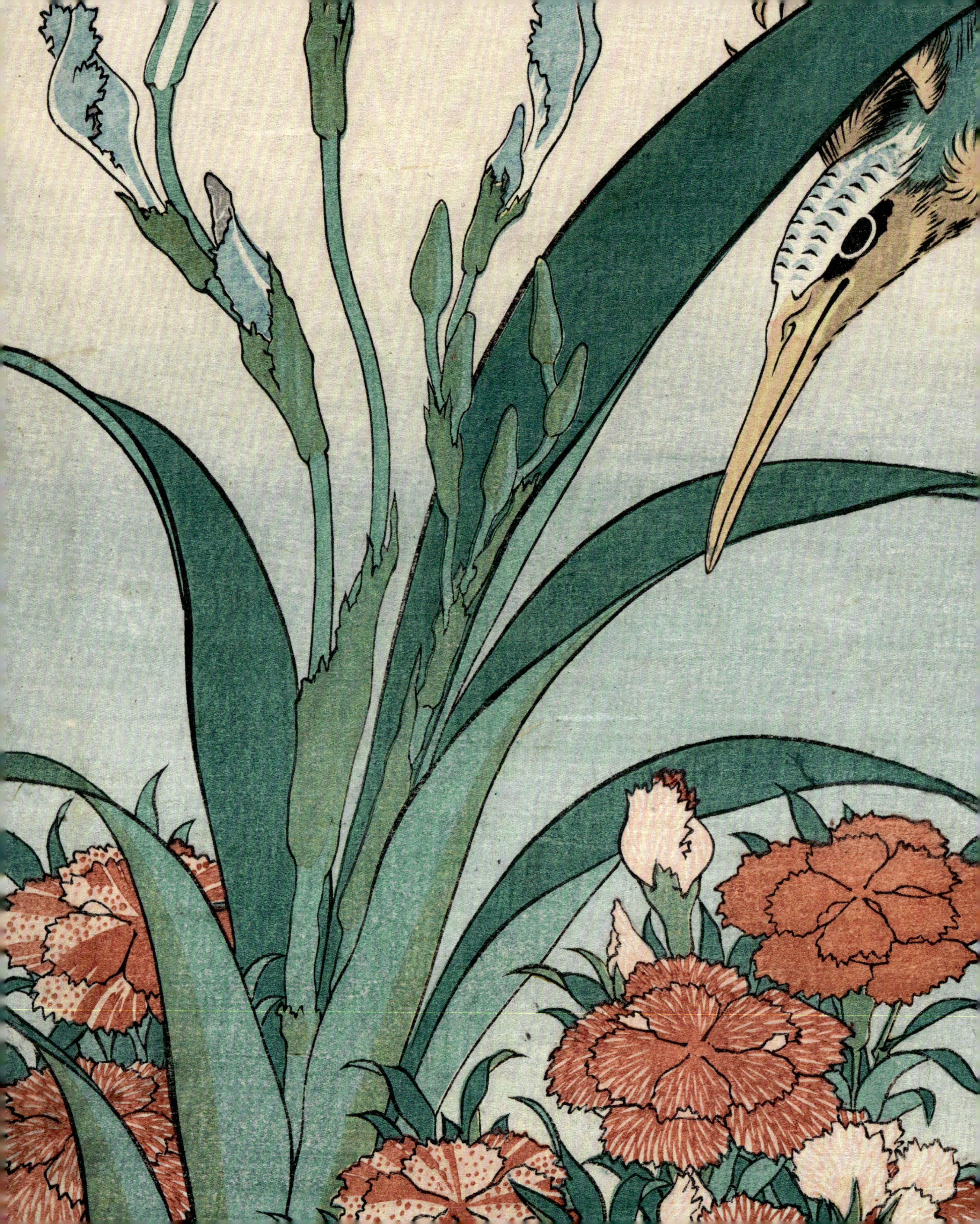

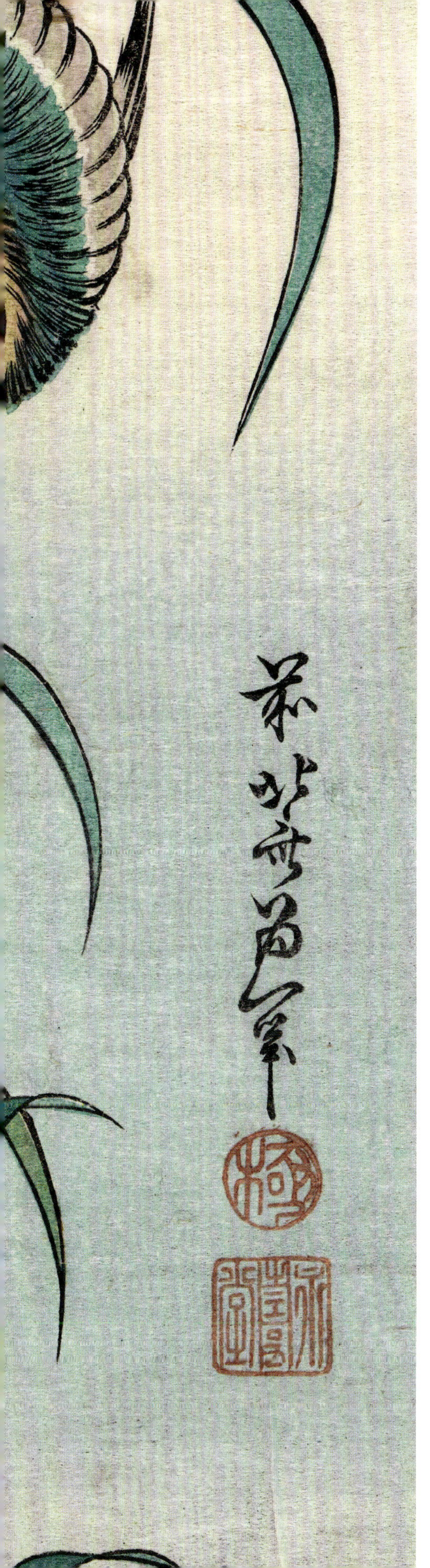

Contents

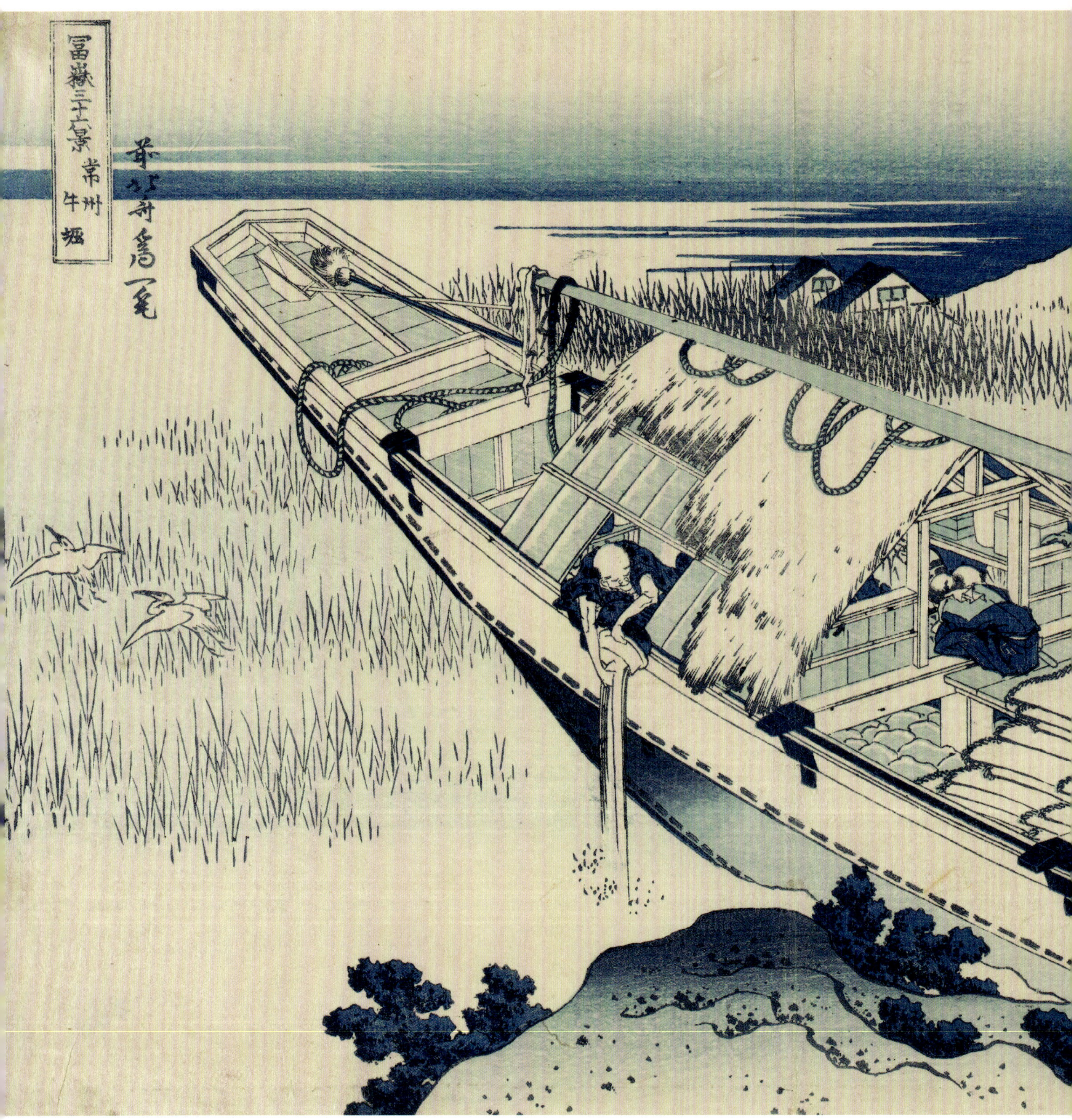

冨嶽三十六景　常州　牛堀
前北斎為一筆

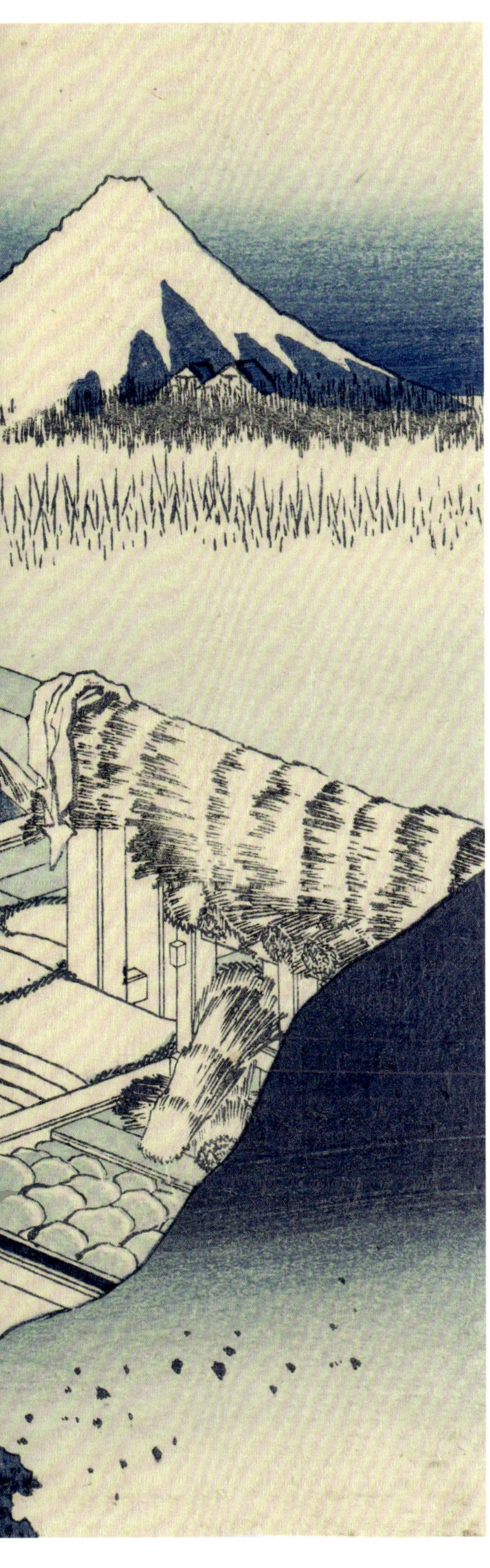

Director's Foreword

Hokusai: Inspiration and Influence looks at the endlessly inventive and versatile Katsushika Hokusai (1760–1849) from the viewpoint of fellow artists, including his own students and contemporaries, along with his many admirers in Japan and around the world from the late nineteenth century to the present. Beginning in his student days and throughout his long career, Hokusai helped to define, reinvent, and elevate every artform he engaged with: painting, book illustration, and above all ukiyo-e color woodblock prints. After Japan reopened to the world in the 1850s, his images traveled far and wide, sparking the global movement known in Europe as Japonisme and inspiring artists such as Monet and Van Gogh. His iconic images — especially the print nicknamed "The Great Wave" — continue to appear in present-day art in a dazzling array of forms, from sculpture, printmaking, and painting to anime and emojis.

The Museum of Fine Arts, Boston, is uniquely positioned to tell this story, thanks to the visionary scholars and donors who established its world-class collection of Japanese prints, at a time when popular ukiyo-e prints were sometimes dismissed as a lesser artform. Because they collected in depth and in breadth, the treasures they brought to the MFA are still yielding fresh insights more than a century after their foundational gifts.

We are pleased to acknowledge our exhibition sponsor, UNIQLO USA, with additional support from the Jean S. and Frederic A. Sharf Exhibition Fund, the Museum Council Artist in Residency Program Fund, the Dr. Terry Satsuki Milhaupt Fund for Japanese Textiles, the MFA Associates/MFA Senior Associates Exhibition Endowment Fund, and the Patricia B. Jacoby Exhibition Fund. Generous support for this publication was provided by the Andrew W. Mellon Publications Fund.

I invite viewers of the exhibition and readers of this volume to enjoy this exploration of the origins and enduring appeal of Hokusai's delightful and inspiring art.

MATTHEW TEITELBAUM
Ann and Graham Gund Director, Museum of Fine Arts, Boston

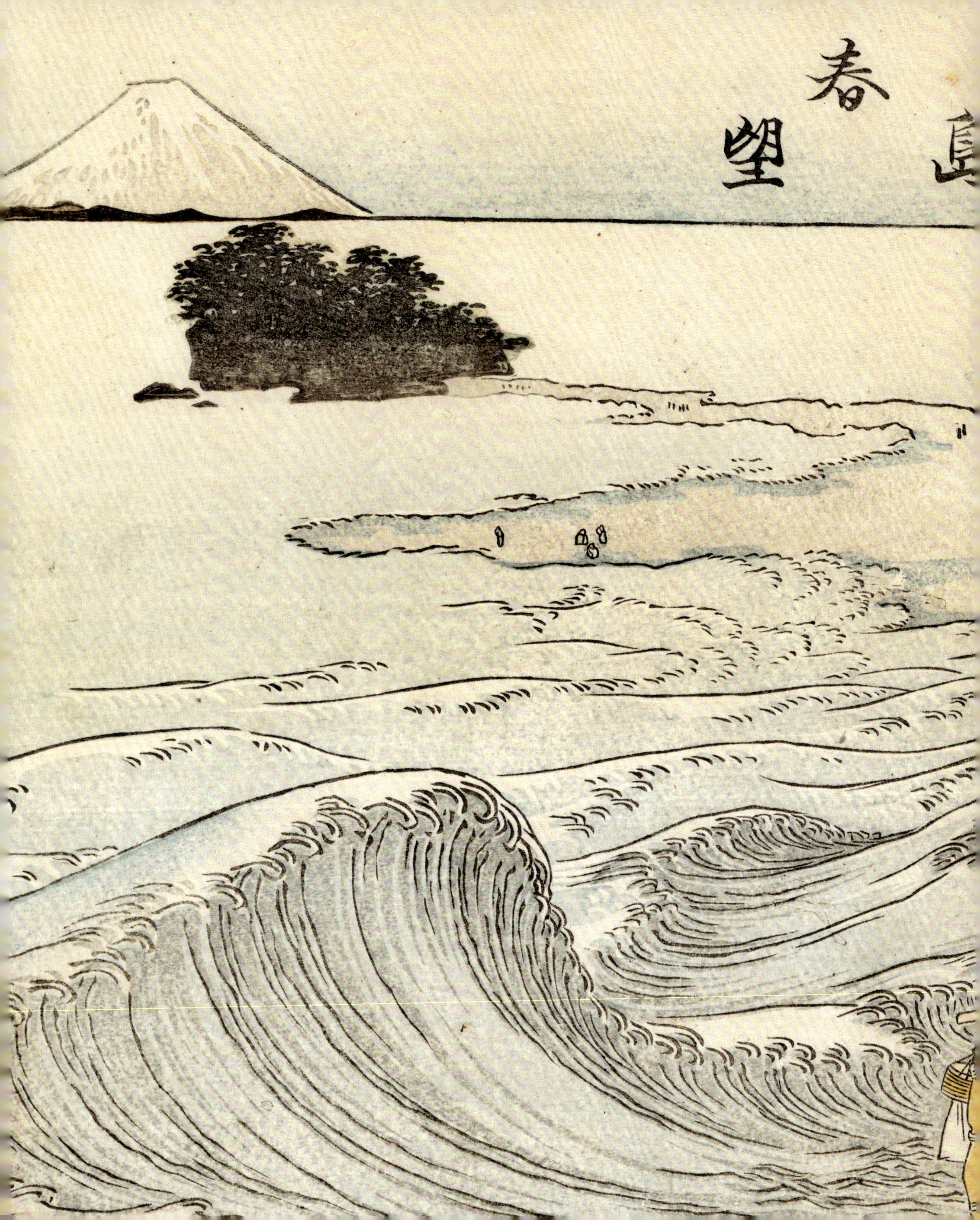

眞
春望

Hokusai's Sources of Inspiration

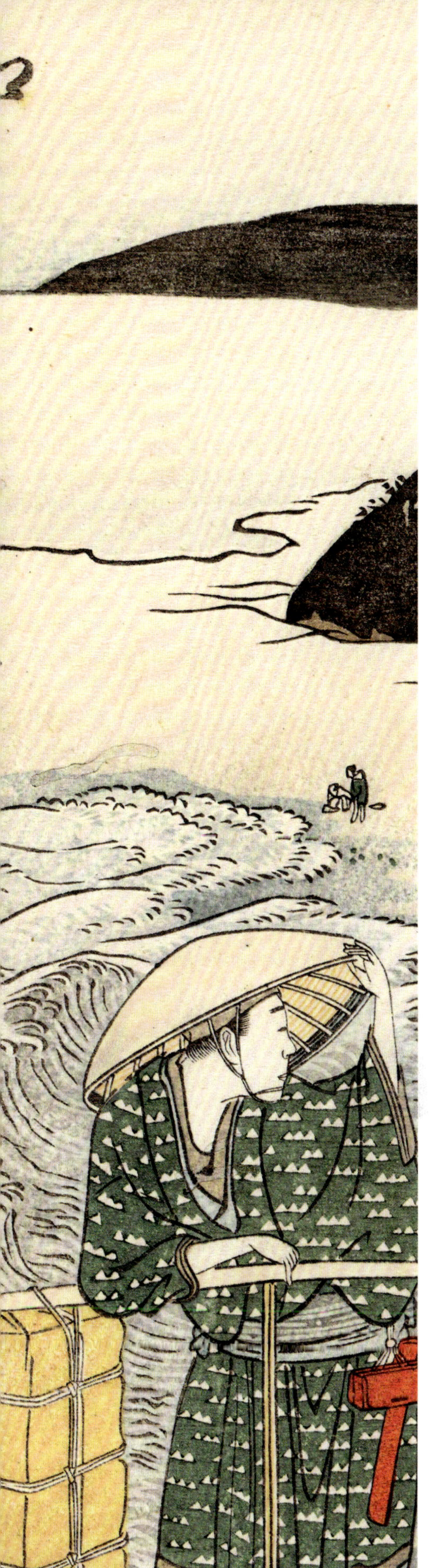

THE GREAT PAINTER, book illustrator, and print designer Katsushika Hokusai (1760–1849) has become the best known of all Japanese artists and one of the most famous and influential artists in the world. He was a key figure in the Japonisme movement in late nineteenth-century Europe, and his iconic images — especially the color woodblock print nicknamed "The Great Wave" — are frequently evoked in present-day art in both serious and frivolous forms. Stylized versions of the Wave have been used as emoji in more than a dozen different text messaging systems, and the visual image is familiar even to people who have never heard of the original artist.

Numerous books in many languages, and exhibitions at museums around the globe, have examined Hokusai's career in detail. This book and the exhibition it accompanies look at Hokusai from the viewpoint of fellow artists who incorporated lessons learned from him into their own work. These artists include Hokusai's own students, and the students of his students; his contemporary rivals, especially the Utagawa school artists, who emulated Hokusai's bestselling print designs and added their own flourishes; and his many posthumous admirers working in a wide range of media, in Japan and around the world, from the late nineteenth century to the present. The theme of artists learning from artists begins with Hokusai's early career, as he learned from his own teacher and other artists as well, synthesizing these influences into a multifaceted style that he passed on to his successors.

One source of the great appeal of Hokusai's works is his eclecticism. Trained in the ukiyo-e school, he was also well aware of other schools of art and incorporated influences from them into his mature style. His range of subject matter included not only scenes of contemporary life (the mainstay of earlier ukiyo-e), but also landscapes, nature studies, and scenes from history, literature, and folklore — something to please almost everyone. Within the large body of work that he produced during his long professional career, his two greatest hits, which made him famous in Japan during his lifetime and around the world shortly after his death, were the multivolume picture book *Hokusai Sketchbooks* (*Hokusai manga*), originally published in 1814–19, and the series of color prints *Thirty-Six Views of Mount Fuji*, published in the early 1830s, when he was already past seventy.

The term *ukiyo-e* means literally "Pictures of the Floating World," as the main subject matter of the paintings, prints, and printed books created by ukiyo-e artists was the "Floating World" of urban popular culture that was enjoyed by the newly affluent and literate middle class that flourished in large Japanese cities during the Edo period (1615–1868). Hokusai, himself a member of this class, had been adopted by his childless uncle, a prosperous maker of fine metal mirrors for the court of the shogun, the head of the elite warrior clans who ruled the country in the name of the emperor. As a teenager, he left his uncle's home and is said to have worked at various jobs, including carving wooden blocks for printing and working in a bookstore. At nineteen, he joined the studio of Katsukawa Shunshō (1726–1792), the leading ukiyo-e artist of the day.

In Edo-period Japan, the various schools of art were organized into clan-like structures — sometimes actual families related by blood or adoption, and sometimes groupings of a master artist in the "parent" role and numerous students who related to the master as "children" and to one another as older or young siblings. The typical method of instruction was for the master to make a drawing while students watched; they would then copy the master's work as closely as possible and receive his critique of their efforts. The students might also copy older works by their teacher's teacher or other artists in the quasi-familial lineage. After mastering the techniques of their chosen school, students would move on to creating compositions of their own. The junior artists in a large studio would assist the master in his projects, and he in turn would introduce them to potential patrons.

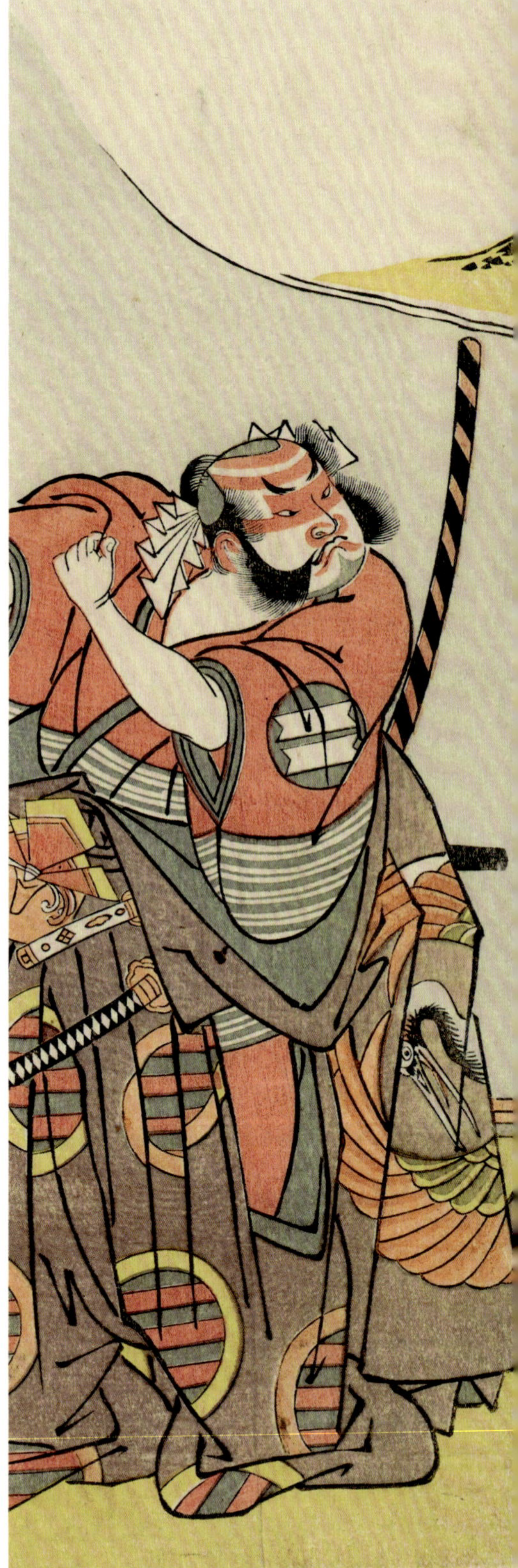

SHUNSHŌ (DETAIL, NO. 3)

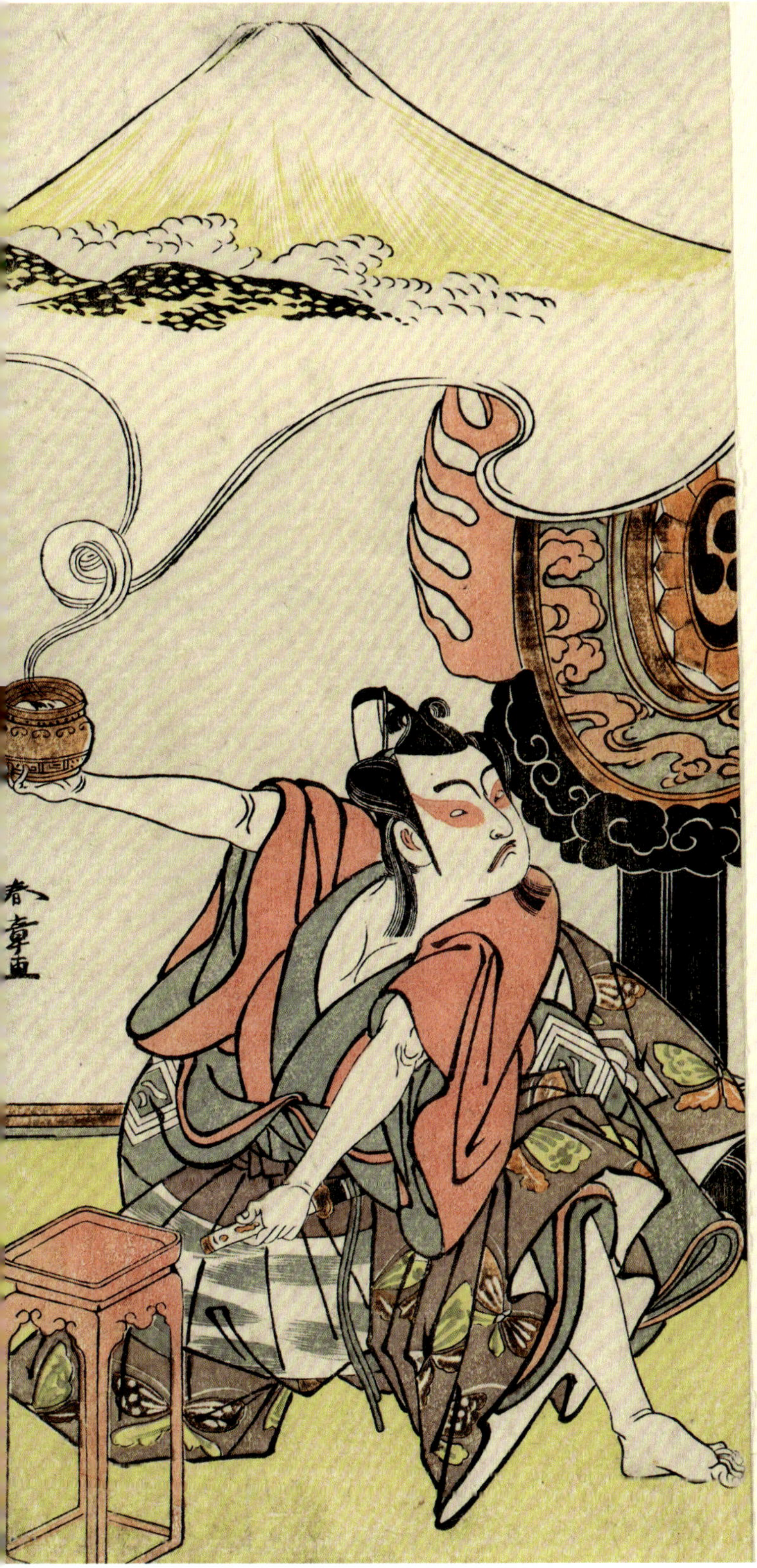

春章画
春章画

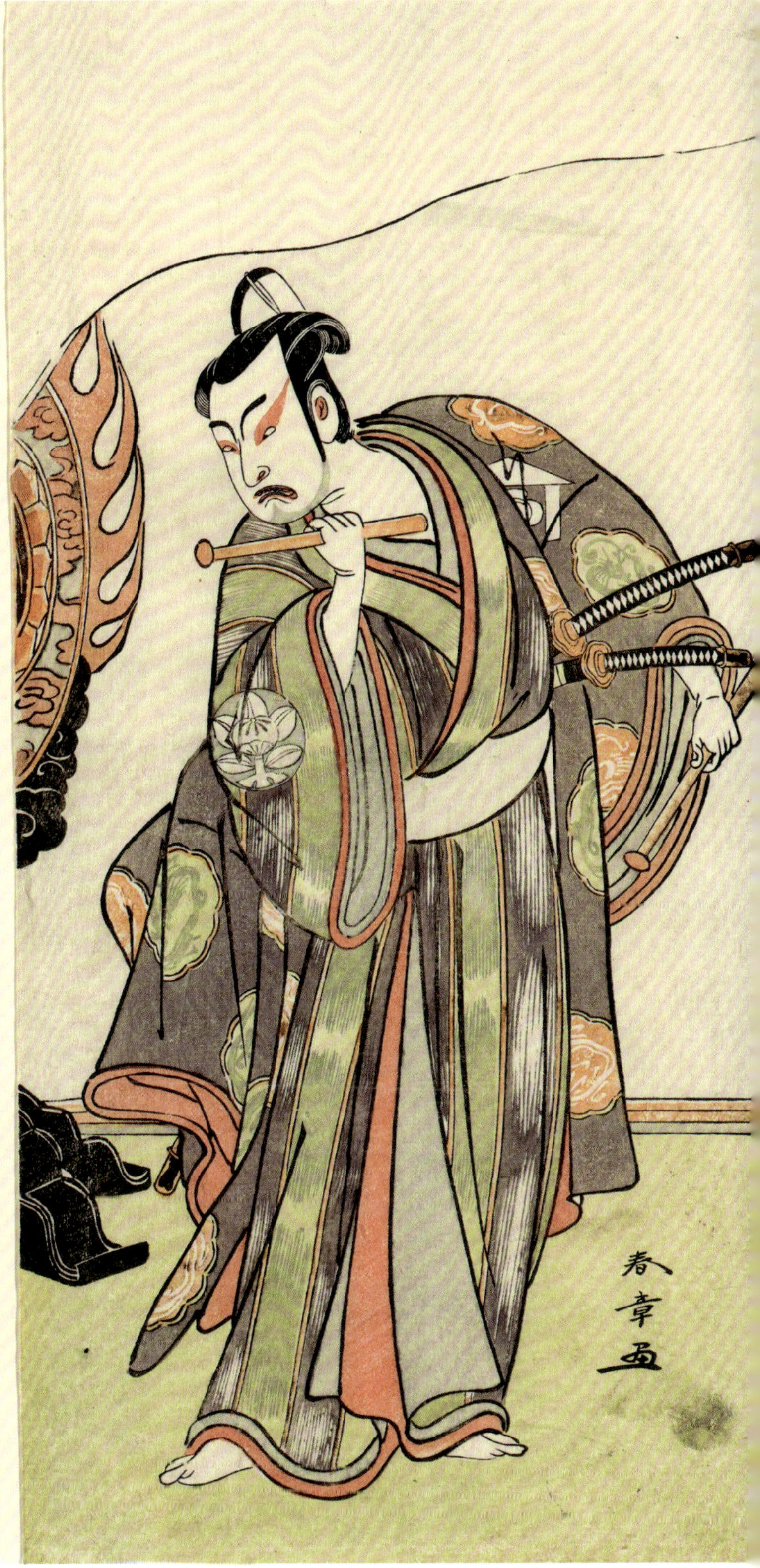

Artists signed their work not with their everyday, legal names but with an assortment of art names that generally indicated their lineage or affiliation and could change from time to time. Hokusai is known to have used some thirty different names in the course of his long career. While in the studio of Katsukawa Shunshō, he was known as Katsukawa Shunrō, an art name that included the family name of his teacher (the surname comes first in Japanese) and a personal name that incorporated part of his teacher's name (*shun*). Later, after Shunshō's death, he left the Katsukawa school and stopped using the name, choosing a series of other art names. For convenience, he is referred to as Hokusai because that was the name that he chose as his main signature when he first became an independent artist unaffiliated with any other school.

The ukiyo-e school was closely connected to the printing industry. Paintings by artists of other schools were sometimes reproduced in printed art books, but the vast majority of book illustrations and especially single-sheet prints were designed by artists of the ukiyo-e school. In fact, the origins of the school in the late seventeenth century were closely linked to book publishing, when single-sheet pictorial prints were introduced around 1680 as a new product line for booksellers. Books and prints were commercial products, turned out as quickly and efficiently as possible by a collaborative production process. The artist contributed a drawing that was carved into a wooden printing block, destroying the original drawing in the process. For the full-color printing process that was perfected in 1765 (when the future Hokusai was five years old), one block was prepared for each color. The blocks were handed over to the printer, who inked each block, placed the paper facedown on it, and rubbed the back of the sheet with a flat pad known as a baren to transfer the ink. The entire process was coordinated by the publisher, who hired the artist, blockcutter, and printer, and sold the finished prints in his bookstore, together with printed books, often illustrated, made by the same method.

Because ukiyo-e artists, unlike most of their contemporary counterparts in Europe, only made the drawings and did not do any printing, they could be enormously prolific. Hokusai is thought to have designed about three thousand prints during his lifetime; his output is actually comparatively low because for much of his career, especially during his later years, he concentrated on painting and book illustrations instead. By comparison, his younger contemporary Utagawa Kunisada (1786–1864), the most prolific (and financially successful) of all ukiyo-e artists, is thought to have designed as many as thirty thousand prints. Hokusai, however, may have had more bestselling individual works.

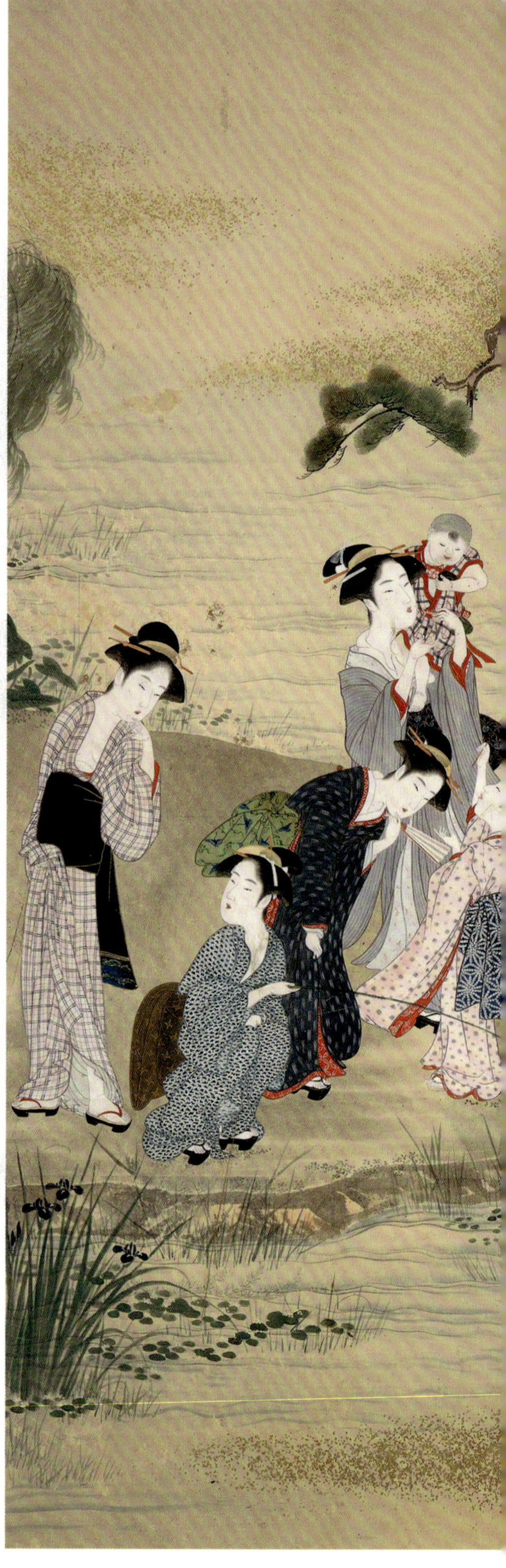

SHUNSHŌ (DETAIL, NO. 5)

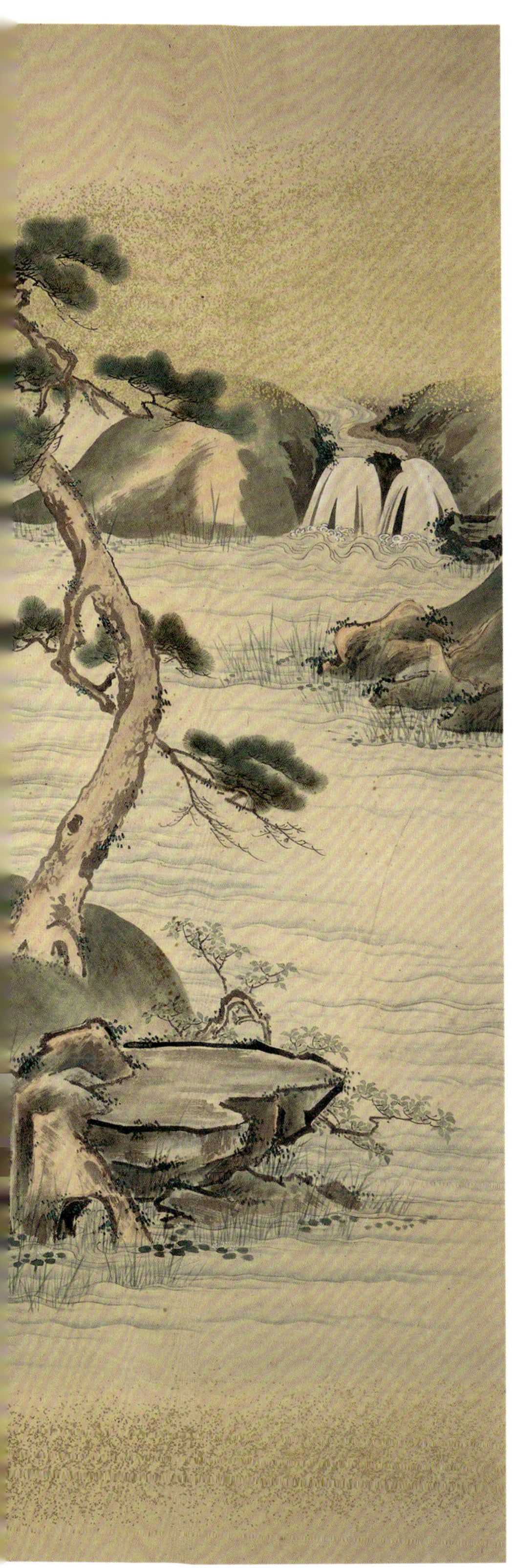

Definite figures are hard to come by, since the prints were not numbered or editioned as present-day artists' prints usually are. They were commercial products for sale to the general public, and publishers naturally wanted to sell as many as they could. During printing, the wooden blocks gradually wear down, so that the quality of the impressions slowly deteriorates and the original blocks become unusable after about five or six thousand impressions. For a series such as Hokusai's enormously popular *Thirty-Six Views of Mount Fuji*, there must originally have been several thousand impressions of each design. But since the prints were used as cheap, disposable decorations (much like posters today), only small numbers of them have survived, and fewer still are in good condition.

Katsukawa Shunshō's art focused on the two main themes that had been the traditional mainstay of ukiyo-e from the beginning: beautiful young women in fashionable clothing—the usual subjects of his paintings—and kabuki actors, most often depicted in woodblock prints. His student Shunrō, the future Hokusai, mastered both painting and print design during more than a decade as a junior Katsukawa artist. He followed a typical pattern of career development for an ukiyo-e artist, first drawing black-and-white illustrations for inexpensive printed books, then the cheaper kinds of color actor prints. Gradually the young artist would be allowed to design more expensive prints and books, which would be produced with more skillful blockcutting and printing. At the same time, he would learn to paint finely detailed, one-of-a-kind paintings, using expensive mineral pigments on paper or silk. Toward the end of a successful career, a master artist might turn over most commissions for print designs to his students while he concentrated on painting, the highest-status artistic activity. This was the pattern followed by Shunshō and some fifty years later by Hokusai as well.

Hokusai continued to use the painting skills learned from Shunshō throughout his life, and he passed them on to his own pupils. But he dropped the making of actor portraits almost completely after leaving the Katsukawa school in 1794. The few theatrical works that he produced in later years show that he was indeed able to draw the kind of realistic, recognizable portraits that had made Shunshō and his disciples the top designers of actor prints in the late eighteenth century. By the beginning of the nineteenth century, that position had been taken over by Utagawa Toyokuni (1769–1825), followed by his student Kunisada. Hokusai seems to have been content to leave the field of theatrical prints to the Utagawa school, though one can't help wondering whether the Katsukawa school might have been more competitive if he had remained a member.

The reasons for Hokusai's break with the Katsukawa school after the death of Shunshō are unknown, although there are various anecdotes and speculations. It is easy to imagine that the senior disciples of Shunshō may have been jealous of his abilities and eager to push him out. Or perhaps young Shunrō was considered disloyal to the Katsukawa school because of his broad interest in many forms of pictorial art, including other branches of ukiyo-e and even completely different schools of art.

During his Shunrō period, Hokusai is rumored to have taken lessons on the side from a painter of the Kano school. Its members, the official painters to the shogunate, worked mainly in a Chinese-derived style. Yet another anecdote suggests that after leaving the Katsukawa, he was briefly employed as an assistant to a Kano painter and then fired for insubordination. Because the Kano school controlled general art education, it is very possible that Hokusai had already received some instruction in Kano-style painting as a child. The repertoire of the Kano painters included subjects that were not common in ukiyo-e but that Hokusai excelled at in later life: landscapes, nature studies, and narrative scenes featuring Chinese figures.

A prominent feature of Hokusai's landscape prints is his use of Western-style perspective, with receding lines converging toward a vanishing point on the horizon — as opposed to traditional East Asian perspective, in which receding lines are parallel and more distant objects are shown higher up in the picture plane. This technique had been known in Japan since the 1740s, derived from both European prints and European-inspired Chinese prints. Since Japan during the Edo period was largely isolated from the outside world, with no foreign travel permitted for any Japanese and only a few Dutch and Chinese traders allowed to bring goods through the port of Nagasaki, foreign pictures were of great interest to Japanese artists. Perspective prints showing landscapes and cityscapes, sometimes intended for use in toy peepshows with imported Dutch lenses and sometimes simply to be enjoyed on their own, rode several waves of popularity in Japan.

In the 1780s, the young Hokusai designed a number of these works, mastering Western perspective in the process. Forty to fifty years later, he incorporated this compositional technique — now thoroughly familiar to his viewers — into his bestselling landscape designs, beginning with the series *Thirty-Six Views of Mount Fuji* in about 1830. Ironically, one of the reasons why his landscapes became so popular in Europe later in the century was that they were easily understandable in terms of Western visual conventions. Hokusai's models for his early perspective prints

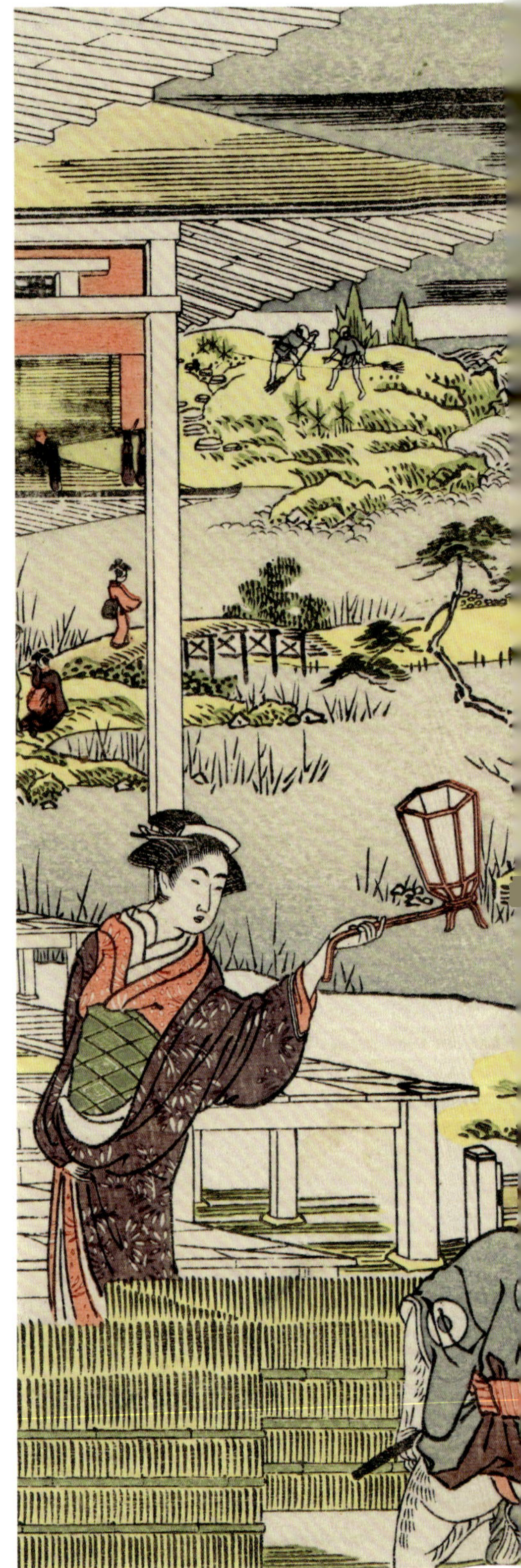

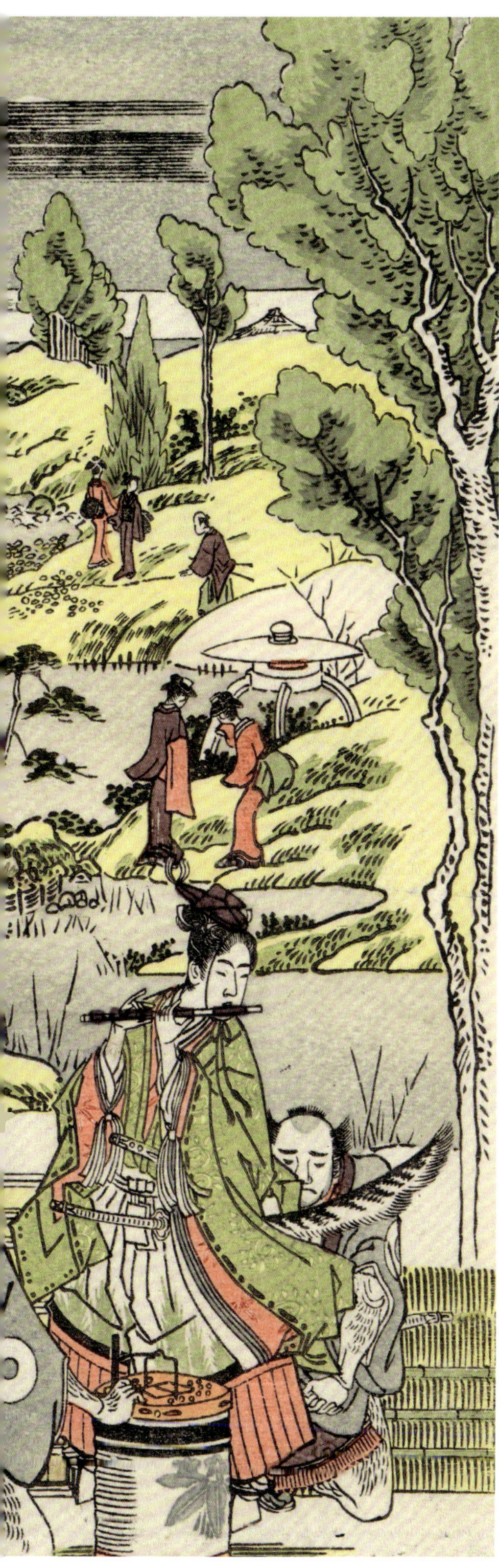

most likely included works of the 1770s and 1780s by Utagawa Toyoharu (1735–1814, the teacher of Utagawa Toyokuni) as well as actual Western prints and works by Japanese artists experimenting with the Western technology of copperplate engraving, notably Shiba Kōkan (1747–1818).

Hokusai made contact with yet another school of Edo-period Japanese painting through his first major job after leaving the Katsukawa school. In 1794 he was hired by the Tawaraya, a small family-run school whose head, Tawaraya Sōri, had died when his son was too young to take over. Hokusai was hired to train the heir and function as the acting head of the school, with permission to use the art name Sōri himself until passing it on to the son of the original Sōri. Happily, the arrangement worked well for all concerned and concluded amicably in 1798. The Tawaraya school, though eclectic in style (and thus a good match for Hokusai), was loosely affiliated with the larger Rimpa school, which had originated in Kyoto as a stylish updating of older Japanese painting styles. Hints of Rimpa influence in Hokusai's later work include swirling patterns of water and flowers depicted entirely in color, without the usual black outlines.

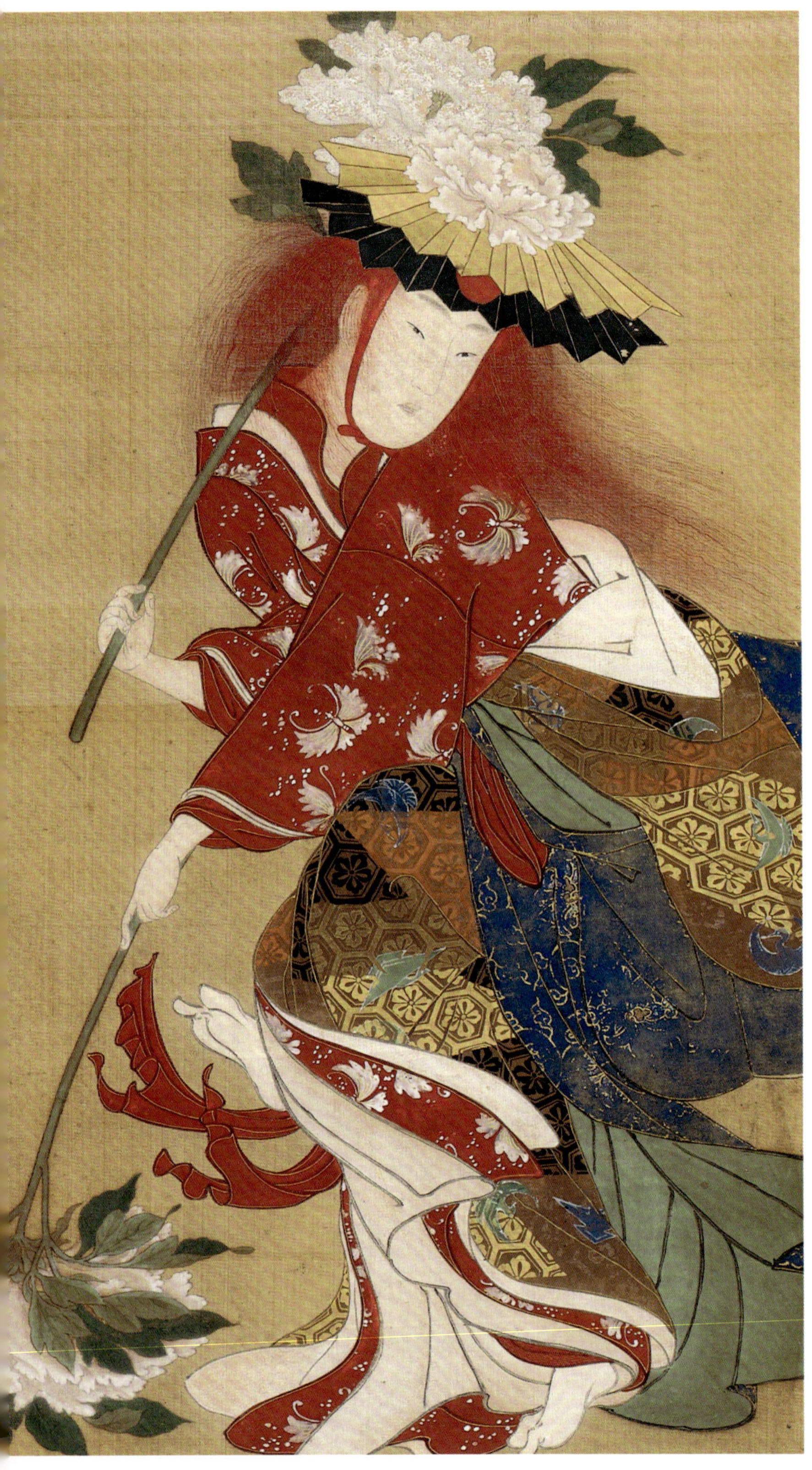

Hokusai's teacher, Katsukawa Shunshō, was famous for two kinds of works: exquisitely detailed paintings of women in fashionable clothing, made on commission for affluent patrons; and designs for woodblock prints of kabuki actors, which the publisher's workshop produced in multiple identical copies for sale to the general public. The young artist who would become Hokusai learned the techniques for both types of art and later passed them on to his own students, continuing the lineage of the ukiyo-e style in general and the Katsukawa school in particular.

In the hanging scroll painting by Shunshō, a beautifully dressed dancer performs the Lion Dance from the story of the Stone Bridge (*Shakkyō*), in which a Japanese Buddhist priest visiting China meets a magical lion that dances among the peonies beside a natural bridge deep in the mountains. The dancer's long red wig symbolizes the lion's mane, with a hat consisting of two fans topped by a peony blossom; the dancer holds long wands with more peonies that are waved during the graceful dance. Around the time that Shunshō made the painting, a hit version of the dance had been performed on the kabuki stage by a male actor who specialized in female roles (because women were forbidden to act publicly). The painting may represent him, or it may show a woman presenting the fashionable dance in a private performance.

Hokusai's painting, using the same materials and brush techniques, presents a romanticized image of a pretty country girl, for the pleasure of urban viewers. The women of Ohara, a rural area on the outskirts of Kyoto, often came into the city to sell bundles of firewood that they had gathered, wearing a distinctive costume that included leggings, laced sandals, and fingerless gloves. Similar figures appear in some of Hokusai's later landscape prints.

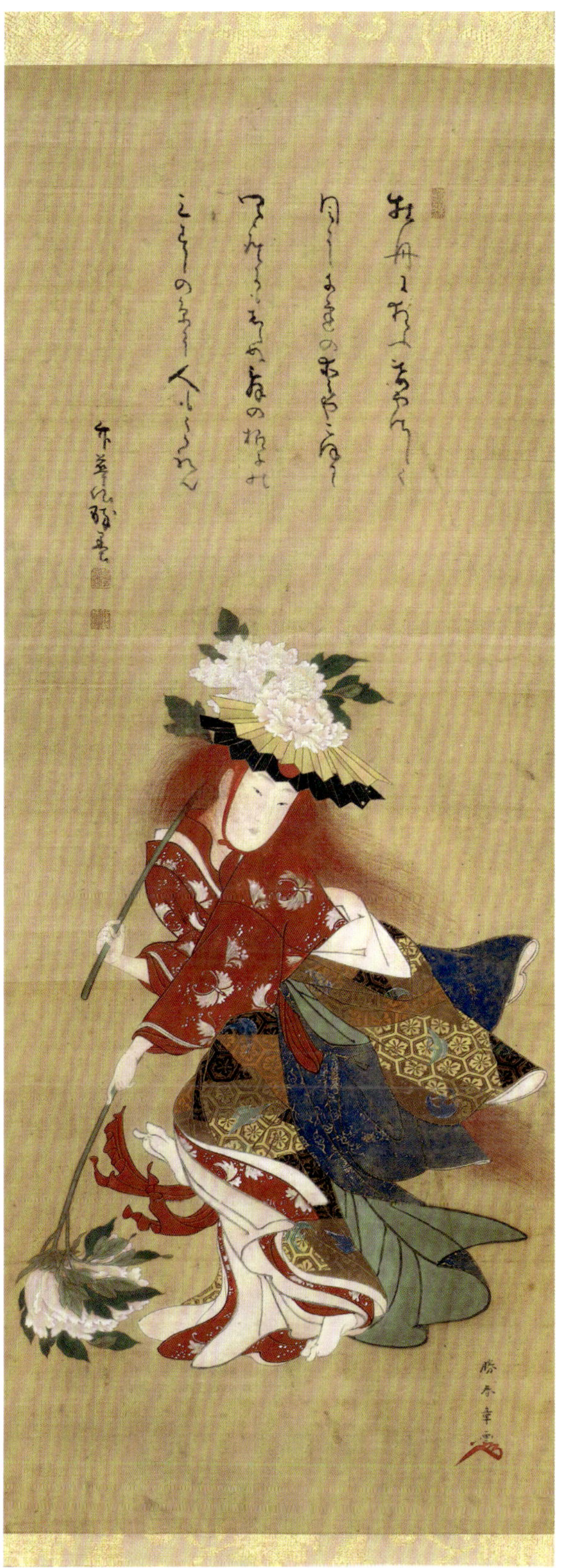

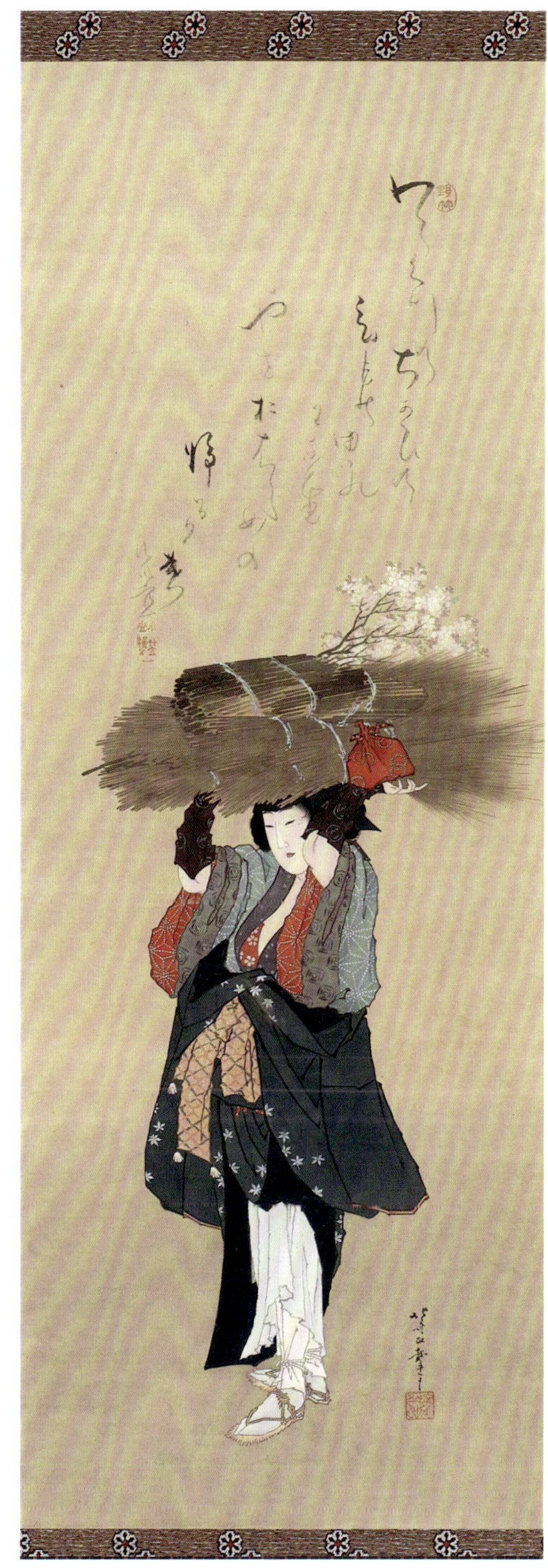

1

KATSUKAWA SHUNSHŌ

Shakkyō, the Lion Dance, about 1787–88. Hanging scroll; ink, color, and gold on silk 82.5 x 32.5 cm (32½ x 12¾ in.)

2

HOKUSAI

Woman from Ōhara Carrying Bundles of Firewood, late 1800s– early 1810s. Hanging scroll; ink and color on silk 92.8 x 33.7 cm (36½ x 13¼ in.)

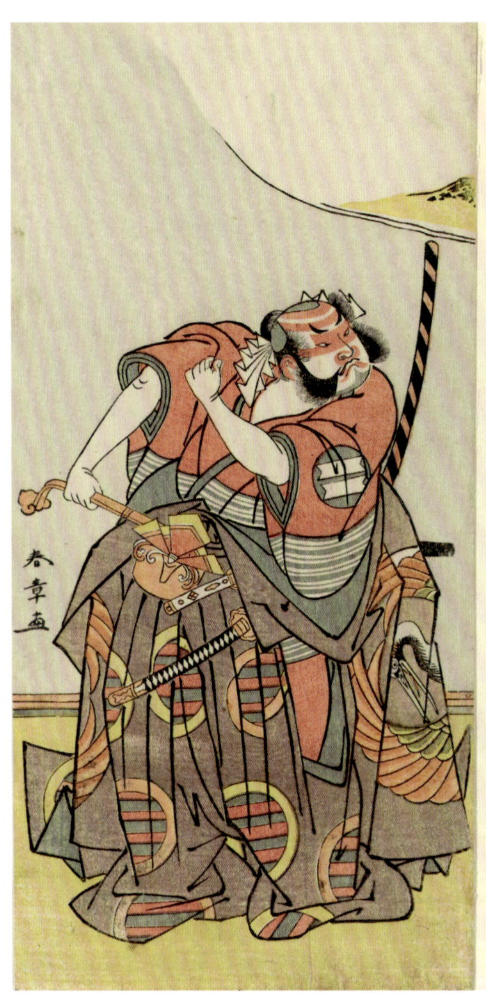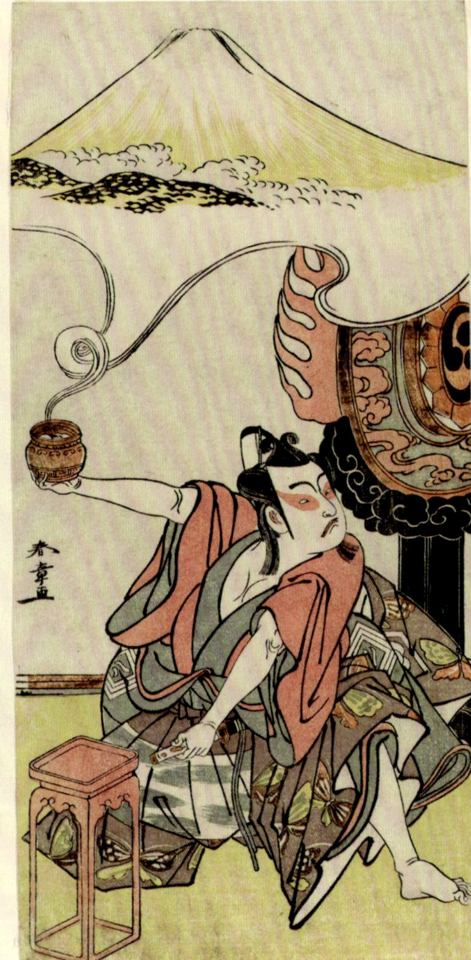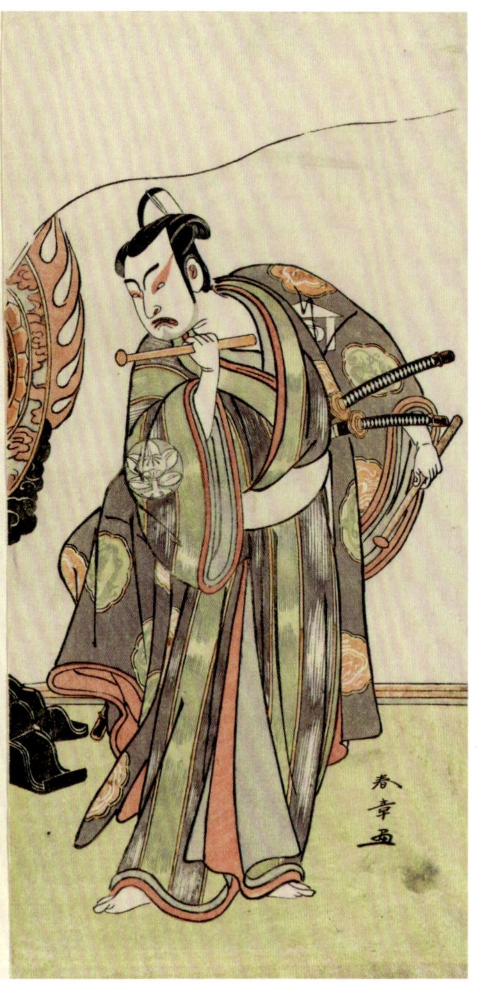

3

SHUNSHŌ
Actors Ichimura
Uzaemon IX as Kudō
Suketsune, Ichikawa
Yaozō II as Soga no Gorō,
and Sakata Hangorō II
as Kobayashi Asahina
(right to left), 1775.
Color woodblock print
30 x 44.1 cm
(11¾ x 17⅜ in.)

n the late 1760s, soon after full-color printing became widespread, Shunshō made the Katsukawa school the leading designers of actor prints by drawing the stars of the popular kabuki theater with recognizable features and not just generic handsome faces. Many of his prints were made in sets showing a group of actors from the same play; customers could buy only their favorite actor, or the entire group. In this triptych, a hero (*center*) confronts the murderer of his father (*right*), with a vision of future vengeance at the foot of Mount Fuji appearing in the incense smoke.

Young Katsukawa Shunrō, the future Hokusai, learned from his master Shunshō the techniques of capturing a likeness, posing multiple figures in a stage setting, and creating a pleasing composition. His earliest known actor prints, made in the early 1780s soon after he joined the Katsukawa studio, are drawn a little awkwardly and were assigned to be produced by less-skilled blockcutters and print-ers. Over the next decade he improved steadily and rose to become one of the most skillful junior art-ists working under Shunshō, creating outstanding works comparable to those of his master. The print shown here is the right sheet of a diptych featuring a nighttime meeting in a graveyard, with a thrilling revelation of the hero's true identity.

Hokusai left the Katsukawa school after Shunshō's death in 1792 and largely gave up designing actor prints. But his ability to draw figures convincingly in many different poses and settings — acquired through more than a decade as a designer of theatrical prints — stood him in good stead for the rest of his career, from the genre scenes of the *Hokusai Sketchbooks*, to the busy workers who populate the landscape prints, to imaginative book illustrations set in distant times and places.

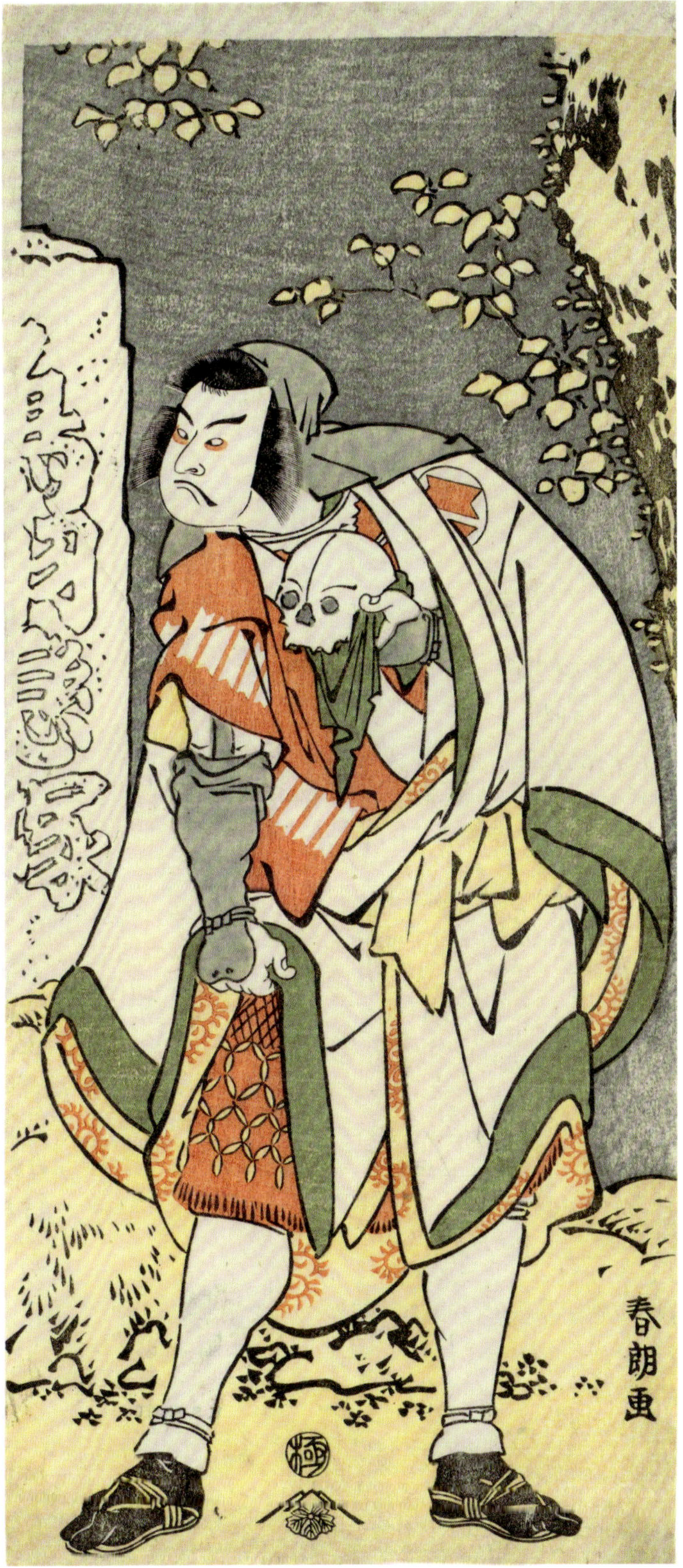

4

HOKUSAI
Actor Sakata Hangorō III as a Traveling Priest, actually Chinzei Hachirō Tametomo, 1791.
Color woodblock print
31.4 x 14.2 cm
(12 3/8 x 5 5/8 in.)

Shunshō depicted fashionably dressed women not only in individual portraits, but also in larger compositions such as these spectacular folding screens, made to be used as room dividers in an elegantly furnished home. In the summer scene, women wearing loose, gauzy garments seek relief from the heat beside a garden stream, lounging on a garden bench or on the veranda of a building. The matching scene of early spring is a panoramic view seen from a greater distance, with well-dressed city dwellers who have traveled to the suburbs to enjoy the scenery and to picnic under the cherry blossoms.

The landscape elements in Shunshō's screen paintings are elegantly drawn and arranged to provide a background for the figures. This was the usual role of landscape in ukiyo-e paintings and prints at the time, although in other Japanese painting traditions, such as the Kano school and the literati school, landscape could be a subject in itself, an idea that Hokusai later pursued in printmaking.

In addition to learning from his teacher how to draw individual figures of well-dressed women, Hokusai also acquired skill at putting many such figures together in a convincing and interesting setting. Hokusai only rarely designed multi-sheet prints, usually preferring to put an entire design on one sheet of paper. This five-sheet interior view of one of the major establishments in the Yoshiwara pleasure quarter (possibly the Ōgiya, the House of the Fan), with many courtesans dressed in their elaborate finery, may have been a special New Year offering. Shunshō's screen paintings use traditional Asian perspective, with receding lines in parallel and distant objects shown higher in the picture plane, while in the pentaptych Hokusai is experimenting with elements of Western vanishing-point perspective. Some of the receding lines converge, helping to give the impression of a very large interior space.

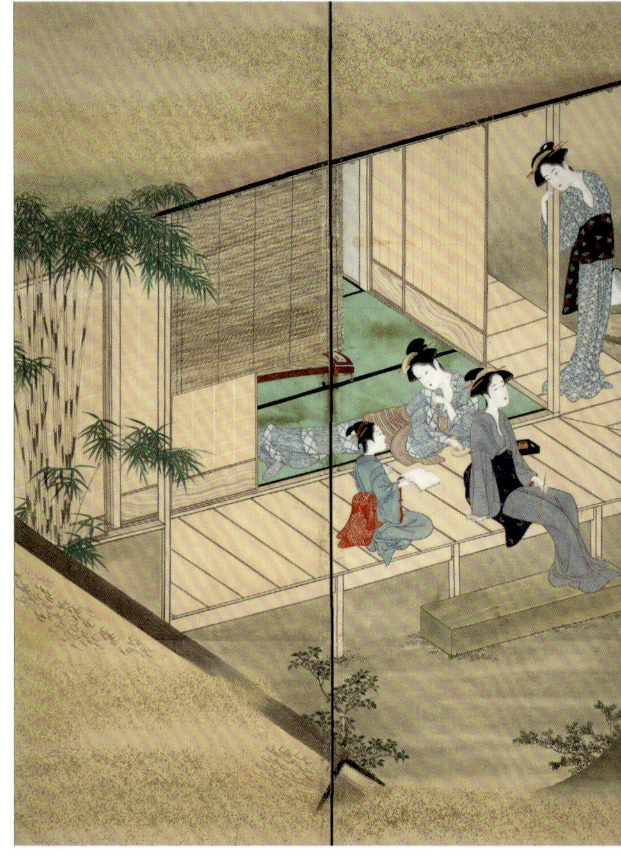

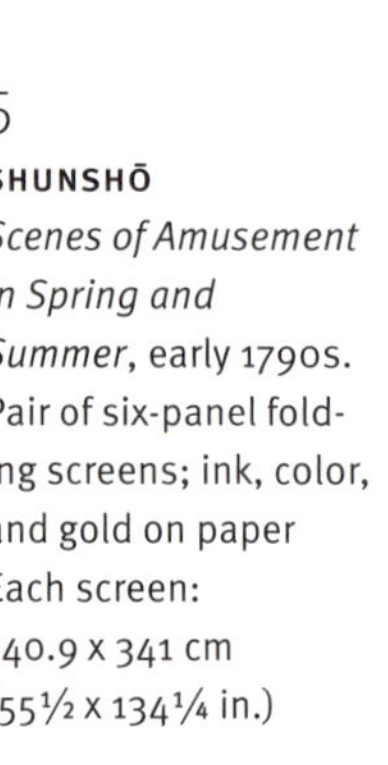

5

SHUNSHŌ
Scenes of Amusement in Spring and Summer, early 1790s. Pair of six-panel folding screens; ink, color, and gold on paper
Each screen:
140.9 x 341 cm
(55½ x 134¼ in.)

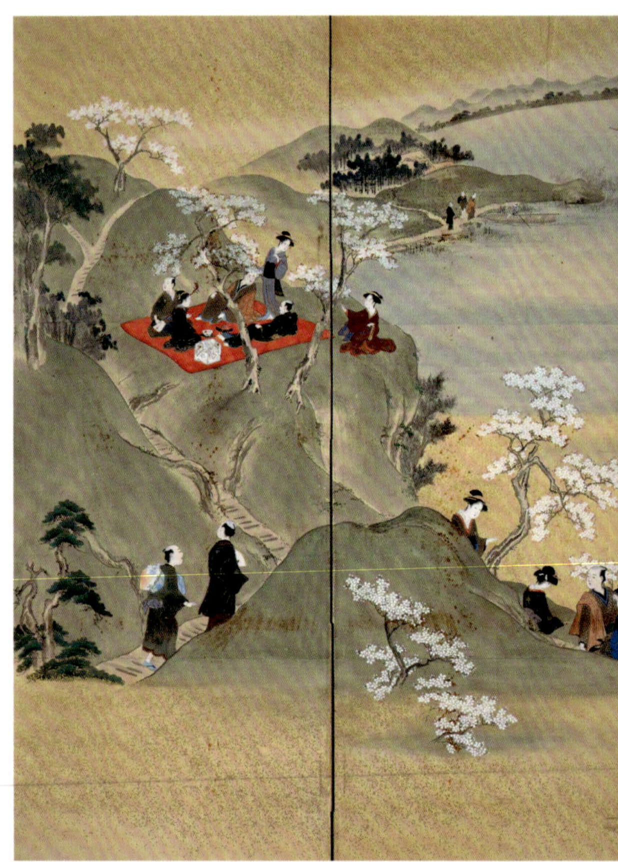

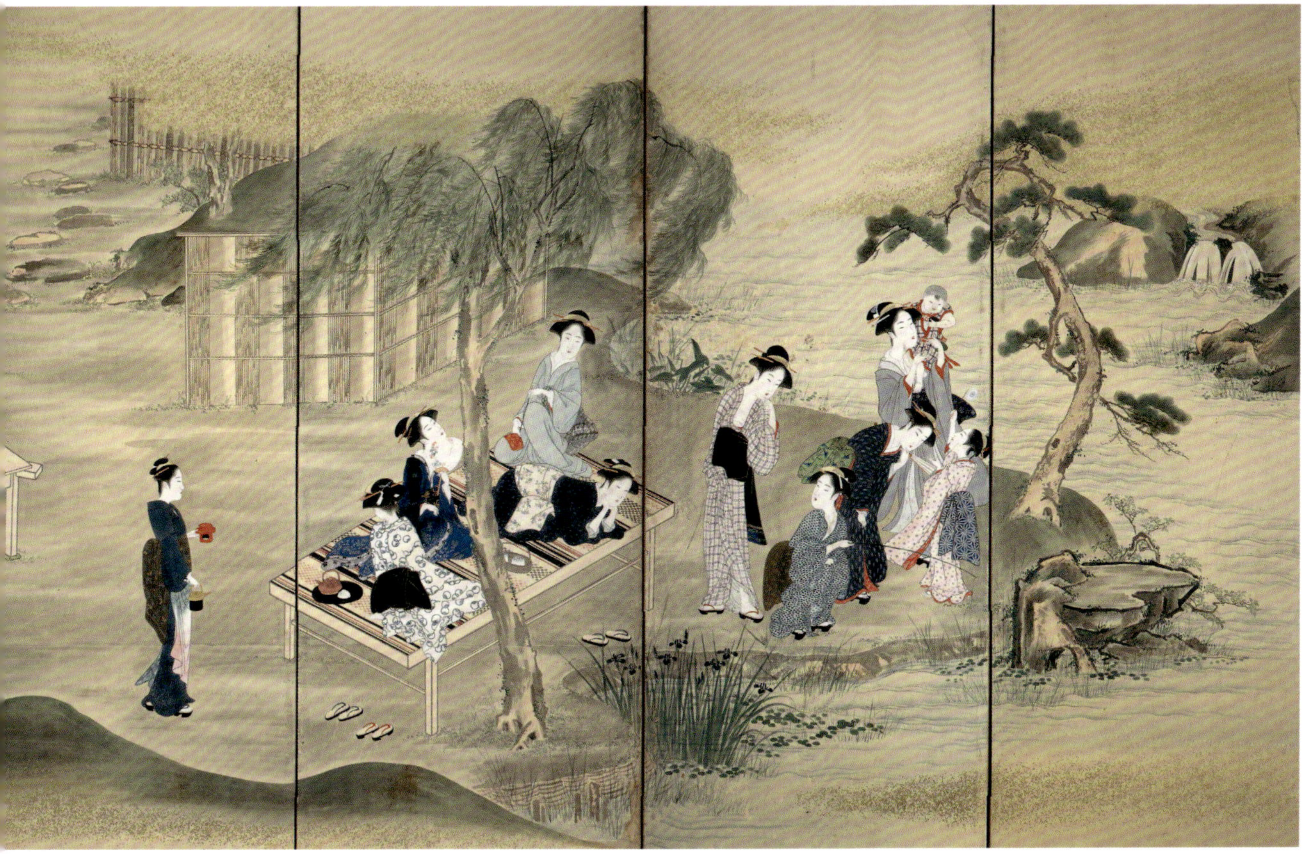

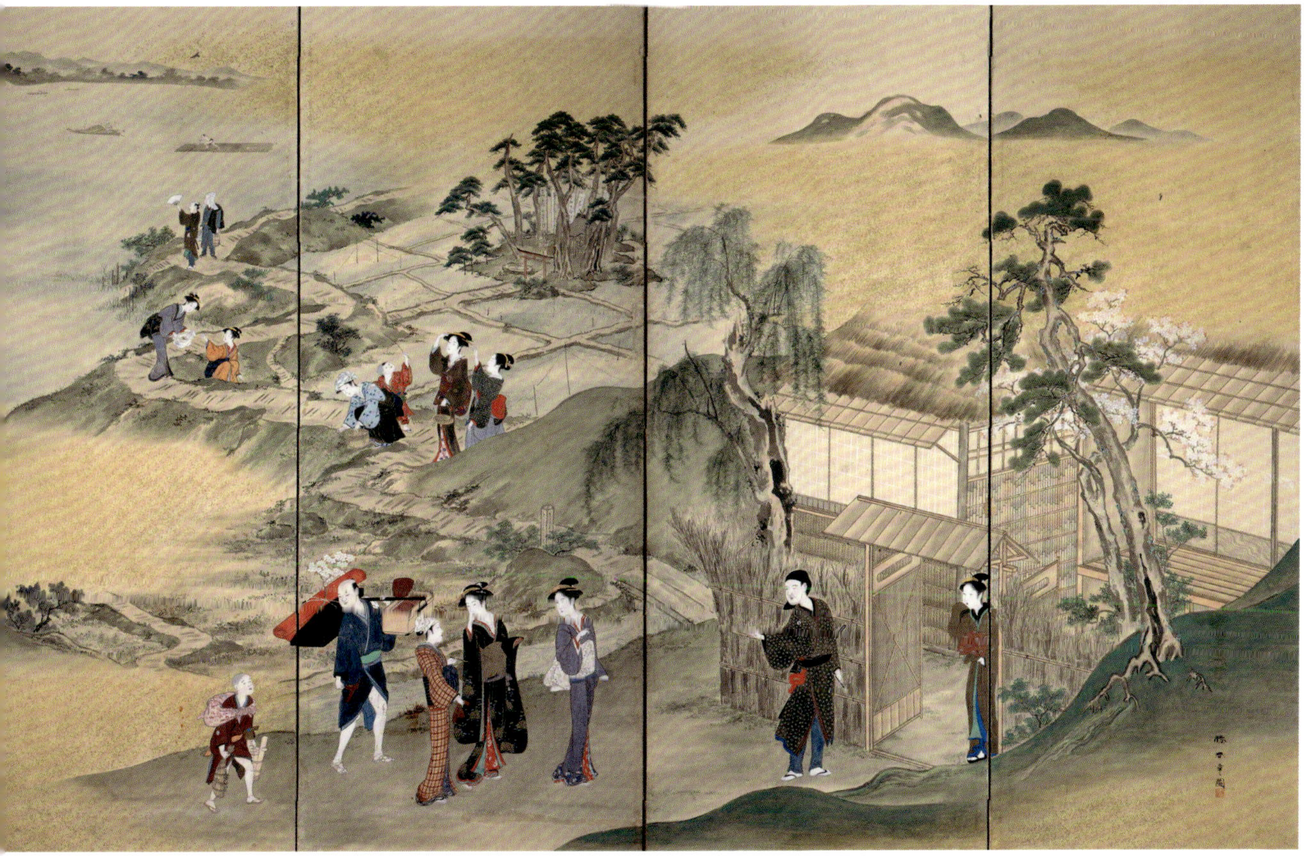

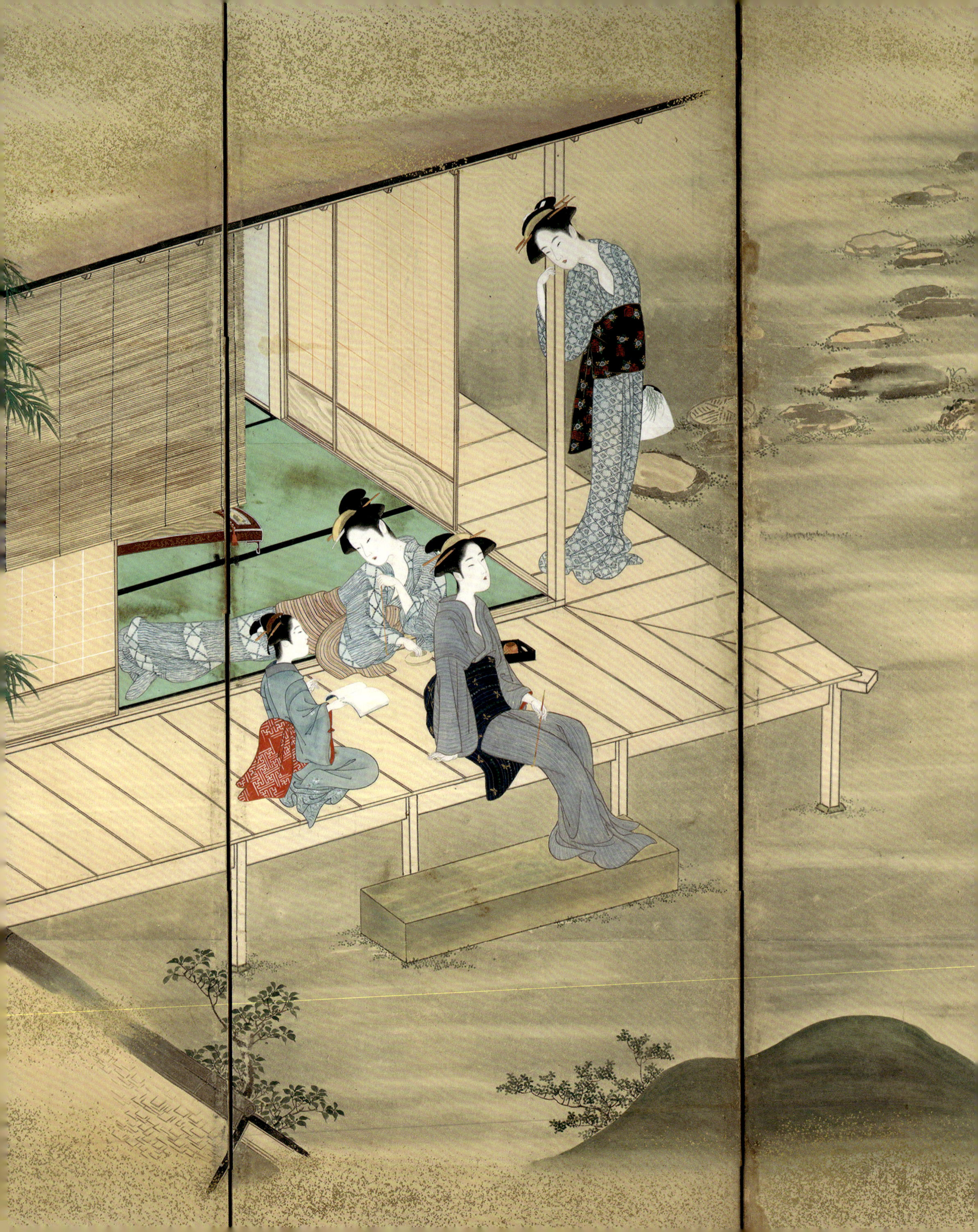

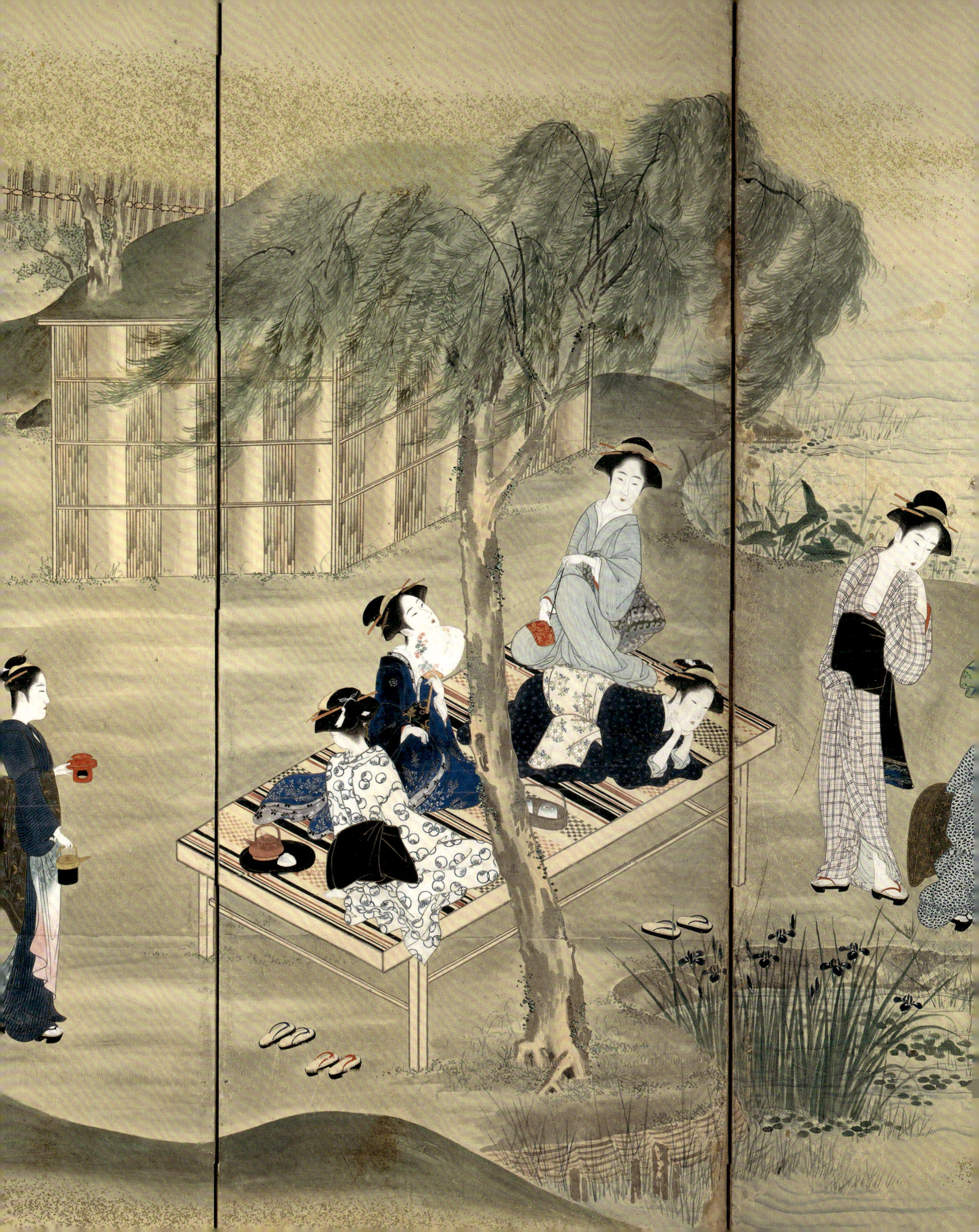

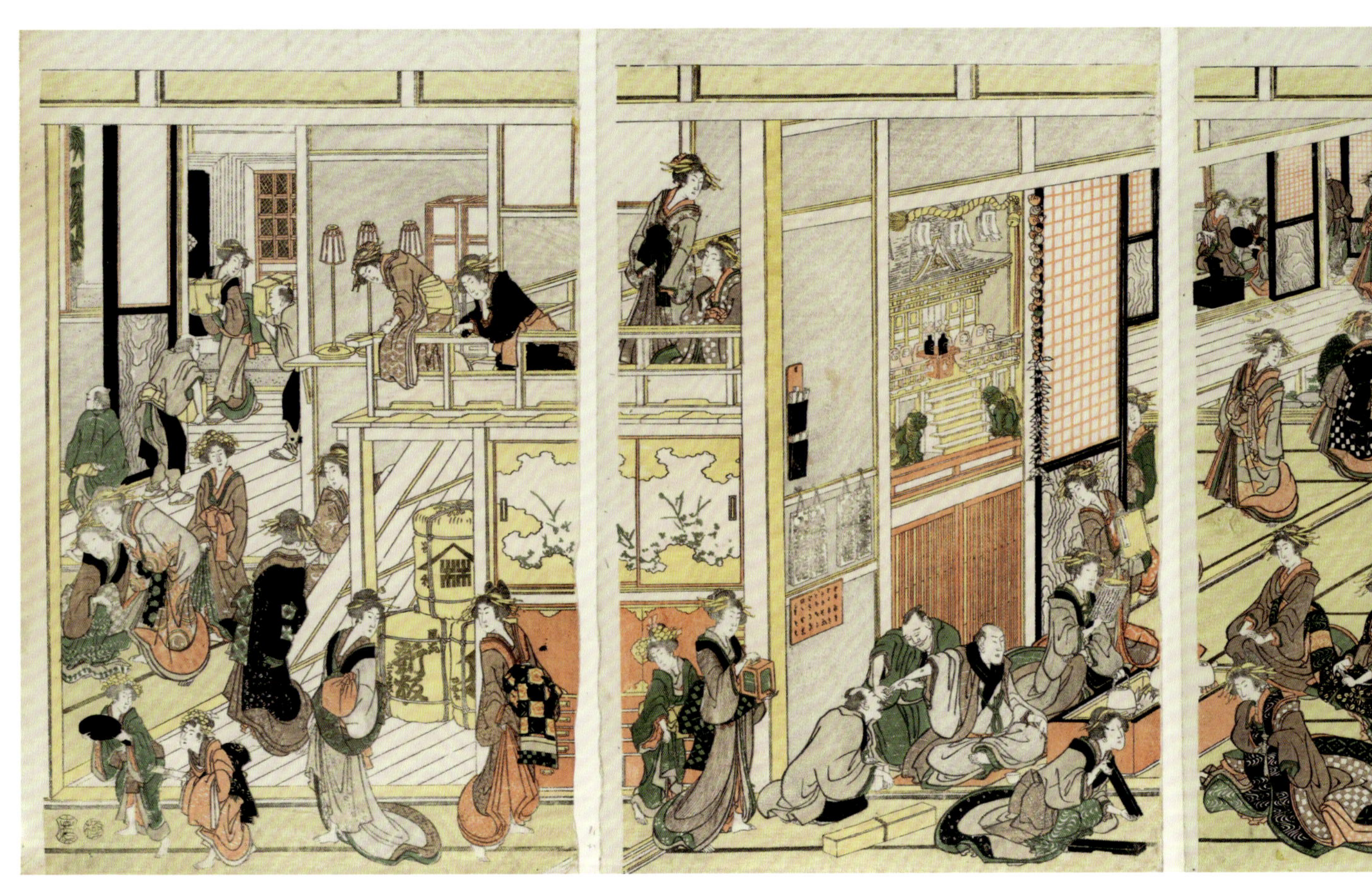

6

HOKUSAI
*New Year's Day at the
Ōgi-ya in the Yoshiwara*,
about 1808–13.
Color woodblock print
pentaptych
38.5 x 130 cm
(15⅛ x 51⅛ in.)

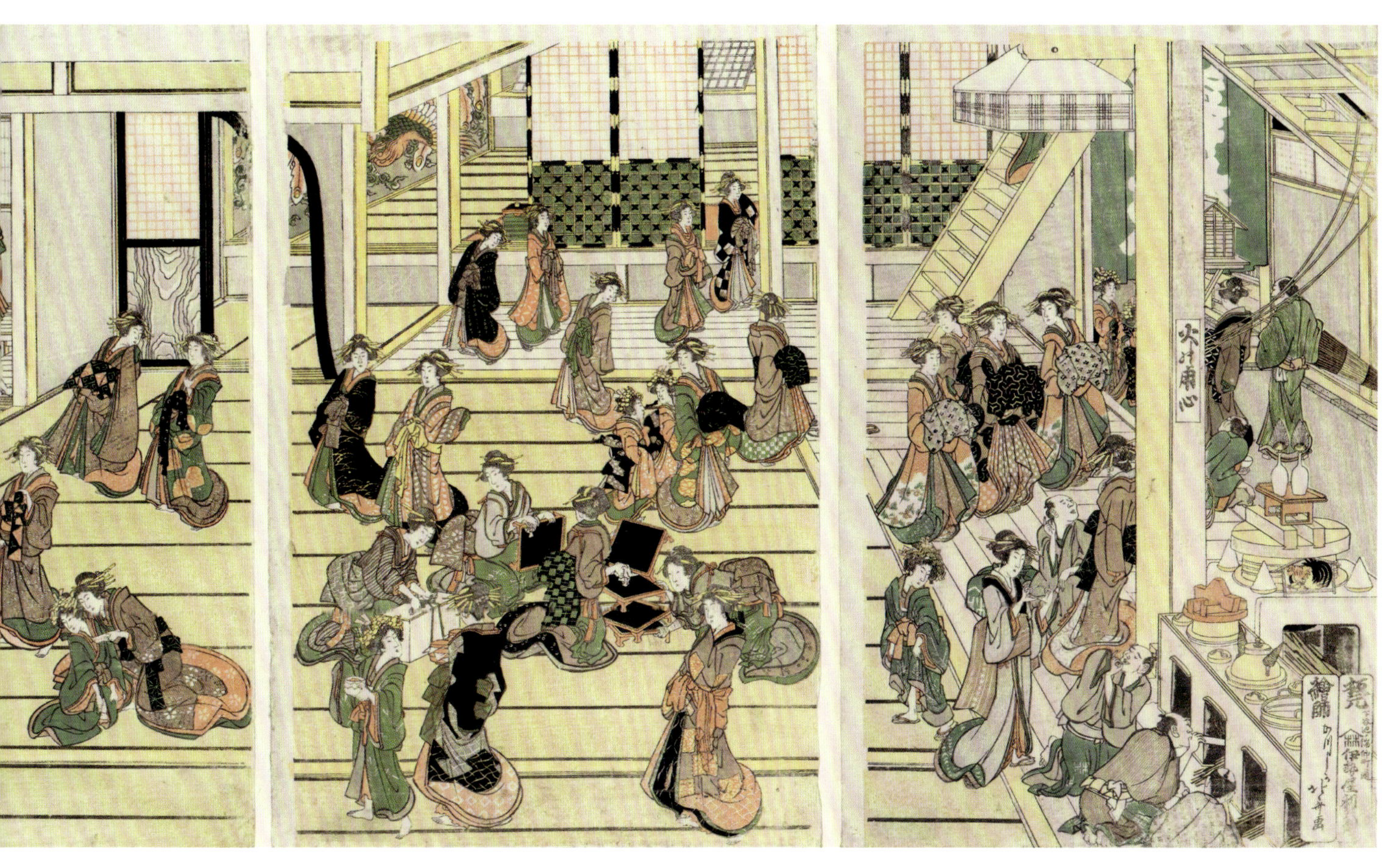

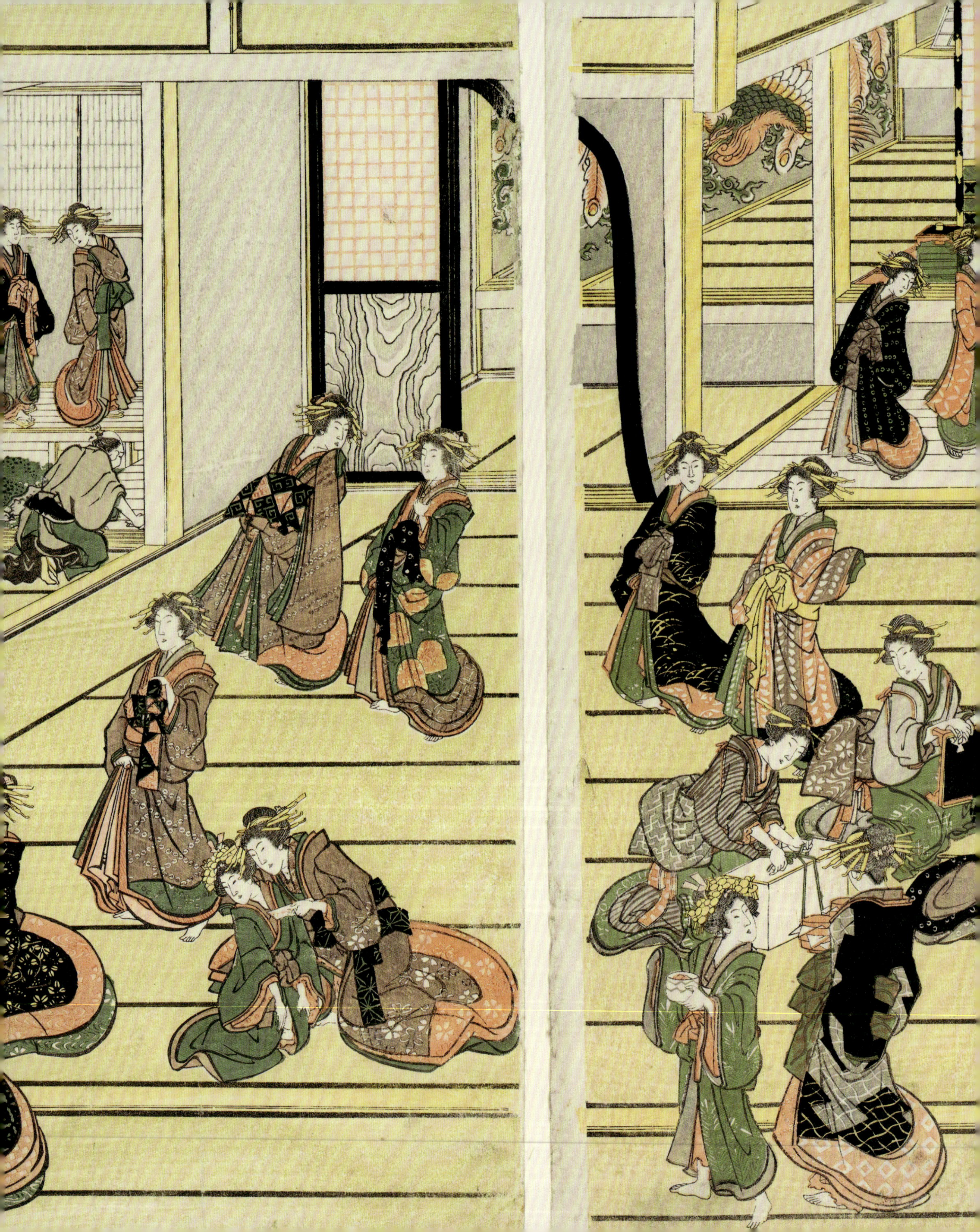

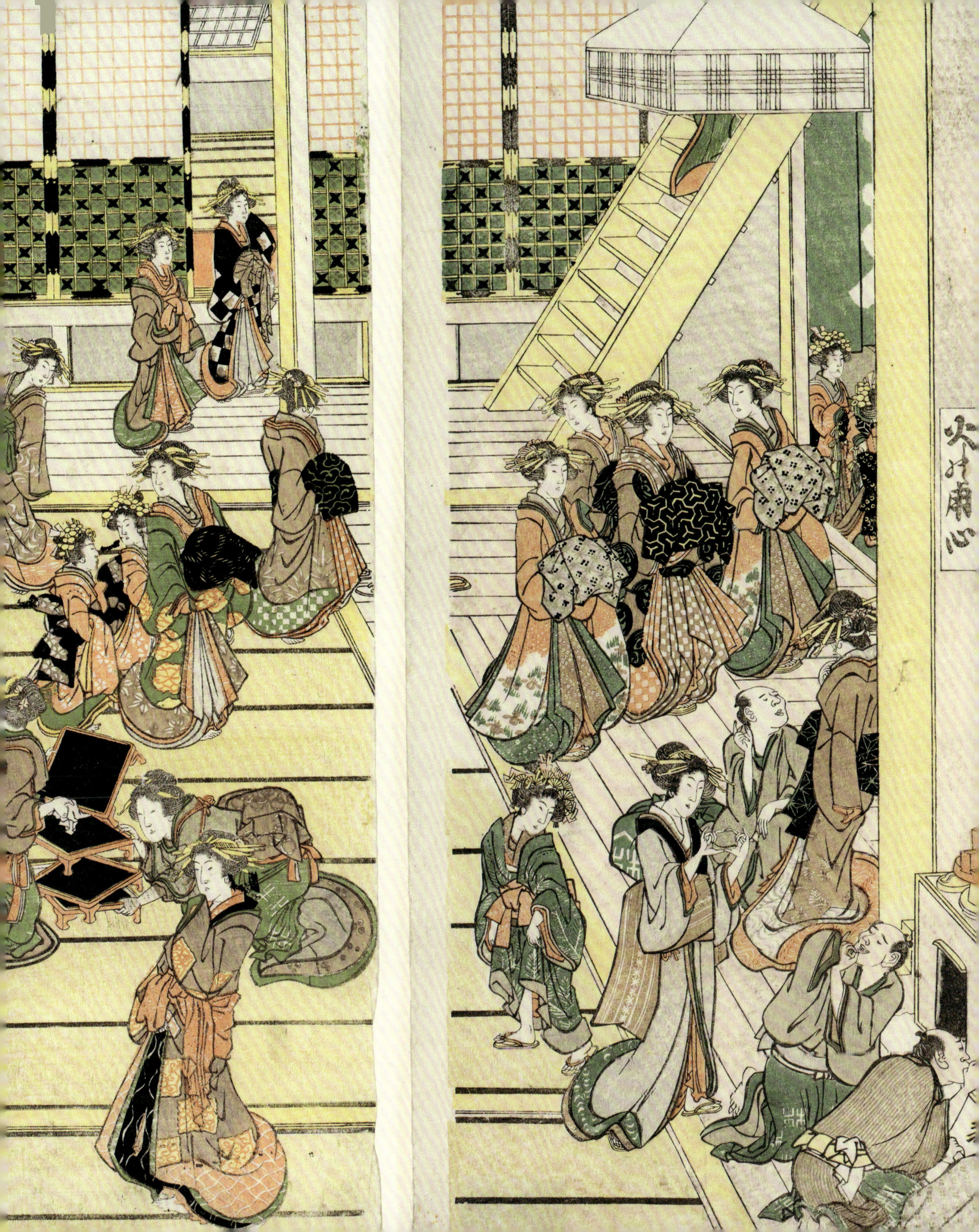
火の用心

Western-style vanishing-point perspective came to the attention of Japanese print designers in the early 1740s, through imported Western books and prints as well as Chinese books and prints with Western influence. While perspective was seen in Europe as a great scientific and artistic advance, in Japan it was regarded as a clever, amusing optical illusion suitable for such uses as stage sets and children's peepshow toys. Prints using exaggerated vanishing-point perspective, with receding lines converging on the horizon, were called *uki-e* or "floating pictures," perhaps because they were sometimes viewed through imported Dutch lenses in which an image would appear to float, as if looking through a porthole into another world.

Various schools of ukiyo-e, including the Katsukawa school, sometimes experimented with this technique. When Hokusai was young, the artist most famous for this approach was Utagawa Toyoharu, the founder of the Utagawa school (which later, under his pupil Toyokuni, came to dominate the field of actor prints). In this example, Toyoharu uses converging lines to emphasize the large scale of a spacious mansion in which a wealthy man is holding a snow-viewing party. The host, dressed in black, plays *go* with his friends as a woman brings refreshments. His two daughters amuse themselves by playing with the cat (*right*) and sculpting a snow rabbit (*left*).

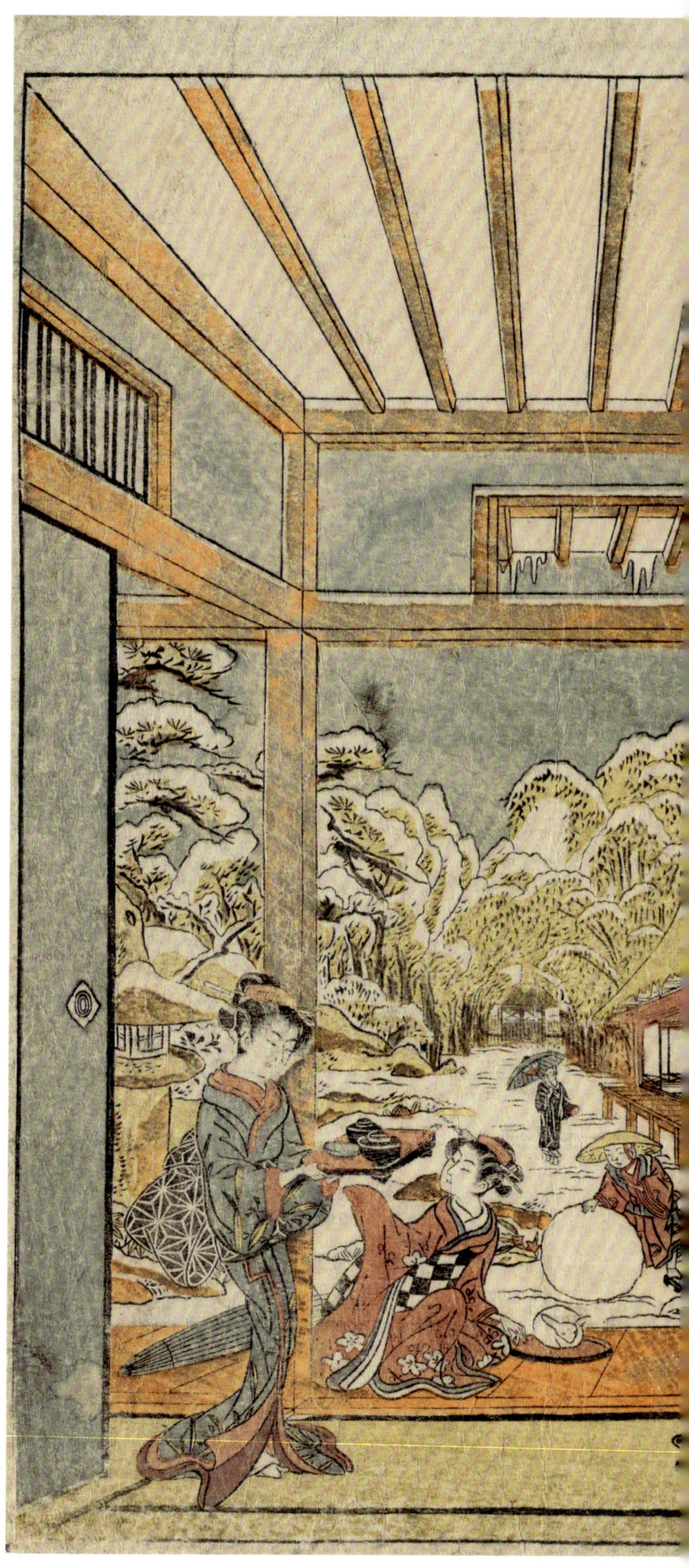

7

UTAGAWA TOYOHARU
*Perspective Picture of
a Snow-Viewing Party*,
1770s–80s.
Color woodblock print
24.5 x 37.1 cm
(9⅝ x 14⅝ in.)

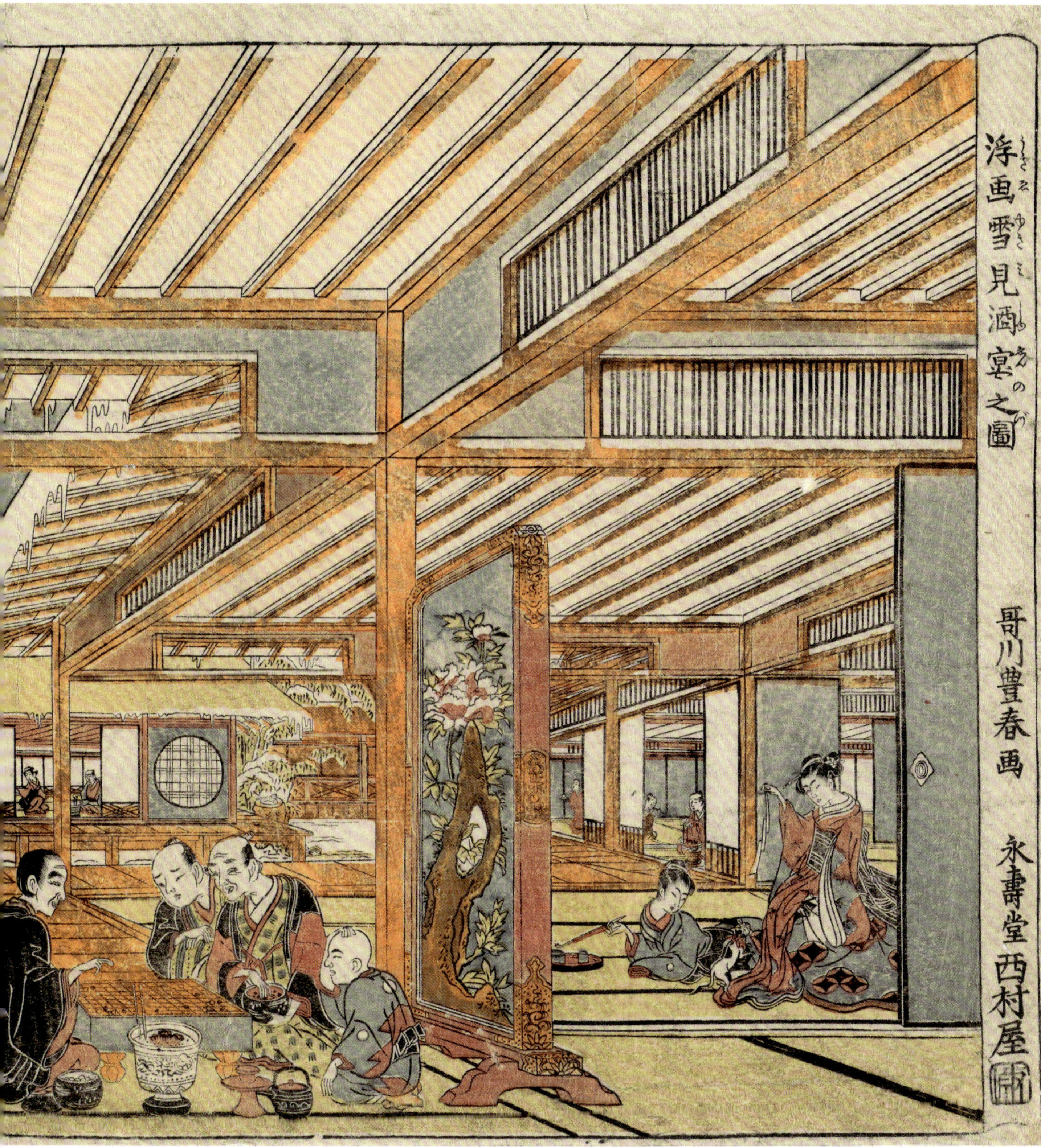
浮画雪見酒宴之圖
哥川豊春画
永壽堂　西村屋

The young Hokusai took an eclectic interest in many forms of art and was especially attracted to uki-e, designing many of them himself. Here he illustrates a famous twelfth-century romance in which the hero, standing outside a palatial mansion, uses his flute to serenade a young lady who plays the *koto* inside. Oddly, the house is shown in vanishing-point perspective, but not the garden. Perhaps Hokusai did not yet fully understand the technique, or deliberately chose to apply it selectively.

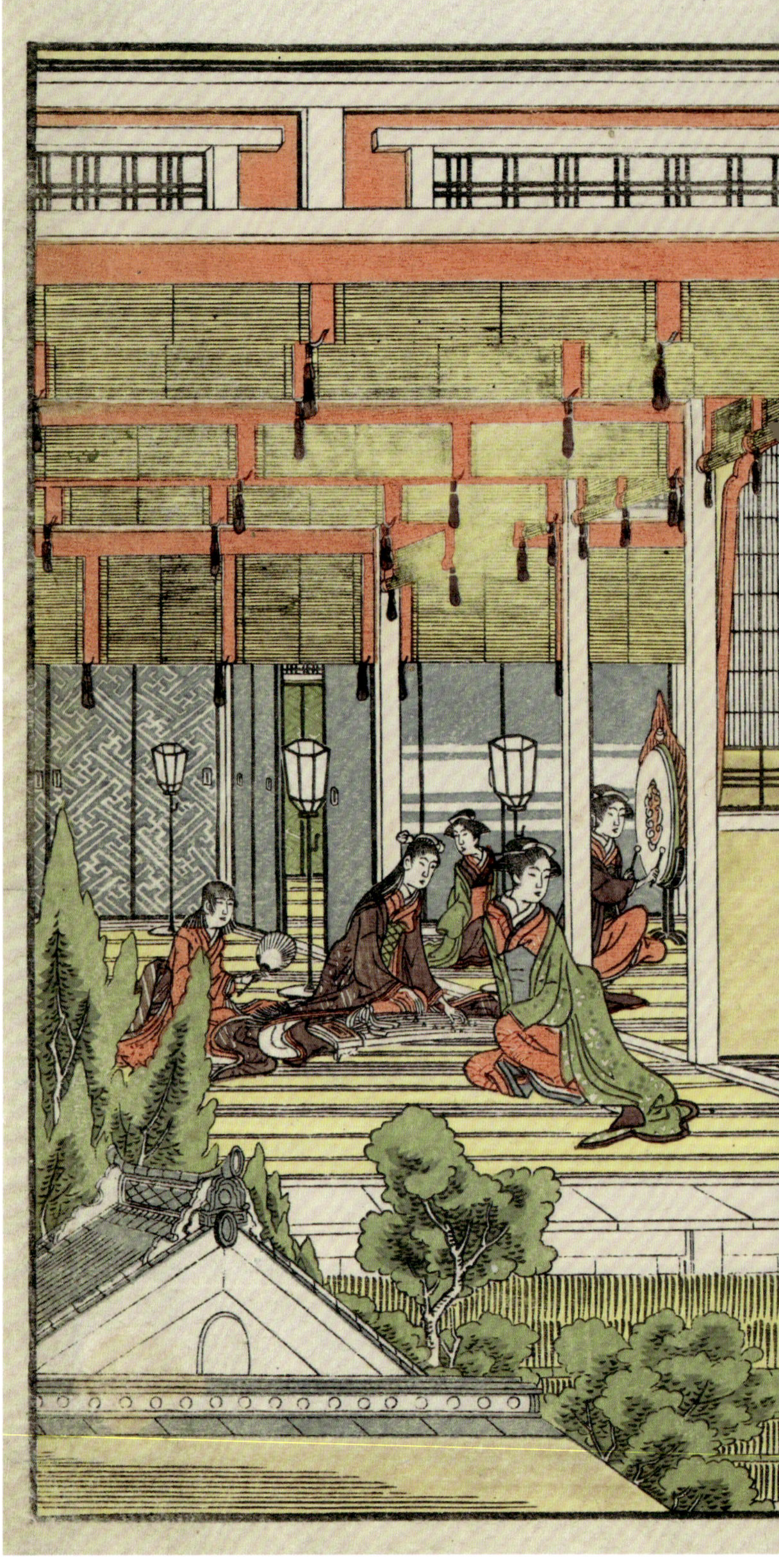

8

HOKUSAI
The Story of Minamoto no Yoshitsune and Jōruri-hime, 1780s.
Color woodblock print
26.3 x 39.5 cm
(10³⁄₈ x 15¹⁄₈ in.)

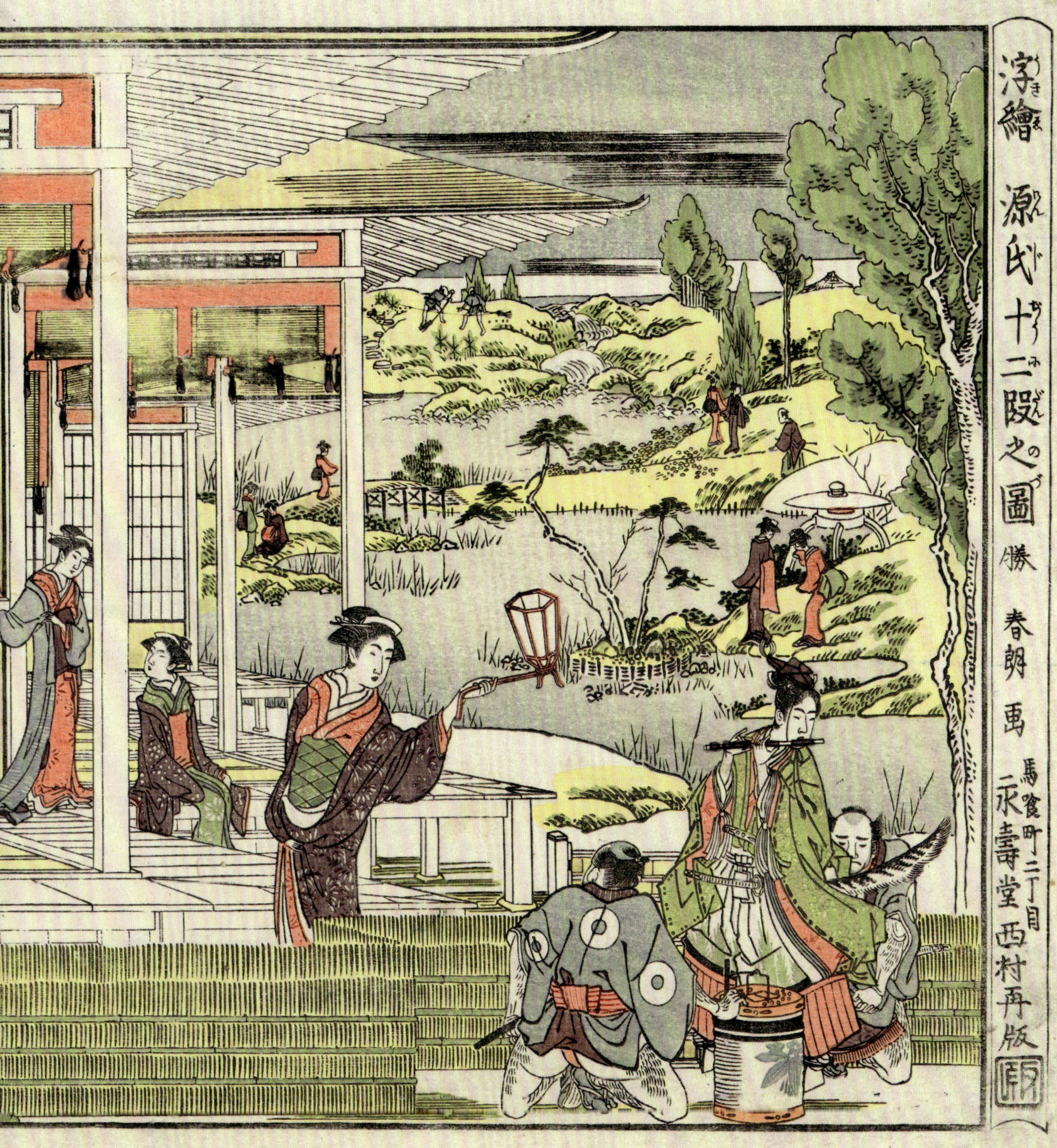

浮繪源氏十二段之圖
勝春朗画
馬喰町二丁目　永壽堂西村再版

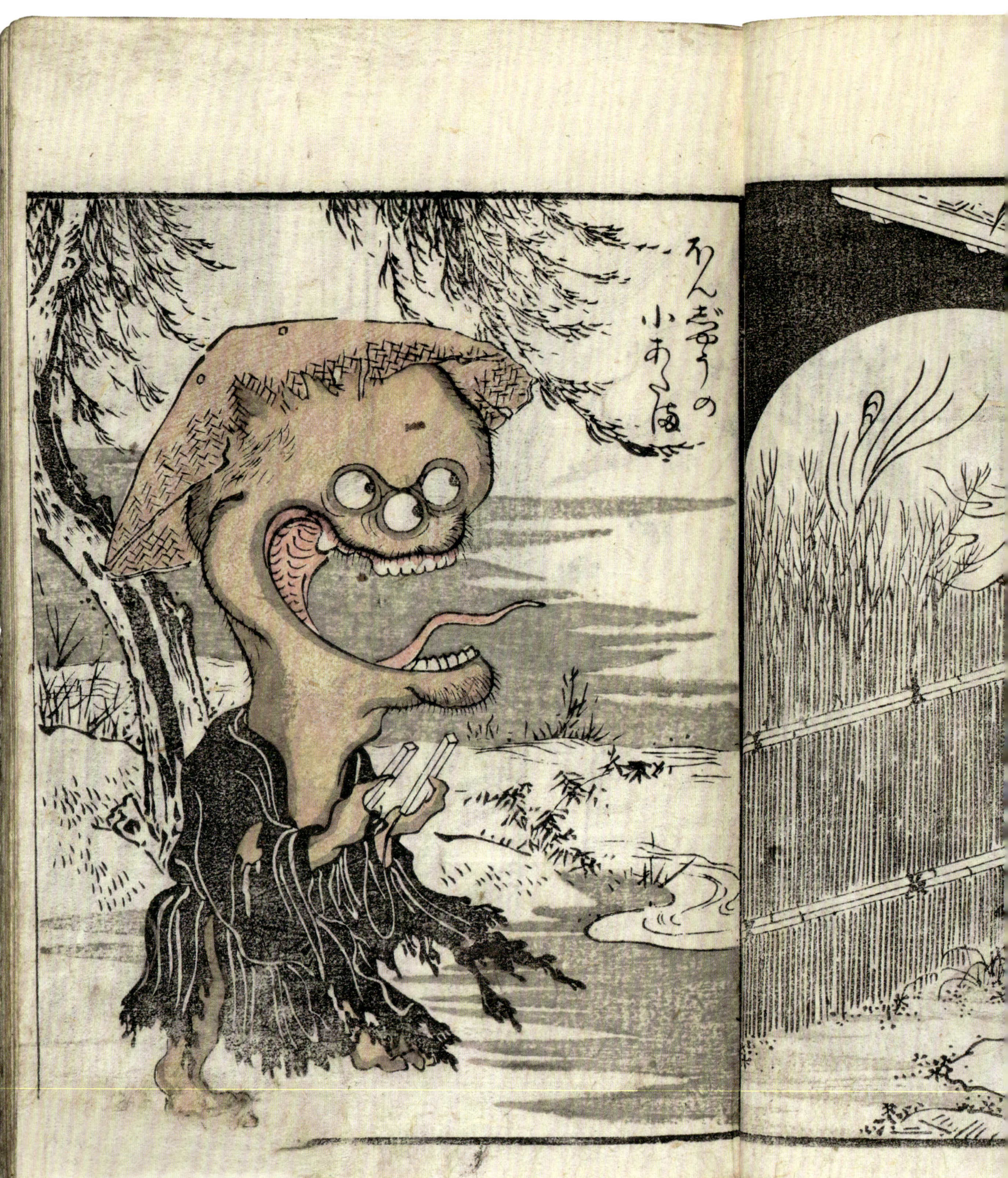

うんぎうの
小あくま

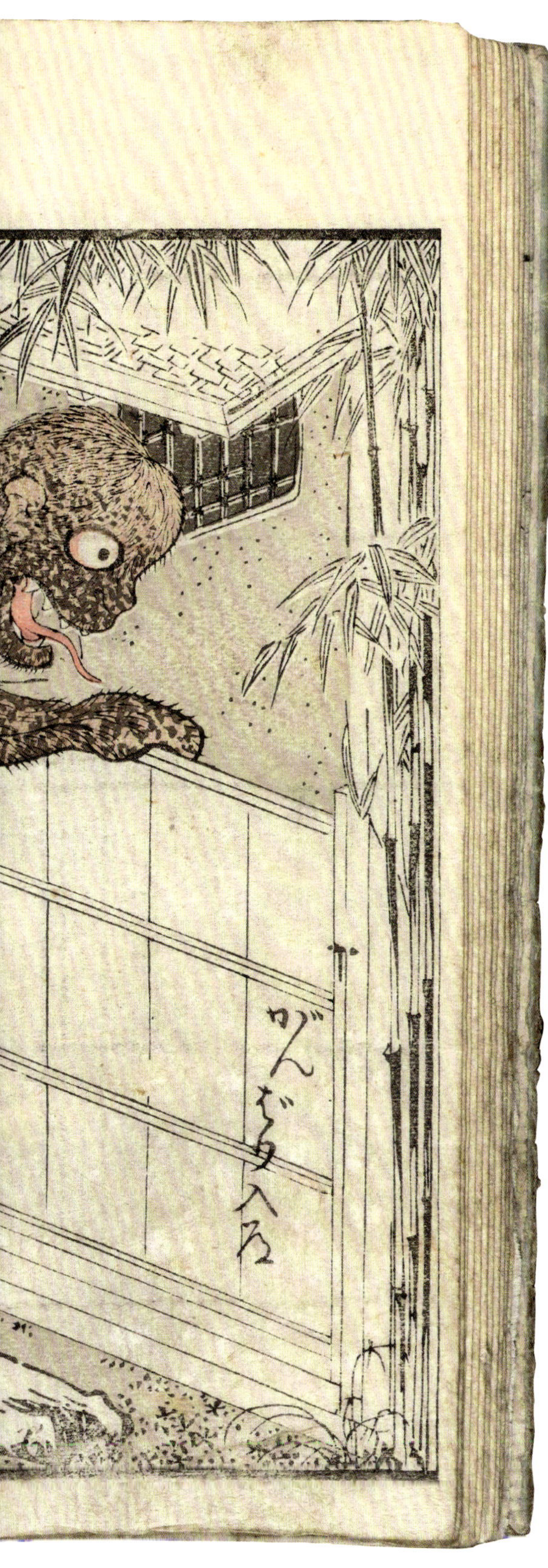

Bizarre monsters frequently appear in Japanese folklore, fiction, drama, and the visual arts, often depicted in ways that are both frightening and humorous. When Hokusai used his vivid imagination to create strange beings, he was joining in a tradition that was already centuries old and has continued to the present day, with familiar monsters still making frequent appearances in films, comics, and games.

While Hokusai was still a member of Shunshō's studio, another of Shunshō's students, Katsukawa Shun'ei, illustrated a delightful book of ghosts and monsters with the help of the master himself. Around the same time, Hokusai incorporated similar creatures into one of his perspective prints (10). The title *One Hundred Ghost Stories* refers to a popular storytelling game played during the summer months, when it was thought that scary stories would help people to forget the heat as they shivered with delicious terror.

In the game, a group of people gather at night to tell ghost stories. As each story is finished, one of the lights in the room is put out. Eventually the stories are finished and the room is completely dark, and then monsters may appear. Hokusai shows a group of well-dressed men gathered for such a party in a large house with a garden. They thought that it was all just a game until the monsters attacked! The meticulously drawn vanishing-point perspective provides an illusionistic setting for the supernatural creatures and makes them all the more believable.

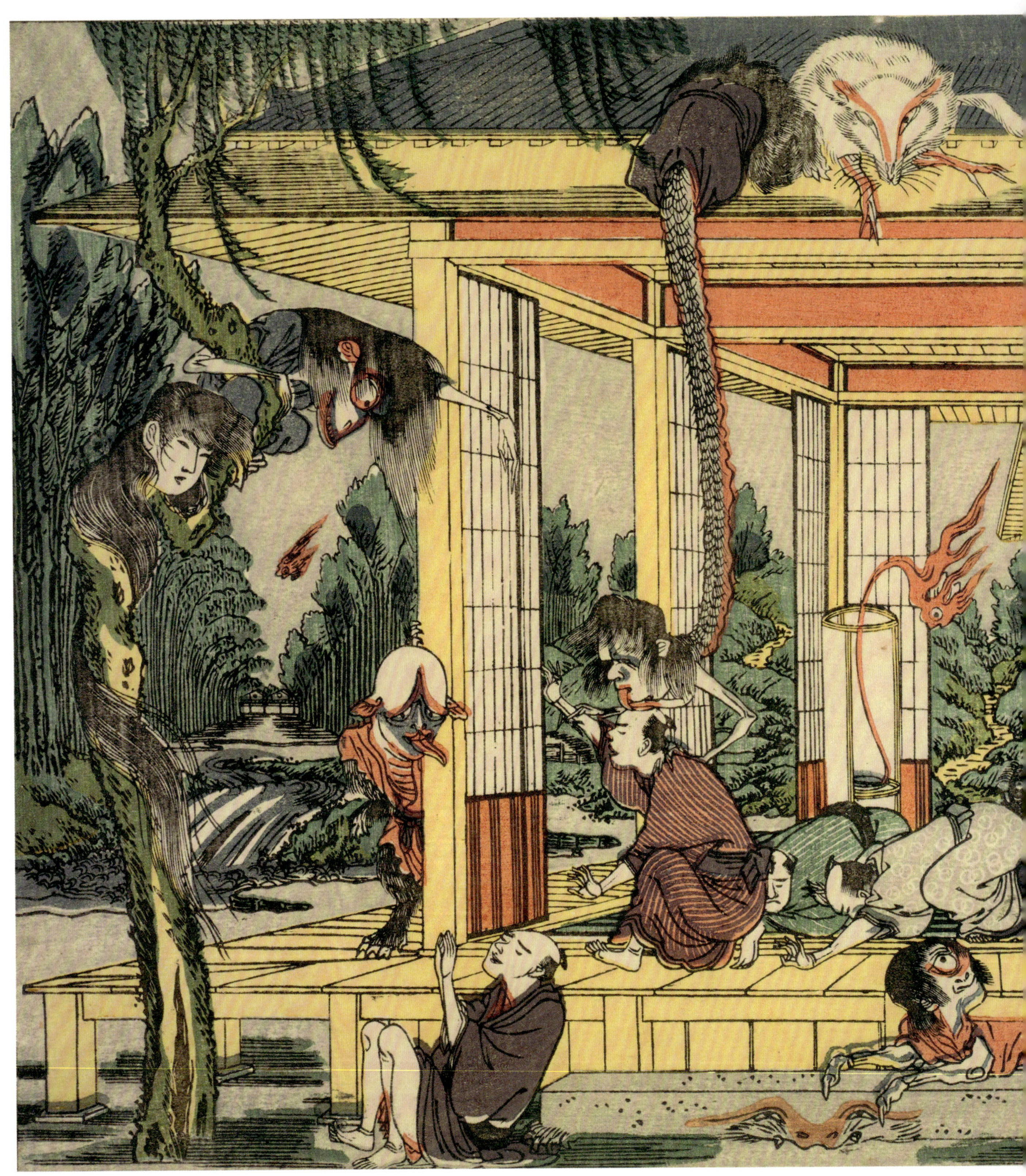

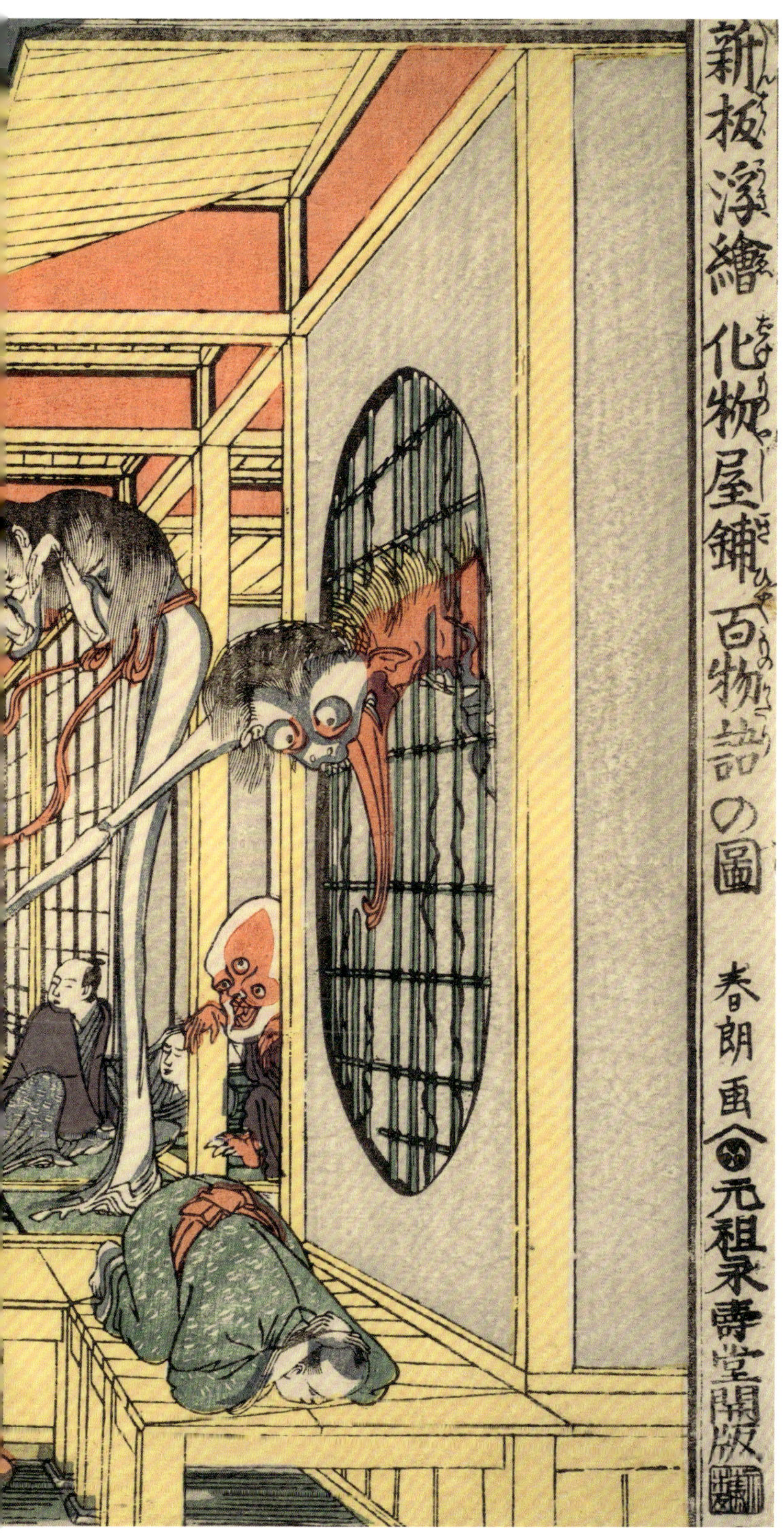

10

HOKUSAI
*Newly Published
Perspective Picture: One
Hundred Ghost Stories in
a Haunted House*, 1780s.
Color woodblock print
23.7 x 35.4 cm
(9 3/8 x 13 7/8 in.)

Hokusai's ideas about the depiction of
landscape — culminating in the Fuji series
that began to appear in about 1830 —
developed gradually as he studied various schools
of art. An important early influence on Hokusai
was Shiba Kōkan, a pioneer in the exploration of
Western methods in art who traveled to Nagasaki
to learn from the Dutch. In 1796, a Western-style
painting by Kōkan that used opaque pigments
imitating oil paints was exhibited at the Atago
Shrine in Edo; a year later, Hokusai copied its
composition in an illustration for *Willow Silk*, an
album of poetry.

Both Kōkan's painting and Hokusai's print
show the beach at Enoshima, a popular pilgrimage
site within easy reach of Edo, using vanishing-
point perspective and a low horizon line in the
manner of Dutch prints. In Hokusai's work, however, the figures on the beach are much larger, in
keeping with the tendency of ukiyo-e at the time to
use landscape as a background for figures rather
than a subject in itself. A few years later, Hokusai
designed a series of small privately commissioned
prints in a Western style that make the landscape the focus of interest — including a scene of
Enoshima with a similar wave elegantly rendered
in embossing, now large enough to threaten the
tiny, ant-like figures on the shore (12).

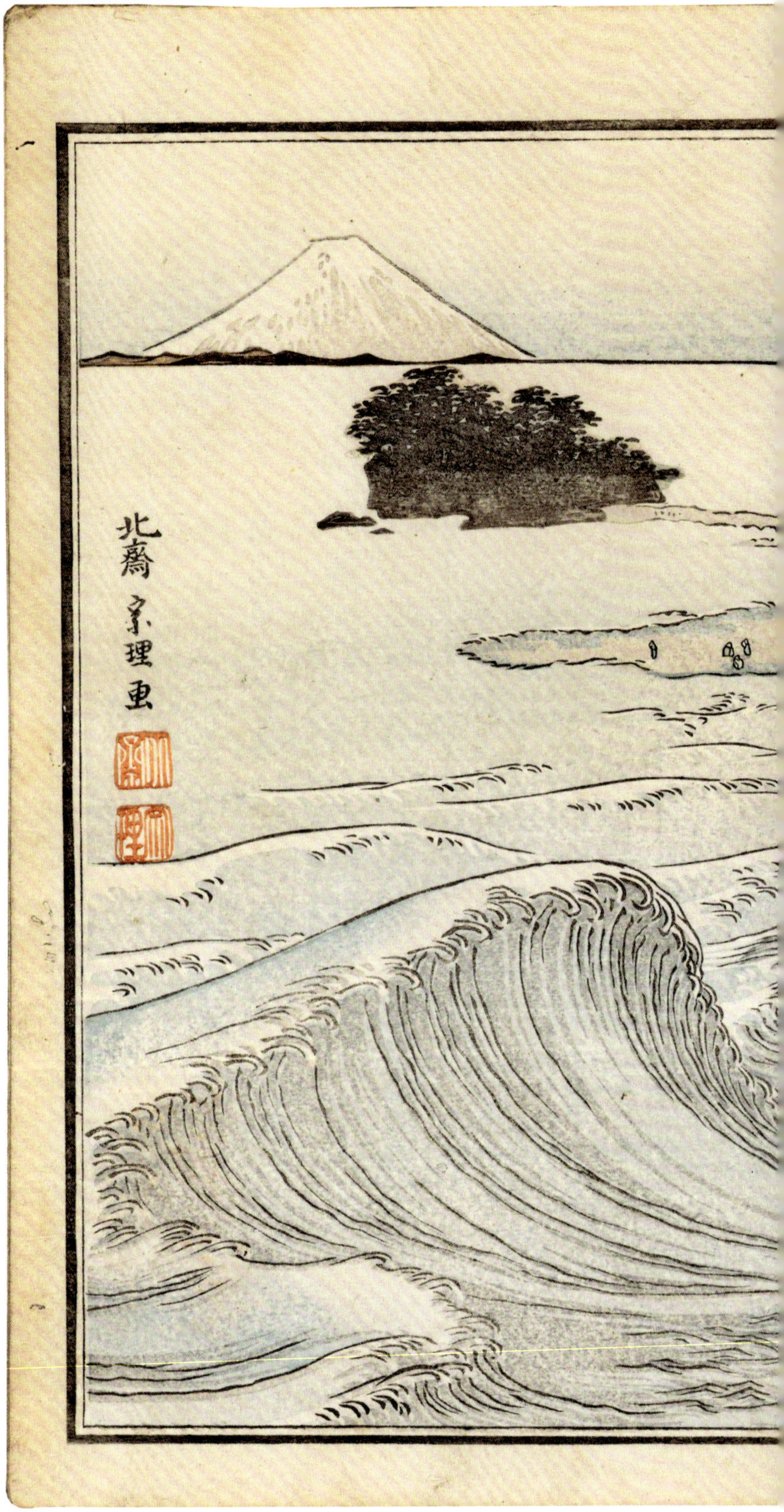

11
HOKUSAI
Spring View of Enoshima,
from *Willow Silk*, 1797.
Color woodblock
printed book
25 x 18.7 cm
(9⁷⁄₈ x 7³⁄₈ in.)

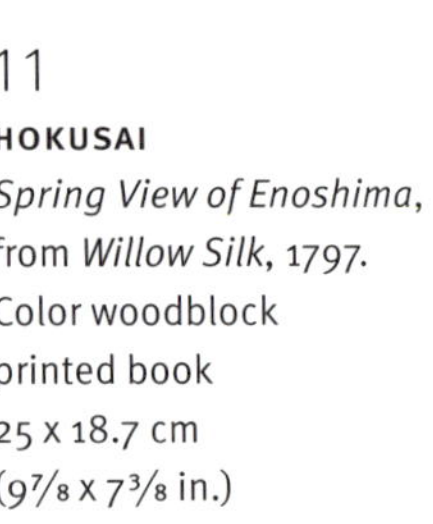

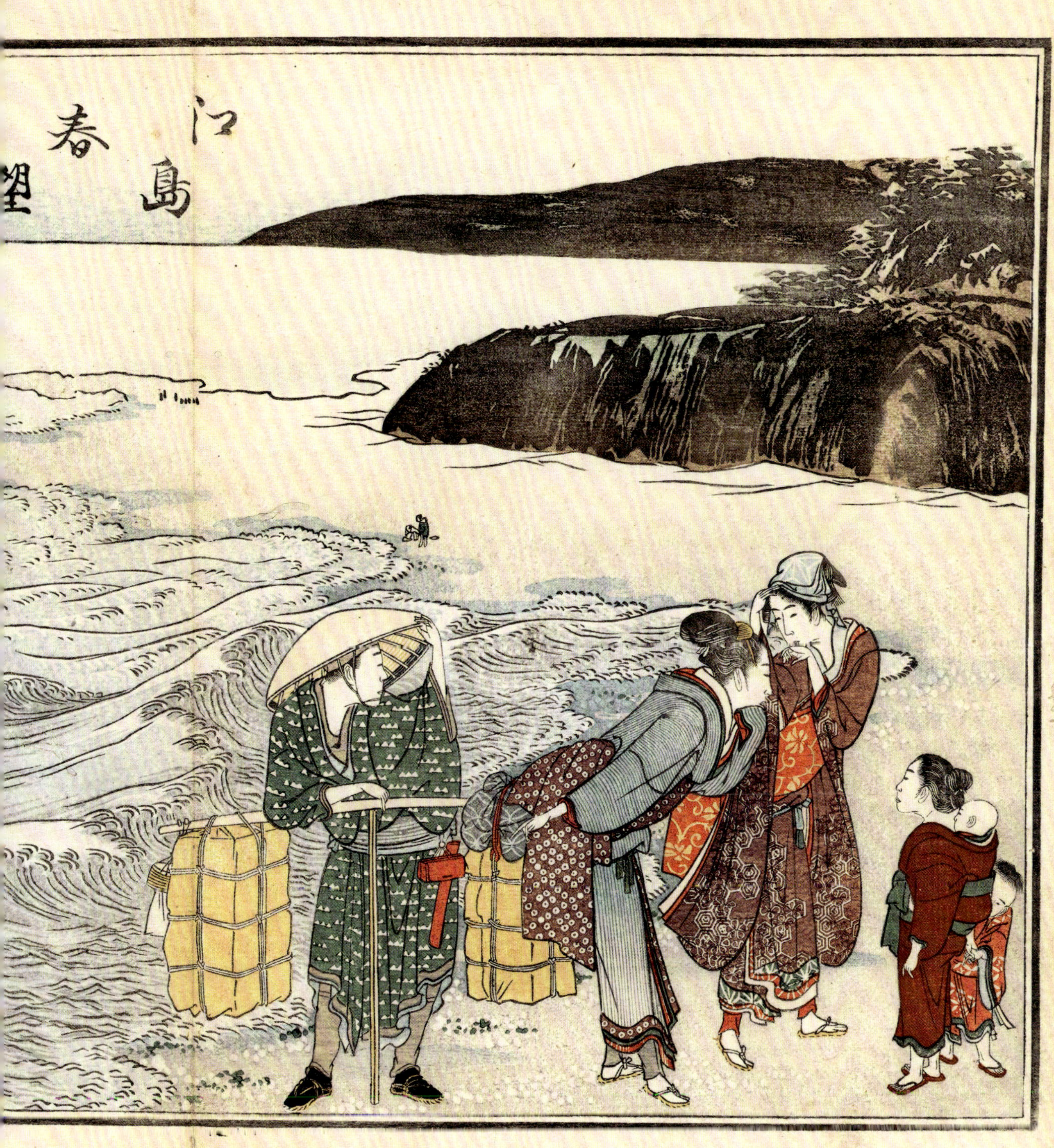

江島
春望

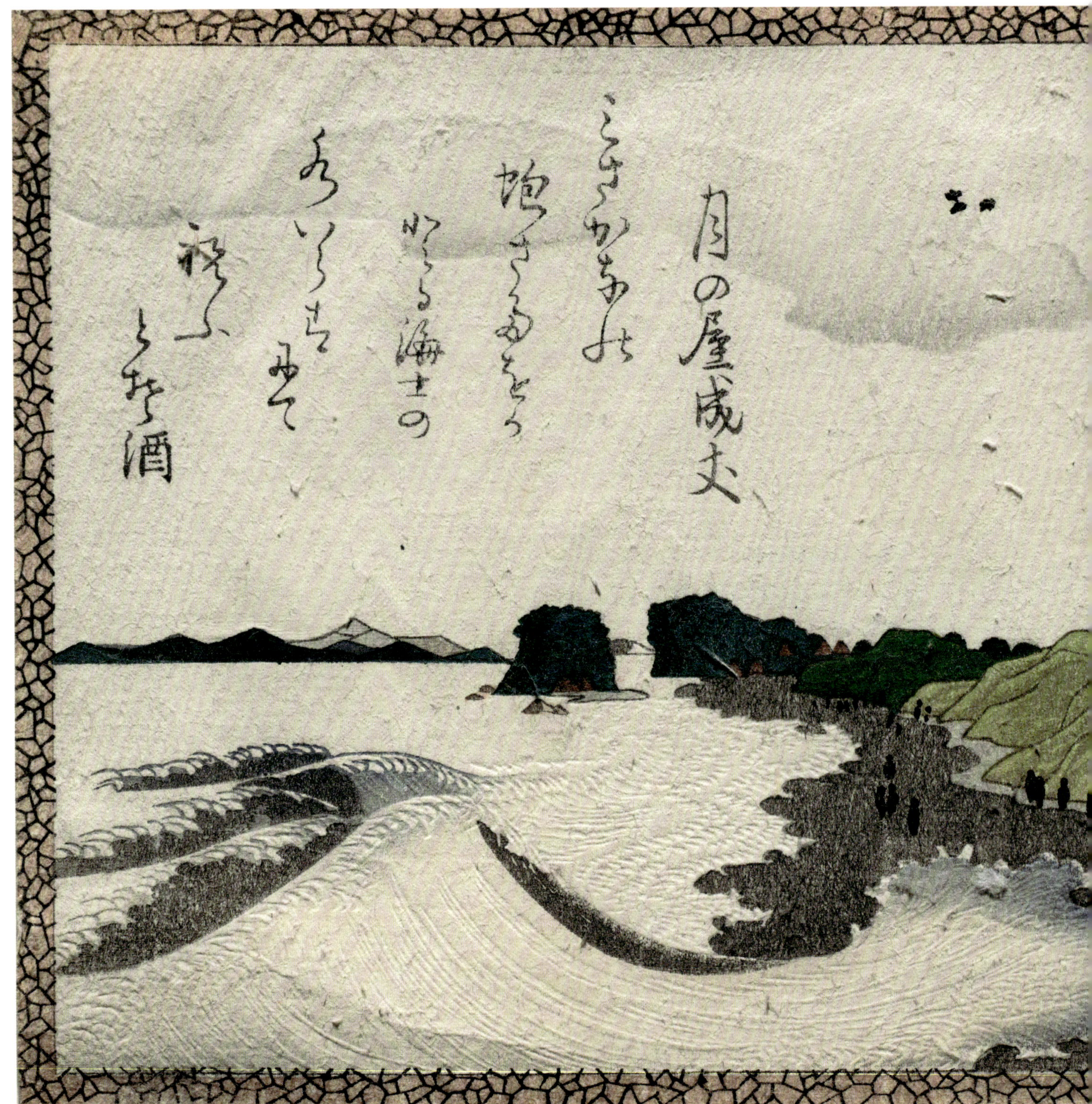

月の屋成丈
ふぐりのまよ
飽きられとろ
ける海士の
あいちも
みて
祝ふ
白酒

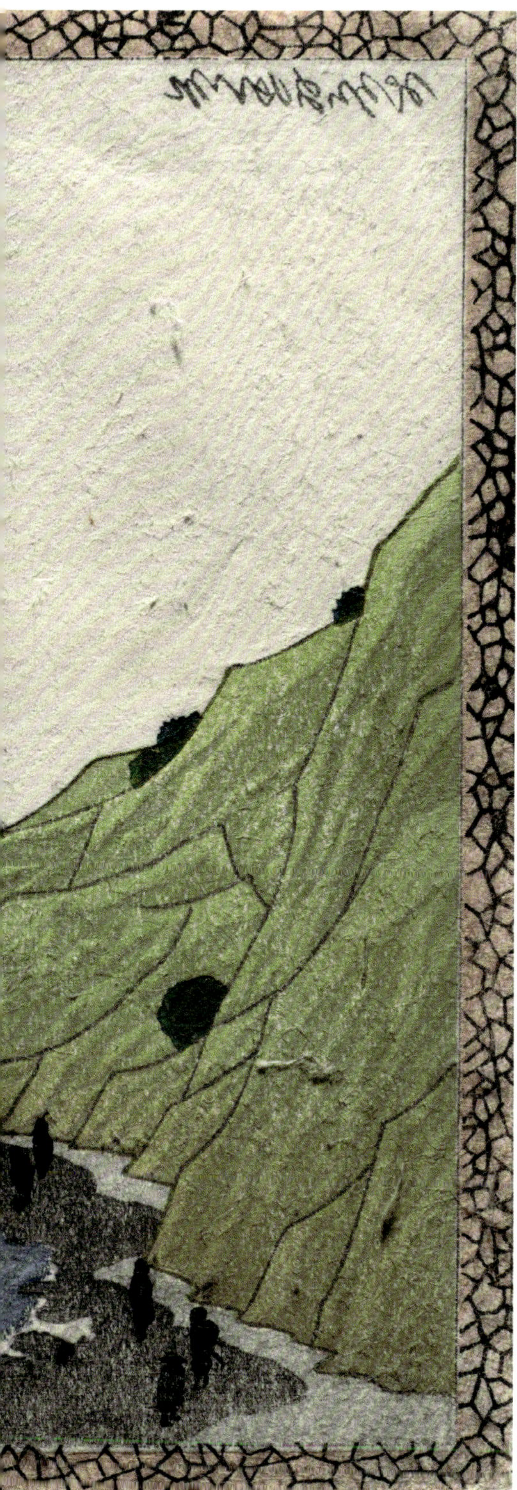

12

HOKUSAI
Panoramic View of Enoshima, about 1804–10.
Color woodblock print
13.5 x 19.1 cm
(5 3/8 x 7 1/2 in.)

13

SAKAI HŌITSU
after **OGATA KŌRIN**
Waves, from *One Hundred Pictures by Kōrin*, 1826.
Woodblock printed book
26.1 x 18.2 cm
(10 1/4 x 7 1/8 in.)

A final key element that would appear in Hokusai's famous "Great Wave" of 1830 — the sinister claw-like shapes of the foam at the crest of the wave — may have come from his interest in the Rimpa school of art: the Tawaraya school that he joined in the mid-1790s was an offshoot of Rimpa. Originally based in Kyoto, the Rimpa school became popular in Edo in the early nineteenth century through the work of Sakai Hōitsu, who in addition to his own paintings published art books presenting woodcut reproductions of the earlier Rimpa master Ogata Kōrin (1658–1716). The image of a screen painting by Kōrin known as "Rough Waves" (now in the Metropolitan Museum of Art) was included in this printed art book of 1826 that Hokusai would surely have seen.

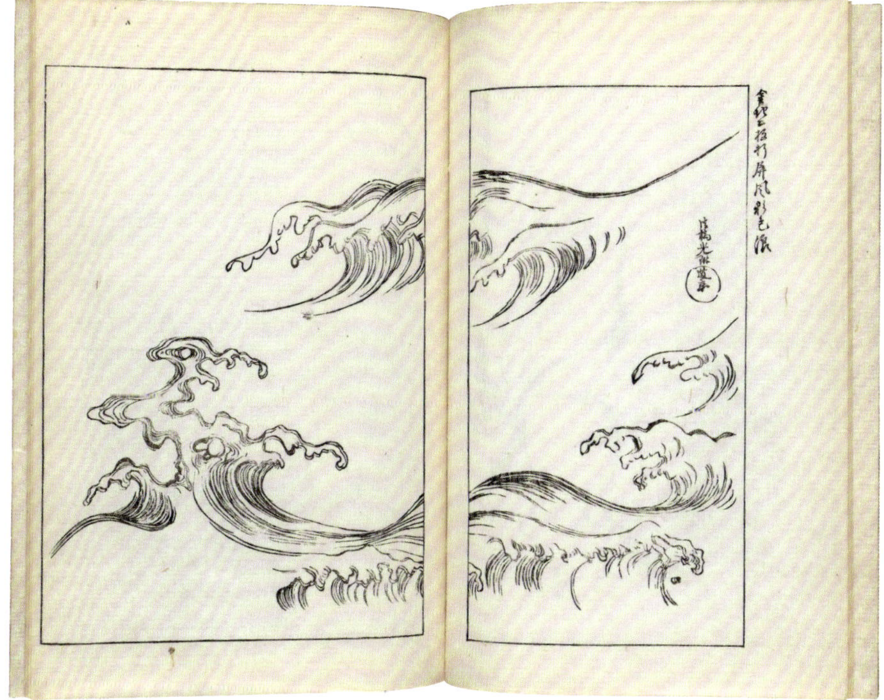

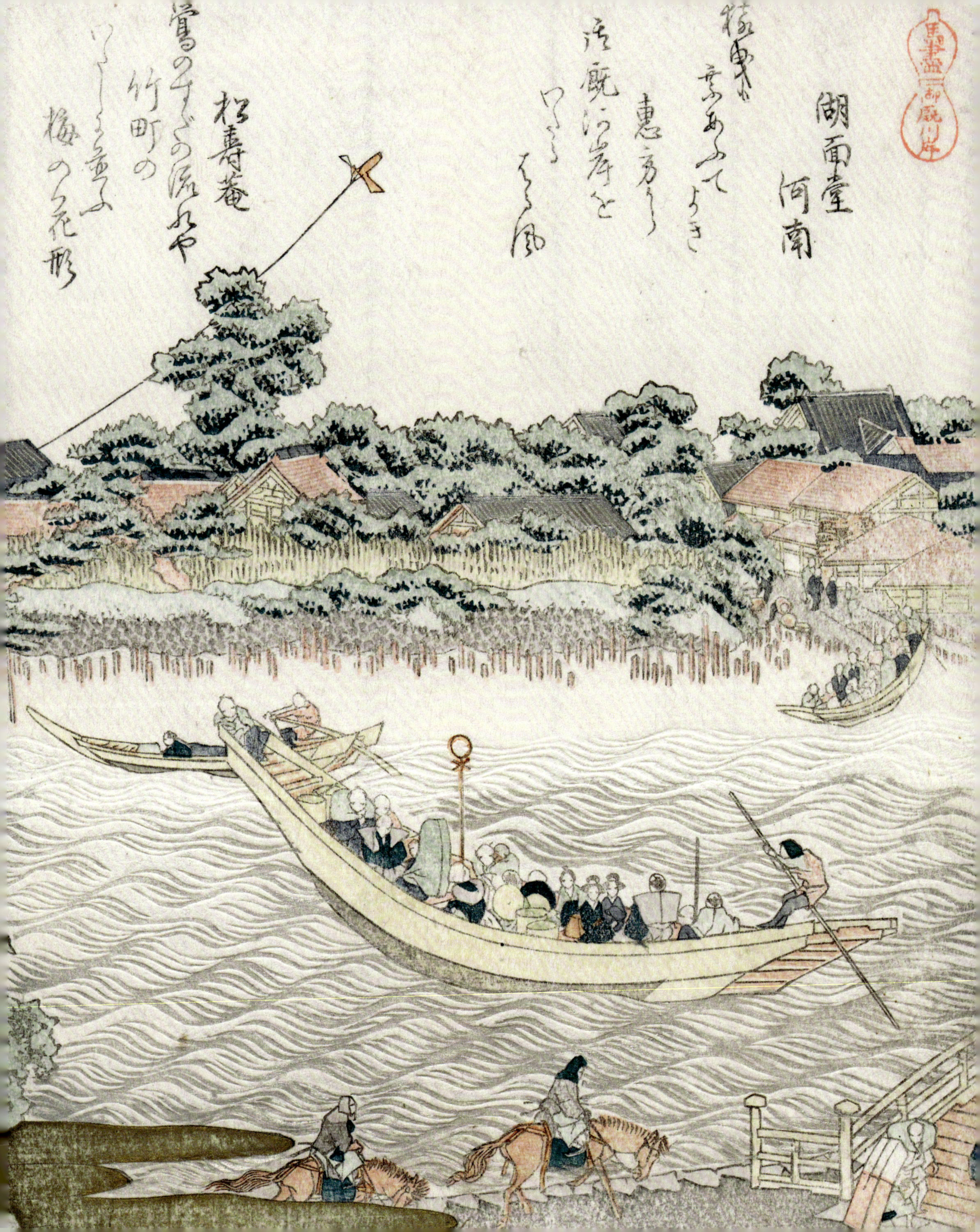

湖南堂
河南

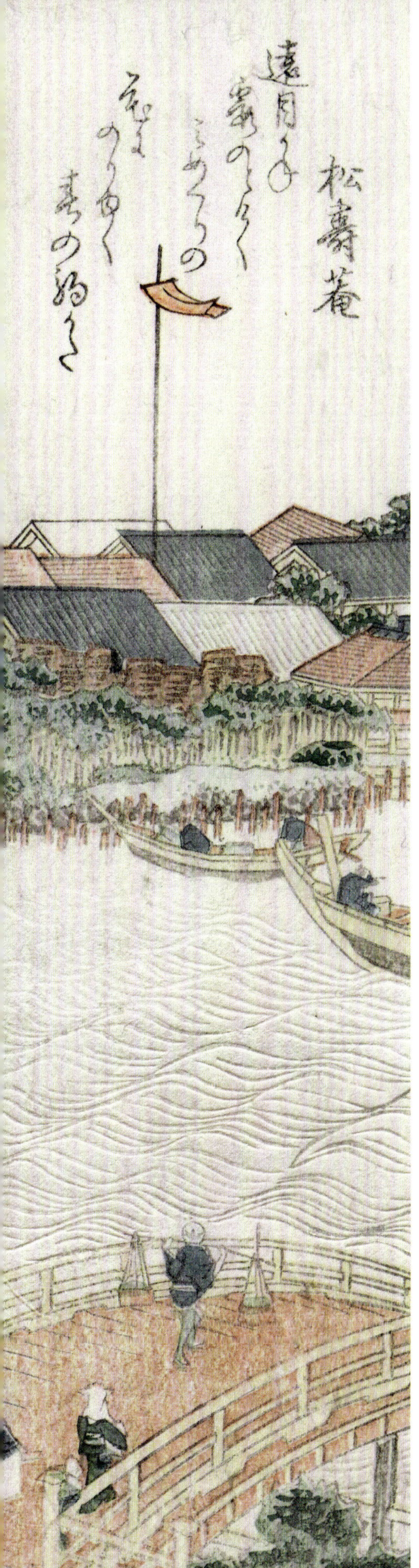

Hokusai's Students

HOKUSAI began training students of his own at least by 1794, when he left the Katsukawa school, and he continued to do so throughout his long life. The names of about 180 of his students are known, although for many there is little biographical information. Rather than assemble a large studio with many student assistants, like Shunshō or Kunisada, Hokusai appears to have trained students individually and encouraged them to develop their own styles. His status after 1798 as an independent artist, one who was part of the ukiyo-e tradition but not associated with any particular school, freed him from the obligation to perpetuate a particular lineage.

While he was acting head of the Tawaraya school, Hokusai, along with his wife and children, presumably lived in the family mansion together with his employers. Some additional students may have lived in the household as well, or come in for instruction during the day. By 1798, when he parted with the Tawaraya family and became an independent artist, Hokusai was doing well financially. The next two decades were the most prosperous time of his life, culminating in the success of the picture-book series *Hokusai Sketchbooks*. This was also probably the period when he took on the greatest number of students, although detailed information is lacking. In later life, after suffering severe financial reversals due to family problems in the 1820s, he may have taken on fewer students because he was living in more cramped quarters; again, there is not much information.

It is possible that while he was still associated with the Katsukawa school, Hokusai may have participated in training the younger members of the studio, although the earliest pupils whose names are known are from the time of his association with the Tawaraya. In addition to the Tawaraya heir, who later took the name Hishikawa Sōri (active 1790s–1810s), these early students included Ryūryūkyo Shinsai (1764?–1820) and possibly Teisai Hokuba (1771–1844) and Shotei Hokuju (1763–1824). Hokuba may have been the first of many students to take an art name referring to his teacher's name Hokusai. Meaning literally "Northern Studio," the name derives from Hokusai's religious devotion to Myōken, the Bodhisattva of the polar stars and an important deity in the Nichiren sect of Buddhism; he used it first as an alternate name together with Sōri, and later as his main name. He also continued to refer to himself as "the former Hokusai" even after moving on to other names.

Many of Hokusai's students, throughout his life, are known for paintings rather than print designs, somewhat unusually for ukiyo-e artists. It may have been that the Tawaraya wanted Hokusai as a teacher for the excellent painting skills he had gained from Shunshō. They may have disdained the cheaper popular prints, since he seems to have given up commercial print design during the time he worked for them—though he also might have been distancing himself from actor prints as part of his break with the Katsukawa school.

There was, however, one form of print that the Tawaraya family thoroughly approved of: the privately commissioned luxury prints known as *surimono*. Made to order for discerning customers, these included decorated programs for events such as concerts and dance performances; pictorial calendars that cleverly evaded the government monopoly on the printing of calendars by concealing calendrical information in a puzzle-picture; and illustrations of amateur verse for their authors to exchange with fellow members of poetry clubs on special occasions such as the annual New Year party. The prints were lavishly produced, often with more expensive paper and pigments than ordinary prints sold in stores, as well as extensive use of special techniques such as embossing. The Tawaraya had social connections with the affluent, well-educated patrons who commissioned such prints, and Hokusai had the skill and talent to create the ingenious designs that appealed to them. He and his students soon became top designers of these luxury prints, as well as of illustrated books of poetry that were privately printed for the same clientele.

Probably the most prolific (and hence the most financially successful) of all Hokusai's students was Totoya Hokkei (1780–1850), who became the leading designer of surimono in the 1820s, after Hokusai

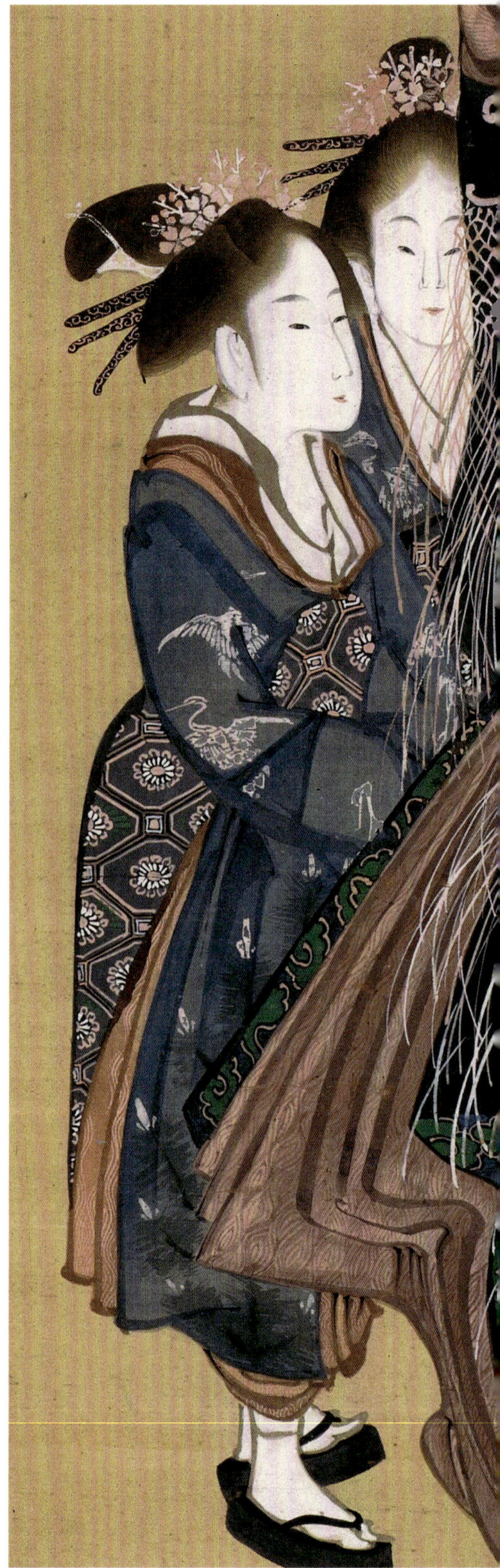

HISHIKAWA SŌRI (DETAIL, NO. 15)

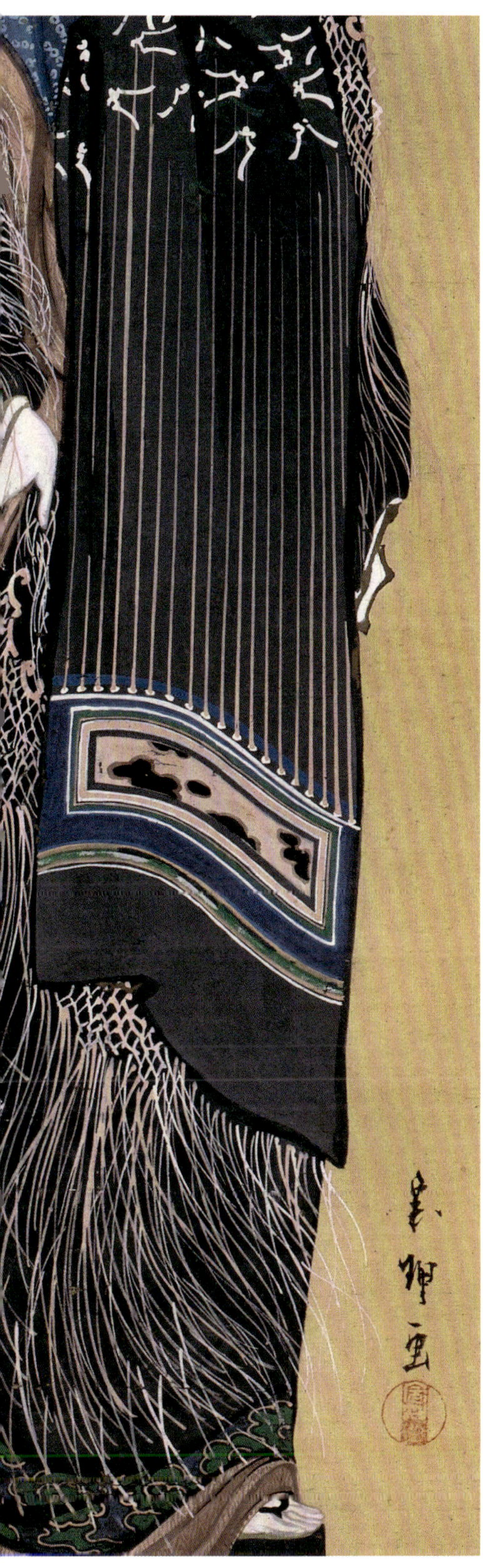

had cut back on activity in this area and the other principal surimono designer, Kubo Shunman (1757–1820), had died. The second most prominent surimono designer at the time was Hokkei's student Yashima Gakutei (1786?–1868), who may also have studied under Hokusai himself, and later moved to Osaka. Although Hokkei and Gakutei are primarily known for surimono, book illustrations, and paintings, they both designed a few outstanding commercial landscape prints following the huge success of Hokusai's Fuji series in the early 1830s.

Little is known about Hokusai's early student Hokuju, who seems to have preceded Hokusai in designing color woodblock landscape prints in the standard ōban size (about 10 by 15 inches, roughly equivalent to two sheets of modern letter-size paper). In the early 1800s, Hokusai had designed a number of small landscape prints, both surimono and commercial, but he does not seem to have produced any full-size landscape prints (other than the early uki-e perspective prints) until the Fuji series. Hokuju, who died in 1824, was apparently the first artist to do so. The numerous extant impressions of his prints, some made from worn blocks, indicate that they sold well, although they did not revolutionize the world of ukiyo-e as Hokusai's works did just a few years later.

The family-like structure of schools of art during the Edo period (which included the lineages of decorative and performing arts as well as pictorial arts) led to the involvement of some of Hokusai's own family in his artistic activities. Hokusai was married twice and had five children, a boy and two girls by the first wife, and a son and daughter by the second wife (and possibly a sixth child, a daughter who died young). The oldest son replaced his father as the heir to Hokusai's uncle and adoptive father, the mirror-polisher whose household Hokusai had left when he was in his (rebellious?) teens. The second son was adopted into a low-ranking samurai family and had a career as a government official, not particularly distinguished but nevertheless prestigious since it made him officially a member of the ruling class.

It was the three girls in the family who became involved in various ways with the art world. The oldest daughter, Omiyo, married Hokusai's student Yanagawa Shigenobu (1787–1832). Hokusai may have arranged the marriage, and he apparently adopted Shigenobu as his son and heir, as his own sons had gone on to other careers. Unfortunately, the marriage ended in divorce and Omiyo returned to her father, but not before the birth of a son by Shigenobu. This grandson was to cause many problems for the family later. Shigenobu himself moved to Osaka for about a year in 1822, perhaps because of the breakup of the marriage, before returning to Edo. A letter written by Hokusai at the beginning of 1830

says that after paying off the enormous debts of his grandson (perhaps
from gambling), he is sending the grandson out of town in the custody of
his father Shigenobu to get him away from bad influences. Shigenobu's
death in 1832 may have been hastened by the difficulties with his son.
A few years later, another letter by Hokusai says that he is setting up the
problem grandson in a business as a fishmonger and has arranged a
marriage for him.

It seems likely that Hokusai's poverty in old age, despite his success
as an artist, was caused by his incurring large expenses on behalf of this
family member, whose name we do not know. Shigenobu did do well in
both Edo and Osaka as a designer of surimono, book illustrations, and
occasionally commercial prints, in a mode that combines the Katsushika
style and the rival Utagawa school style, which he passed on to students
including Yanagawa Shigenobu II (active 1820s–1850s).

Omiyo, the mother of the problem grandson, may have been the
same person as the painter Jofū, one of many pupils of Hokusai for whom
we have little information beyond their signatures and painting styles.
Hokusai's second daughter, who may have been named Otetsu, is said
to have been good at painting; she died as a young adult, soon after
her marriage to a merchant. A mysterious female artist signing her work
Tatsu-jo (literally "Ms. Dragon," using a character also found in some
of Hokusai's many art names), made excellent paintings of elaborately
dressed women and sometimes included the phrase "daughter of
Hokusai" in her signature, but we do not know whether she was this
second daughter.

The most successful artist among Hokusai's children was Oei, the
youngest daughter (or at least the youngest who survived into full adult-
hood), who used the art name Katsushika Ōi. Like her older sister Omiyo,
she was married to another artist and then divorced him and returned
to her father's home. She does not seem to have had any children. Her
mother, Hokusai's second wife, died in the late 1820s, and Oei may have
moved in with her father around that time. She stayed with him until
his death in 1849 and never remarried. There is much debate as to how
much of Hokusai's late work may in fact be by her, and even the works
that bear her own signature — such as a painting of three women playing
musical instruments (see no. 16) — are clearly by a highly accomplished
artist whose style is similar but not identical to that of Hokusai.

Some of Hokusai's students were located outside Edo, particularly
in Osaka and Nagoya. These students may have studied with him while
they were visiting Edo, and in some cases it was Hokusai who traveled
to other cities and taught students there. In 1818 Hokusai visited Osaka,

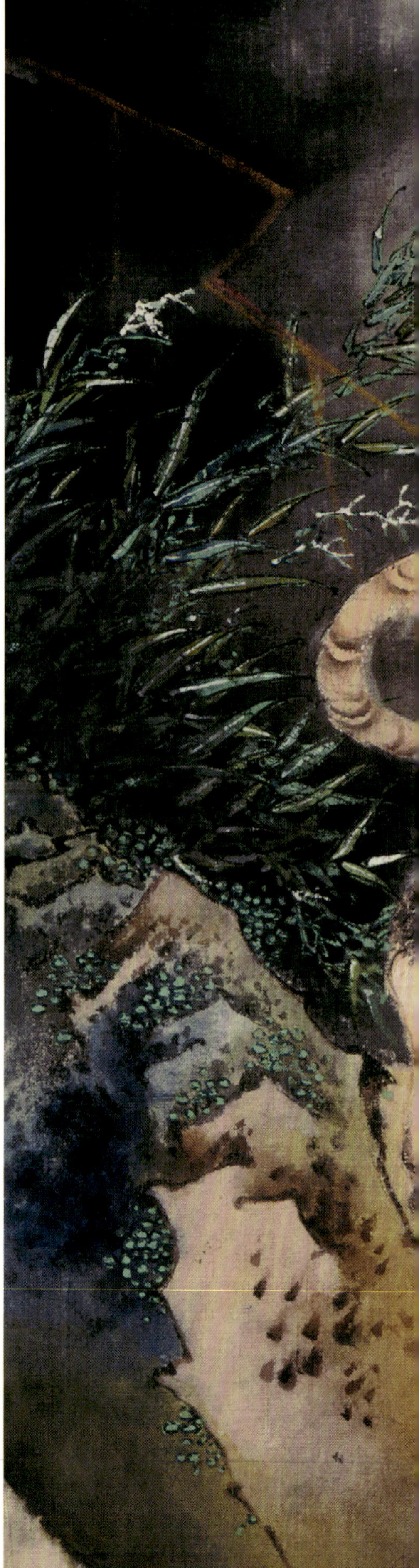

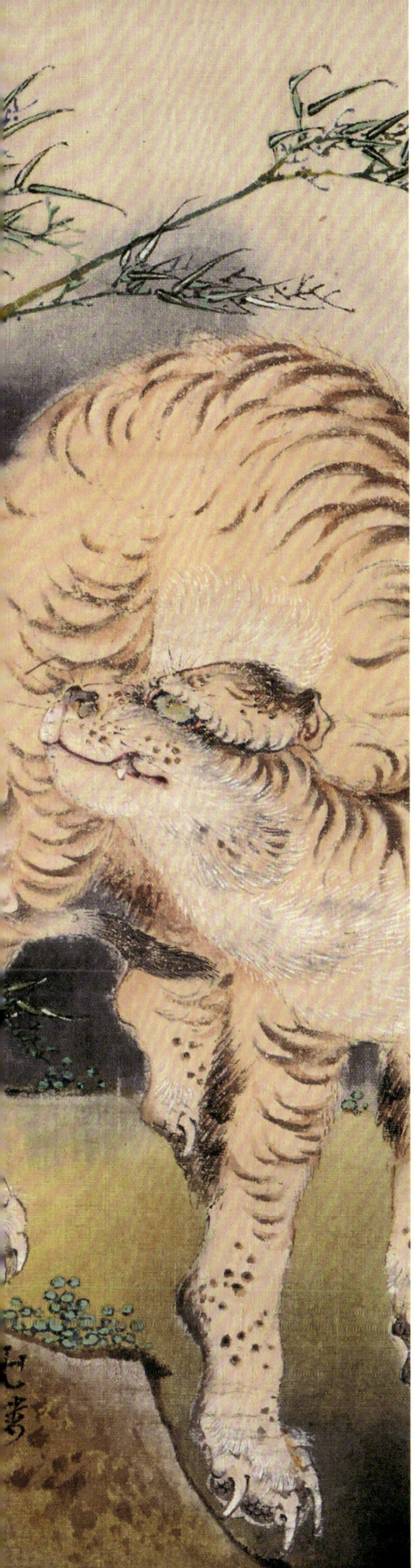

where he apparently taught the artist known as Shunkōsai (active about 1808–32), who took the additional name Hokushū in Hokusai's honor. Shunkōsai Hokushū went on to become one of the most important ukiyo-e artists in Osaka and passed on the Hoku component of the name to his own pupils, including Hokuei (died in 1837) and Hokuchō (active about 1822–30). When Yanagawa Shigenobu went to Osaka in 1822–23, he would have benefited from the connections made by his former father-in-law Hokusai. Shigenobu also trained some Osaka artists, notably Ryūsai Shigeharu (1803–1853).

The pupils in Nagoya were especially important because they were responsible for the publication of Hokusai's first bestseller, the picture book *Hokusai Sketchbooks*, with ten volumes issued in 1814–19 and five more added much later by enterprising publishers. The book originated as a collection of sketches made by Hokusai at a gathering with students when he visited Nagoya in 1812, staying with his student Maki Bokusen (1736–1824). It was the students who collated the drawings and prepared them for publication as a manual of model drawings for aspiring artists like themselves.

The Japanese title of the book, *Hokusai manga*, is a little misleading for modern readers because the meaning of the word *manga* has shifted somewhat over the past two centuries. Today it refers specifically to comics or graphic stories with pictorial narration; in Hokusai's time it simply meant informal drawings of any kind. Some of the drawings in the *Hokusai Sketchbooks* do have narrative content, often humorous, that link them to modern manga. Even closer parallels are found in Hokusai's illustrations for popular novels, reinterpreted as color prints by his own pupils and by his younger colleague and competitor Kuniyoshi, one of the many students of Utagawa Toyokuni.

MANJIRŌ HOKUGA (DETAIL, NO. XX)

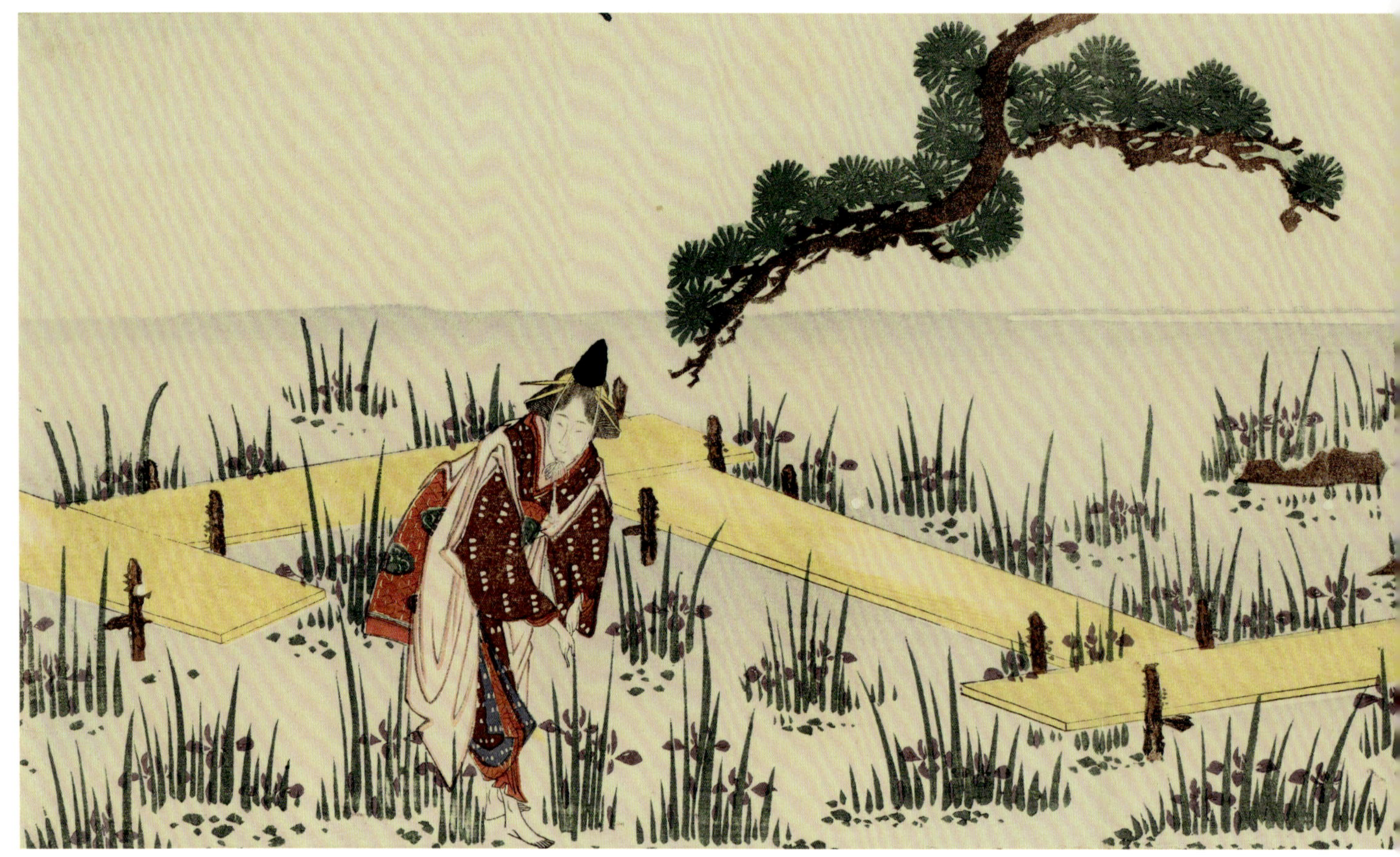

14

HOKUSAI
Women Imitating the Story of Narihira at Yatsuhashi, late 1790s. Color woodblock print (surimono)
19.2 x 51.9 cm
(7½ x 20⅜ in.)

15

HISHIKAWA SŌRI
Courtesan with Child Attendants, about 1798–1810s. Hanging scroll; ink and color on silk
85.5 x 33.2 cm
(33⅝ x 13⅛ in.)

Following the death of Shunshō in 1792, Hokusai was not on good terms with the other artists of the Katsukawa school and had difficulty making ends meet. He is even supposed to have considered giving up art; fortunately, the opportunity to work for the Tawaraya family arose, thanks to his abilities as a teacher. From 1794 to 1798, Hokusai used the art name Tawaraya Sōri II while instructing the family's young heir. In 1798 the young man took the name Sōri, while Hokusai became an independent artist, no longer affiliated with any one school.

Hokusai trained the Tawaraya heir and several other pupils in the techniques he had learned from Shunshō, so that they, too, could produce gorgeous paintings of women attired in luxurious kimono. Hokusai's teaching was so successful that it is sometimes difficult to determine which artist created works with the Sōri signature. This sumptuous depiction of a top-ranked courtesan of the Yoshiwara pleasure district, painted in subdued tones to emphasize the lavish fabrics, was once attributed to Hokusai himself but is now considered to be the work of his talented pupil.

The Tawaraya family introduced Hokusai not only to patrons for his paintings, but also to the affluent literary types who were members of amateur poetry clubs and often commissioned

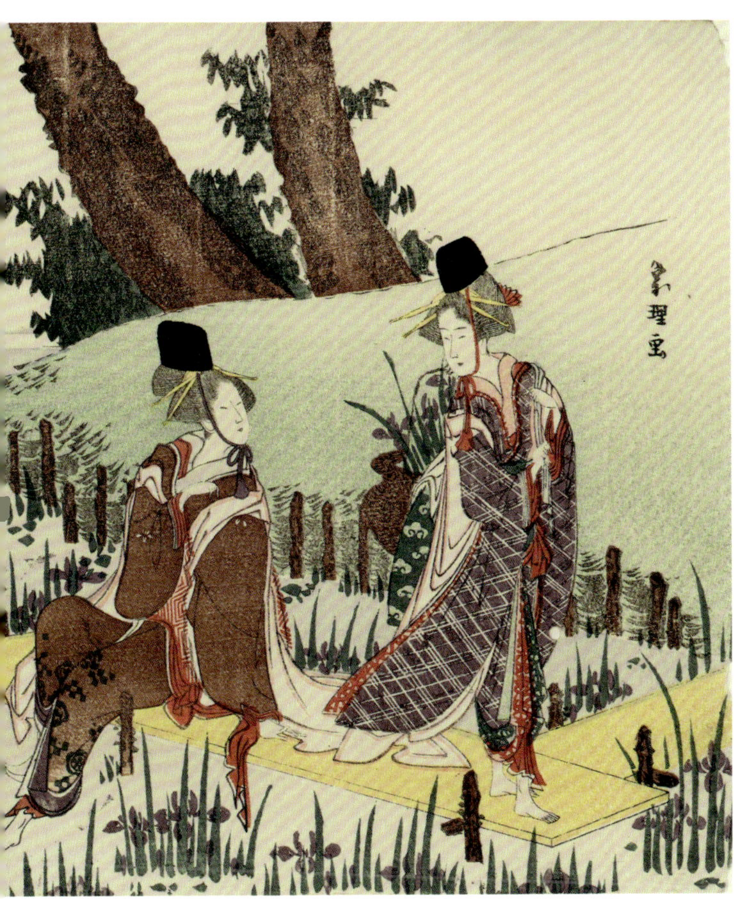

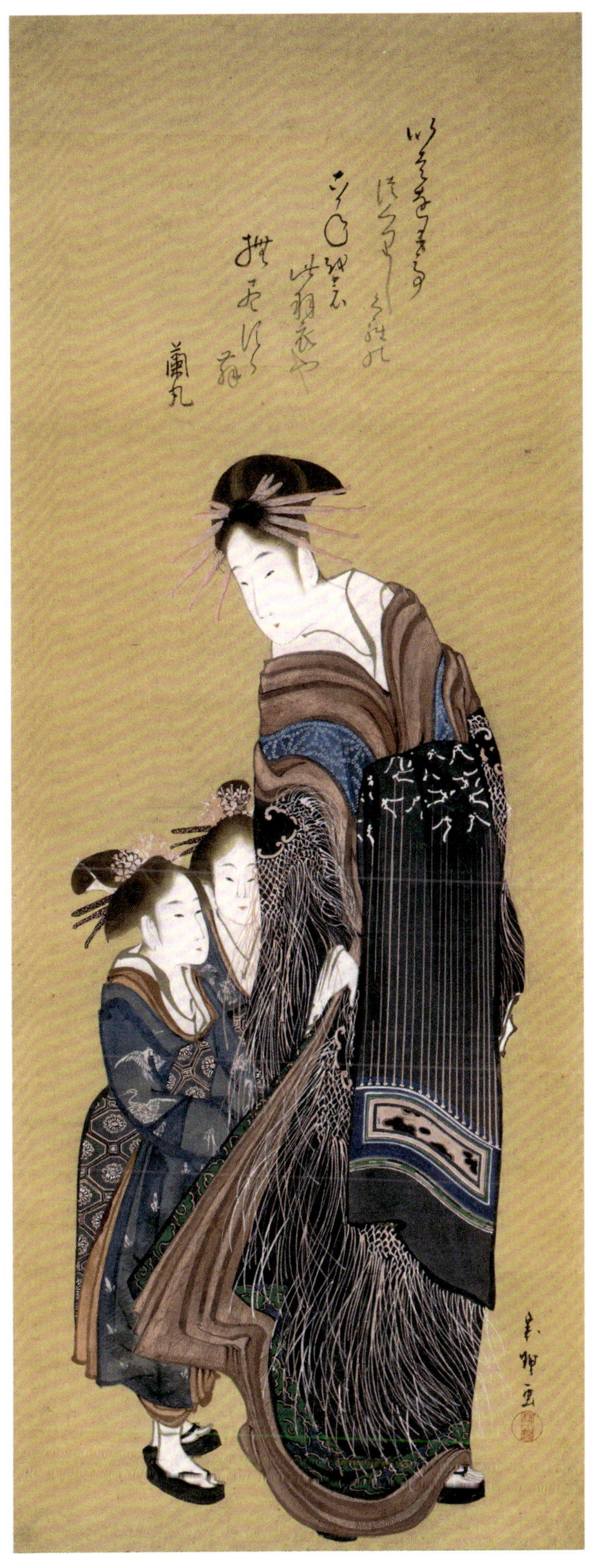

privately produced prints (surimono) to illustrate their poems. Hokusai became one of the top artists in this specialized field. This surimono print with the Sōri signature, most likely by Hokusai himself, is a witty gender-bending parody of a famous occasion in literary history, when a nobleman going into exile wrote a poem about a zigzag bridge among irises. Three young women wear the hats and white jackets of the ancient poet's servants over their modern clothes.

One of the most talented of all Hokusai's pupils was his own daughter, who used the art name Katsushika Ōi and was known as Oei in everyday life. During the Edo period, women artists were rare but not unknown; they were generally the daughters or wives of successful male artists, as family connections were the only way they could obtain the necessary training.

Like one of her older sisters, Oei was married briefly to another artist, although both marriages ended in divorce. She lived with her widowed father for some twenty years, likely from the late 1820s until his death in 1849, and it is not known what happened to her afterward.

Surviving works signed by Katsushika Ōi, such as this splendid image of three women playing music, show that her style was similar to that of her father but not exactly the same; for example, she makes greater use of delicate shading to give a sense of three-dimensionality to her figures. Both of the works shown here juxtapose different types of women in Edo-period society. The painting depicts a musical trio of three women who would probably not have played together in real life: a middle-class townswoman (*left*), a geisha (*right*), and a courtesan (*center*). Additional types of women are shown in the color frontispiece of a book on etiquette and general cultural knowledge for women, first published in 1692 and reissued with new illustrations by Ōi in 1847 (17).

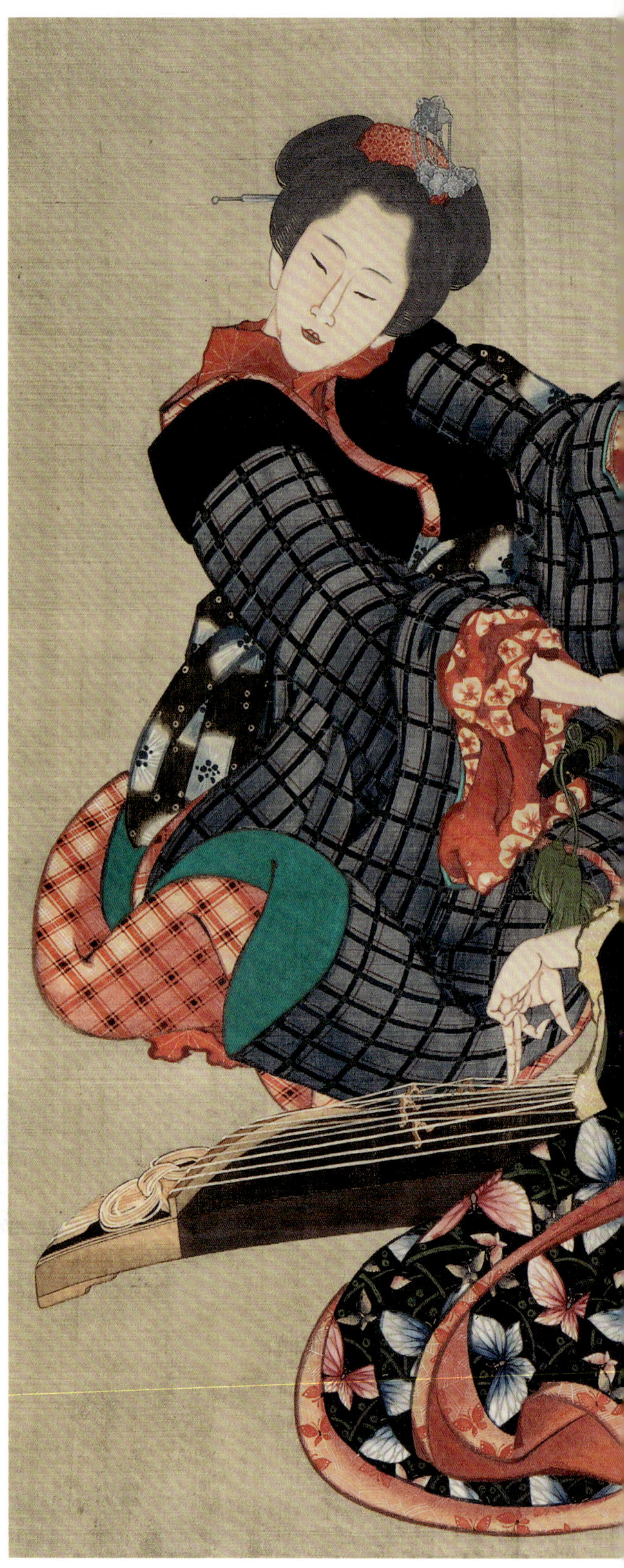

16

KATSUSHIKA ŌI
Three Women Playing Musical Instruments, 1820s–1830s. Hanging scroll; ink and color on silk
46.5 x 67.5 cm (18¼ x 26⅝ in.)

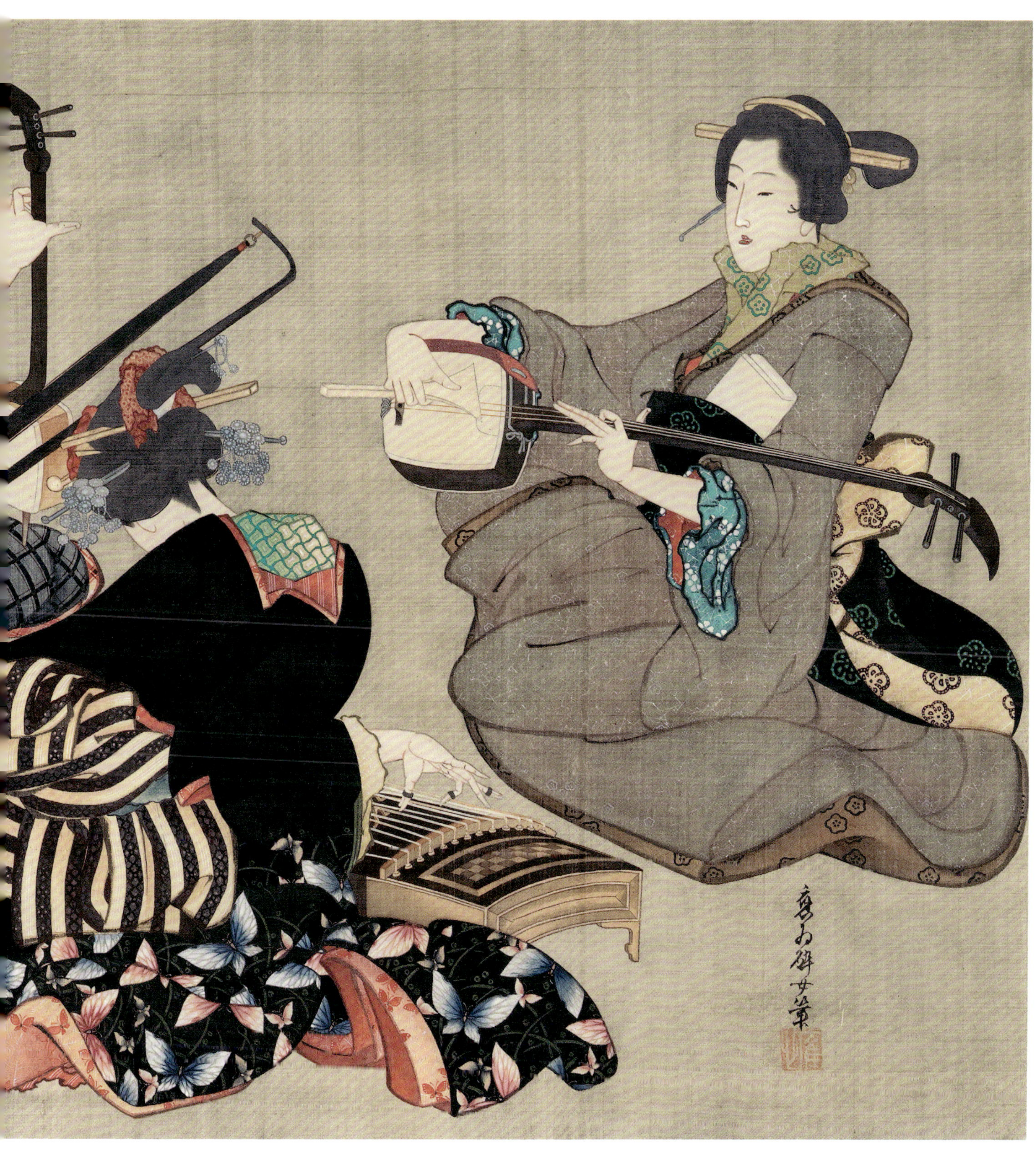

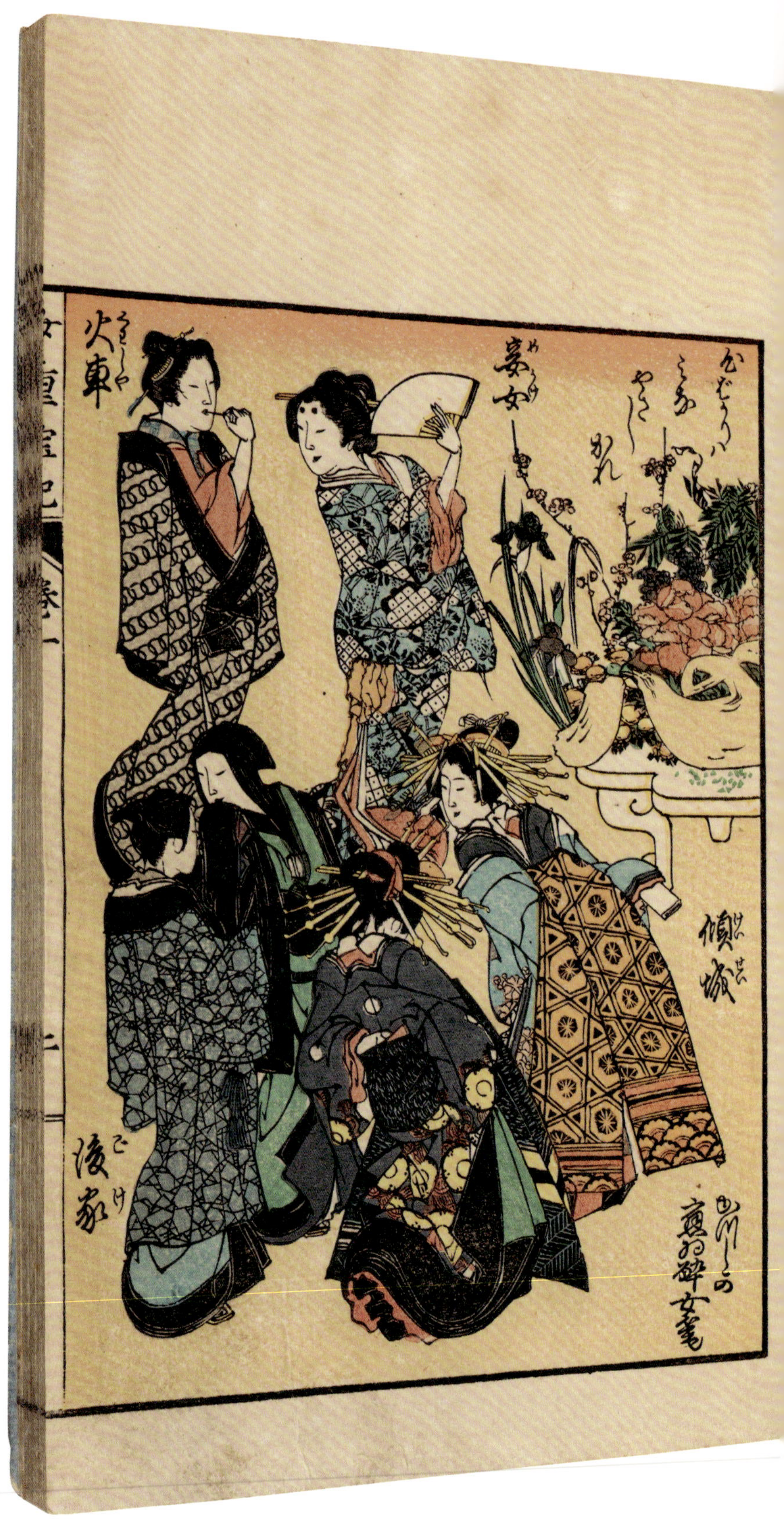

17
ōi
Types of Women,
frontispiece to
A Woman's Treasury,
1847. Color woodblock
printed book
25.3 x 17.9 cm
(10 x 7 in.)

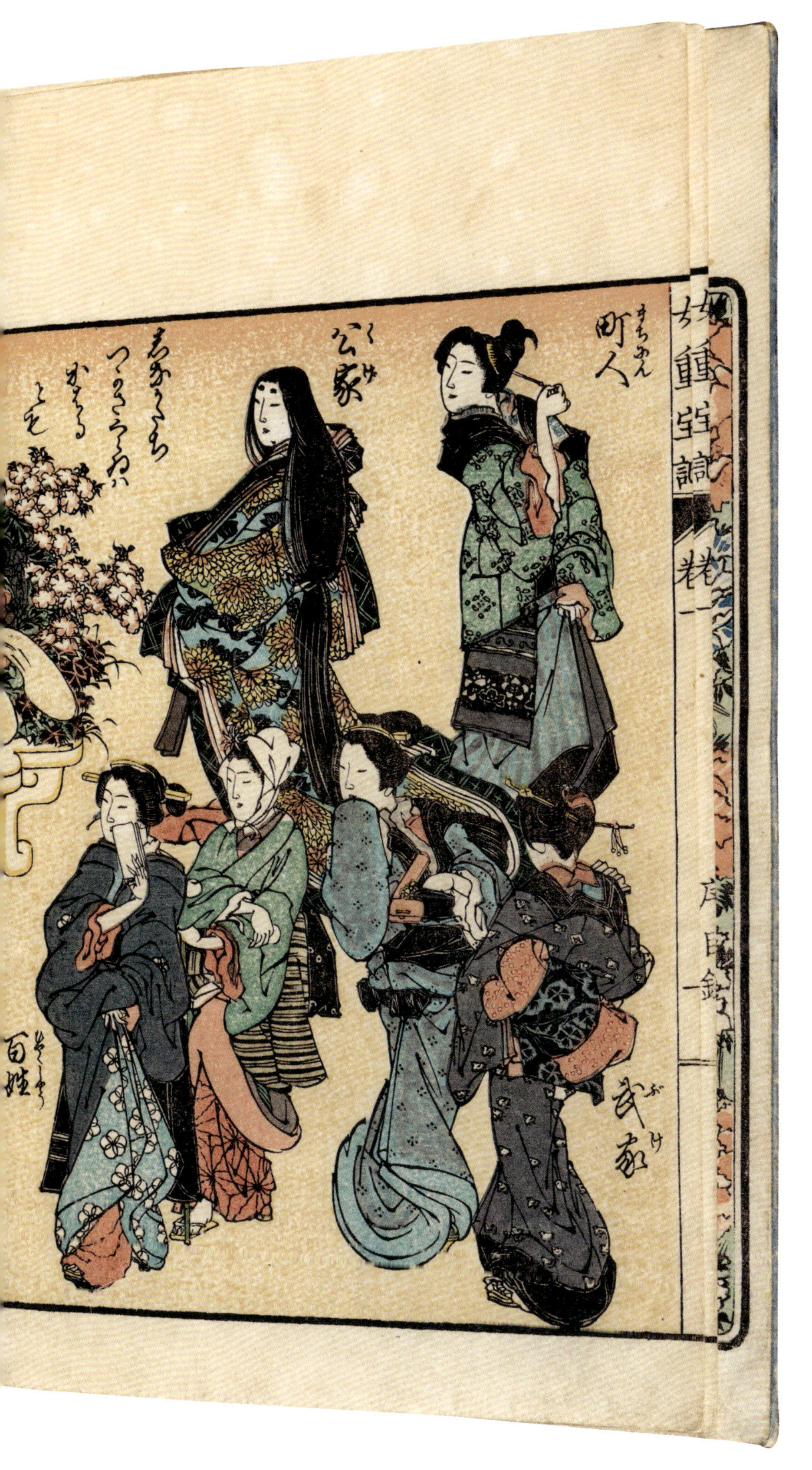
女重宝記　巻一
公家
町人
武家
百姓

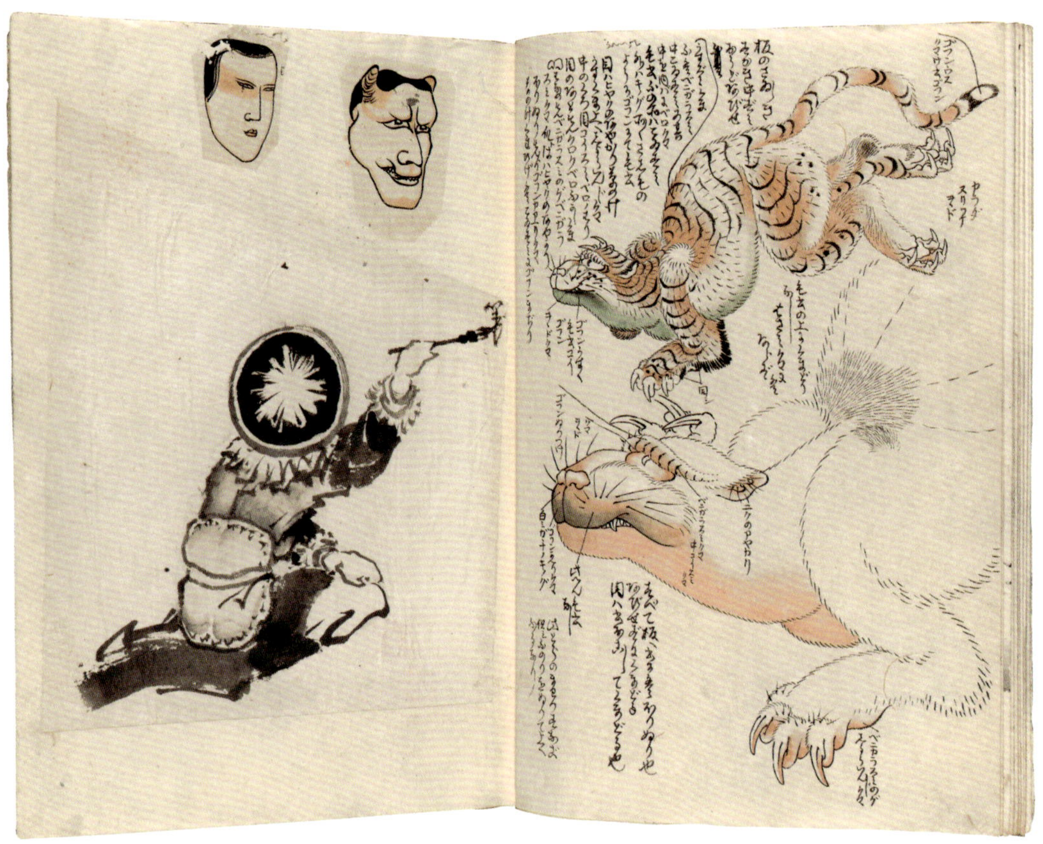

18
**ATTRIBUTED TO
MANJIRŌ HOKUGA**
How to Paint a Tiger,
1856. Ink and color
on paper
32.4 x 23.9 cm
(12¾ x 9⅜ in.)

19
MANJIRŌ HOKUGA
Tiger in a Thunderstorm,
late 1840s–mid-1850s.
Hanging scroll; ink and
color on flax
53.8 x 34.2 cm
(21⅛ x 13½ in.)

igers in East Asian art are magical animals, often paired with dragons because together they control the weather: dragons produce or withhold rain, while the roar of a tiger generates the wind. In Japan, tigers were almost as mythical as dragons since they are not native to the Japanese islands. Artists had to imagine what they might look like based on tiger skins imported from Korea, where real tigers were common, and local domestic cats, who were thought to resemble miniature tigers.

Manjirō Hokuga seems to have been a late pupil of Hokusai who specialized in paintings depicting legendary figures, and also made a few prints of the same subject. He was the second of Hokusai's pupils to use the name Hokuga, having inherited it from another obscure Katsushika-school artist later known as Hōtei Gosei. Manjirō Hokuga may have been a pupil of this first Hokuga as well as of Hokusai. A small album of drawings

by Hokusai in the MFA's collection has a hand-written preface by Manjirō Hokuga stating that Hokusai gave him the drawings when they were living together in the Fukagawa district in 1836.

Two unsigned albums of color sketches, dated 1855 and 1856, have been attributed to Hokuga because they resemble paintings by him. Although made a few years after Hokusai's death in 1849, they seem to be studies of paintings by the master, suggesting that Hokuga still wanted to learn from Hokusai even though he could no longer receive instruction in person. There may also be a connection between Hokuga and Hokusen, another late pupil of Hokusai's who died about 1885 or 1886. The contents of Hokusen's studio were acquired by William Sturgis Bigelow and eventually donated to the MFA. The studio is the likely source of many drawings and albums by Hokusai's students in the Museum's collection.

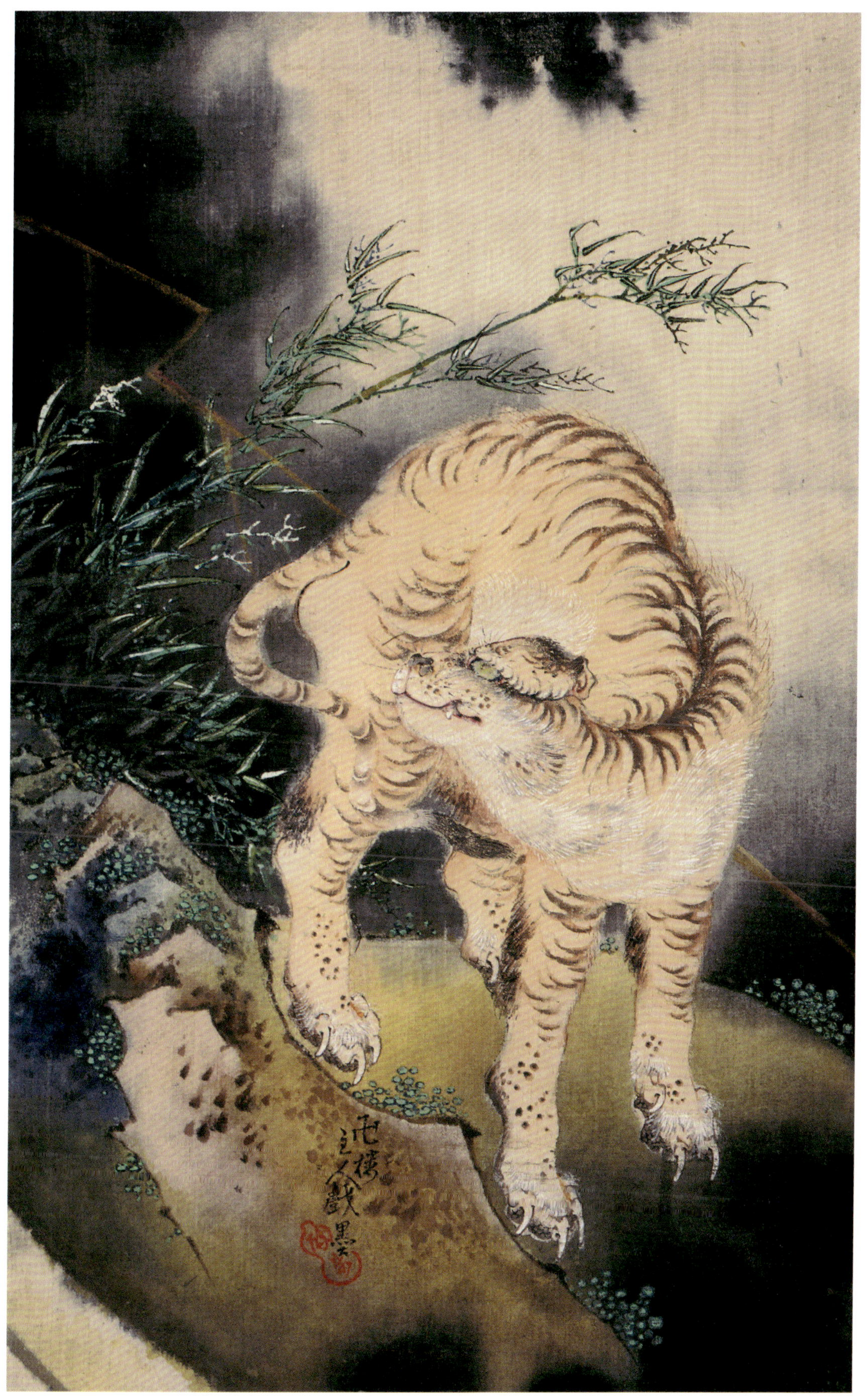

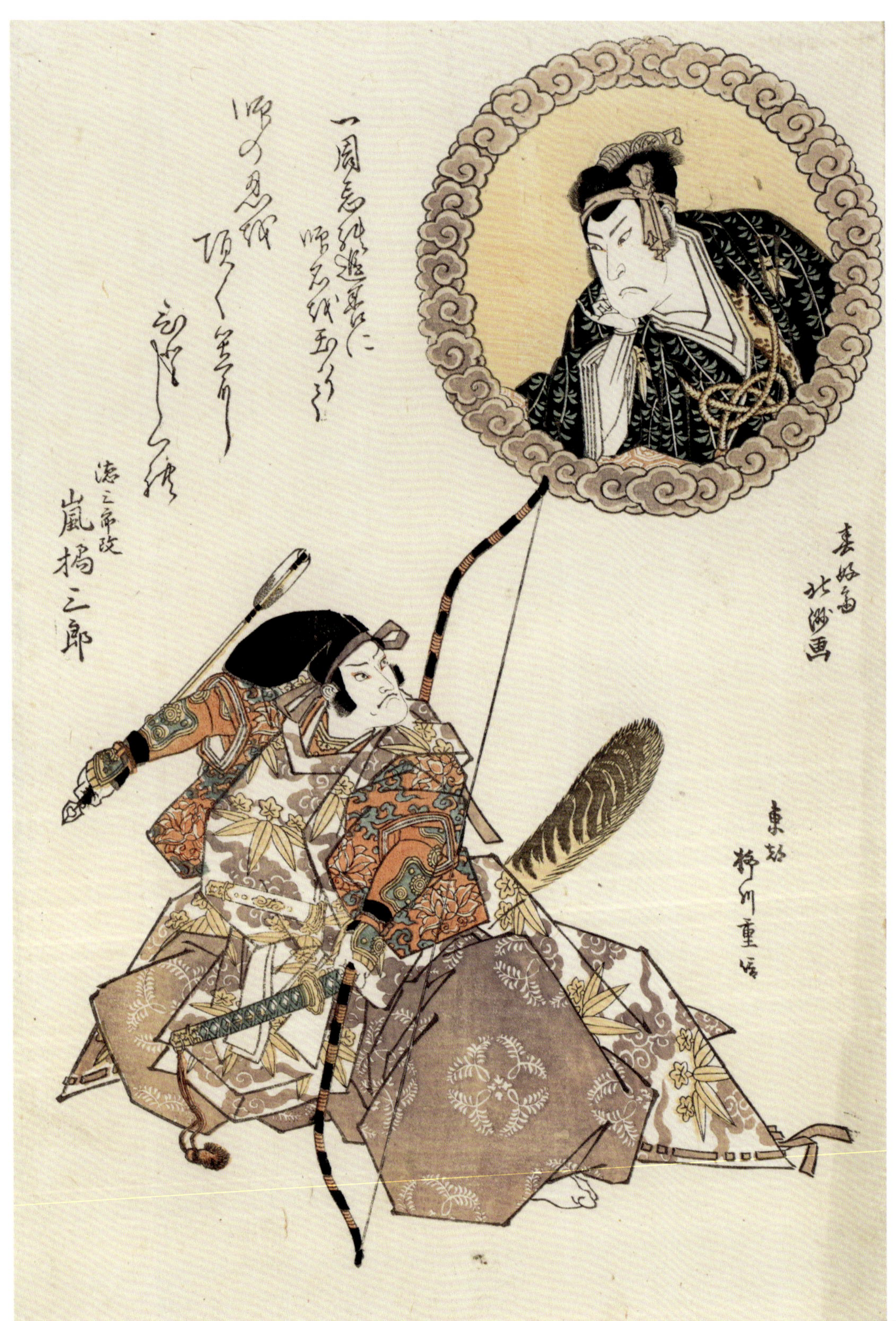

20

YANAGAWA SHIGENOBU I
and
SHUNKŌSAI HOKUSHŪ
*Memorial Portrait of Actor
Arashi Kitsusaburō I
(Rikan) as Yorimasa*,
1821.
Color woodblock print
37.7 x 26 cm
(14⅞ x 10¼ in.)

21

NUMATA GESSAI
*The Female Captain of
the Boat*, about 1818–30.
Hanging scroll; ink and
color on silk
91.9 x 33 cm
(36⅛ x 13 in.)

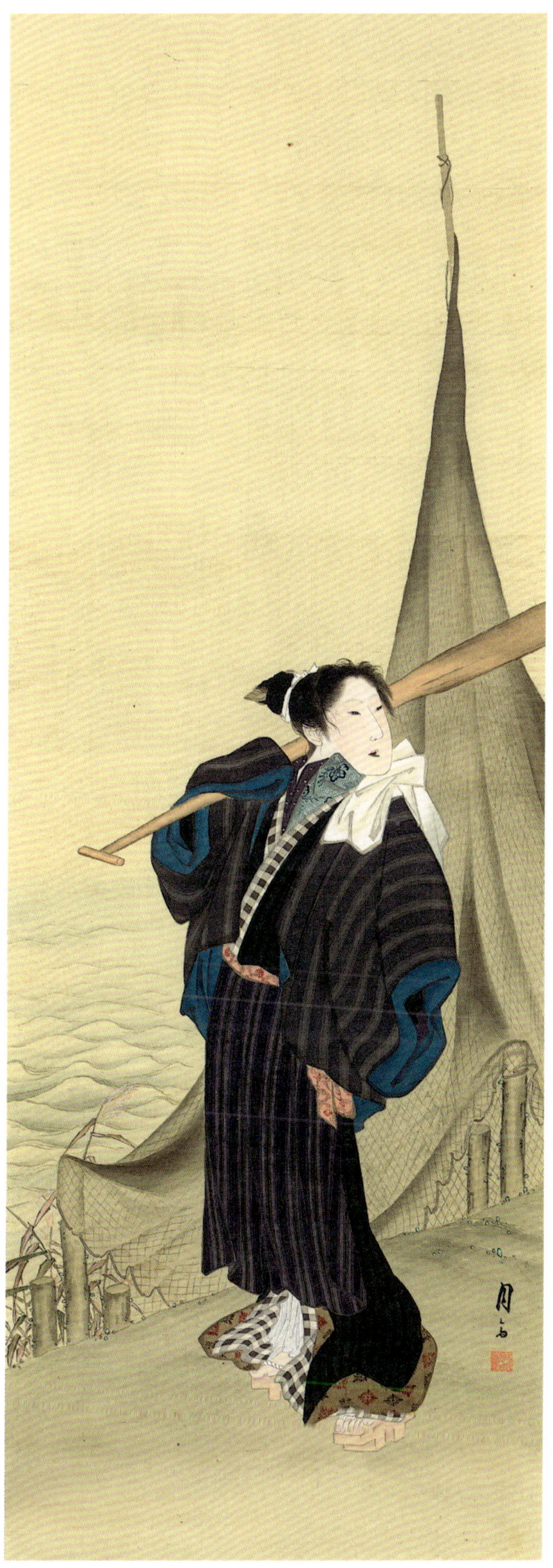

The network of Hokusai's students, loosely identifiable as the "Katsushika school," extended beyond Edo to other major cities such as Osaka and Nagoya. Hokusai had visited both cities and instructed pupils there, and some had probably studied under him in Edo. In Osaka, the connection was preserved in the names of a number of ukiyo-e artists, as a result of Hokusai's visit to the city in 1818. The artist Shunkō changed his name to Shunkōsai Hokushū after studying with Hokusai and went on to become the leading designer of actor prints in Osaka in the 1820s. Several artists who later studied under Hokushū also took names beginning with Hoku, a proud acknowledgment of their secondary connection to the great Hokusai, although there are few visual traces of Hokusai's influence in their work.

Yanagawa Shigenobu spent a year in Osaka in 1821–22 after his divorce from Hokusai's oldest daughter and probably took advantage of his former father-in-law's connections there. His own style combines features of the Katsushika style and the Utagawa style, as seen in a joint work with Hokushū, a memorial to a recently deceased actor. Shigenobu shows the star in one of his last roles, posed dramatically as a valiant archer, while Hokushū draws him in a wreath of heavenly clouds, with a purple headband (now some- what faded) symbolizing his final illness, in the caricature-like Osaka style.

Some of Hokusai's students in Nagoya were wealthy amateur painters of the samurai class, such as Maki Bokusen (1736–1824), who had once studied under Utamaro in Edo, and his student Numata Gessai (1787–1864). During Hokusai's extended visit to Nagoya in 1812, both Bokusen and Gessai became his students. This painting by Gessai shows a bold fisherwoman standing in front of nets hung over tall poles to dry. Her shaved eyebrows indicate that she is married with children, and the oar over her shoulder shows that she also works to bring in the catch. Her confident manner suggests that she may be the captain of a fishing boat.

Hokusai's devoted students in Nagoya became the driving force behind his first great hit, the bestselling multivolume picture book known as *Hokusai Sketchbooks*. According to the preface to volume 1, published in 1814, the project originated when Hokusai visited Nagoya and stayed at the home of Maki Bokusen. There he met with other students and made more than three hundred drawings of many different subjects, which the students decided to collate and publish. Various students are listed as collaborators with Hokusai in each of the ten volumes that make up the first edition; five extra volumes — some of them issued after Hokusai's death — were later added by publishers. The exact role played by these students is unclear: did they simply do layout and pasteup of Hokusai's drawings, or did they also trace over the originals to make the final drawings for the blockcutter? The books were enormously successful, running through many editions and referred to by numerous artists in Japan and, from the 1850s on, overseas as well. In addition to their value for artists, humorous illustrations such as this had great appeal for general viewers.

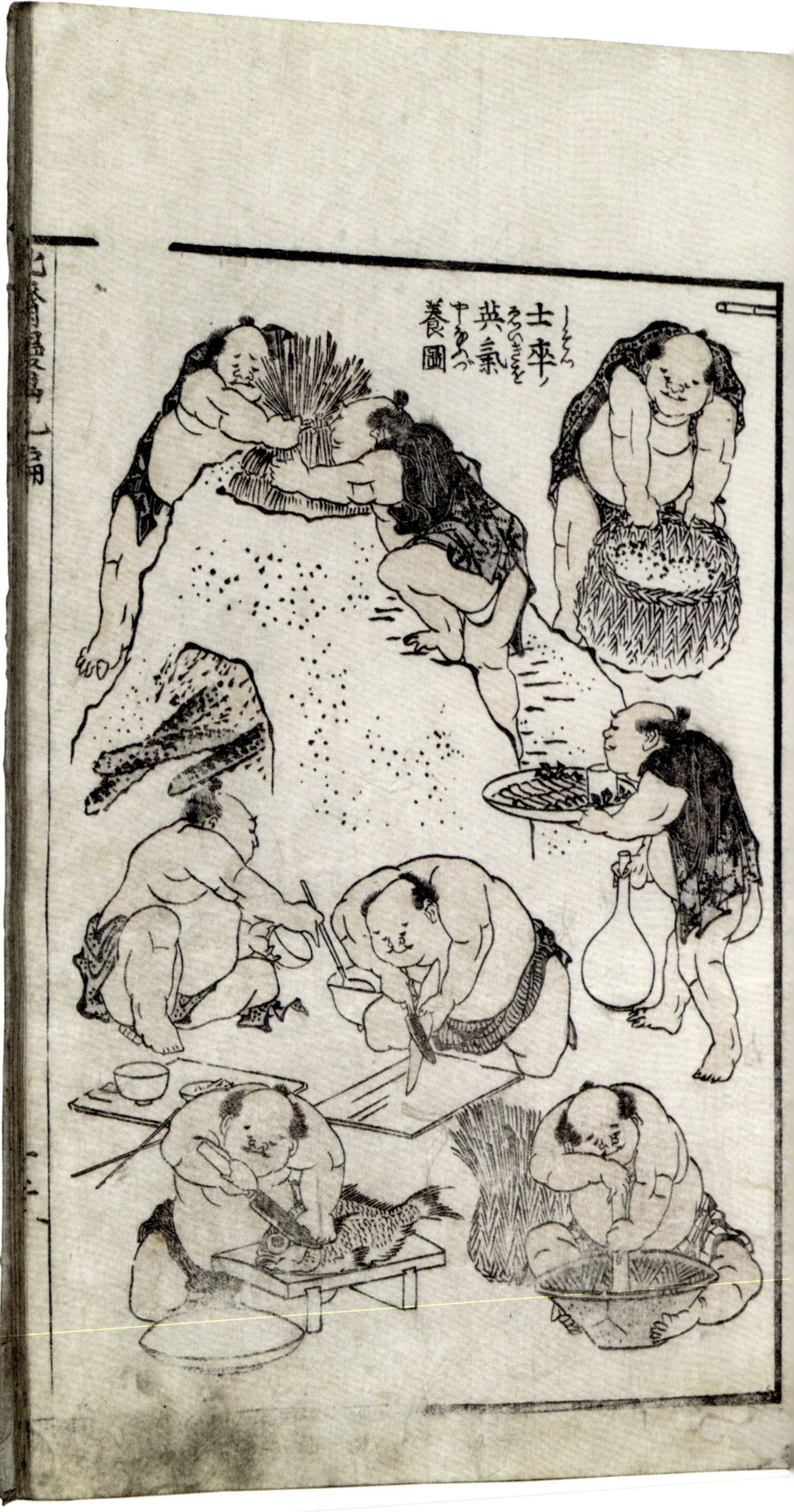

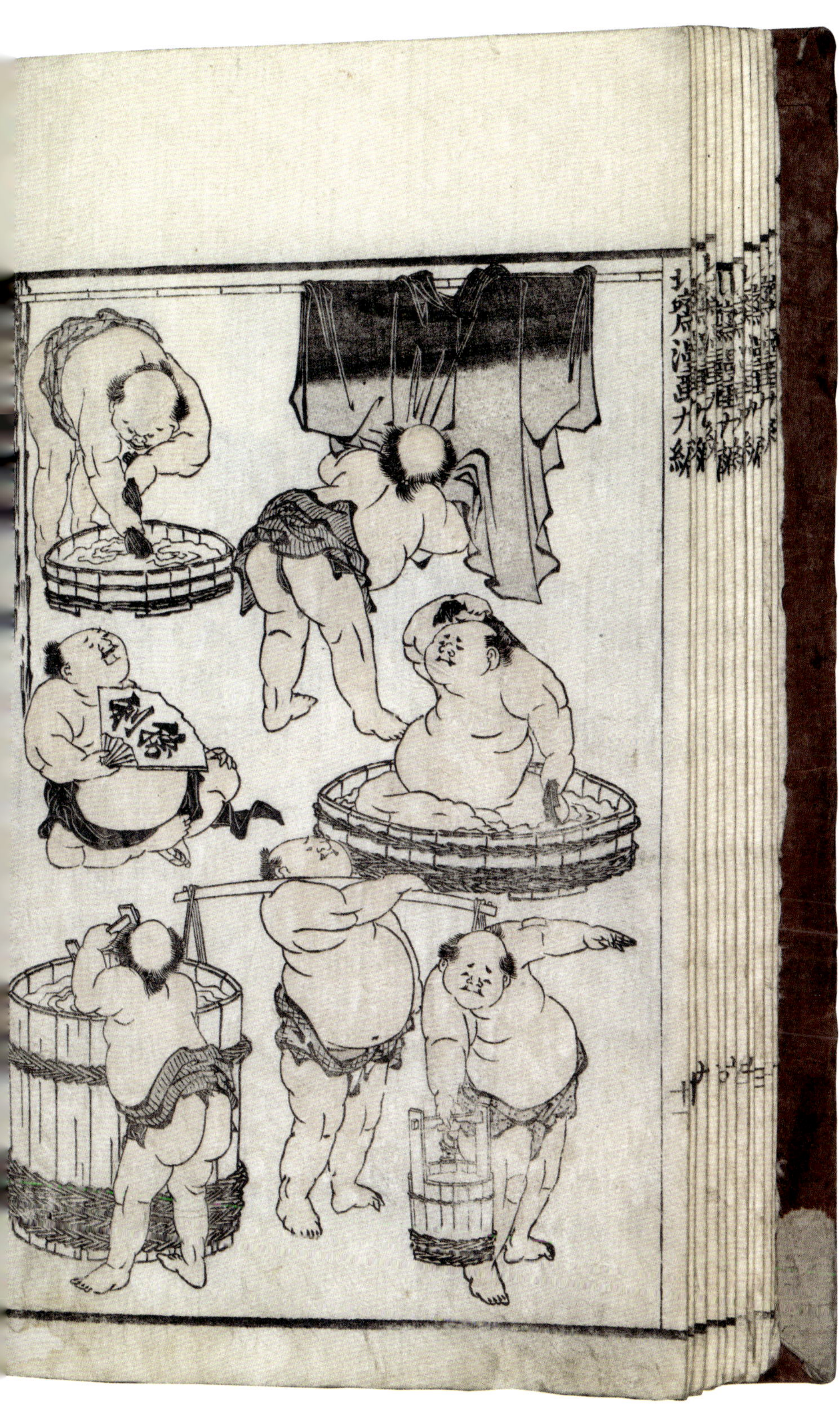

22

HOKUSAI
Sumo Wrestlers Doing Chores, from *Hokusai Sketchbooks*, 1819.
Woodblock printed book
Each page
about 23.5 x 16 cm
(9¼ x 6¼ in)

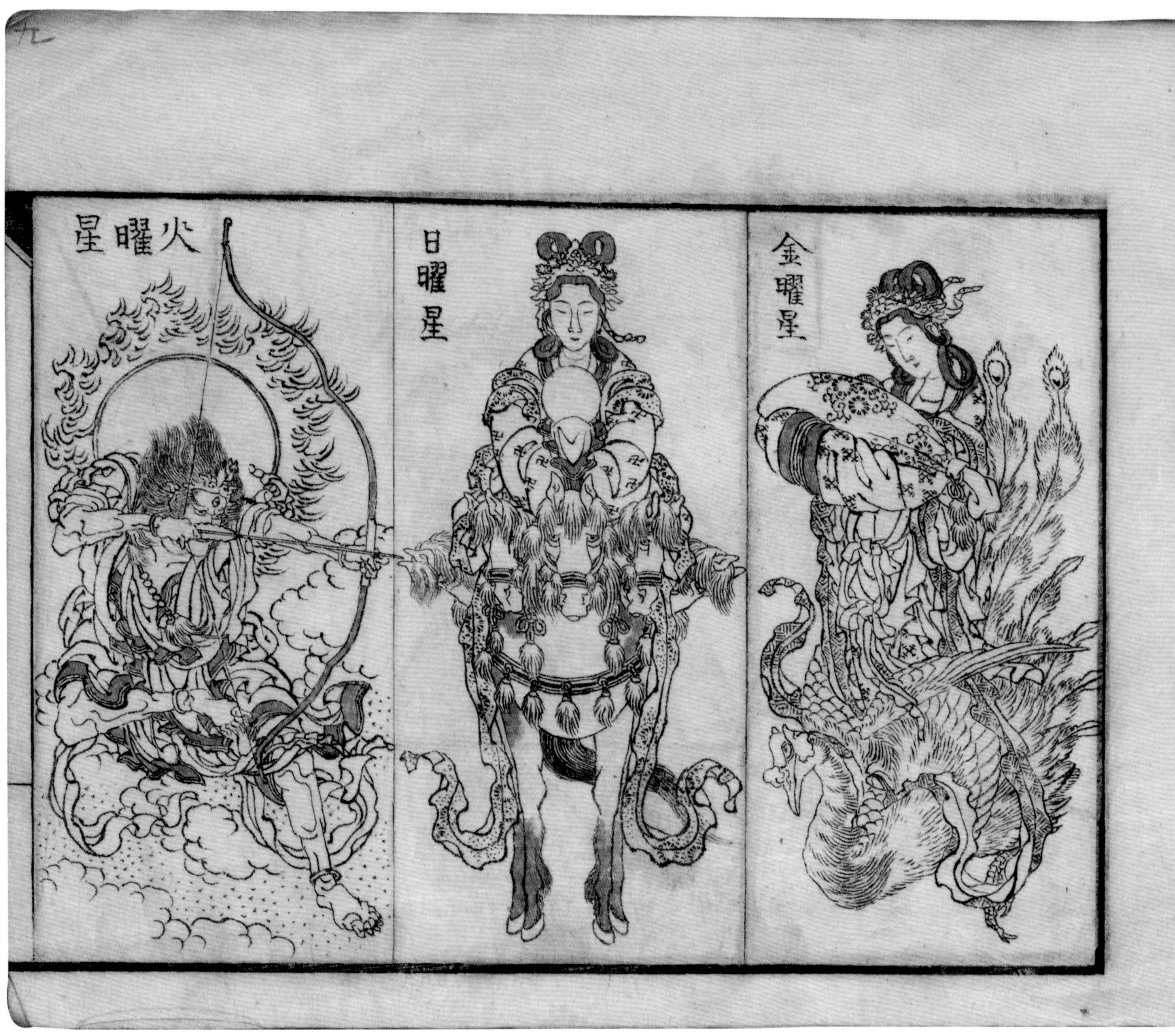

23

HOKUSAI
Deities of the Planets,
from an album of draw-
ings for a picture book,
1820s–40s. Ink on paper
Each page:
13.8 x 20.4 cm
(5³⁄₈ x 8 in.)

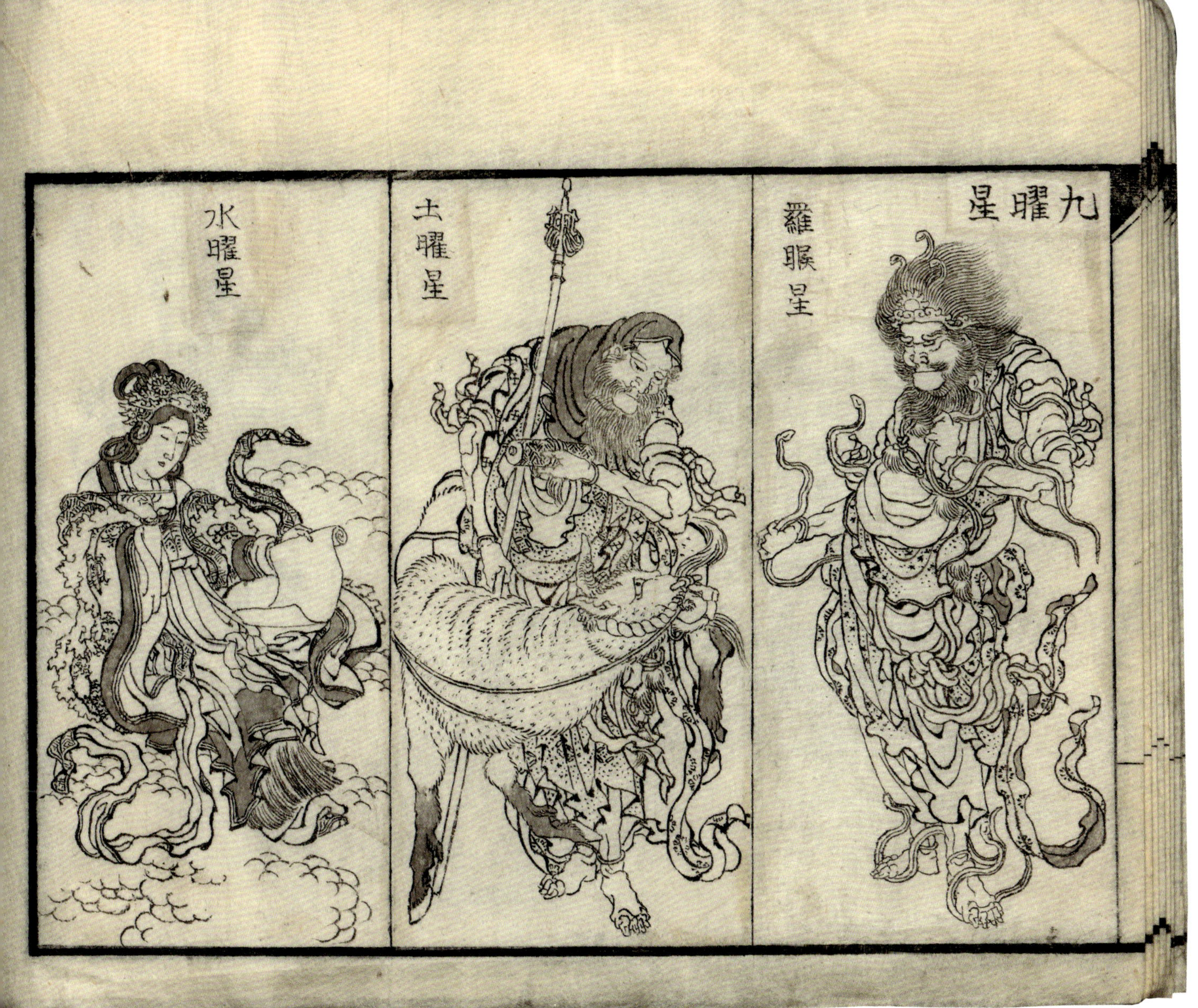
九曜星
羅睺星
土曜星
水曜星

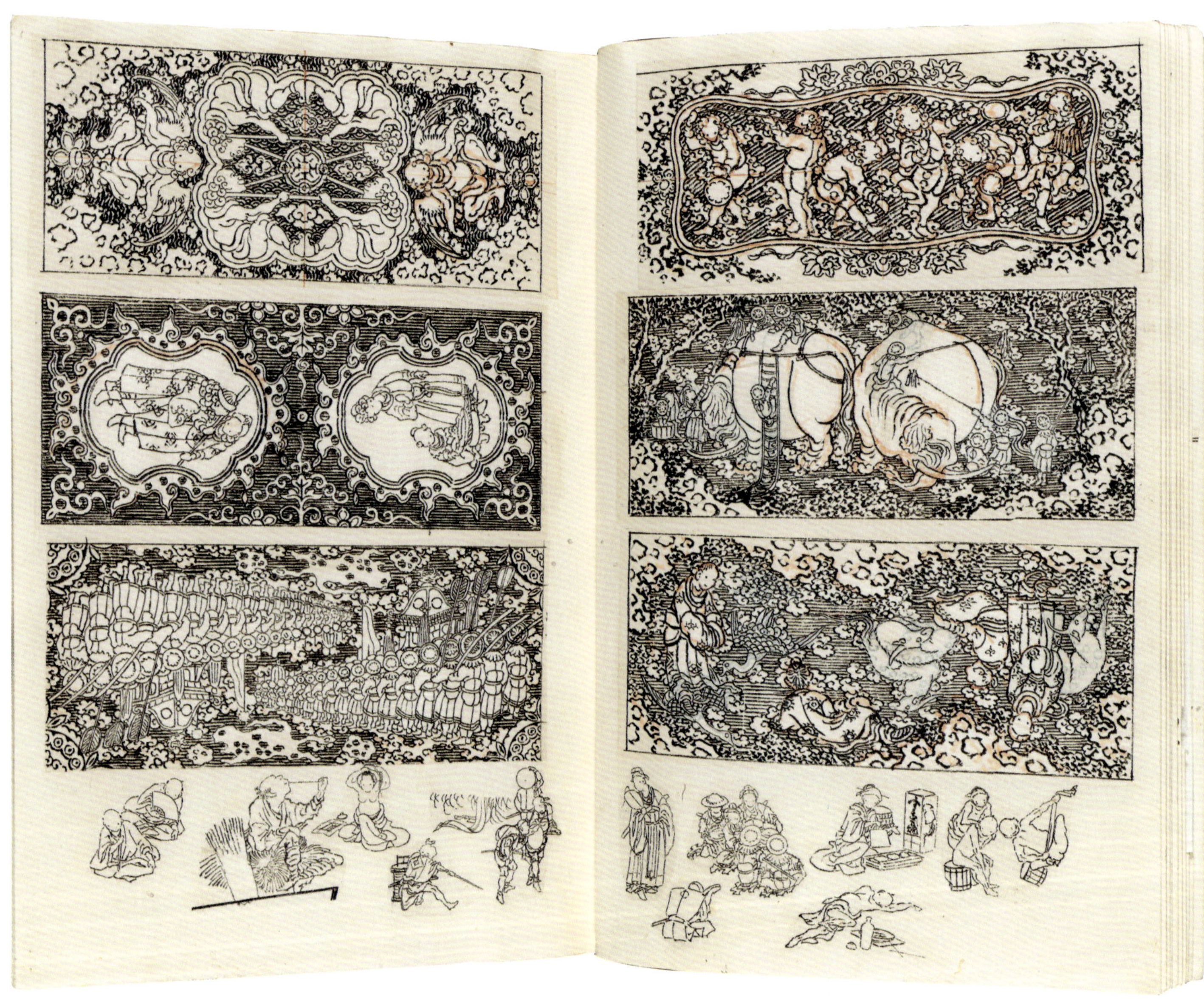

Hokusai seems to have prepared another ambitious multivolume book of model drawings for both art students and general audiences that was never published. A three-volume album survives, containing 177 block-ready drawings by Hokusai, works that would have been destroyed in the printing process (23). Like the *Sketchbooks*, these drawings show many different subjects, some of which are similar to elements in Hokusai's color prints of the 1830s. Another group of 103 drawings that appear to be from the same set has recently been acquired by the British Museum, with the title *The Great Picture Book of Everything* (*Banmotsu ehon daizen*), mentioned in two letters from Hokusai to his publisher in the 1840s. More remains to be discovered about what seems to have been a grand project, never quite finished, late in Hokusai's career.

Still more drawings probably by Hokusai have recently been identified, part of a large group of

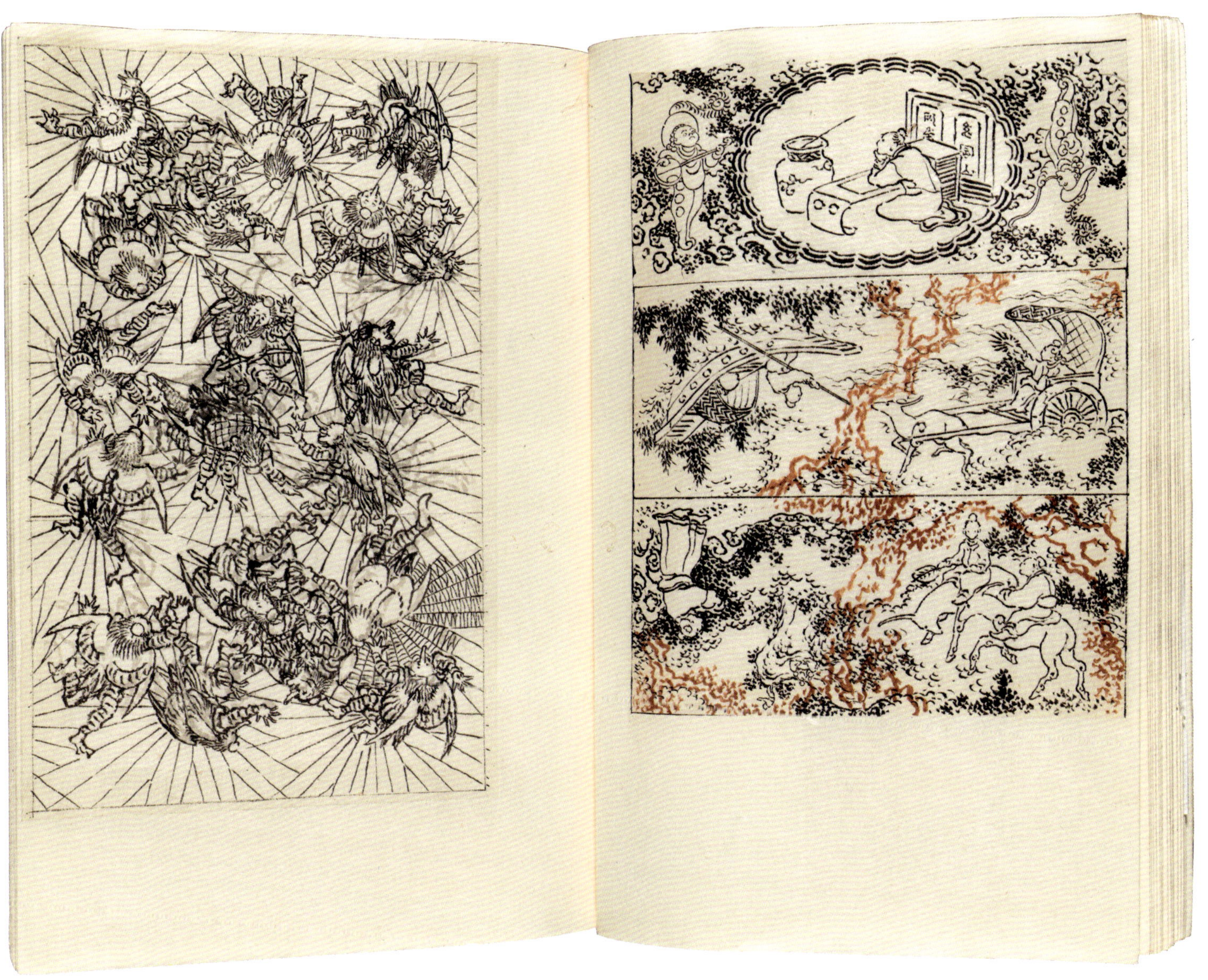

sketches, both loose and mounted in albums,
purchased by William Sturgis Bigelow in the 1880s
from a former student of Hokusai and now in the
MFA's collection. The album shown here has many
intricate designs for craft work — possibly lacquer,
metalwork, textiles, or all of the above — that
appear to be by Hokusai, with less elaborate
sketches by unidentified artists, in both the
Katsushika and the Utagawa styles, pasted in
the margins of some of the pages.

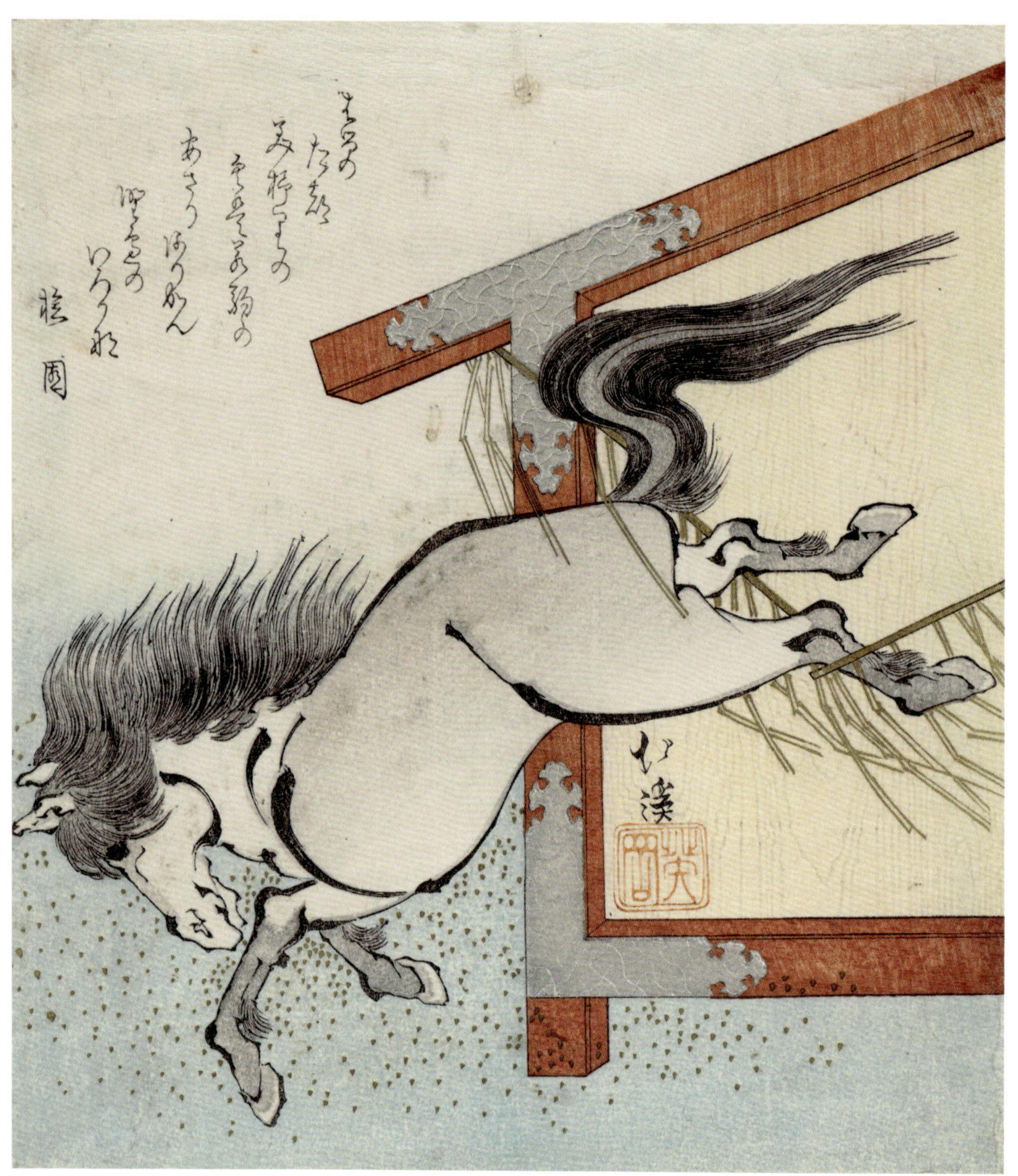

25

HOKKEI
*Painted Horse Escaping
from Ema*, 1834.
Color woodblock print
(surimono)
20.3 x 18.1 cm
(8 x 7⅛ in.)

26

TOTOYA HOKKEI
The Hall of Immortality,
1831. Color woodblock
print (surimono)
42.6 x 18 cm
(16¾ x 7⅛ in.)

62

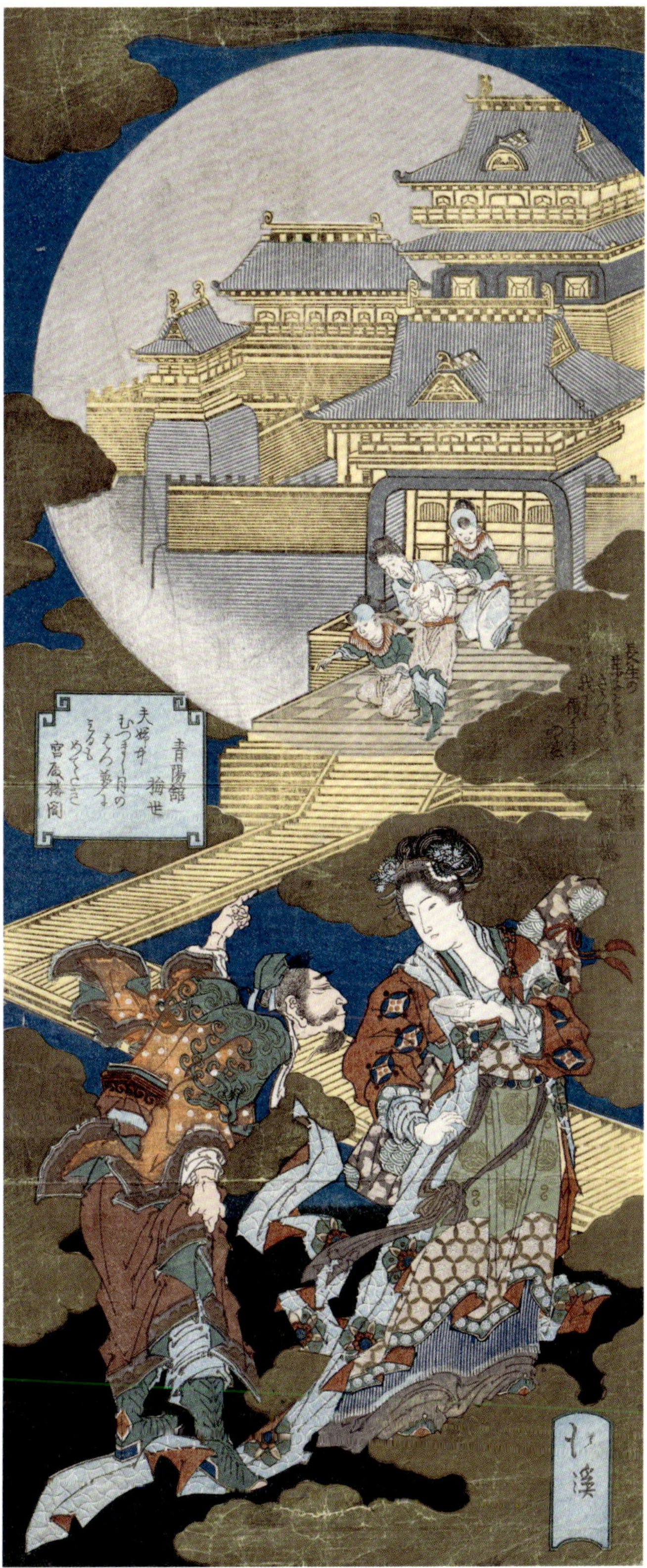

The most successful of Hokusai's students, Hokkei, became one of the most important designers of surimono. These privately commissioned high-quality prints typically incorporate numerous colors including metallic pigments, as well as special techniques such as embossing, often on heavier paper than was generally used for commercial prints.

The main patrons for these prints were members of amateur poetry clubs — a popular hobby among affluent intellectuals — who exchanged the prints with each other on special occasions such as New Year. Surimono prints depicted a wide range of subjects, frequently including clever parodies and jokes, according to the wishes of their sophisticated patrons. Hokusai himself became known to these circles during his time with the Tawaraya school, and he passed on the connections on to his pupils.

Hokkei, who came from a family of fish sellers (as indicated by the surname Totoya), studied under a Kano school painter before switching to Hokusai in the late 1790s. In a clever design made for New Year of 1834, a year of the horse in the East Asian zodiac, Hokkei illustrates an old story of a Kano painter so skillful that a horse he painted on a votive plaque (*ema*) donated to a temple came to life at night to graze. The horse escaping from the picture is drawn in the Kano ink-painting style.

In the 1820s and 1830s, when Hokkei and his student Gakutei dominated the field of surimono design, a square format was standard. Occasionally, a double-size sheet of paper was used, as in Hokkei's spectacular version of a famous scene from Chinese literature. On behalf of the emperor, a Taoist magician searches the heavens for the spirit of the emperor's dearly beloved, deceased concubine and finds her at last in the Moon Palace.

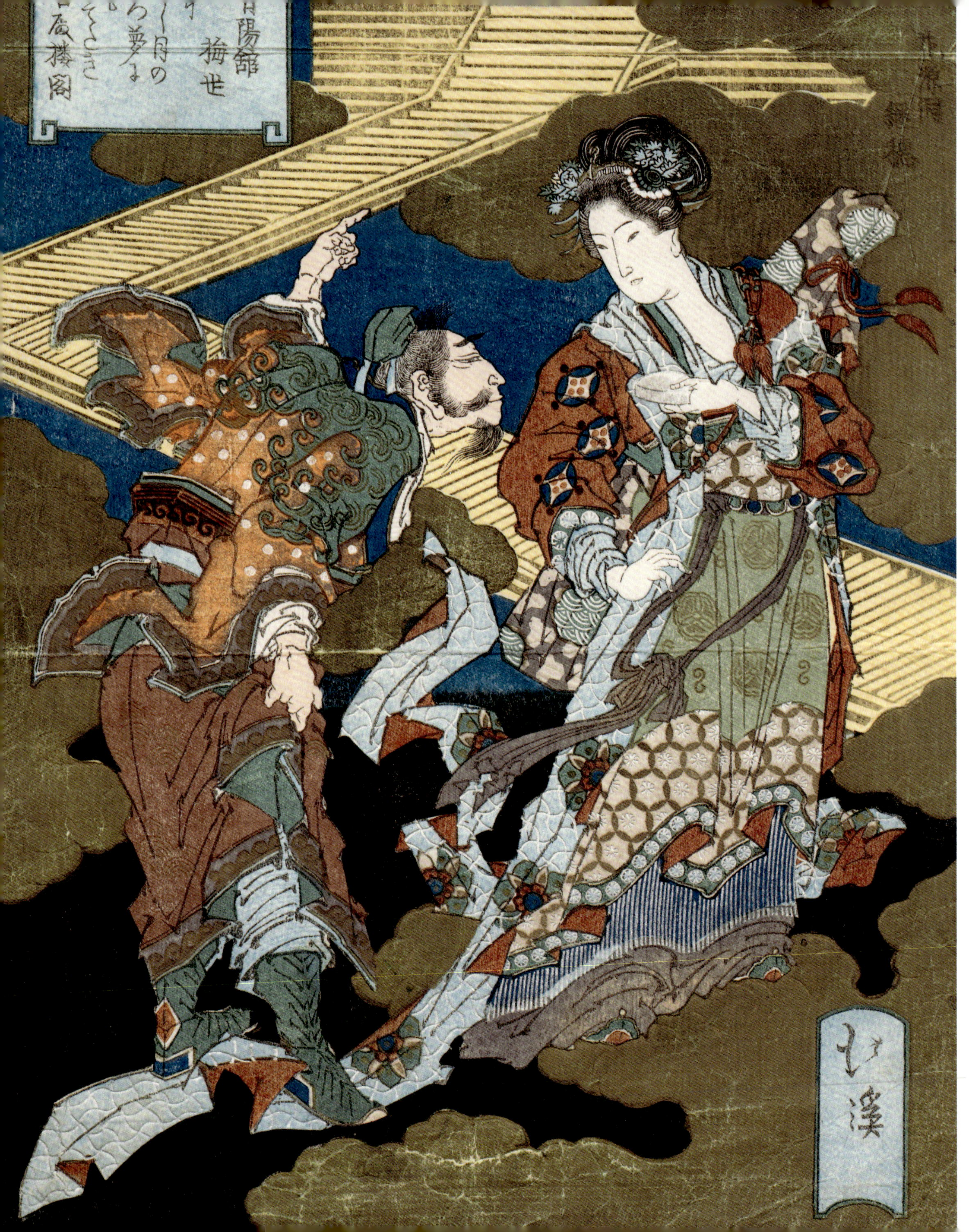

陽舘　梅世
り
く月の
夢よ
そこき
辰揆閣
北溪

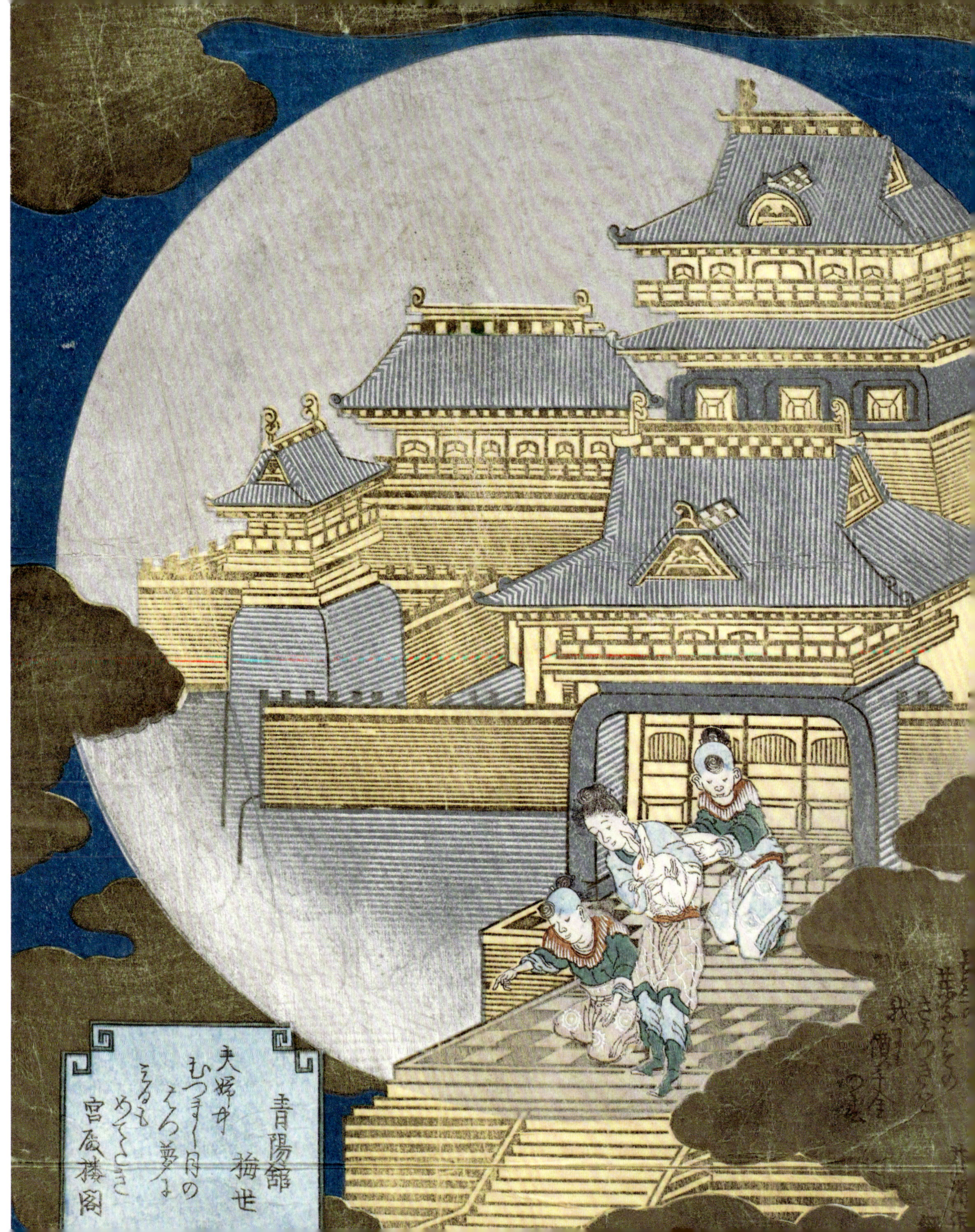
青陽舘
梅世
夫婦中
むつまし月の
ゝゝろ夢よ
ゐるも
めでたき
宮辰楼図

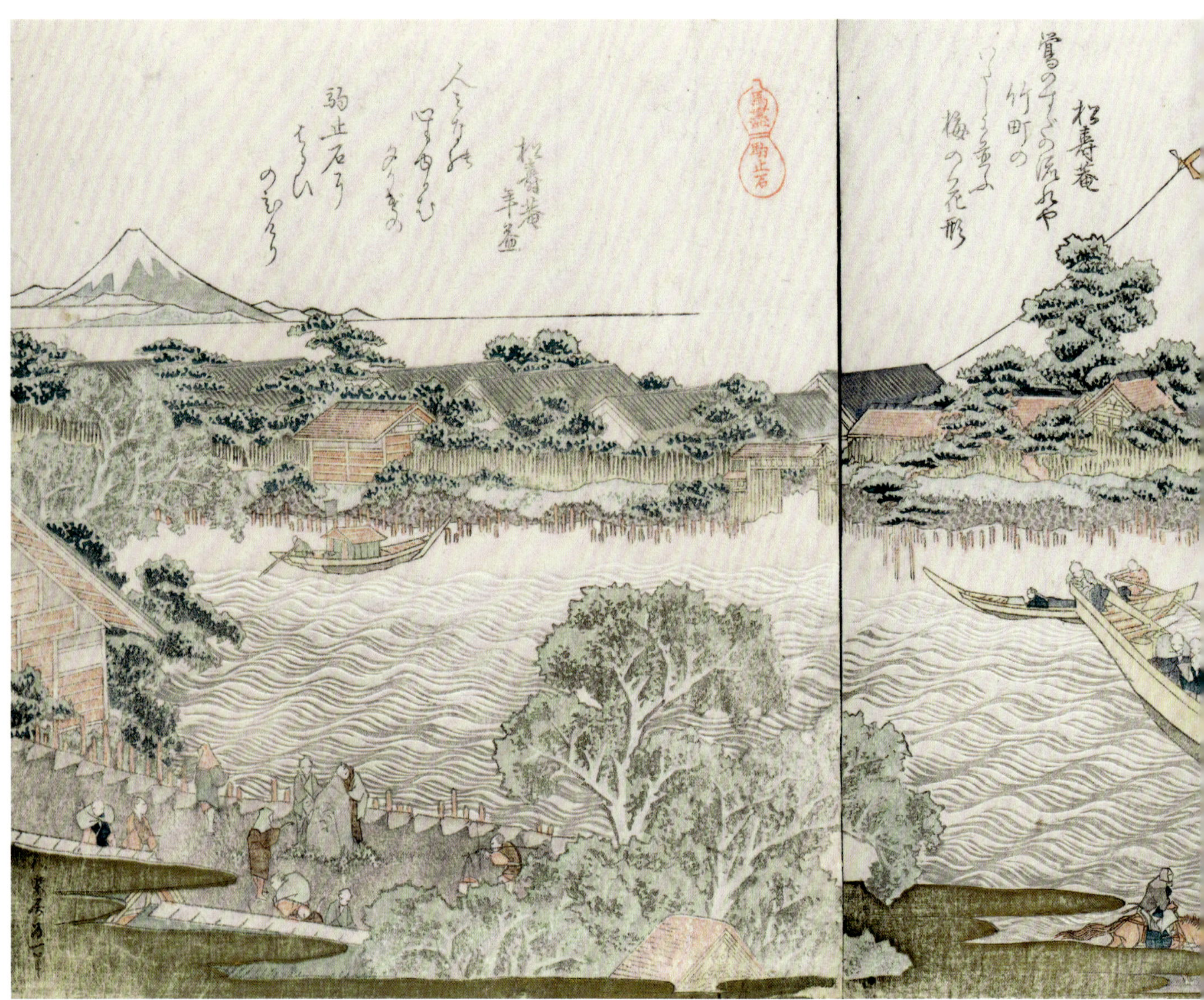

松壽菴年盛
駒止石
松壽菴
梅の花形
竹町の

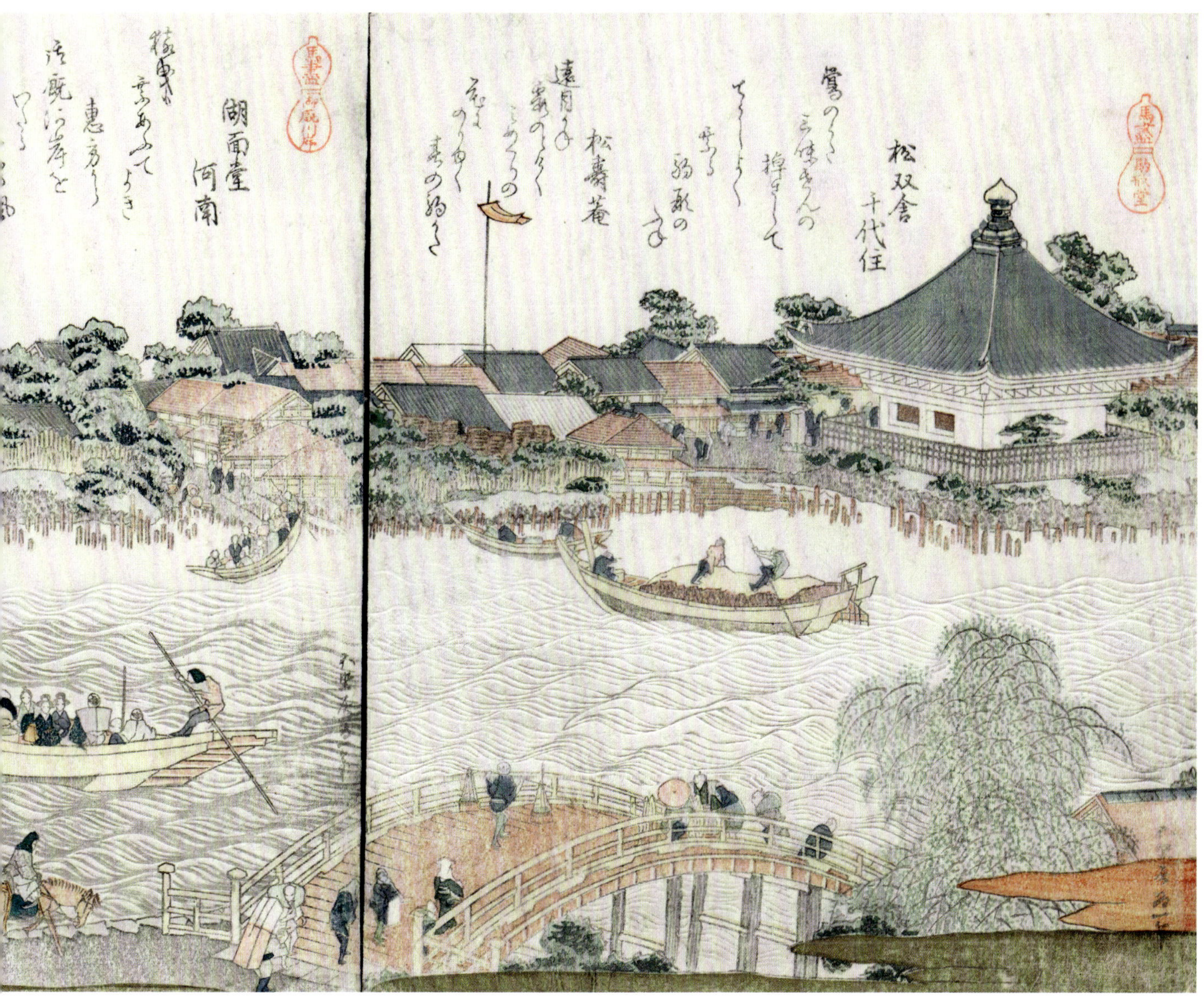

andscapes appeared in surimono before they became popular in commercial prints, as part of the broad repertoire of subject matter that patrons might request. This triptych by Hokusai, made up of three scenes along the Sumida River in Edo that fit together in a panoramic view, is part of a large surimono series commissioned by the Yomo poetry group for New Year of 1822, a horse year in the calendrical cycle. Each of the thirty prints in the set shows something related to horses: here, a temple building whose name includes the word *koma* (pony); an embankment named for the official stables once located there; and an upright stone where a shogun surveying flood damage once tethered his horse. Hokusai's detailed renditions of the landscapes, and the glimpse of Mount Fuji at the left, hint at the best-selling commercial landscape prints that he would design a few years later.

27

HOKUSAI

Komagata-dō Temple, Onmaya Embankment, and the Hitching Stone (right to left), 1822. Color woodblock print (surimono)

21 x 55.1 cm (8¼ x 21¾ in.)

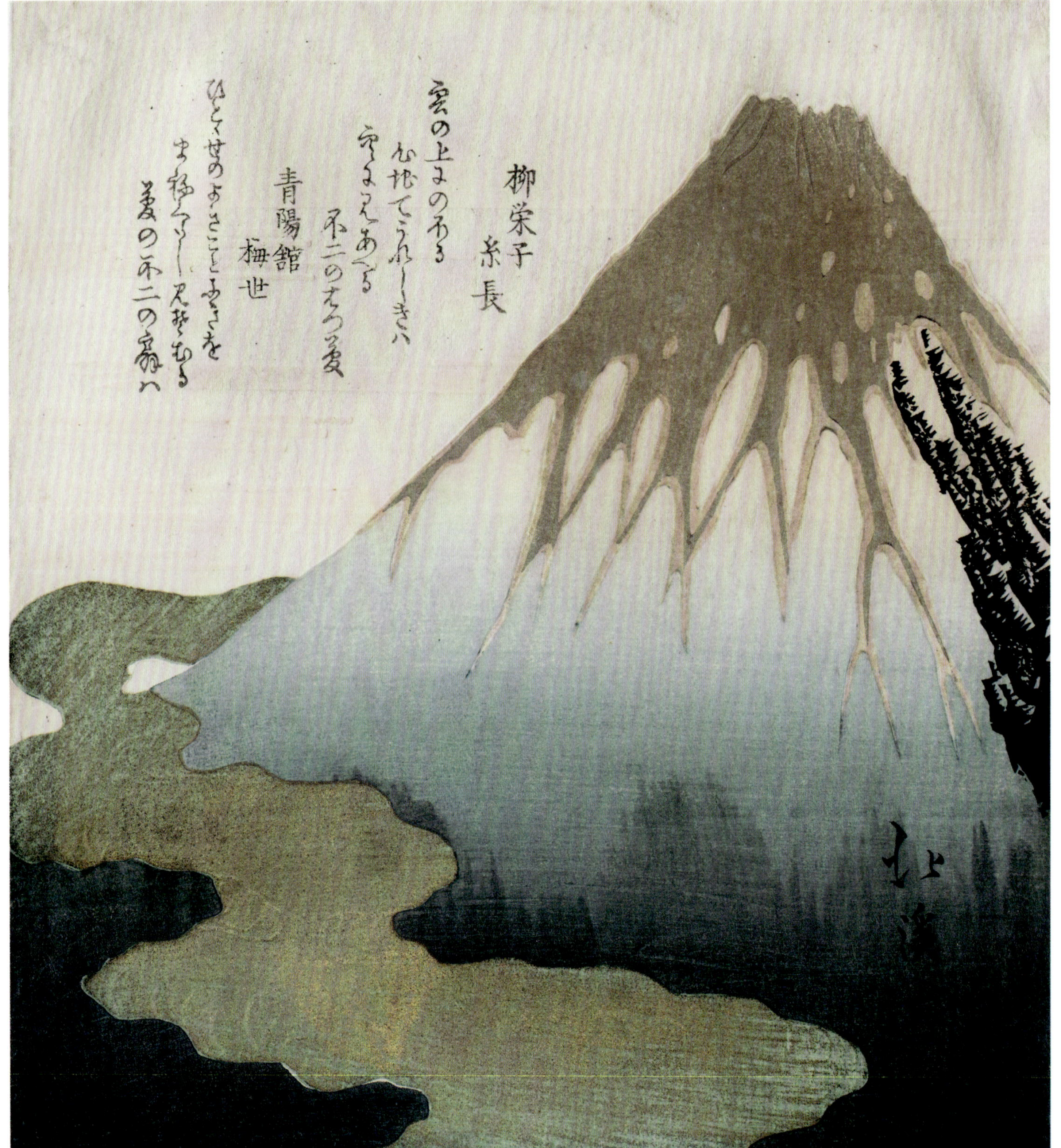

柳栄子　糸長

雲の上よのわる
ゝゝ地てうれしき八
空もえあてる
不二のそつ麦

青陽館
梅世

ひとゝせのあさこと
ゝゝさを
まもらし尺ゝむる
麦の不二の家ゐ

28
HOKKEI
Mount Fuji, 1820s.
Color woodblock print
(surimono)
20.8 x 18.7 cm
(8¼ x 7⅜ in.)

29
SHŌTEI HOKUJU
*True Depiction of the Fuji
River*, about 1804–24.
Color woodblock print
23.3 x 36 cm
(9⅛ x 14⅛ in.)

After the horse series, Hokusai seems to have cut back drastically on the number of surimono commissions that he accepted, turning over much of that work to Hokkei, who designed an especially elegant view of Mount Fuji as part of a series showing the three most fortunate subjects of dreams to have at New Year: Mount Fuji, falcons, and eggplants. Hokkei's surimono is reminiscent of some of Hokusai's most striking images of Fuji, but since the exact date of Hokkei's work is not known, it is uncertain whether he was inspired by his teacher Hokusai or whether Hokusai may have taken inspiration from his brilliant pupil.

Another pupil whose work may have influenced that of his teacher was Hokuju, who before his death in 1824 was already designing landscapes in the full-size horizontal ōban format. Several show scenes of the Tōkaidō Road, although he did not produce a complete set. Hokuju's landscapes seem to have sold fairly well: numerous impressions survive, some of them showing wear to the blocks that indicates a long print run. However, Hokuju did not attain the bestselling status achieved later by his teacher, and landscape remained a minor subgenre within ukiyo-e until the appearance of Hokusai's Fuji series in 1830.

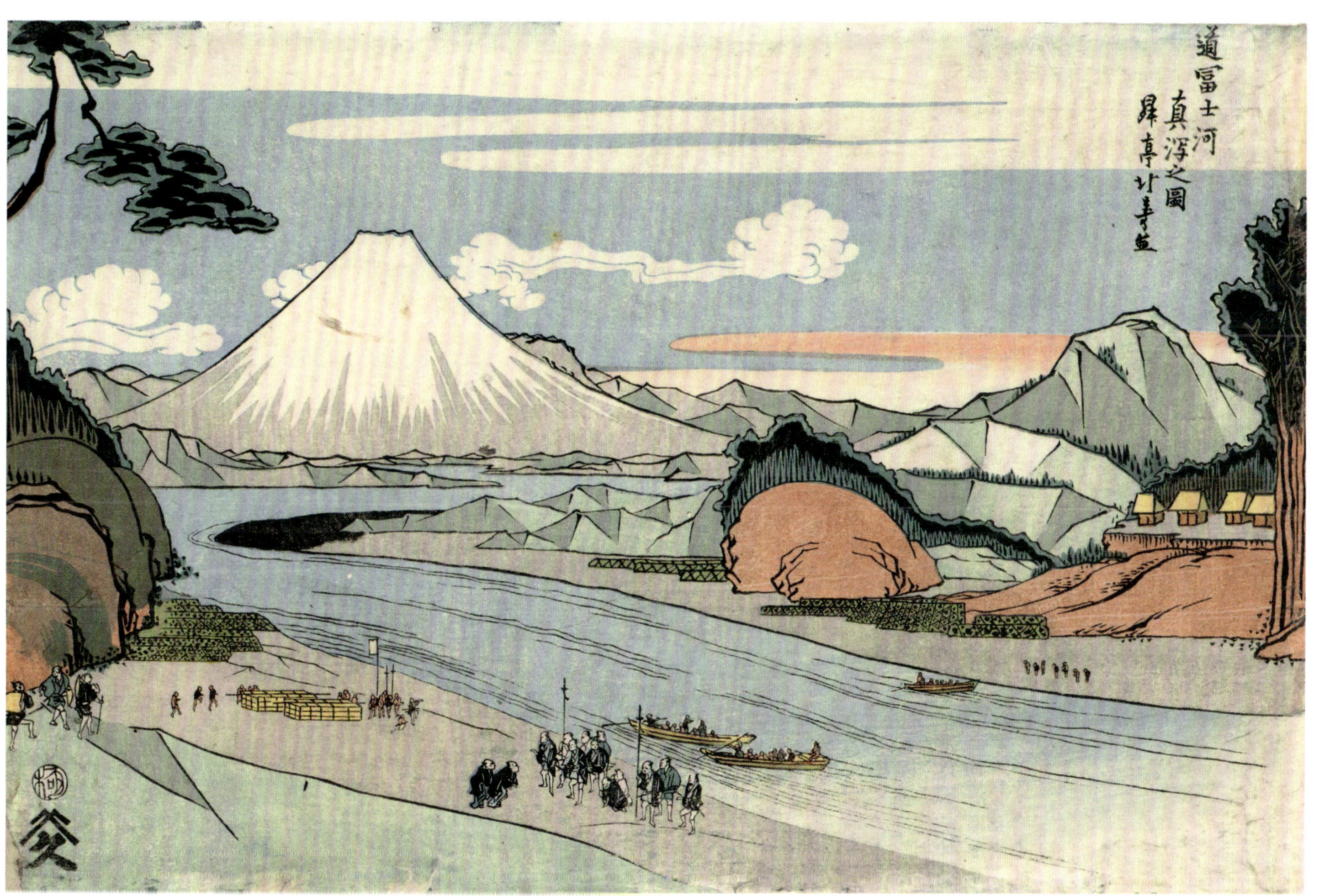

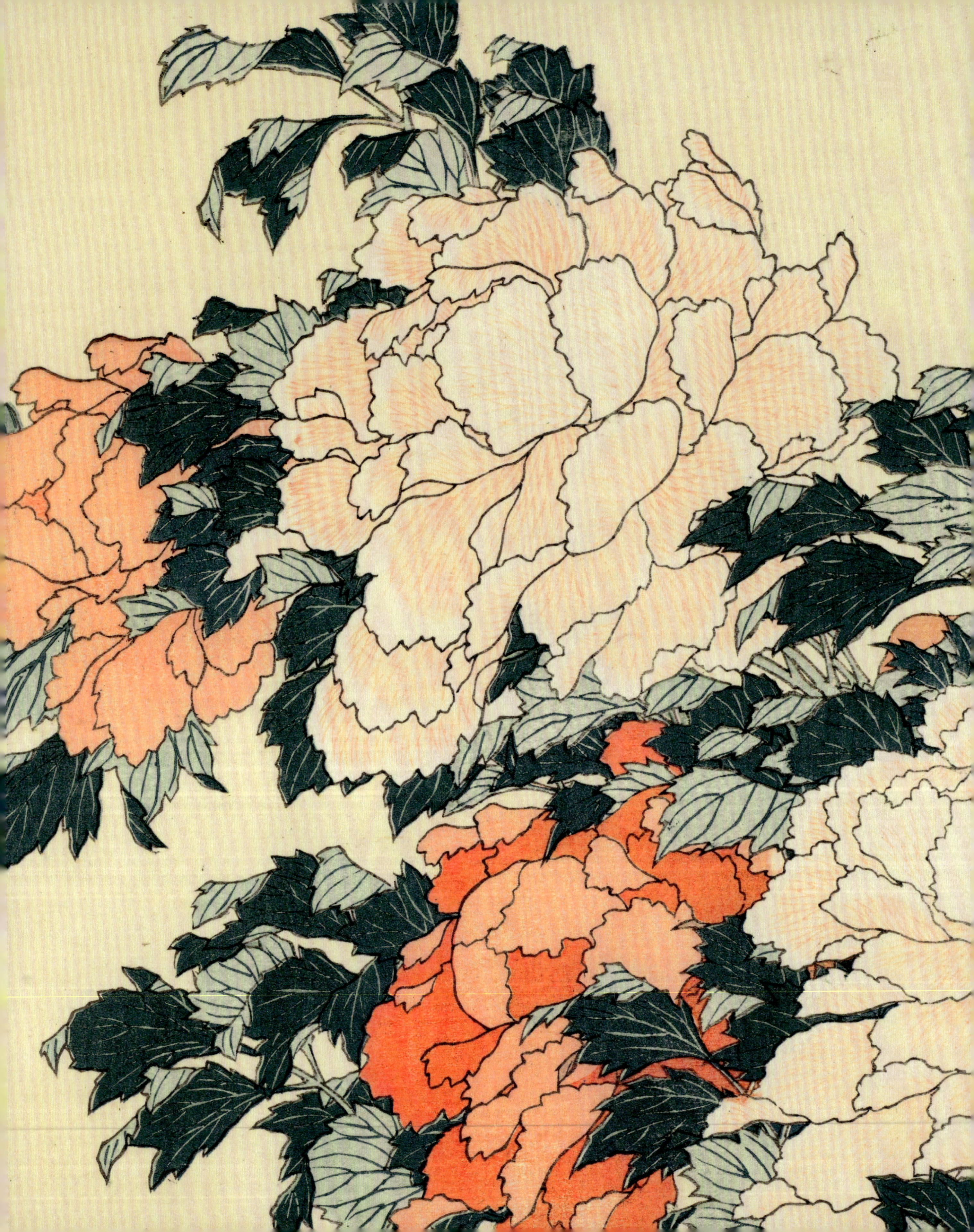

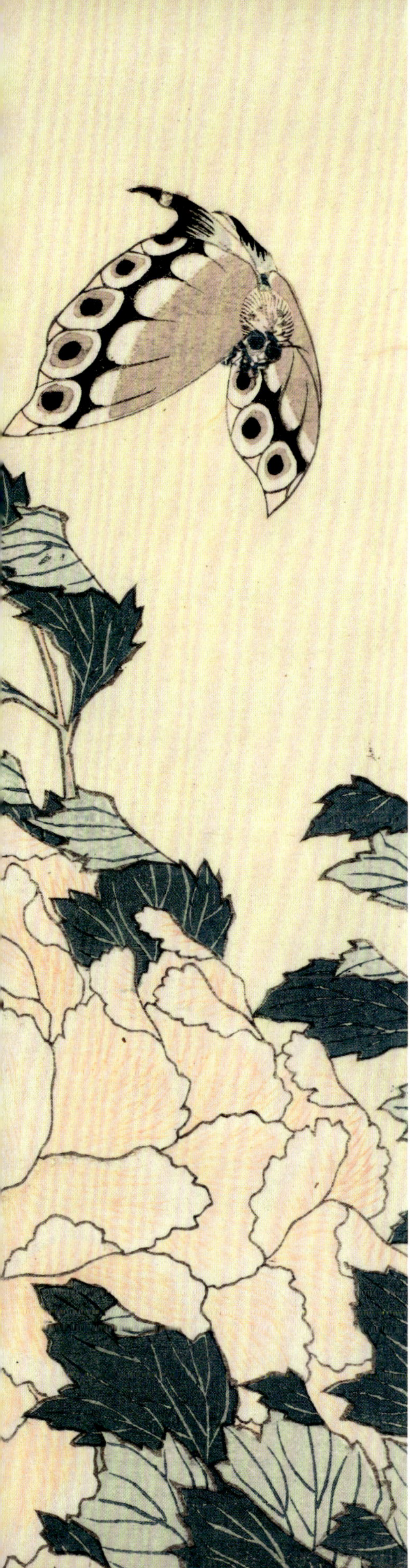

Hokusai's Rivals

AFTER HIS DEPARTURE from the Katsukawa school, Hokusai mostly evaded the highly competitive world of print publishing by concentrating on painting and designing surimono. As privately commissioned works tailored to the taste of individual patrons, they were not subject to the same commercial pressures. In the early decades of the nineteenth century, Hokusai became famous and influential as a book illustrator. His own career is reflected in the many surviving works of his students in the genres of paintings, surimono, and illustrated books.

But Hokusai's greatest impact on the world of Japanese printmaking (and later on the art world at large) came with the enormous success of his single-sheet color prints of the 1830s — first landscapes, then nature studies, followed by scenes from history and literature. By the time he re-entered the field of color prints, the lineup of potential competitors had changed drastically. The Katsukawa school in which he was trained had been eclipsed by the Utagawa school, which dominated the production of both actor prints and prints of fashionable beauties. To compete with the Utagawa artists, Hokusai needed to find a completely different angle of approach, and landscapes proved to be the answer. Two of the younger Utagawa artists, Hiroshige (1797–1858) and Kuniyoshi, faced the same problem when they found themselves in competition with the top Utagawa artist, Kunisada (1786–1864), and both of them took inspiration from Hokusai to create highly successful works of their own.

The Utagawa school had been founded in the eighteenth century by Utagawa Toyoharu, whose landscapes and cityscapes with Western-style vanishing-point perspective were emulated by the young Hokusai. Toyoharu's most successful student was Hokusai's contemporary Toyokuni, under whose leadership the Utagawa school gradually surpassed the Katsukawa school to become the top designers of actor prints, around the time that Hokusai left the Katsukawa school and gave up depicting actors. Toyokuni's students Kunisada and Kuniyoshi in turn carried on his very successful style. Another student of Toyoharu was Toyohiro, a fellow student of Toyokuni and teacher of Hiroshige, so that in the quasi-familial system of Japanese art lineages, Hiroshige was a kind of cousin to the siblings Kunisada and Kuniyoshi.

Hiroshige's breakthrough into the top ranks of ukiyo-e artists was directly inspired by Hokusai. Following the enormous success of Hokusai's *Thirty-Six Views of Mount Fuji*, the first landscape series to achieve bestseller status (actually forty-six prints, because the series was so successful that ten extra designs were added), Hiroshige designed *Fifty-Three Stations of the Tōkaidō Road*. This series depicted the official highway rest stops on the main road between Edo and Kyoto, with a total of fifty-five scenes including the two cities at each end. Since Fuji is clearly visible from many of the stations, some of Hiroshige's designs are very similar to Hokusai's. The success of this series — which, like Hokusai's Fuji series, is still well known and influential today — confirmed the position of landscape as a major subject within ukiyo-e.

After designing several additional successful landscape series between about 1830 and 1836, including sets of waterfalls and bridges, in the final decade of his life Hokusai concentrated primarily on painting and left the field of print design to others. Hiroshige, in contrast, remained an extremely prolific print designer and went on to produce many additional Tōkaidō series (the first and most famous is nicknamed the "Great Tōkaidō" or the "Hōeidō Tōkaidō" after its publisher, to distinguish it from other series with similar titles) as well as series on subjects such as the sixty-odd provinces of Japan and a vertical-format version of *Thirty-Six Views of Mount Fuji*. Hiroshige's final masterpiece, *One Hundred Famous Views of Edo*, was on the verge of completion at the time of the artist's sudden death in the cholera epidemic of 1858. The inventive and unusual viewpoints of the scenes became a source of inspiration for other artists in the Japanese print world, and later for artists in Europe as well.

Hiroshige explicitly acknowledged his debt to Hokusai in a print of 1836, based on one of the images in Hokusai's Fuji series, redesigned

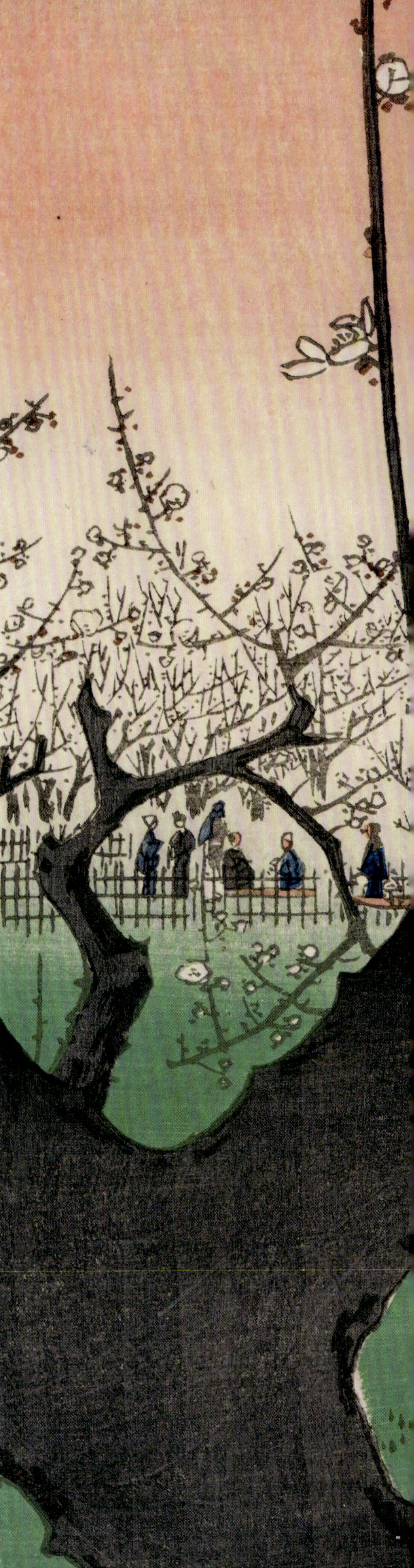

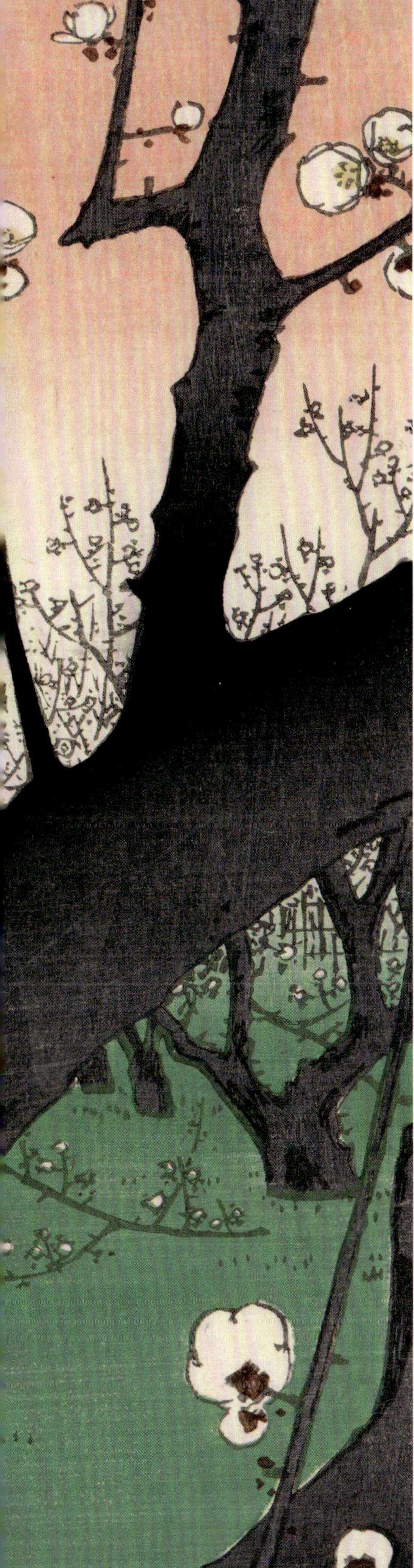

for use on a flat fan. Both prints show a cooper at work on a very large wooden barrel, with a distant landscape visible through the circle of the barrel: Mount Fuji in Hokusai's work, and a riverside lumberyard in Edo in Hiroshige's design. Hiroshige's print includes the inscription "Copied from a Picture by Old Master Katsushika" (38). In 1858, which would be the final year of his life, Hiroshige created two other works referring explicitly to Hokusai, who had died almost a decade earlier: a series in the vertical ōban format entitled *Thirty-Six Views of Mount Fuji* (the Japanese title is worded slightly differently from Hokusai's), which includes a spectacular print of a large wave based on an illustration in volume 2 of Hokusai's book *One Hundred Views of Mount Fuji*; and Hiroshige's own picture book of views of Fuji (whose title translates the same in English but is slightly different in Japanese), with a preface that describes how inspiring he found Hokusai's work.

Another major artist who did landscape print designs in the style pioneered by Hokusai was Keisai Eisen (1790–1848), who like Hokusai was an independent ukiyo-e artist not affiliated with any particular school. He seems to have been a personal friend of Hokusai's family. Eisen specialized in prints of women as well as landscapes, and collaborated with Hiroshige in designing a series showing the sixty-nine stations of the Kisokaidō road, another major highway known for its gorgeous mountain scenery. He also patterned his work directly on Hokusai's when he designed a set of scenic views in the vicinity of Nikkō, the shrine in northern Japan dedicated to the deified founder of the Tokugawa shogunate; it includes several images of waterfalls inspired by Hokusai's series (41).

Hiroshige followed Hokusai's lead in designing not only landscapes but also bird-and-flower pictures, the name conventionally given to nature studies in East Asian pictorial art dating back to the Song dynasty in China (960–1279). The theme had been present from the earliest days of ukiyo-e prints, but like landscape, had been only a minor subject until Hokusai's brilliant designs became bestsellers in the early 1830s. Hokusai did two main series, both untitled; the set nicknamed the "Large Flowers" is in the same standard ōban size as the Fuji series (about 10 by 15 inches), while the slightly later "Small Flowers" are in the chūban format, half of the ōban size. Hokusai's Small Flowers include inscribed poems in both Japanese and Chinese, and Hiroshige also incorporated this feature in most of his own designs. His numerous bird-and-flower prints are typically in narrow vertical formats that suggest the hanging scroll format of paintings.

Hiroshige's most famous nature series of all, known as the "Large Fish," originated as a privately commissioned poetry album, with

beautifully printed horizontal ōban-size sheets folded in half and glued
together to make a booklet. Like the single-sheet surimono prints also
commissioned by wealthy amateur poets, they feature inscribed poems
by the patrons. Later the Large Fish were reissued as single-sheet commercial prints, with some additional designs. They strongly resemble
the much smaller black-and-white images of fish in the *Hokusai
Sketchbooks*, a major source of inspiration for Hiroshige.

Hokusai's illustrations for popular novels were closely connected to
the rise of a third kind of subject matter that became prominent around
1830, so-called warrior prints (*musha-e*), which depict not only warriors
but historical subjects of all kinds. The first artist to design a bestselling series in what had previously been a relatively obscure genre was
not Hokusai himself but Kuniyoshi. Kuniyoshi had struggled for years to
compete with the star student of Toyokuni, the very successful Kunisada,
who throughout his career dominated the fields of actor prints and
prints of fashionable women. Kuniyoshi was equal in skill to Kunisada in
draftsmanship, composition, and design, but Kunisada had a special gift
for capturing the likenesses of popular actors. In the days before photography, these prints were hugely popular with theater fans. Kuniyoshi
found his own niche in 1827, when he became a star artist thanks to a
series based on the beloved Chinese martial arts novel *The Water Margin*
(*Suikoden* in Japanese, *Shuihuzhuan* in Chinese).

Considered one of the four greatest novels in the history of Chinese
literature, *The Water Margin* is a tale of 108 heroic bandits fighting corrupt officials in twelfth-century China; their hideout on Mount Liang is
protected by the marsh around a lake, hence the title. Japanese transla-
tions that had been available since the early eighteenth century were
intended more for scholars of Chinese literature than for the general
public. The first popular edition appeared in 1805–7, when the initial ten
volumes of *A New Illustrated Edition of the Water Margin* were issued,
translated by Kyokutei Bakin (1767–1848), a top author of popular fiction, and illustrated by none other than Hokusai. This new work was an
enormous success because it fitted perfectly the new trend in Japanese
popular literature: long historical adventure novels, known as *yomihon*
(literally "books for reading"), that avoided potential censorship issues
by being set in distant times and places and emphasizing the traditional
samurai virtues of courage and loyalty. Publication was halted before
the translation was complete, allegedly because the translator and the
illustrator quarreled over who had been primarily responsible for the
book's success. However, Bakin and Hokusai did continue to collabo-
rate on other similar projects, such as Bakin's Japanese historical novel

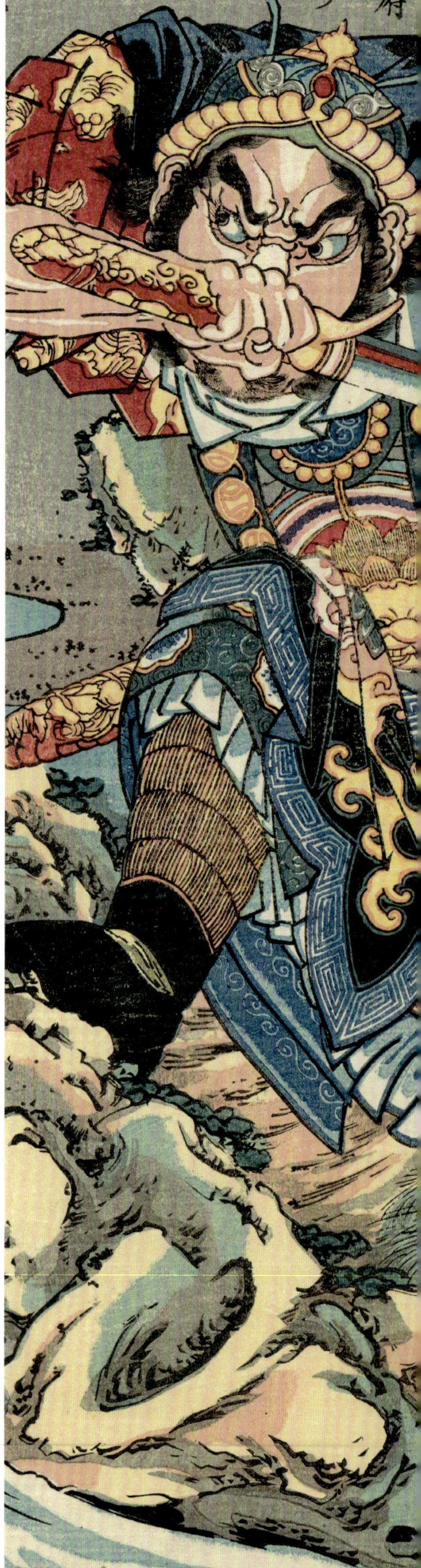

74

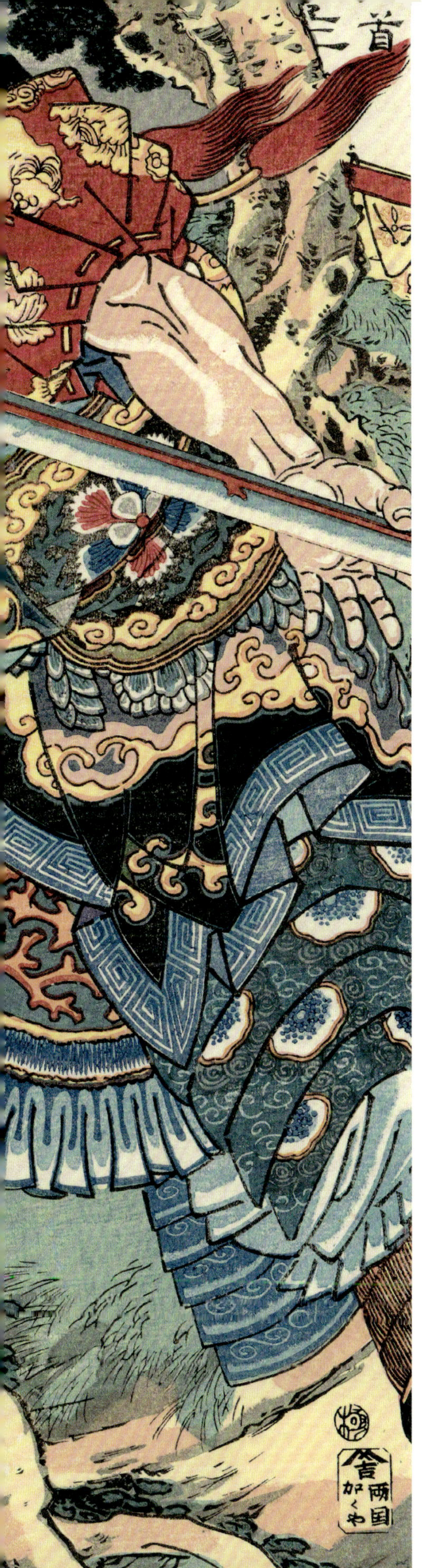

The Crescent Moon Bow, published in 1807–11 and inspired in part by *The Water Margin*. The author and artist appear together — looking as they had some decades earlier — in an illustration by Kuniyoshi for his 1845 book *Extraordinary Persons of Japan* (49).

A New Illustrated Edition of the Water Margin may have been a childhood favorite of the future artist, since Kuniyoshi chose it as the subject for his breakout color print series twenty years after it was first published. The volumes illustrated by Hokusai typically had portraits of the main characters at the beginning, with panoramic two-page spreads scattered throughout the text that illustrate the action of the story in landscape or interior settings. Kuniyoshi's color prints combine these two types of illustration by showing the individual heroes in close-up action scenes with the focus on the figures, deliberately drawn so large that they crowd the edges of the sheet. He followed up on the success of the first *Water Margin* series with similar series showing Japanese heroes, and other artists also followed the trend.

Hokusai himself returned to the *Water Margin* theme as a result of Kuniyoshi's series, in an example of how competition can lead to circularity. After a twenty-year gap, the publication of *A New Illustrated Edition of the Water Margin* resumed, still with Hokusai's illustrations but with a different translator continuing the story. Hokusai and his students made additional picture books of the *Water Margin* heroes and still more of Japanese warriors, now that Kuniyoshi's success had made the action-adventure theme popular. In color prints, as opposed to monochrome book illustrations, Hokusai designed just one gorgeous vertical ōban series of warriors in combat. He himself is not known to have designed any warrior print triptychs like those by Kuniyoshi and his pupils; some of his students, including Hokuga and Hokui, did design such prints, using the Katsushika style of figure drawing rather than the Utagawa style. Perhaps Hokusai might have gone in this direction had he not, after about 1836, abandoned print design for painting.

There is one very late and unusual work by Hokusai that shows he was still thinking fondly of *The Water Margin*. In 1844 and again in 1845, Hokusai, now in his mid-eighties, traveled with Oei to the town of Obuse, northwest of Edo, at the invitation of his student and patron, the wealthy sake brewer and amateur artist Takai Kōzan (1806–1883). Among other artistic activities there, he supervised the redecoration of the town's two festival floats. For one of them he designed a life-size sculpture of the *Water Margin* hero Gongsun Sheng, accompanied by a winged dragon that refers to his nickname, "Dragon in the Clouds."

Hokusai had become a household name in
Japan following the phenomenal success
of the *Hokusai Sketchbooks* in the 1810s,
but the 1820s found him beset with health
problems, family troubles, and financial difficulties. Beginning in about 1830, his circumstances
improved as he was inspired to create his second
great masterpiece: the color print series *Thirty-Six
Views of Mount Fuji*, showing the sacred mountain
from many different viewpoints, throughout the
year, in a variety of different weather conditions.
The series was an enormous sensation and went
through many printings. Hokusai even added ten
extra designs, probably at the request of the publisher, so that there are actually a total of forty-six
prints in the series.

The success of a second great landscape print
series, *Fifty-Three Stations of the Tōkaidō Road*
by Utagawa Hiroshige, confirmed the new status
of landscape prints as one of the most popular
ukiyo-e print genres, comparable to the established genres of kabuki actors and fashionable
women. In the early 1800s Hokusai had already
done several series of small prints showing all of
the official rest stops on the great Tōkaidō highway
that ran between Edo and Kyoto, and his student
Hokuju had designed prints of the subject in the
larger, standard ōban size, but not a complete
set. Hiroshige, following the example of Hokusai's
Fuji series, created a complete series of fifty-five
prints (the fifty-three stations plus the two cities
at the ends) showing a variety of seasonal scenes
and weather conditions such as a wintry night
in Kanbara (31).

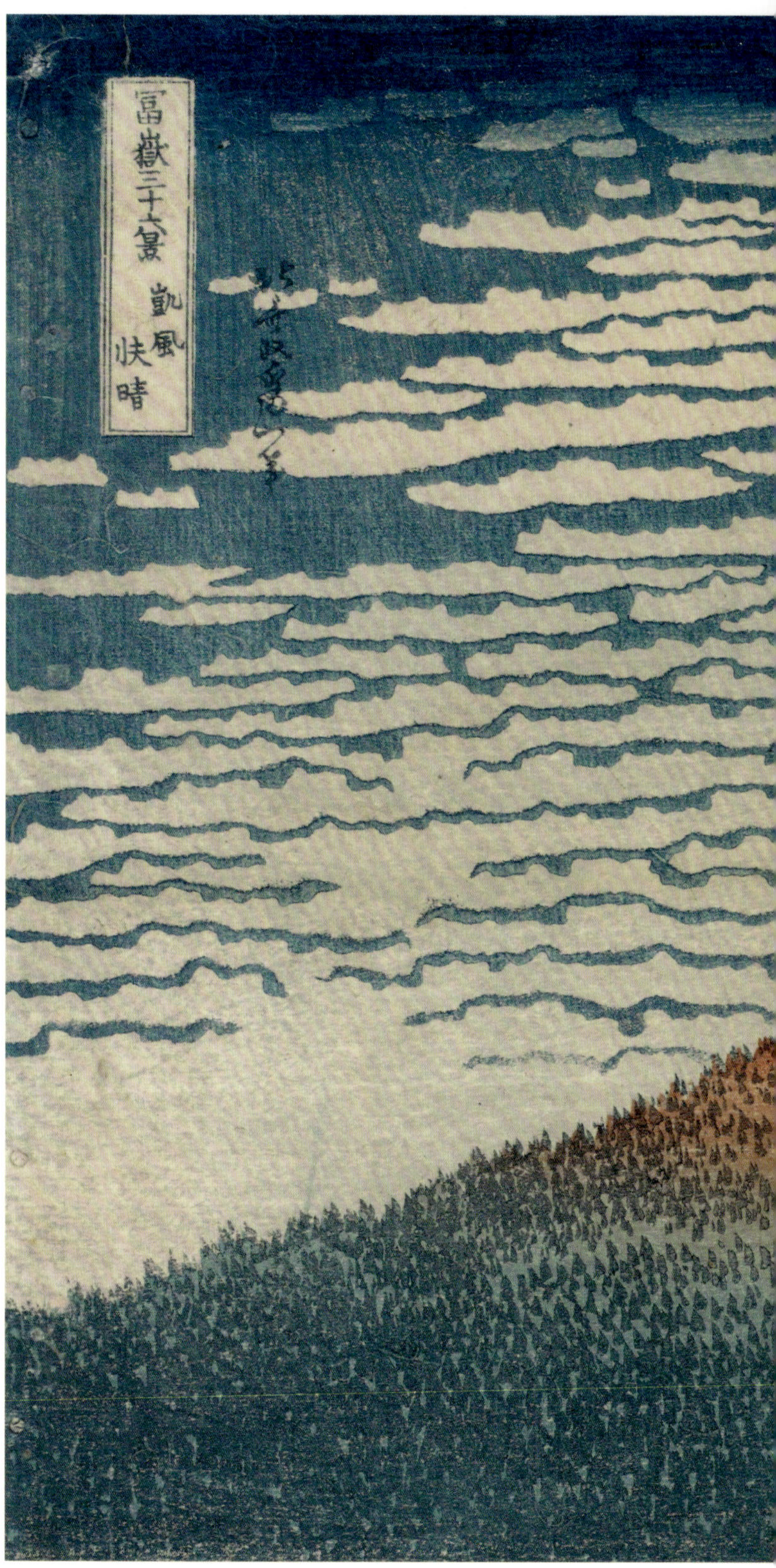

30
HOKUSAI
Fine Wind, Clear Weather,
also known as "Red Fuji,"
about 1830–31.
Color woodblock print
23.9 x 36.5 cm
(9³⁄₈ x 14³⁄₈ in.)

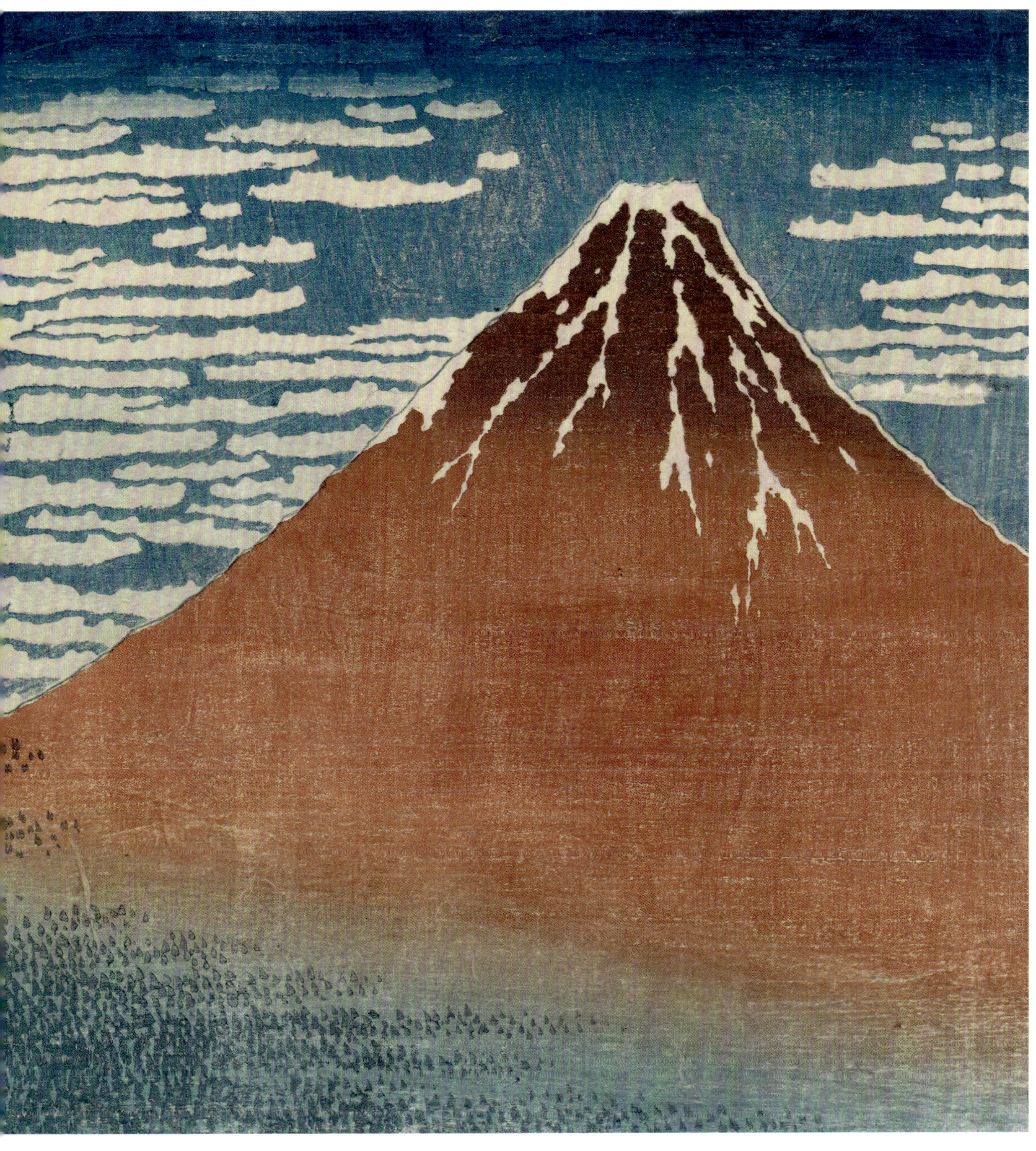

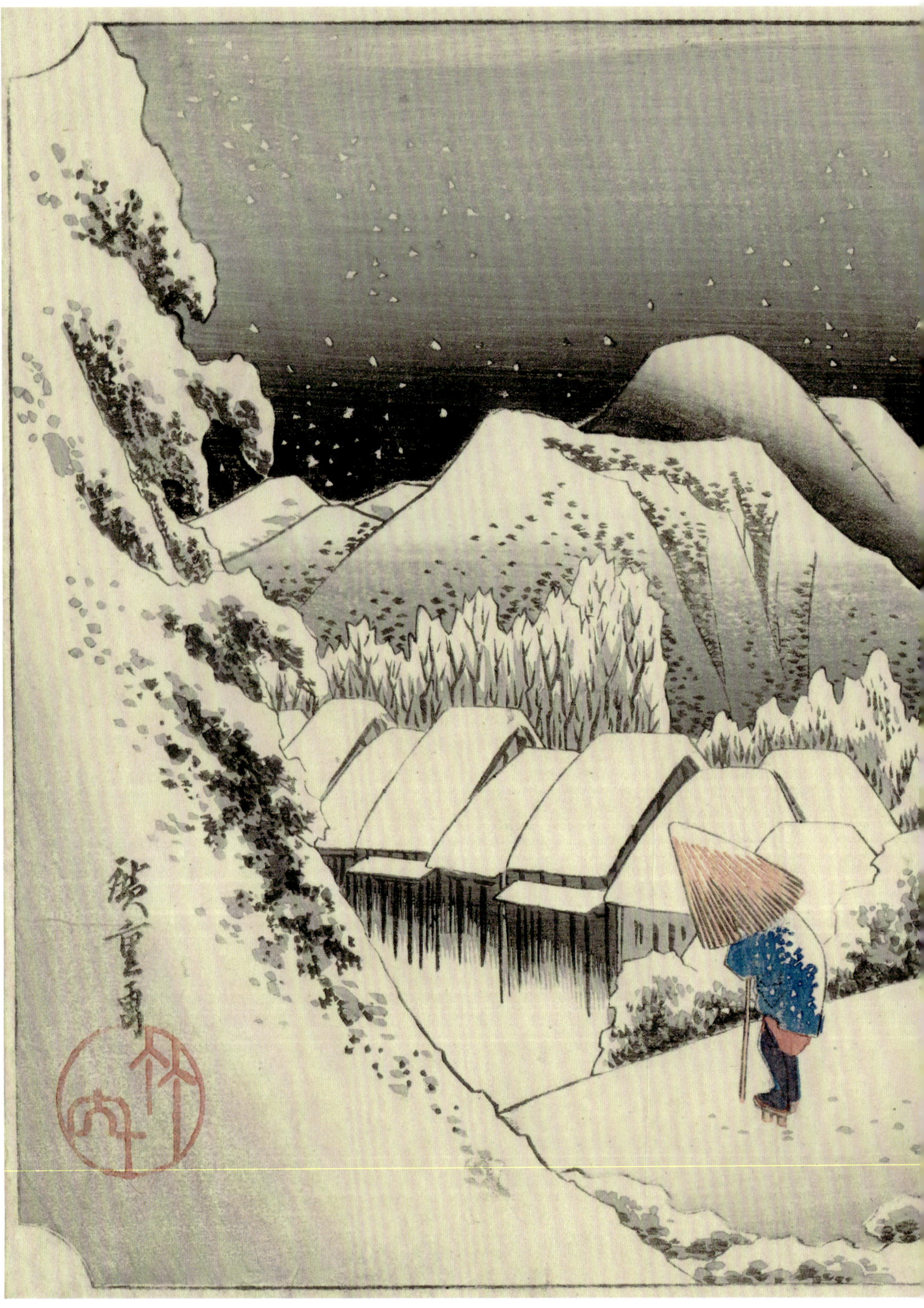

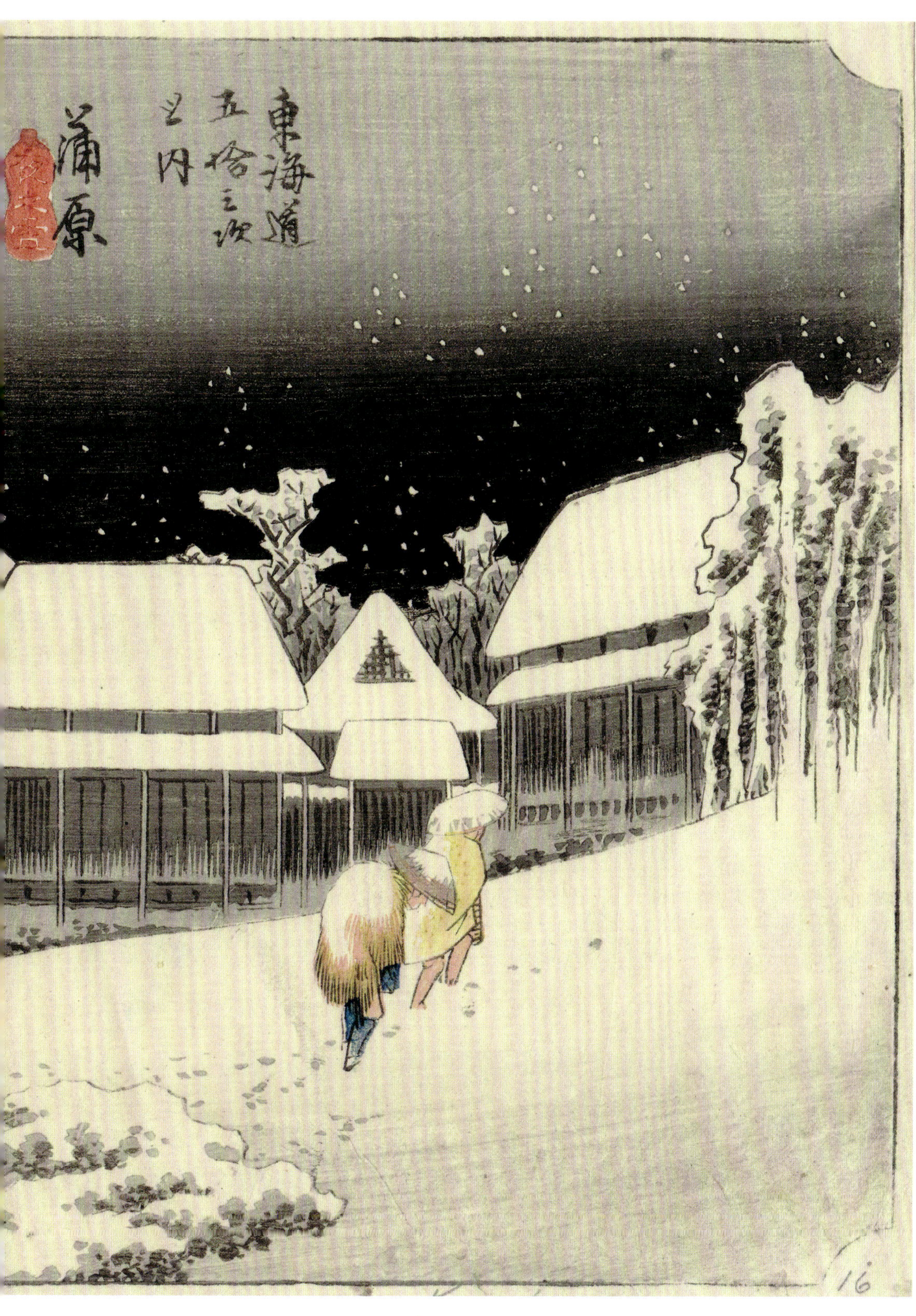

31
UTAGAWA HIROSHIGE I
Kanbara. Night Snow,
about 1833–34.
Color woodblock print
24 x 36 cm
(9½ x 14⅛ in.)

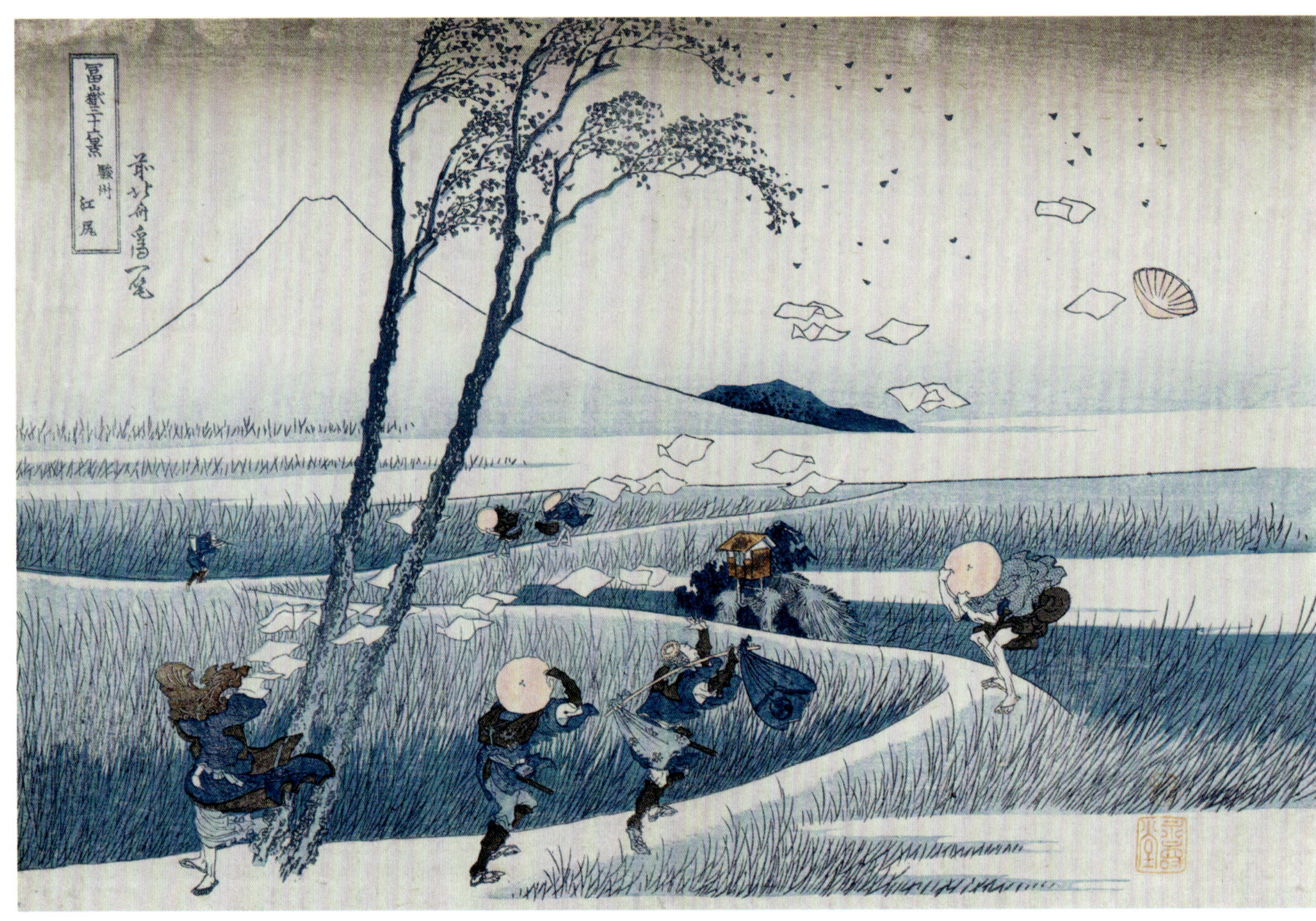

32

HOKUSAI

Ejiri in Suruga Province,
about 1830–31.
Color woodblock print
25 x 37.7 cm
(9⅞ x 14⅞ in.)

Because Mount Fuji is visible from much of the route of the Tōkaidō, some of the scenes in the two series are similar in their general appearance. Both Hokusai and Hiroshige enjoyed populating their landscapes with human figures, sometimes in amusing situations, as in two scenes showing travelers inconvenienced by a windstorm. After Hokusai largely gave up print design in the 1830s, Hiroshige continued to design landscapes in large quantities for the rest of his life. Because many of his Tōkaidō series have similar names, they are distinguished by nicknames; this one is known as the "First Tōkaidō," the "Great Tōkaidō," or by the name of the publisher as the "Hōeidō Tōkaidō."

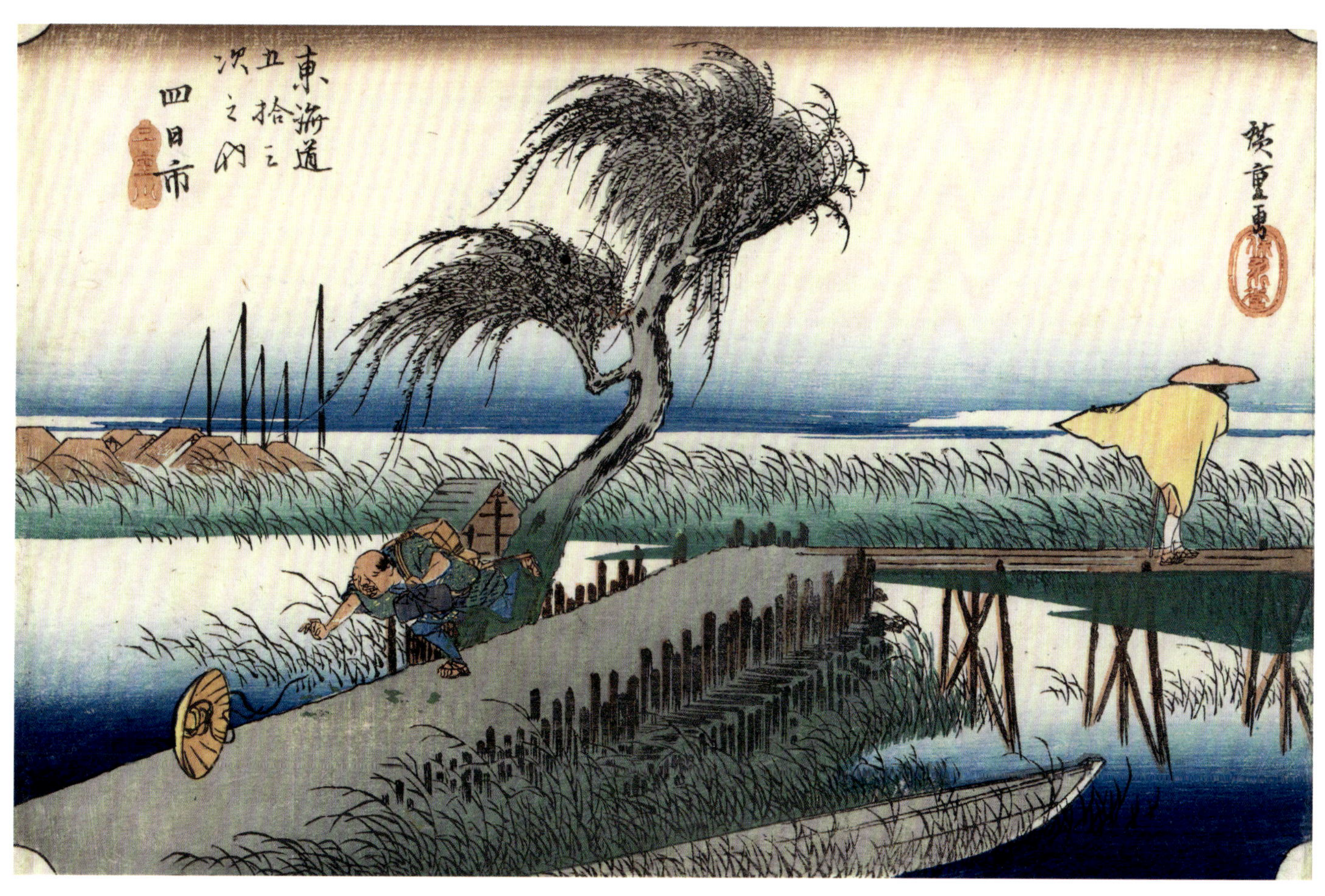

33
HIROSHIGE
Yokkaichi: Mie River,
about 1833–34.
Color woodblock print
22 x 34.6 cm
(8⅝ x 13⅝ in.)

The mesmerizing spiral composition and the simultaneous evocation of beauty and terror have made Hokusai's print *Under the Wave off Kanagawa* one of the most celebrated images in world art. Often referred to by its nickname, "The Great Wave," the scene of express fish-delivery boats threatened by a rogue wave in the vicinity of present-day Yokohama continues to be a source of inspiration for artists today. Its extreme popularity outside Japan seems to date from around the turn of the twentieth century in Europe; until recently, the image known as "Red Fuji" (30) was the favorite in Japan, although the Wave may now have overtaken it.

Among the designs in the Fuji series, the Wave attracted the attention of fellow ukiyo-e artists from the time of its first publication, and similar depictions of rough water appear in the work of a number of Hokusai's contemporary rivals. An especially fine example was made by Hiroshige almost a decade after Hokusai's death, as part of a series of views of Fuji whose title deliberately evokes the title of Hokusai's groundbreaking series, but with slightly different terminology in Japanese. Working in the vertical format that he favored in his later years, Hiroshige shows the tendrils of foam at the crest of the wave merging visually into a flight of seabirds (35). His design is a reworking of an earlier monochrome book illustration by Hokusai, *Fuji at Sea*, in the picture book *One Hundred Views of Mount Fuji*, published in 1835 after the completion of the color-print series (36). Even after producing forty-six designs for the print series, Hokusai had many more ideas for depictions of the great mountain, which he compiled in this book. Like the *Hokusai Sketchbooks* published some twenty years earlier, *One Hundred Views of Mount Fuji* became a major source of visual concepts for later artists.

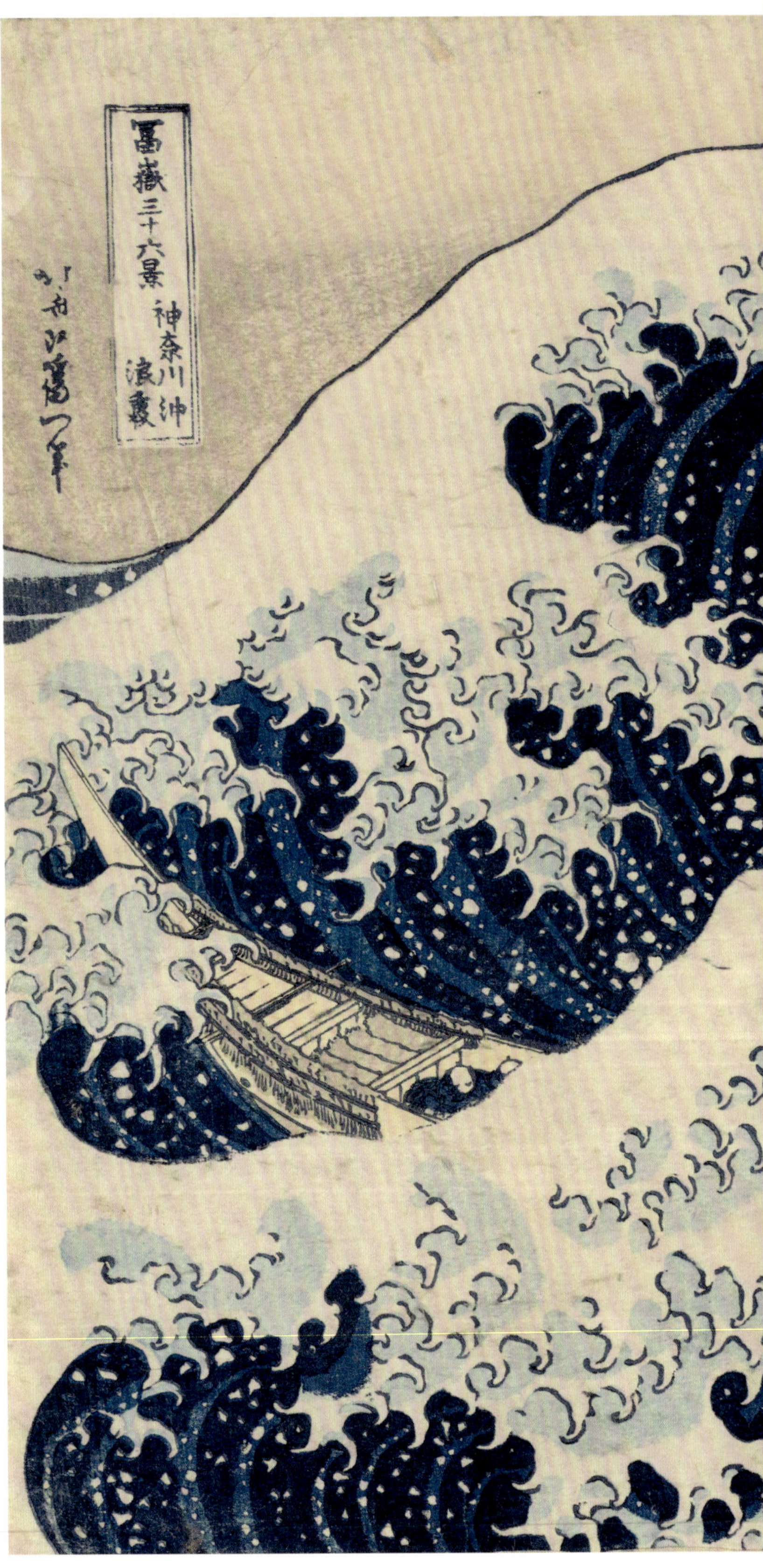

34
HOKUSAI
Under the Wave off Kanagawa,
also known as "The Great
Wave," about 1830–31.
Color woodblock print
25.2 x 37.7 cm
(9⅞ x 14⅞ in.)

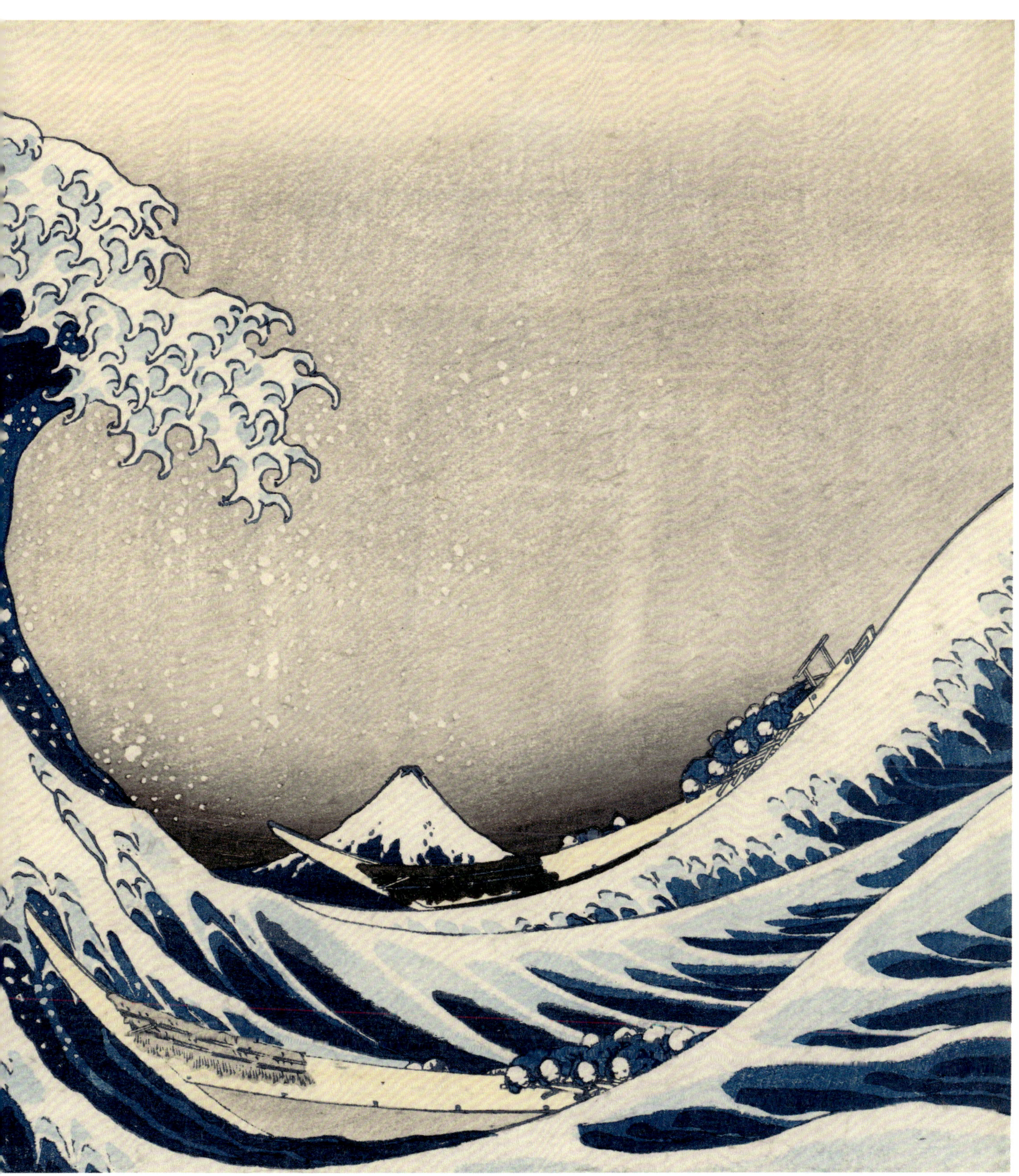

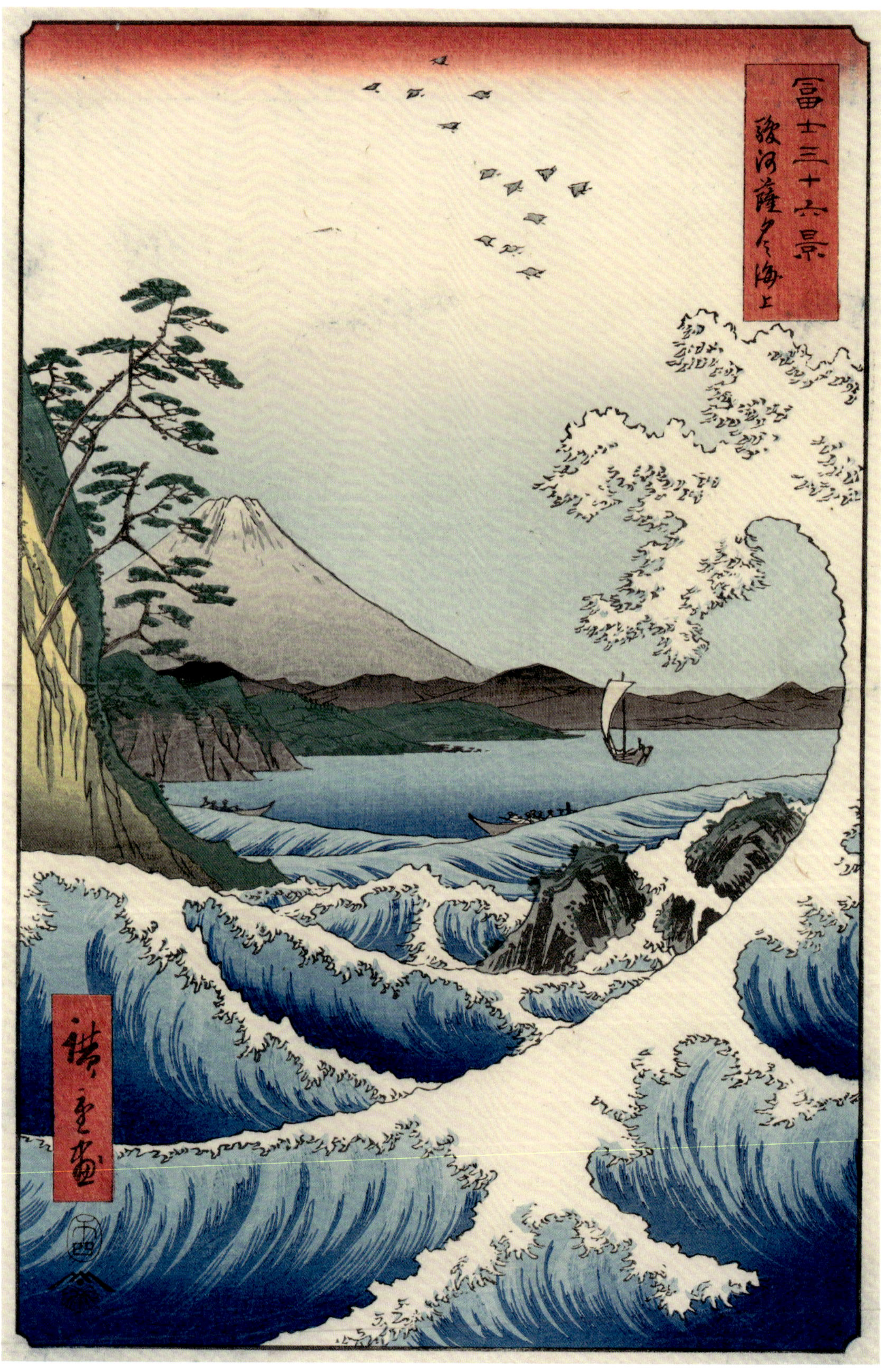

冨士三十六景
駿河薩タ海上
廣重画

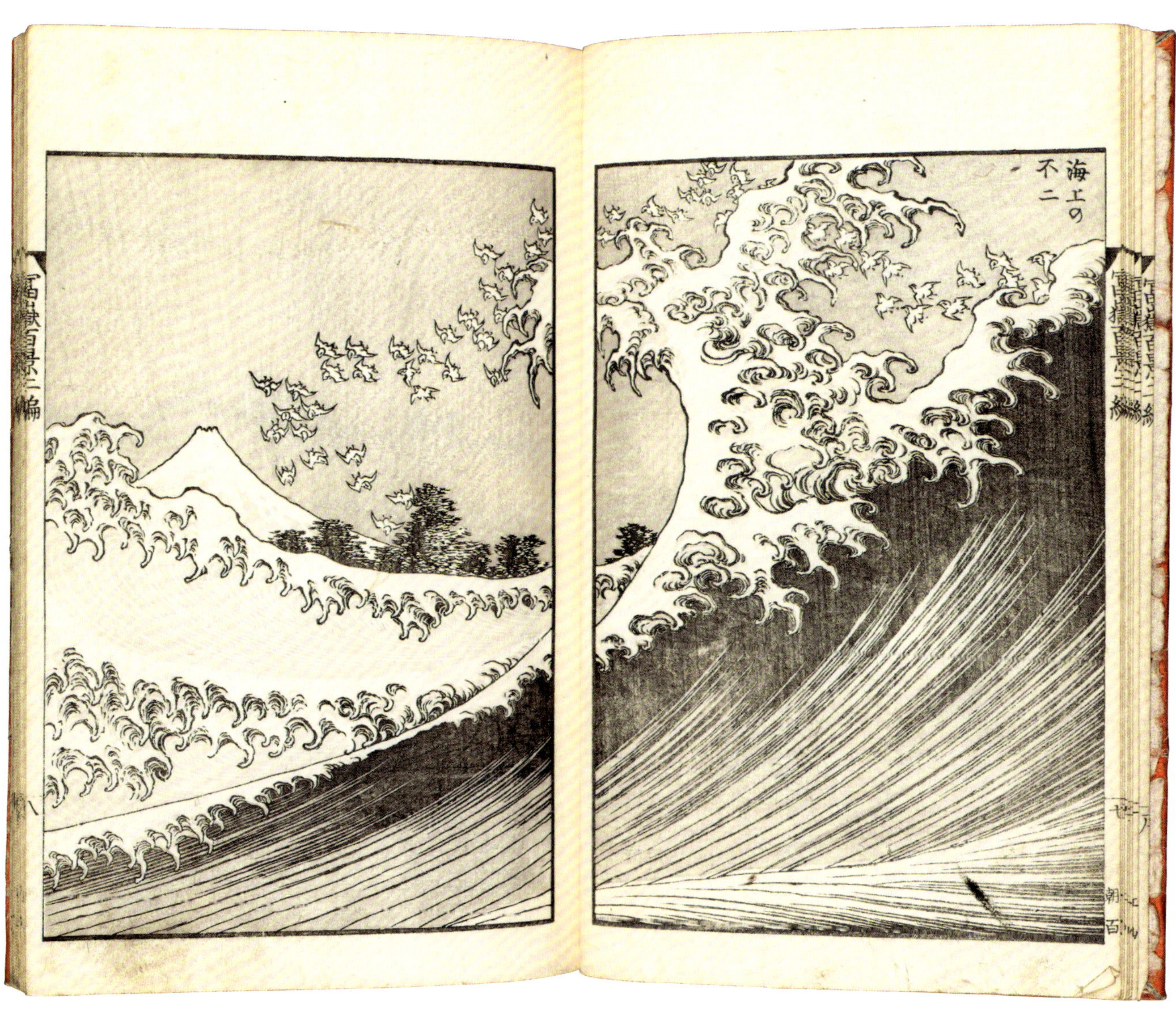

35

HIROSHIGE

*The Sea off Satta in
Suruga Province*, 1858.
Color woodblock print
35.8 x 24.7 cm
(14⅛ x 9¾ in.)

36

HOKUSAI

Fuji at Sea, from
*One Hundred Views
of Mount Fuji*, 1835.
Woodblock printed book
Each page:
22.6 x 15.7 cm
(8⅞ x 6⅛ in.)

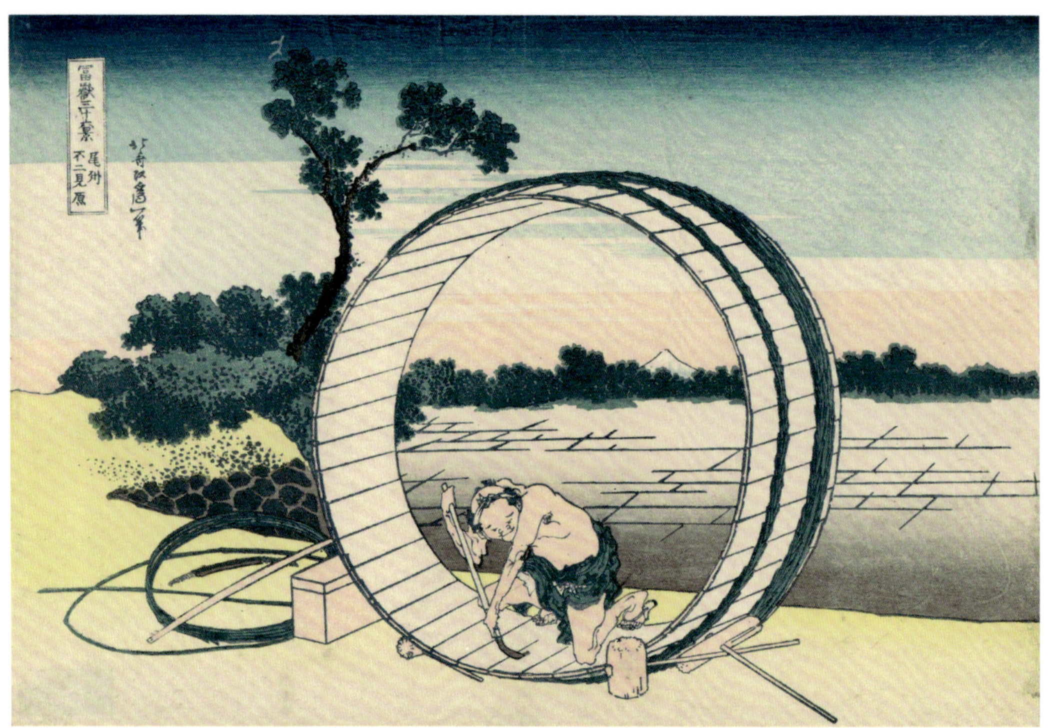

37

HOKUSAI
Fuji View Plain in Owari Province, about 1830–31.
Color woodblock print
25.2 x 37.7 cm
(9⁷⁄₈ x 14⁷⁄₈ in.)

38

HIROSHIGE
Barrel-Maker; Copied from a Picture by Old Master Katsushika, 1836.
Color woodblock print
21.1 x 28.2 cm
(8¼ x 11⅛ in.)

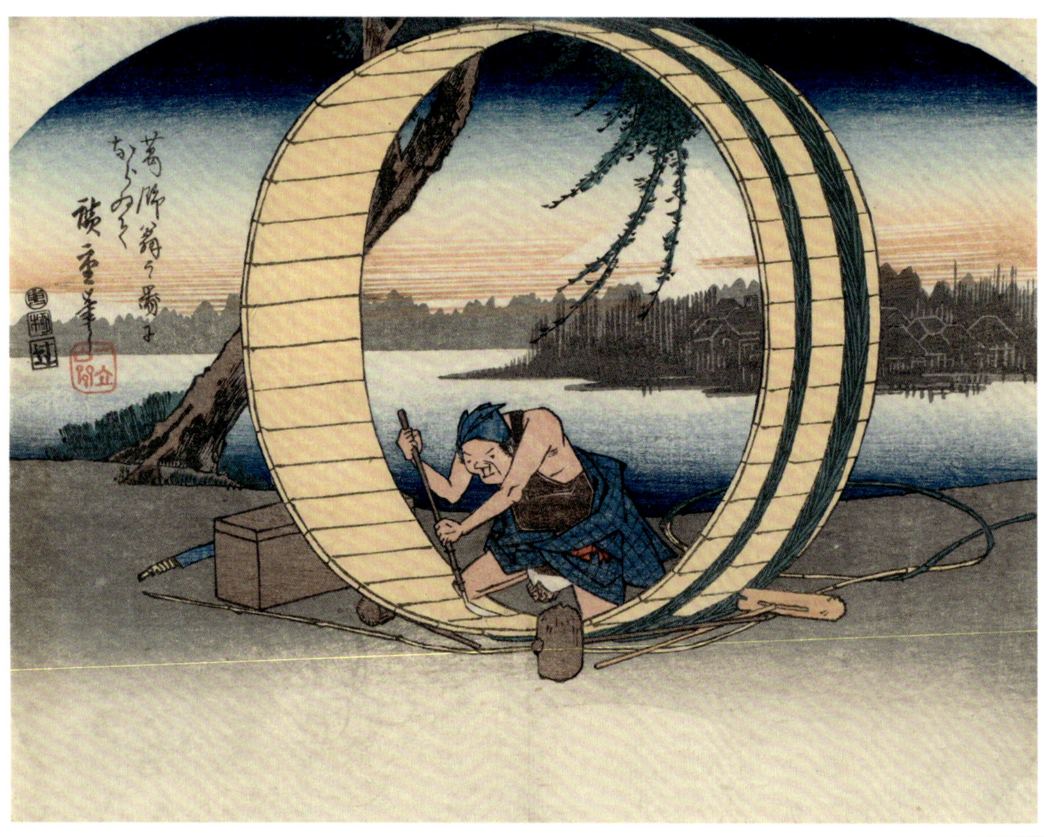

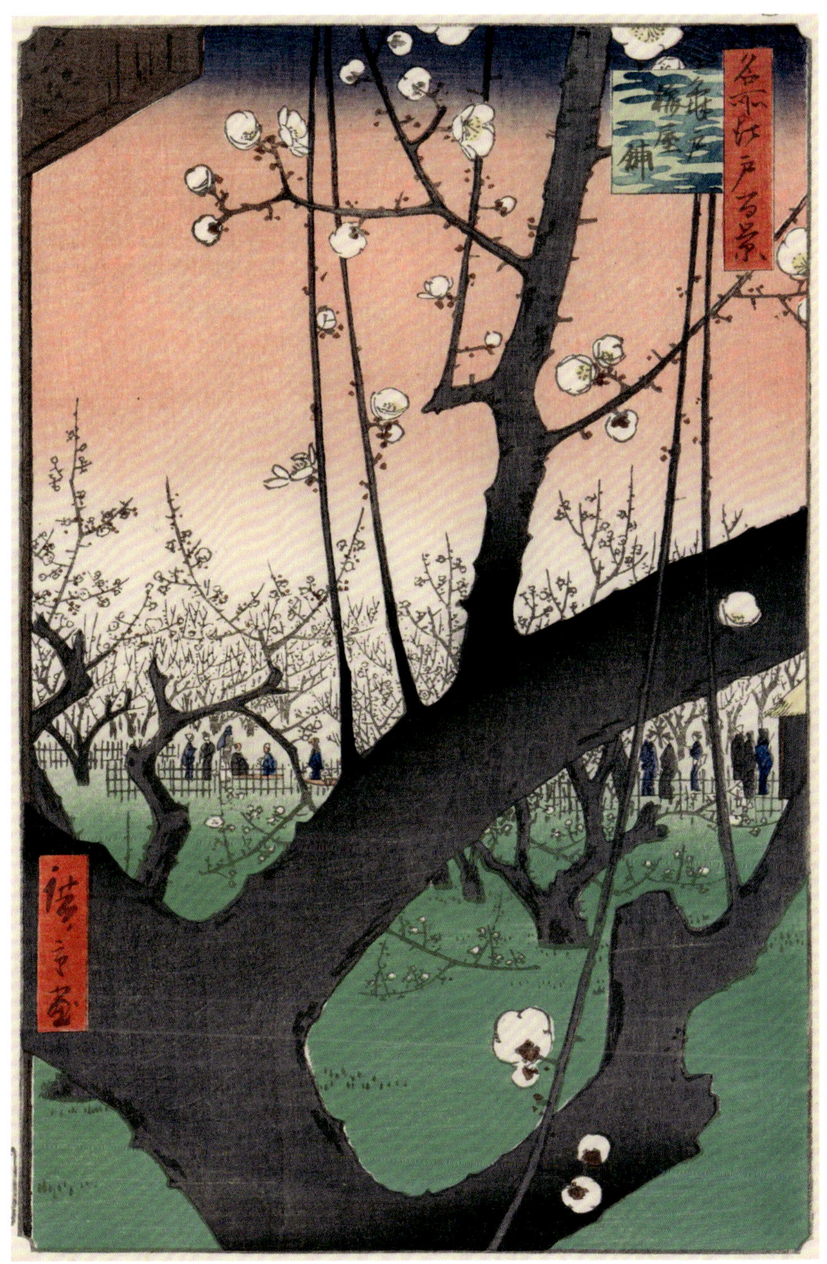

39

HIROSHIGE
Plum Estate, Kameido, 1857.
Color woodblock print
37 x 25.7 cm
(14⅝ x 10⅛ in.)

One source of the great appeal of Hokusai's landscape compositions is his skillful deployment of underlying geometrical forms: the triangle of Mount Fuji, the rectangular shapes of distant fields, and here the perfect circle of a giant barrel under construction by a skilled cooper, which the viewer is invited to look through to spot the mountain on the horizon. We know that Hiroshige was especially intrigued by this print because he copied the composition for a design of his own, a fan print published in 1836 with the acknowledgment that it was copied from Hokusai's work. Hiroshige transferred the scene of a cooper working inside a huge barrel from distant Owari Province (in the area of modern Nagoya) to the banks of the Sumida River in Edo, with lumber yards in the distance.

Hiroshige continued to push Hokusai's ideas for innovative compositions with unusual viewpoints further. His final masterpiece, the series *One Hundred Famous Views of Edo*, includes high viewpoints (in one case a literal bird's-eye view from a hovering eagle); low, ground-level viewpoints; and startling juxtapositions of close foregrounds and distant backgrounds, with the viewer required to look around or even through an object such as the plum tree in this well-known example. The Sleeping Dragon Plum, a gnarled but still blossoming tree, was in a private garden in the Kameido district, open to the public for a small fee. The wooden signpost, topped by a plaque identifying the famous tree, is just visible along the left edge of the print; in the distance low fences mark the paths through the garden, filled with visitors admiring the plum blossoms.

Compositions such as this one were new and exciting to print buyers in Edo in the late 1850s, and over the next few decades, they were received with enthusiasm in Europe as well. In 1887–88, this print and another from the same series were copied in oil by Vincent van Gogh.

Hokusai's interest in showing water in motion included not only waves but waterfalls, which are plentiful in mountainous Japan. His only vertical landscape series, a set of eight prints of waterfalls, was probably the second series that he designed and may have overlapped with his work on the later designs in the Fuji series. Like early printings of the Fuji series, the Waterfall series uses indigo blue, rather than the usual black, for the key block outlines. The waterfalls, not necessarily famous, were selected for their wide variety in appearance.

Of the many ukiyo-e artists who depicted waterfalls in ways that suggest the influence of Hokusai, the clearest examples are found in the work of Keisai Eisen, who like Hokusai was an independent artist not affiliated with any particular school within ukiyo-e. In a hypothetical ranking of the top ukiyo-e artists of the late Edo period, Eisen would probably be in fifth place, after Hokusai and the three top Utagawa-school artists, Kunisada, Kuniyoshi, and Hiroshige. Although his main specialty was prints of beautiful women in high-fashion kimono, he was also an excellent designer of landscapes, including a series of scenes of the Kisokaidō Road (another of the major highways of Edo-period Japan) that was started by him in 1835 and later completed by Hiroshige. In the 1840s, Eisen designed a series of scenic views in the mountains near Nikkō, north of Edo, the location of the elaborate mausoleum of the first Tokugawa shogun — a popular pilgrimage destination at the time and still a major tourist attraction. Three prints in the series focus on waterfalls, and falls appear in some of the other views as well.

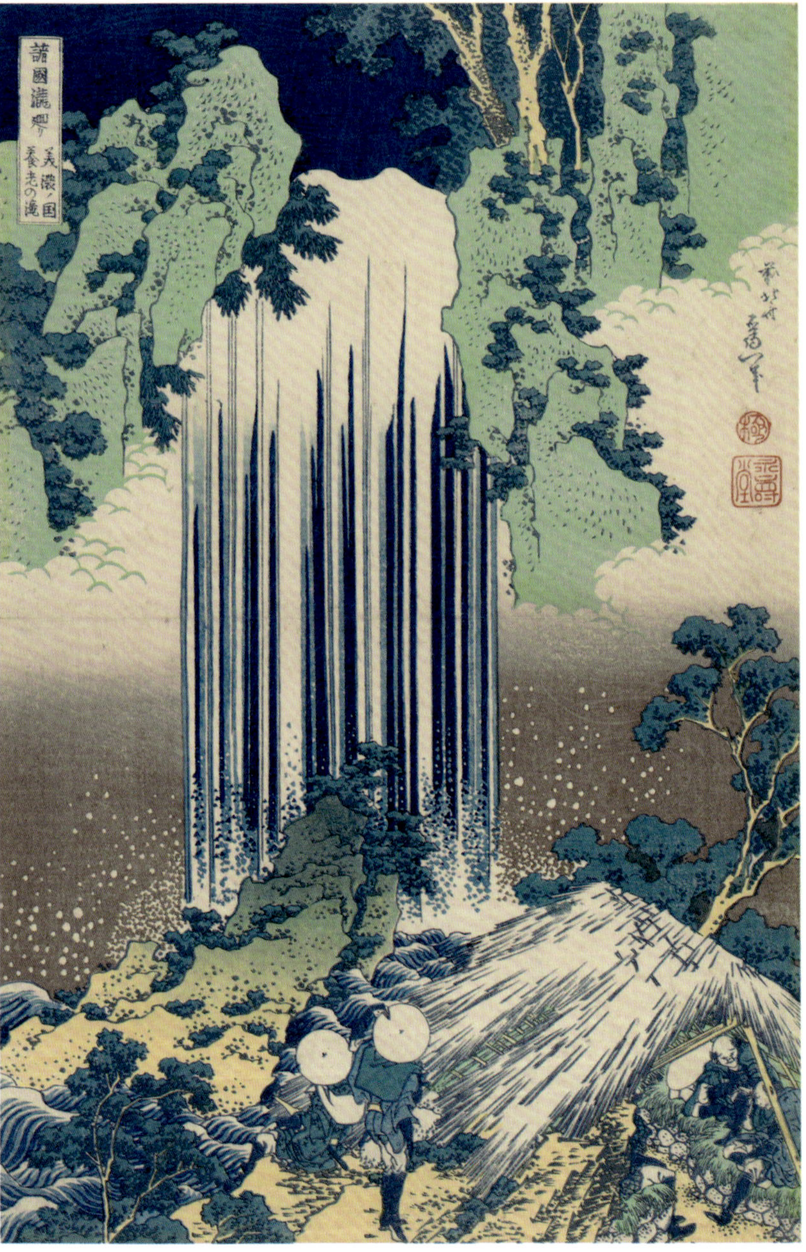

40

HOKUSAI
*The Care-of-the-Aged
Falls in Mino Province*,
about 1832. Color wood-
block print
36.7 x 24.3 cm
(14¹⁄₂ x 9⁵⁄₈ in.)

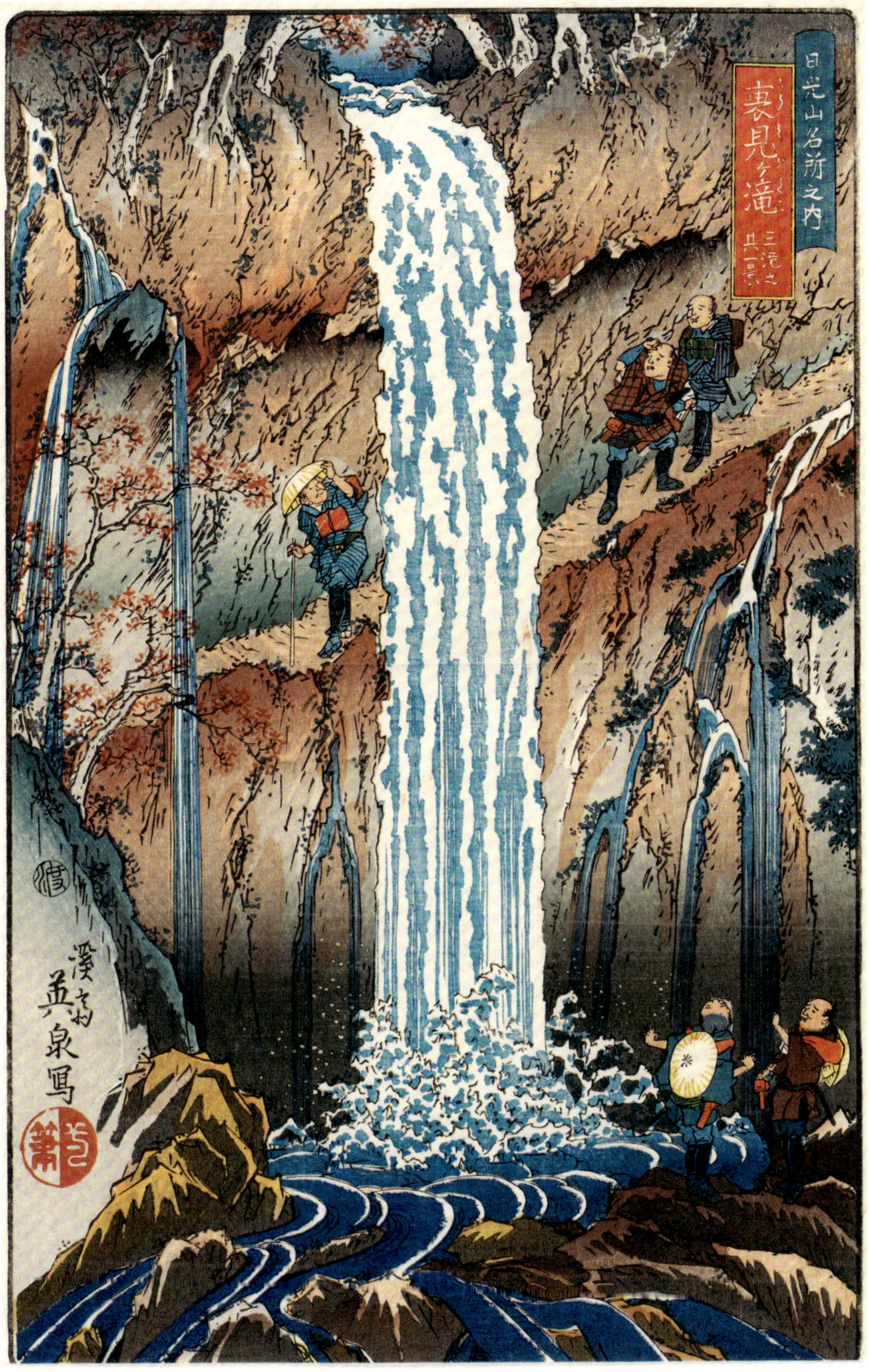

41

KEISAI EISEN
Backward-Viewing Falls, One of the Three Waterfalls, 1843–47.
Color woodblock print
35.5 x 24.4 cm
(14 x 9⅝ in.)

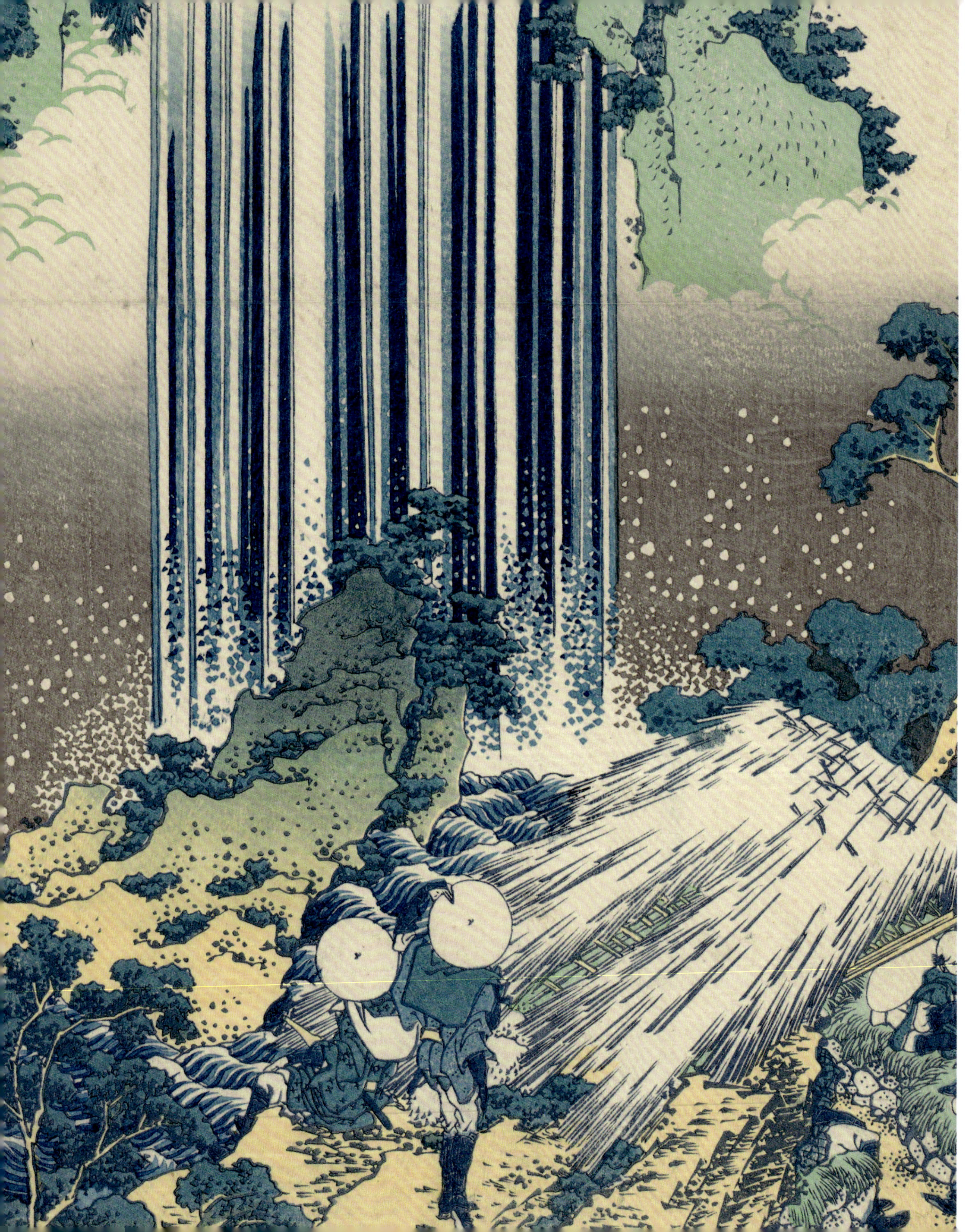

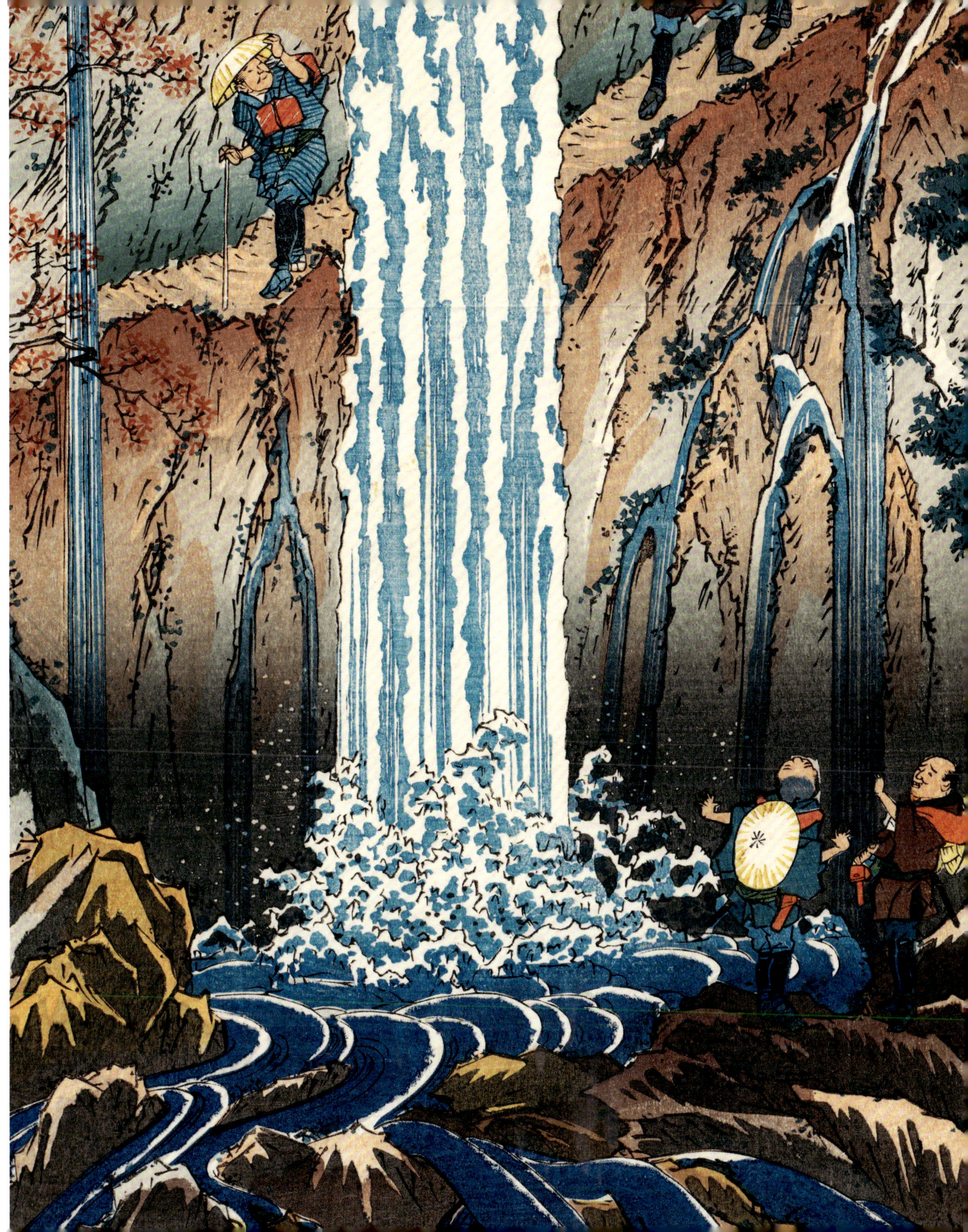

Detailed close-up depictions of flora and fauna are known in Japanese as "bird and flower pictures," although they may also include insects, animals, fish, and miscellaneous plants. The tradition of nature painting dates back to China's Song dynasty (960–1279) and was widely practiced in Korea and Japan as well. In Hokusai's time, this ancient tradition had been further reinforced by the importation of European books and prints with scientific illustrations of botanical and zoological subjects.

Like landscape, the genre of bird-and-flower pictures had been a minor one within ukiyo-e prints — present from the beginning but not very important. Hokusai's untitled series known as the "Large Flowers" did for nature studies what his Fuji series had done for landscape, making the genre into a potential bestseller. In the series the flowers are shown at eye level, as if the viewer were sitting on the ground beside them; they blow in the wind as they are visited by birds and insects. The "Large Flowers" were followed by a series of "Small Flowers," half the size but equally beautiful (71).

As he did in the case of landscape prints, Hiroshige followed up on Hokusai's pioneering work with many attractive designs of his own, continuing to produce both nature studies and landscapes in large quantities. Many of Hiroshige's bird-and-flower designs include inscribed poems that enhance the understated elegance of the prints. His serene image of a pair of mallard ducks on a winter pond (one upended behind the other as it searches for food beneath the surface) includes the haiku poem: "A duck is calling — / the wind blows ripples over / the water's surface."

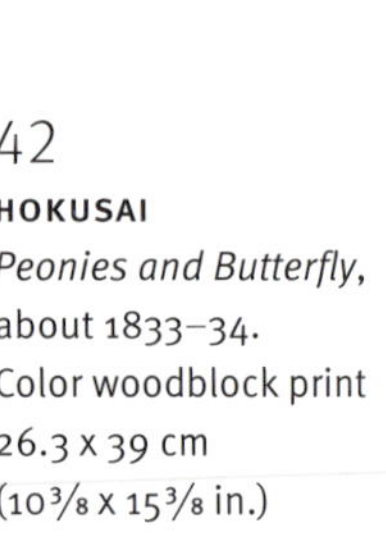

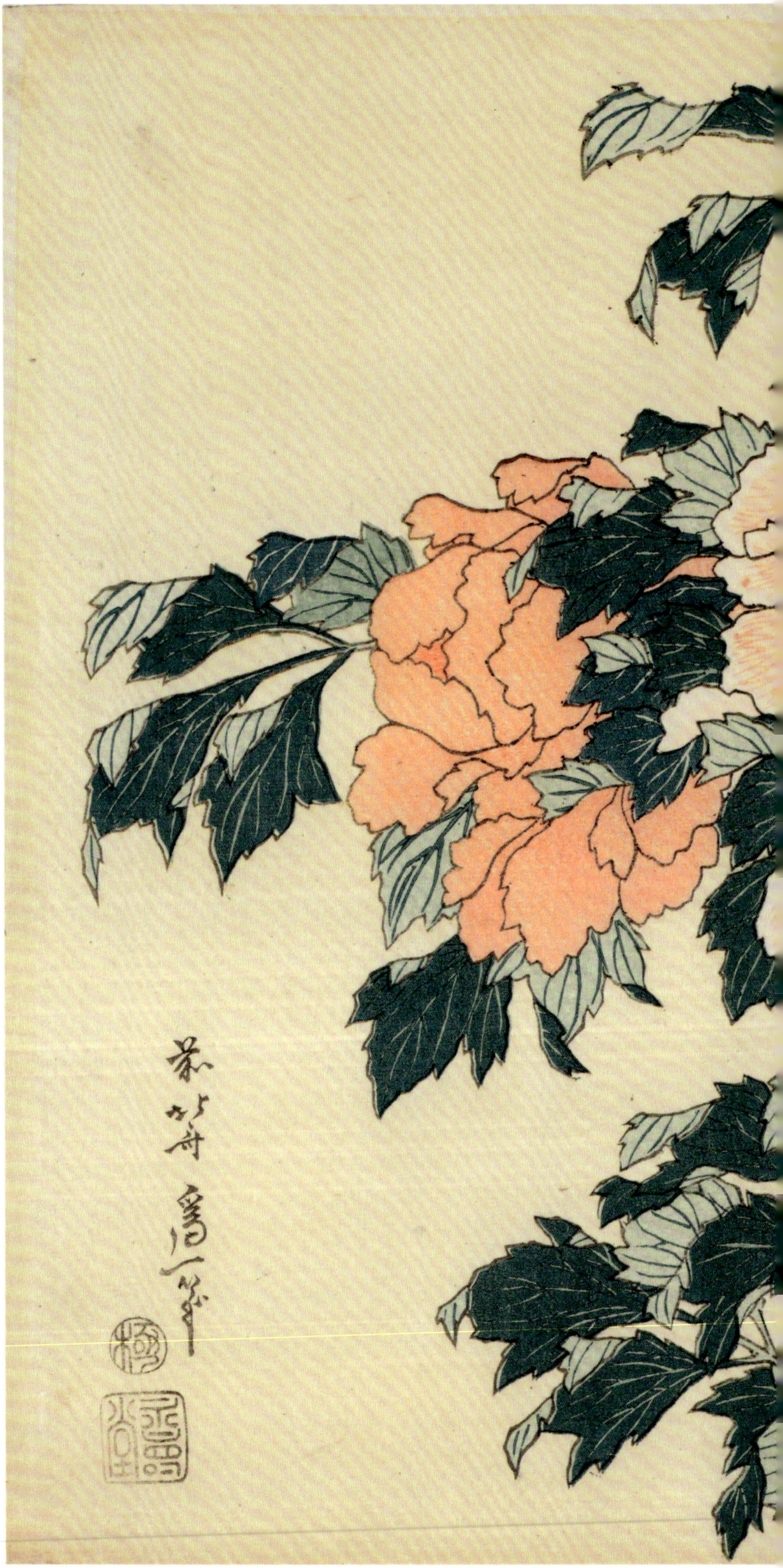

42
HOKUSAI
Peonies and Butterfly,
about 1833–34.
Color woodblock print
26.3 x 39 cm
(10⅜ x 15⅜ in.)

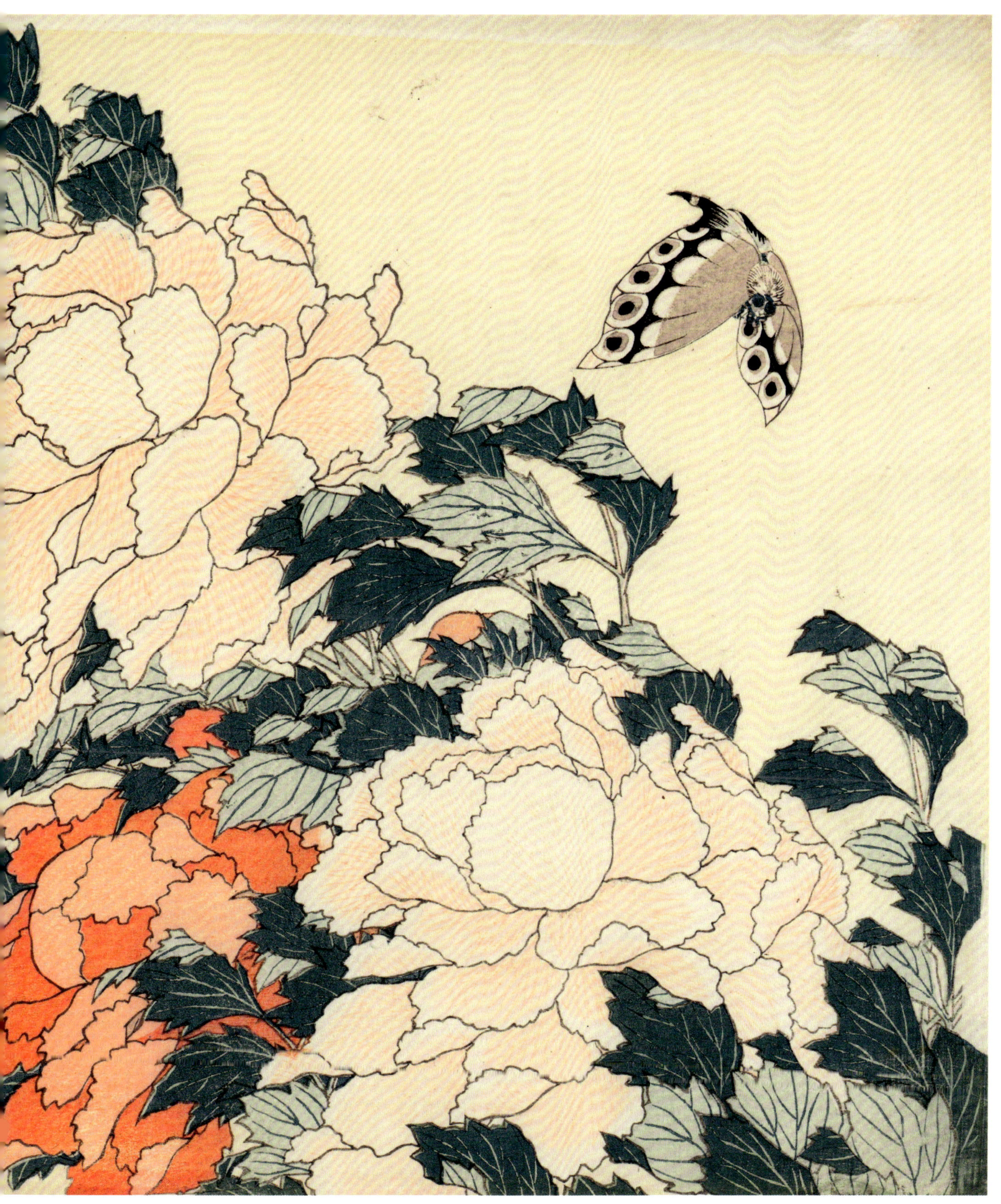

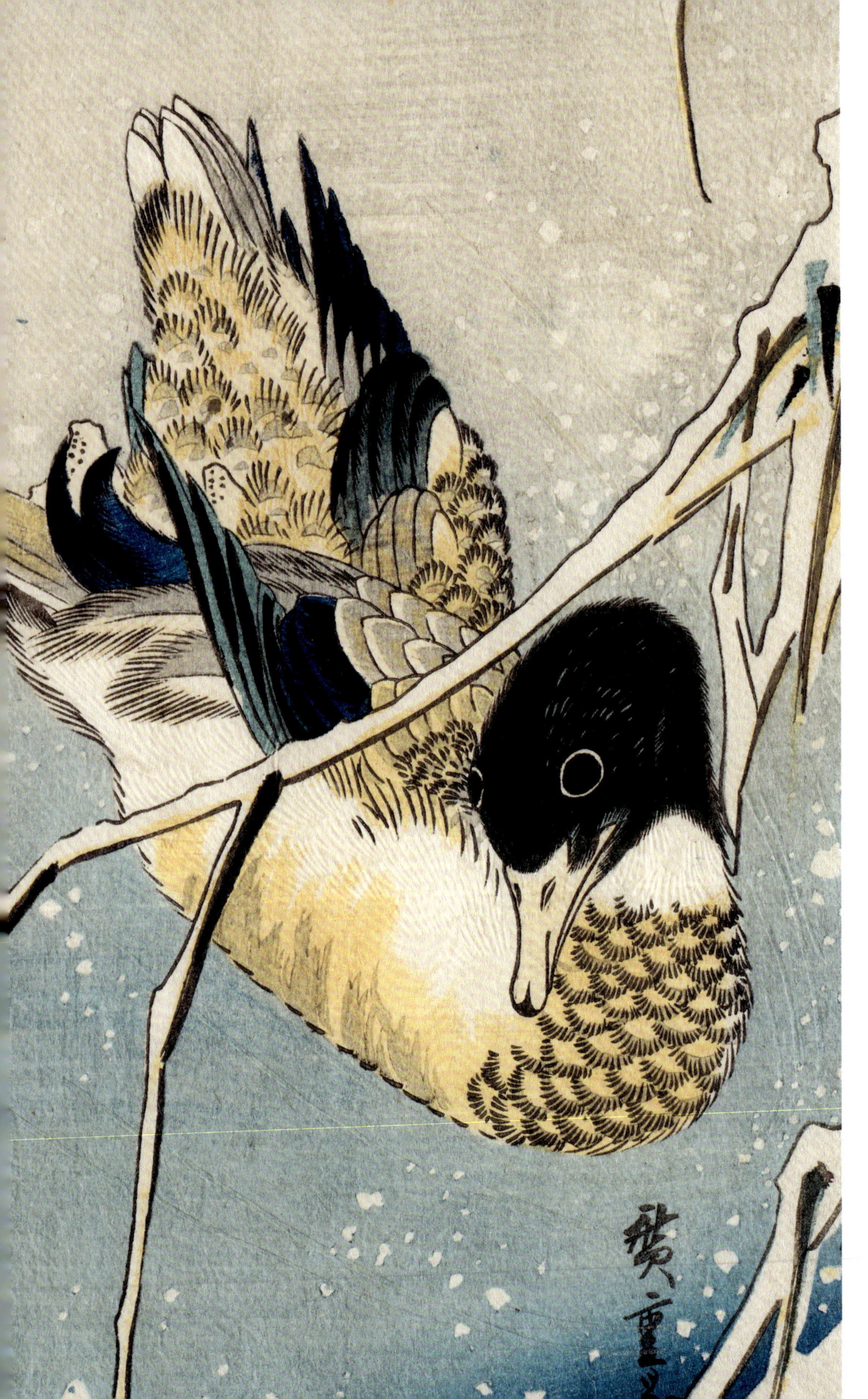

43

HIROSHIGE
Hibiscus, 1843–47.
Color woodblock print
33.5 x 11.3 cm
(13¼ x 4½ in.)

44

HIROSHIGE
*Mallard Ducks and
Snow-Covered Reeds*,
about 1836.
Color woodblock print
37.6 x 17.2 cm
(14¾ x 6¾ in.)

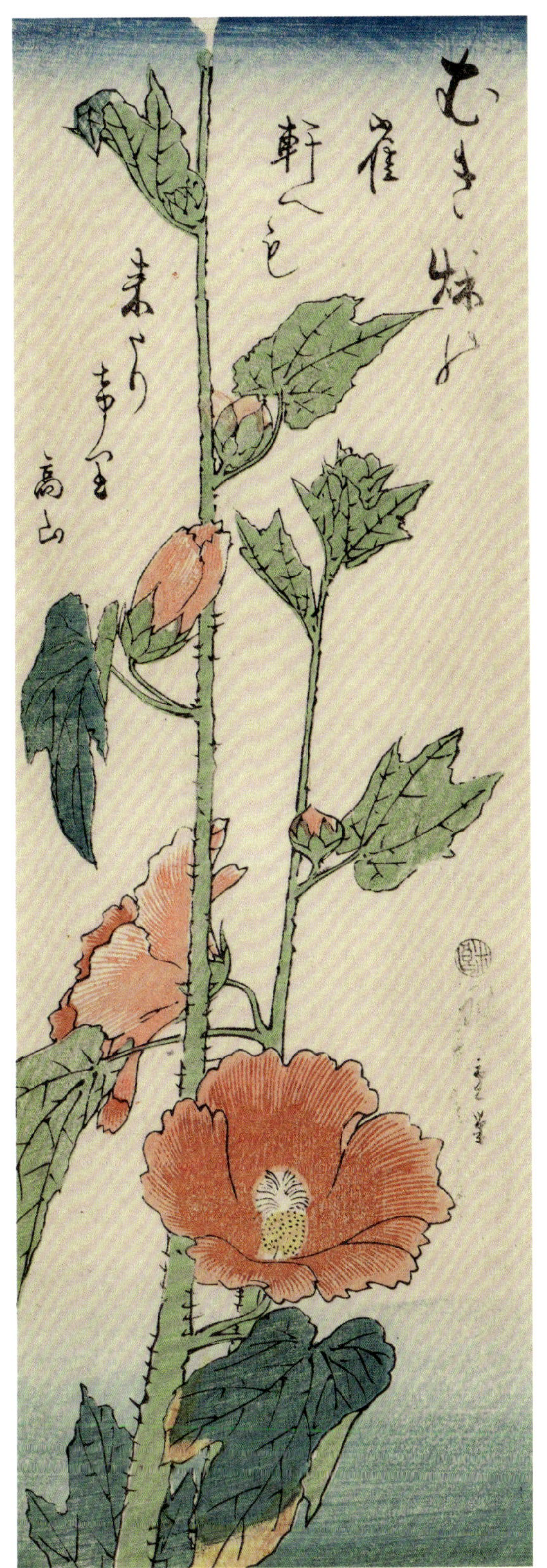

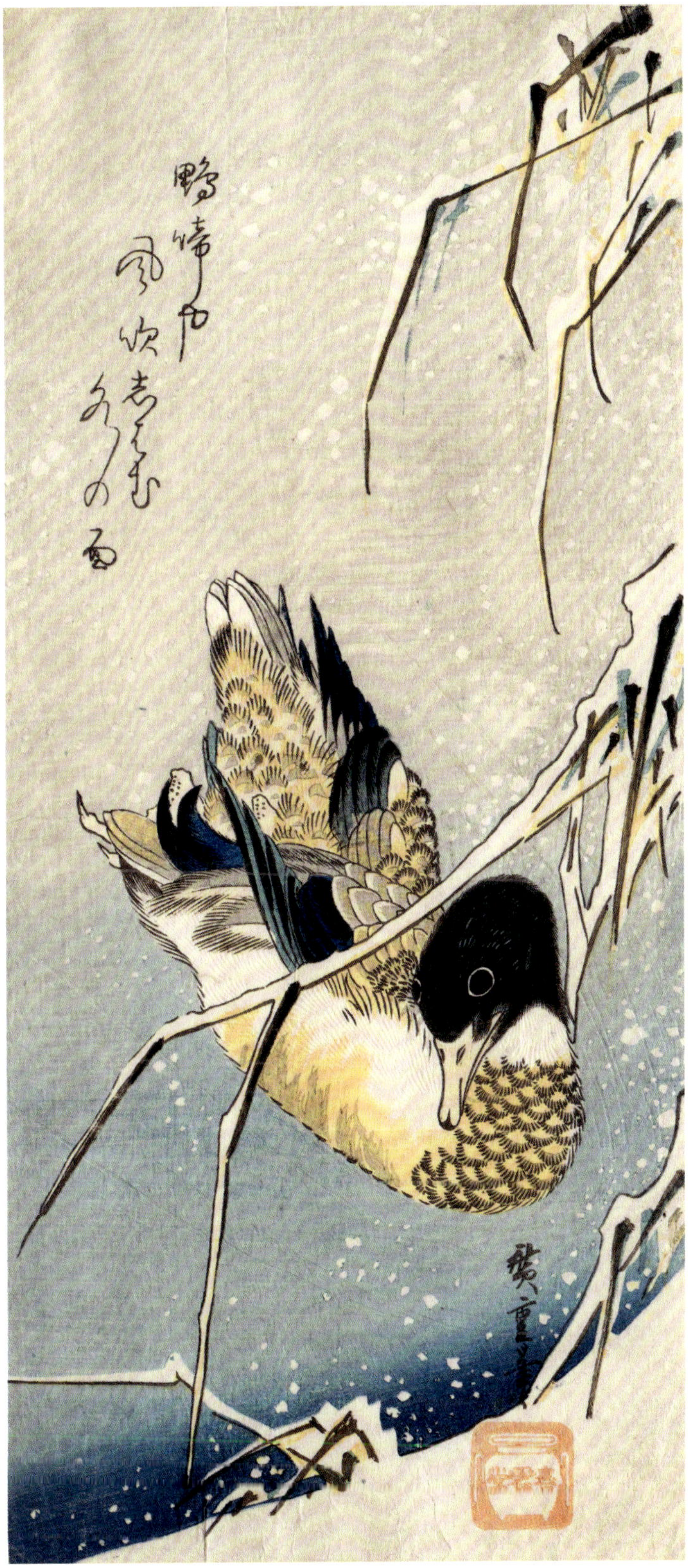

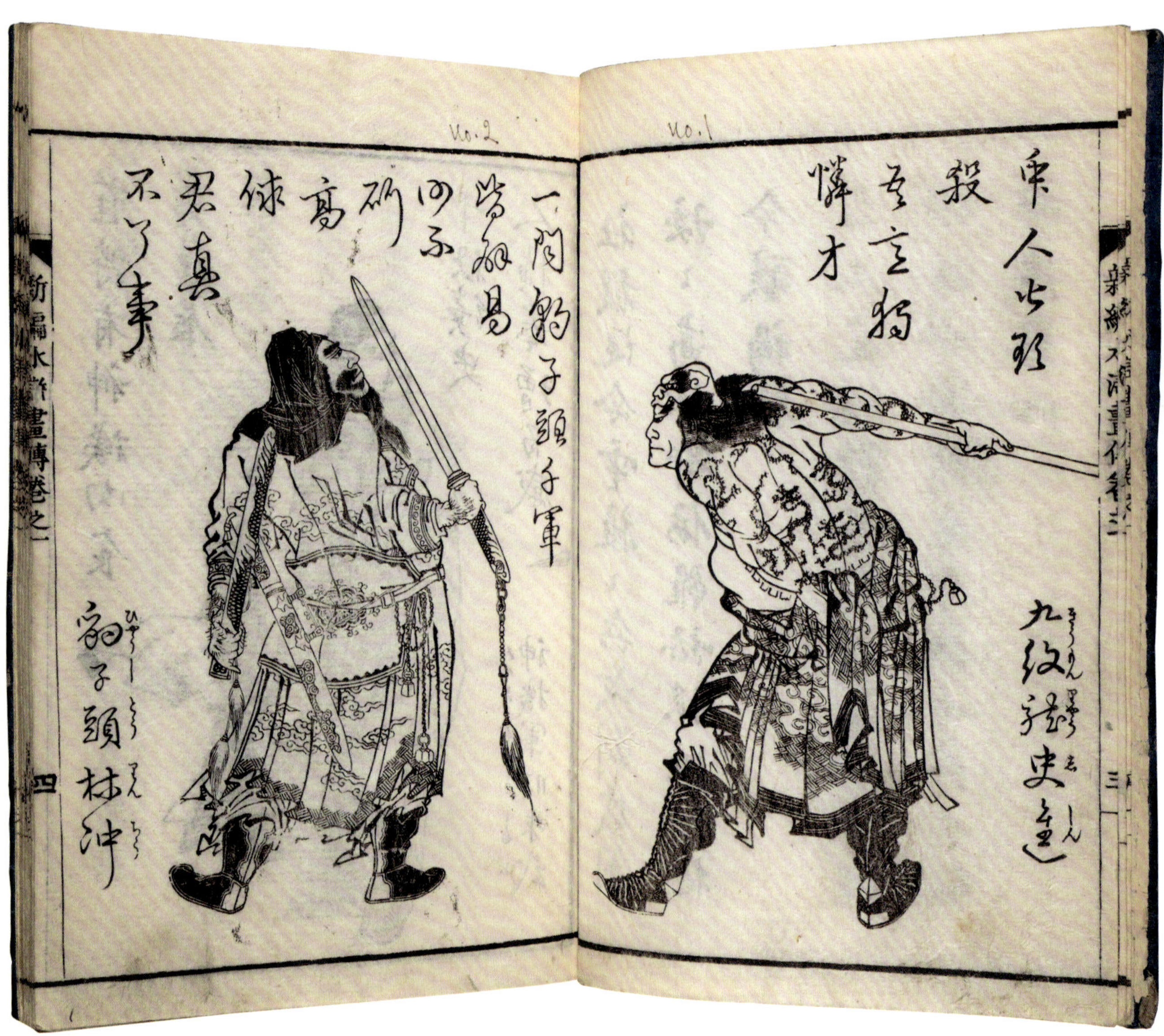

45

HOKUSAI
Illustrations from
*An Illustrated New Edition
of "The Water Margin,"*
after 1838.
Woodblock printed book
Each page:
22.3 x 15.5 cm
(8¾ x 6⅛ in.)

Another type of subject matter that had always been part of the ukiyo-e repertoire but became enormously popular only around 1830, was the warrior print (*musha-e*), actually a broad category of historical and literary scenes. In this case, the elevation of a hitherto minor genre to bestselling status was due to Utagawa Kuniyoshi, who from 1827 on designed a bestselling series of prints based on the great Chinese martial arts novel known in English as *The Water Margin* (*Shuhuzhuan* in Chinese, *Suikoden* in Japanese). Written in China in the fourteenth century, based on legends of the twelfth century, the story tells of

108 heroic bandits who use their martial arts skills to battle corrupt officials. Their headquarters on Mount Liang is in the middle of a lake surrounded by a swamp, the "water margin" of the title.

Hokusai was closely connected to the boom in warrior prints as well. Kuniyoshi's main source of inspiration was a new, easy-to-read Japanese translation of the book by the popular novelist Bakin, with illustrations by Hokusai, first published in 1805–7 when Kuniyoshi was still a child. Perhaps the adult Kuniyoshi, searching for a way to compete with his senior colleague Utagawa Kunisada, the greatest master of actor prints, remembered the

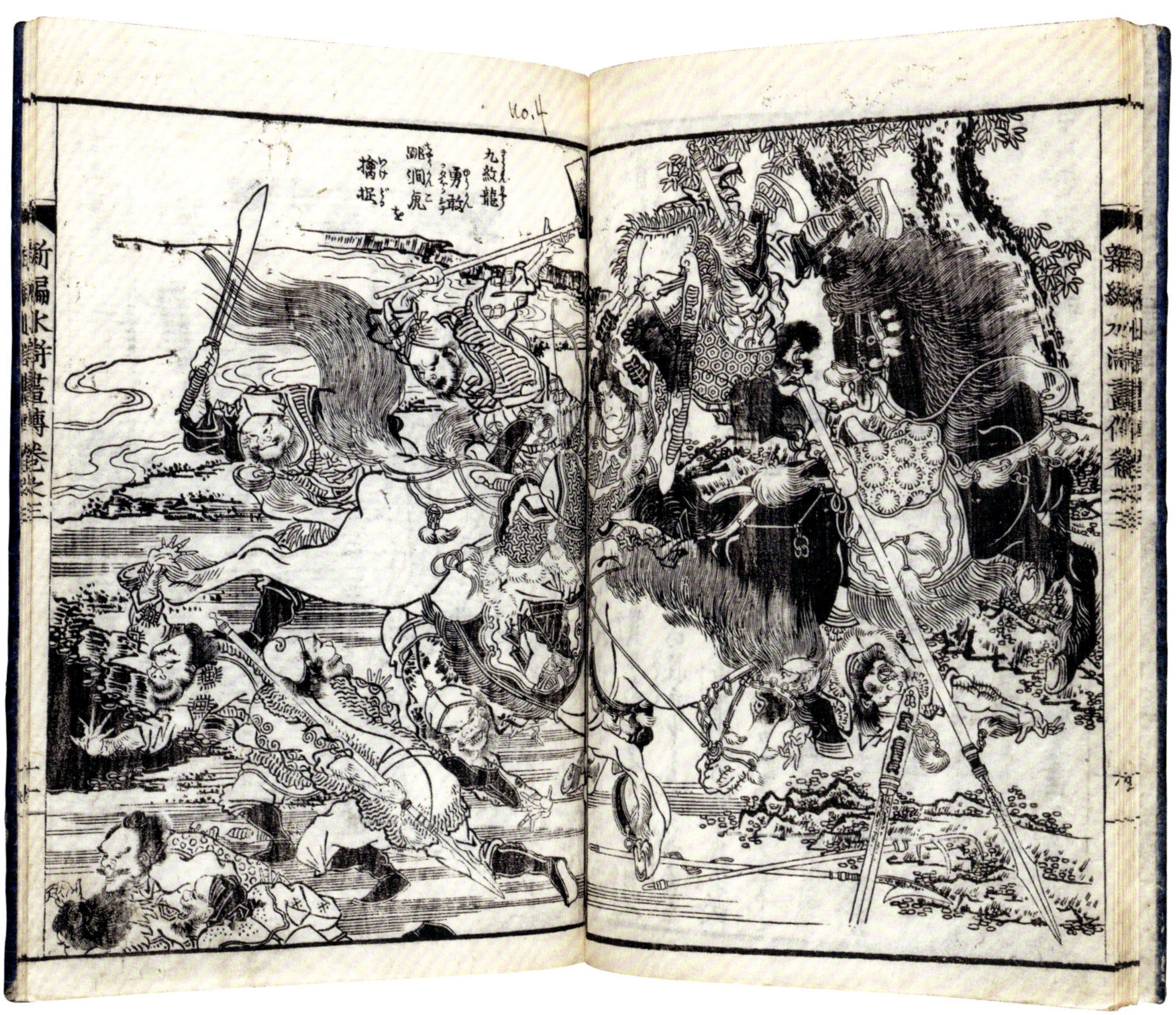

book that he loved as a child and decided to make full-size color prints of the Chinese heroes. He combined two types of illustrations that Hokusai had done: portraits of the individual heroes at the beginning of each volume, and the action-packed illustrations of battles scattered throughout the text. Kuniyoshi showed the heroes in close-up portraits, one or two at a time, in the middle of action scenes with detailed backgrounds (46). Much later, in 1845, Kuniyoshi portrayed the author-artist team of Bakin and Hokusai in a book of notable personalities in Japan, looking as they had several decades earlier at the time of their collaboration (49).

Following up on the great success of the first Water Margin series, Kuniyoshi and his many students designed numerous additional series showing Japanese heroes as well as the original Water Margin characters. In panoramic triptychs and single-sheet portraits, the heroes battle each other or fabulous monsters such as the giant snake vanquished by Saginoike Heikuro (47). In response to the new popularity of this type of print, Hokusai himself designed a series of five brilliantly colored prints of warriors in combat, so complex that viewers must study the image carefully to see who is doing what to whom (48).

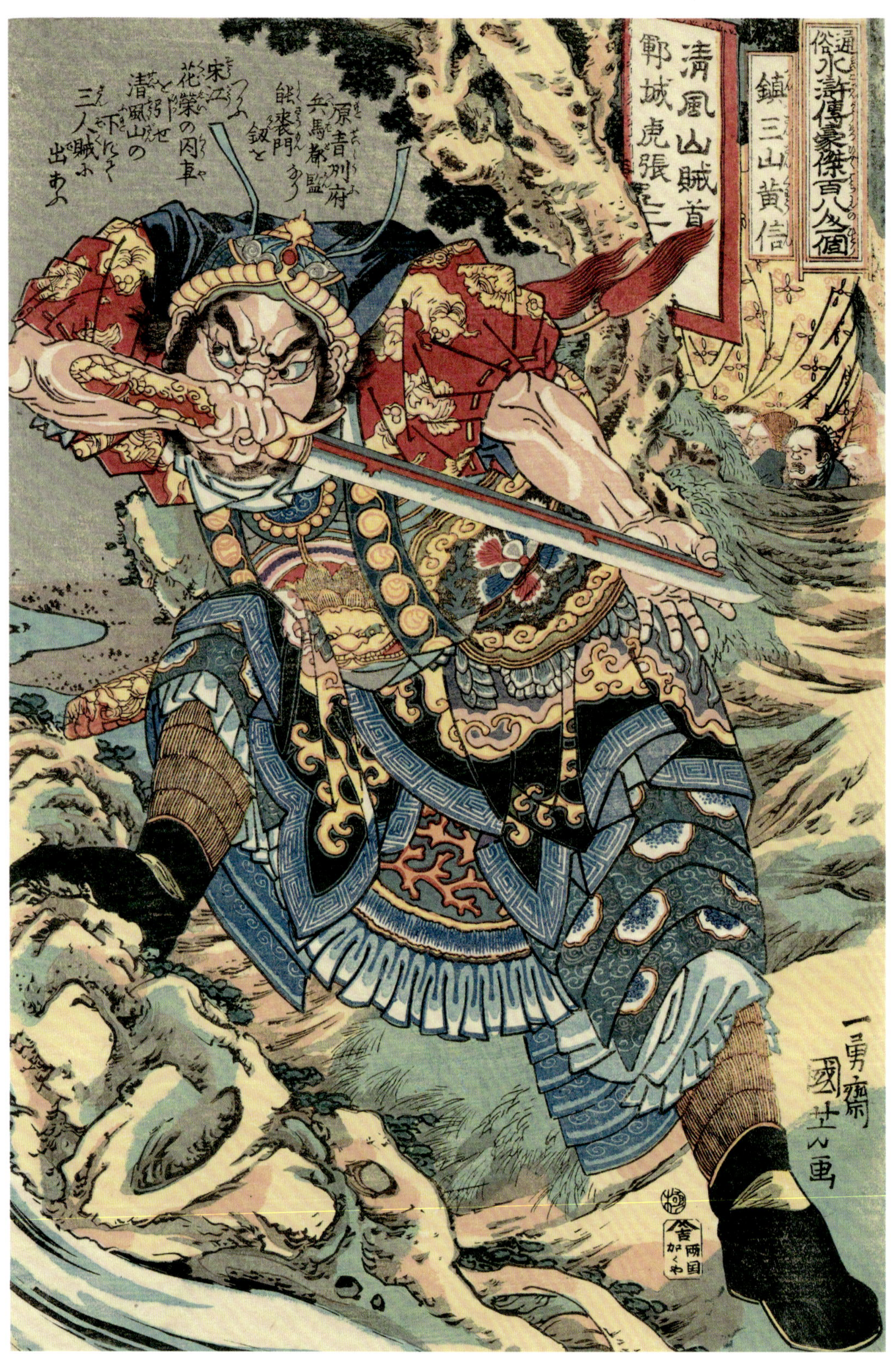

46

UTAGAWA KUNIYOSHI
*Huang Xin, Guardian
of Three Mountains*,
about 1827–30.
Color woodblock print
36.3 x 25.3 cm
(14¼ x 10 in.)

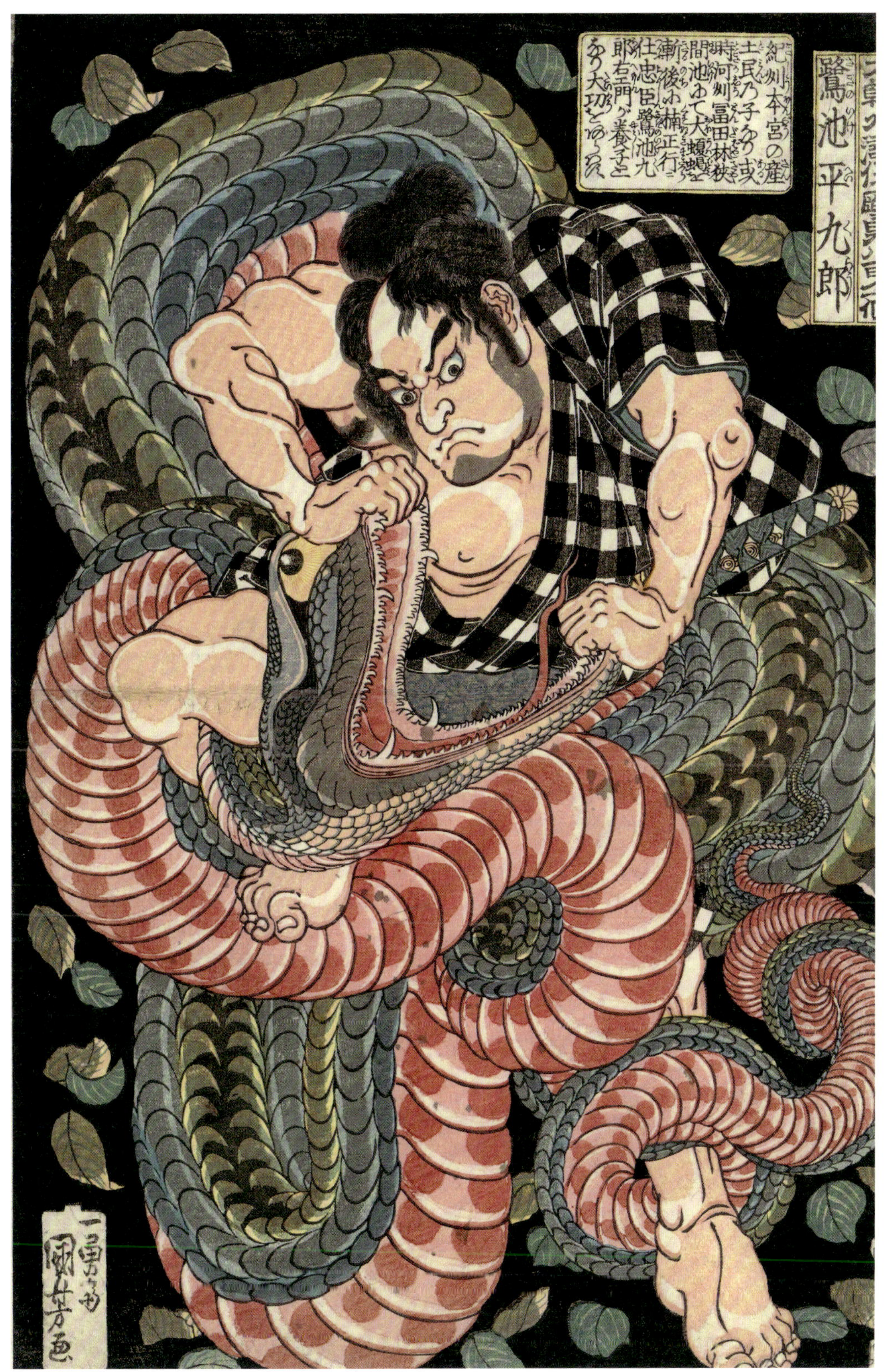

47
KUNIYOSHI
Suginoike Heikurō,
about 1834–35.
Color woodblock print
36.3 x 25.3 cm
(14¼ x 10 in.)

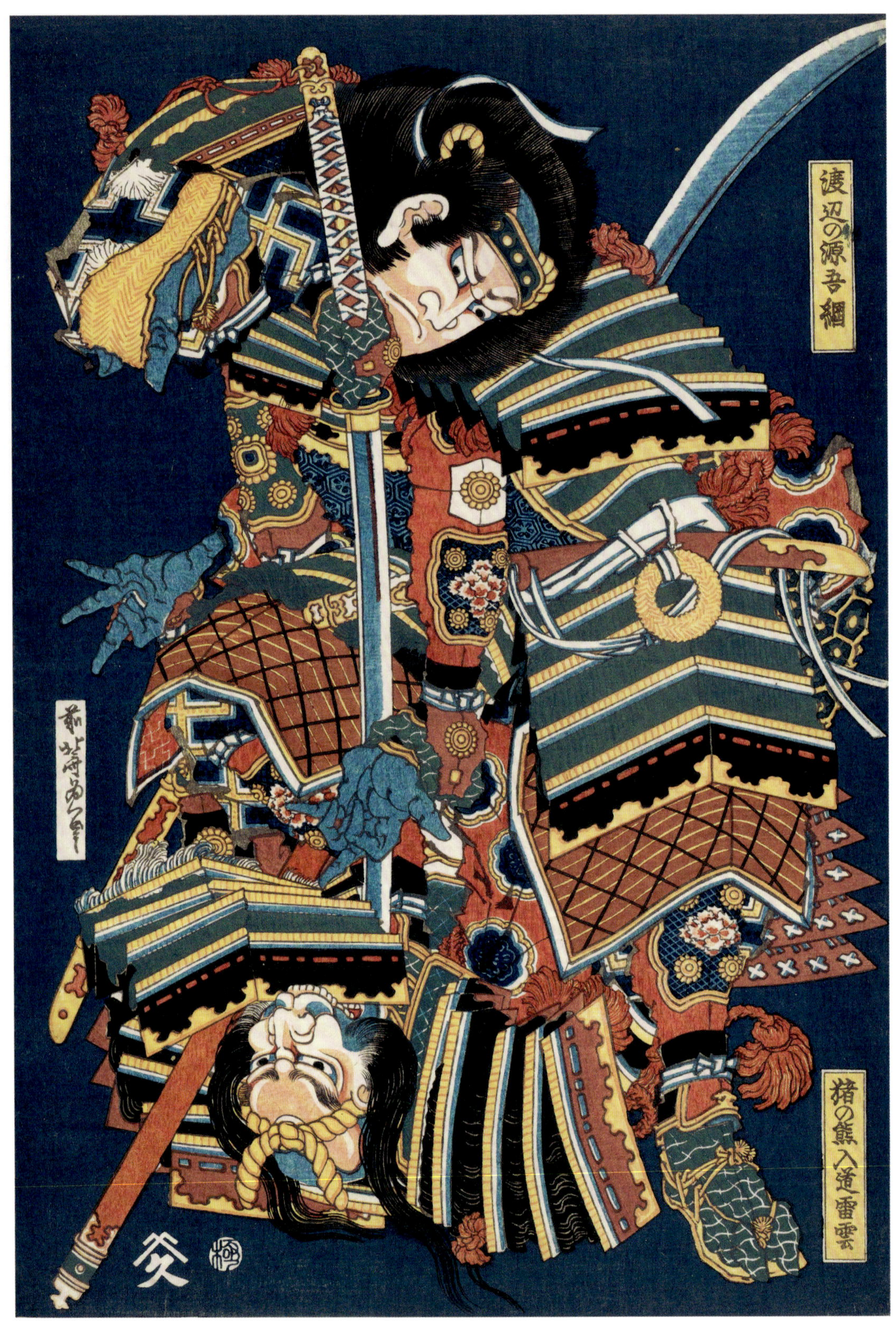

48
HOKUSAI
*Watanabe no Gengo
Tsuna and Inokuma
Nyūdō Raiun*, about
1833–35.
Color woodblock print
37.4 x 26.5 cm
(14¾ x 10⅜ in.)

100

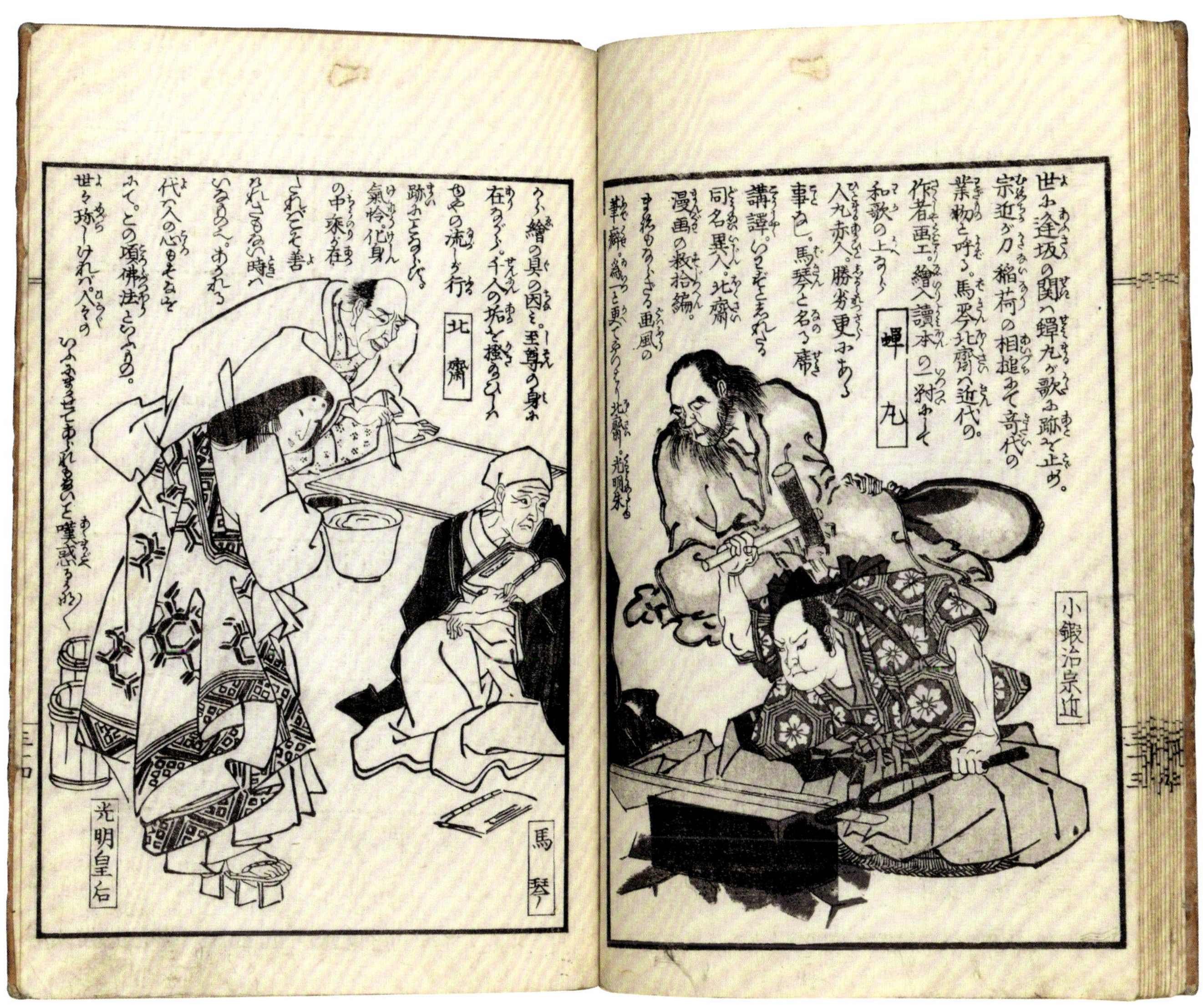

49

KUNIYOSHI

Hokusai and Bakin,
with historical figures,
from *Extraordinary
Persons of Japan*, 1845.
Woodblock printed book
22.6 x 14.2 cm
(8⅞ x 5⅝ in.)

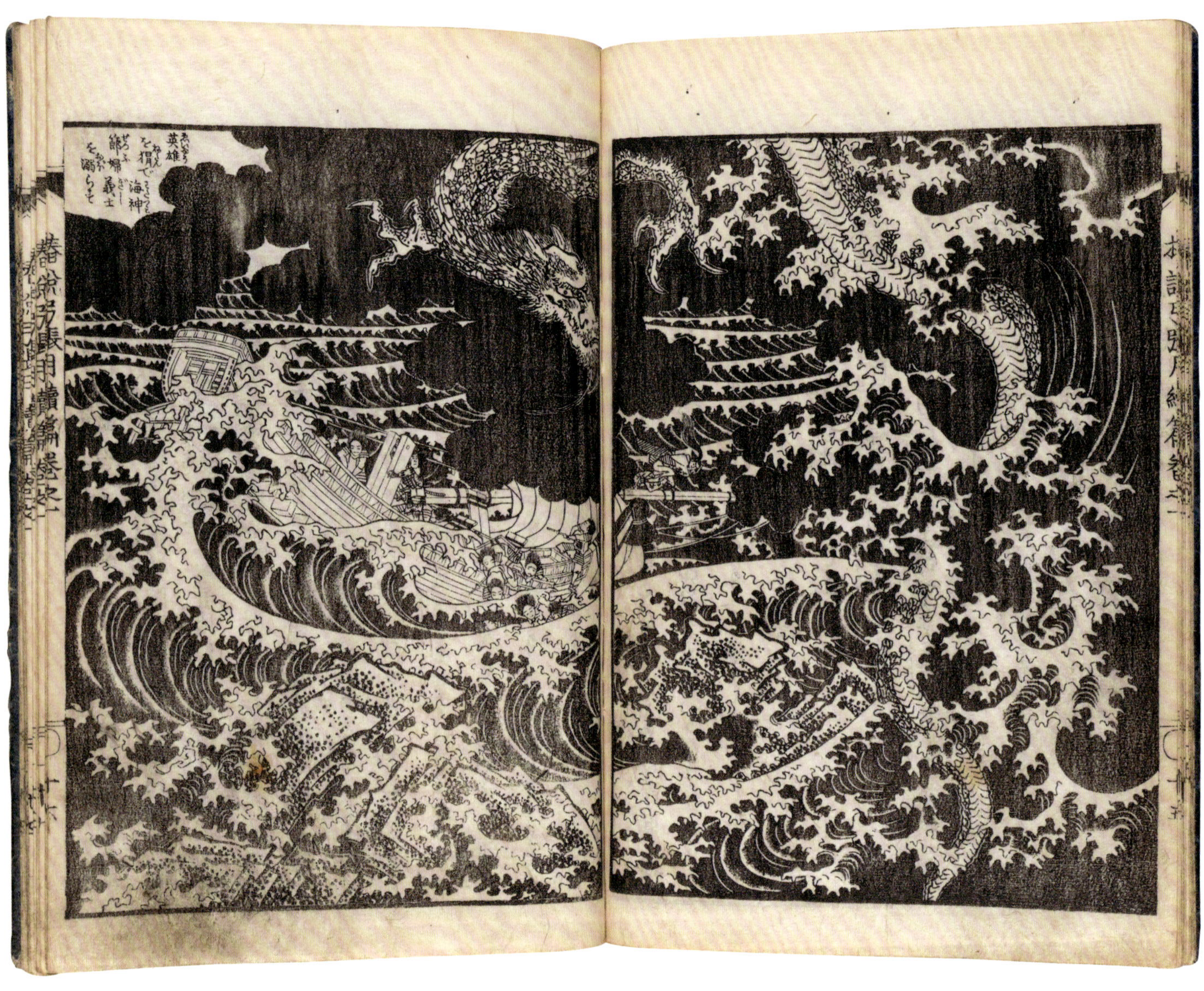

A

50

HOKUSAI

Tametomo's Shipwreck,
from *The Crescent Moon
Bow*, 1807–8.
Woodblock printed book
Each page:
22.9 x 16.1 cm
(9 x 6⅜ in.)

The bestselling Japanese historical novel *The Crescent Moon Bow*, written by Bakin and published in 1807–11 with illustrations by Hokusai, was a major source of inspiration for Kuniyoshi, as seen in two triptychs depicting the same scene from the novel.

The hero Minamoto Tametomo is based on a real historical figure who died in exile after his faction lost one round of the twelfth-century civil wars, but in Bakin's story he escapes and seeks vengeance on his enemies. Unfortunately, his ship is sunk during a storm when it is rammed by a sea monster, in a lengthy scene so exciting that Hokusai devoted four illustrations to it, interspersed with text pages, in the original book: first, a storm dragon menaces the ship (A); then Tametomo is rescued by winged bird-demons (*tengu*) sent by the ghost of his former lord, Retired Emperor Sutoku (B); a doomed couple who were also passengers on the ship wash up on a rock (C); and finally, a faithful retainer rescues Tametomo's infant son by riding on the back of the very monster that sank the ship (D).

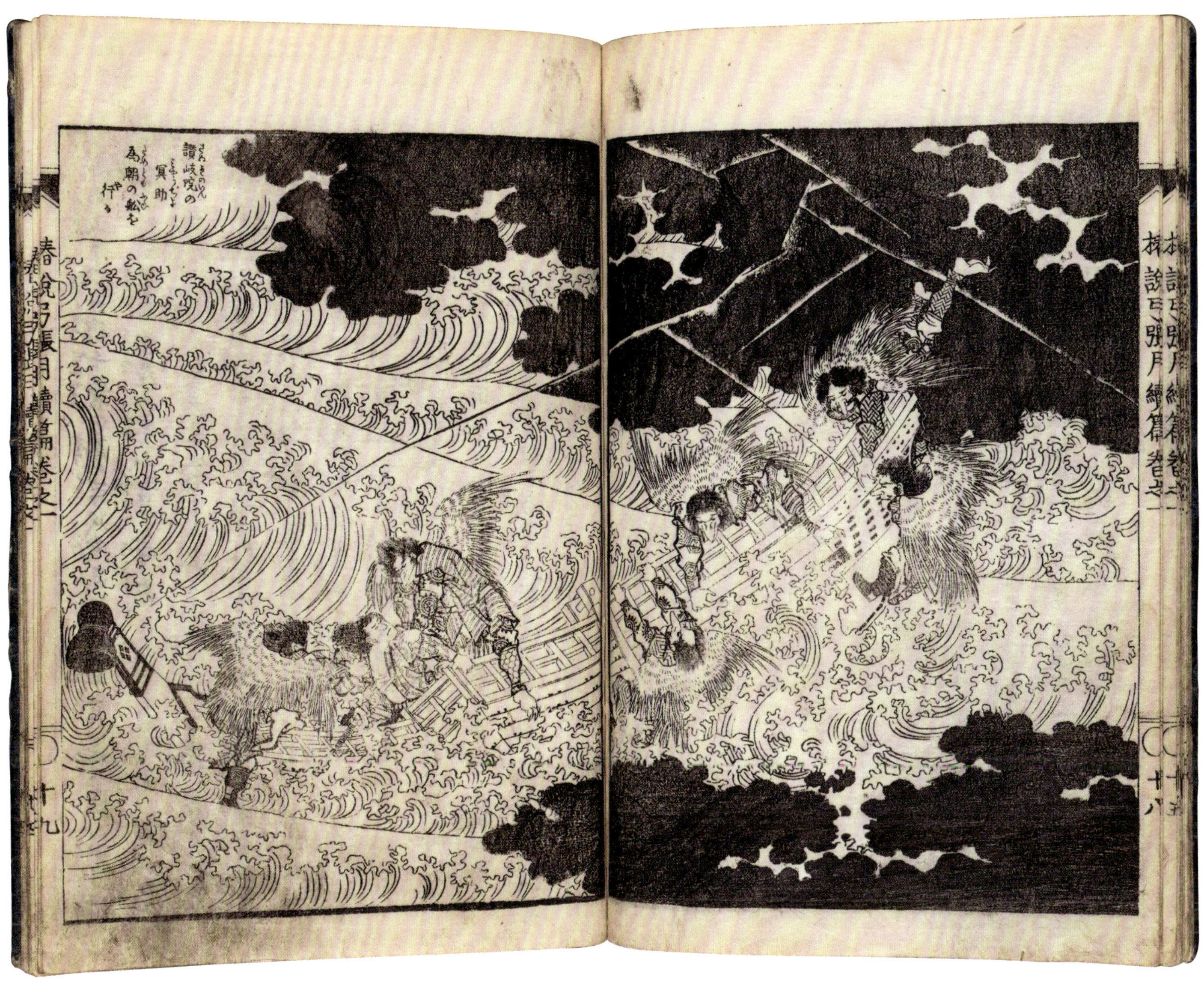

B

Kuniyoshi's first color-print version of the scene combines elements from three of Hokusai's pictures — the dragon hovering above, the couple on the rock, and the retainer on the monster's back, holding the baby — with his own version of the tengu flying in to rescue Tametomo (51). Some fifteen years later, he did another version that is one of his most famous triptychs, with a tighter, better-balanced composition and a more fish-like depiction of the sea monster (52). As in an illustration by Hokusai that Kuniyoshi had not used previously, he shows the moment when the tengu take hold of Tametomo to fly him to safety. Kuniyoshi's clever depiction of them could only be shown in color: he renders the tengu as transparent ghosts, since they are the reincarnated spirits of Tametomo's dead comrades.

In the 2021 television anime series *Godzilla Singular Point*, Kuniyoshi's triptych is reworked to show the monsters that appear in the anime: the sea monster is Godzilla, and the tengu become the pterodactyl-like creatures called Rodan.

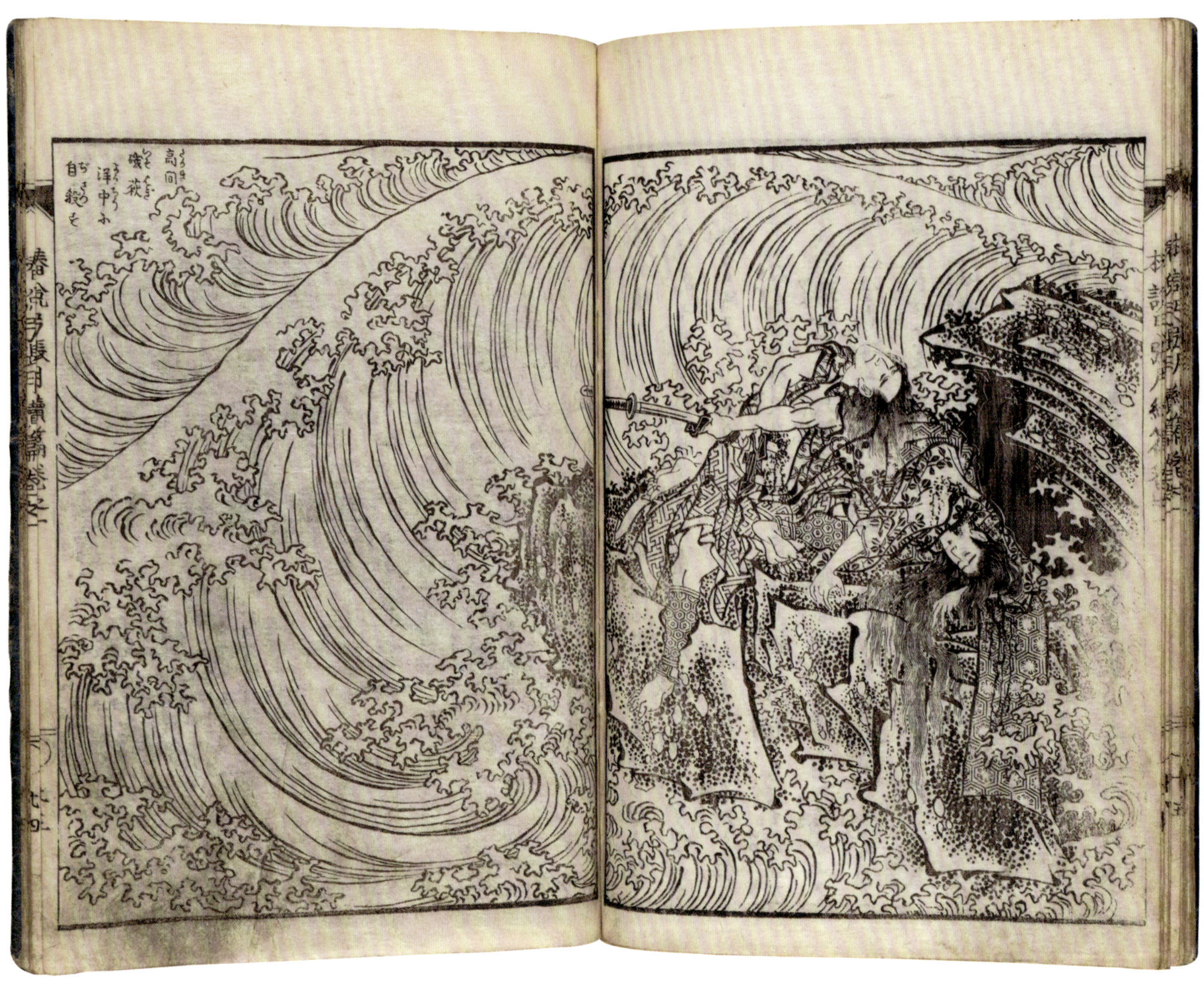
高間
磯萩
洋中ふ
自殺を
春宵弓張月賣編卷之一

半身を水の上にあらはし。その赫奕（かくやく）たるに彼が眼の光るあてを
ありつれ。紀平次これをみて大に驚き。鳴呼（ああ）主従この悪魚の腹
を肥（こや）すよ。腰の刀を佩（は）かされども。稚君を抱きまゐりて殿
ろんぱじや殺らうとも。外に援れのなられぞ。とても活ざ死ざも
あらぬみ怕（おそ）ろ事ろとあるくみやびさえかれもやらび退きもせぞ
むらろ浪間に泅（およ）ぐわどに。悪魚を忽地（たちまち）紀平次をくく崖わひし泥
に汝開れ劔を栽（うゑ）うべうれどに歯をあらひ潮を蹴（け）つ
春る折しもあれ高間夫婦が形體。煙のごとく立あらはれ俄頃（にはか）は二ッ
の燐火となるく。悪魚のはみ入るくくえし怪しられ聴らる沙魚（さめ）に
猛み開くる蕳に閙波を潜りて紀平次を秡（ぬ）ぎあげ。女をみ背上
小助乗して走るみ船よりも速うけり。紀平次をとの欣勢をくくく。

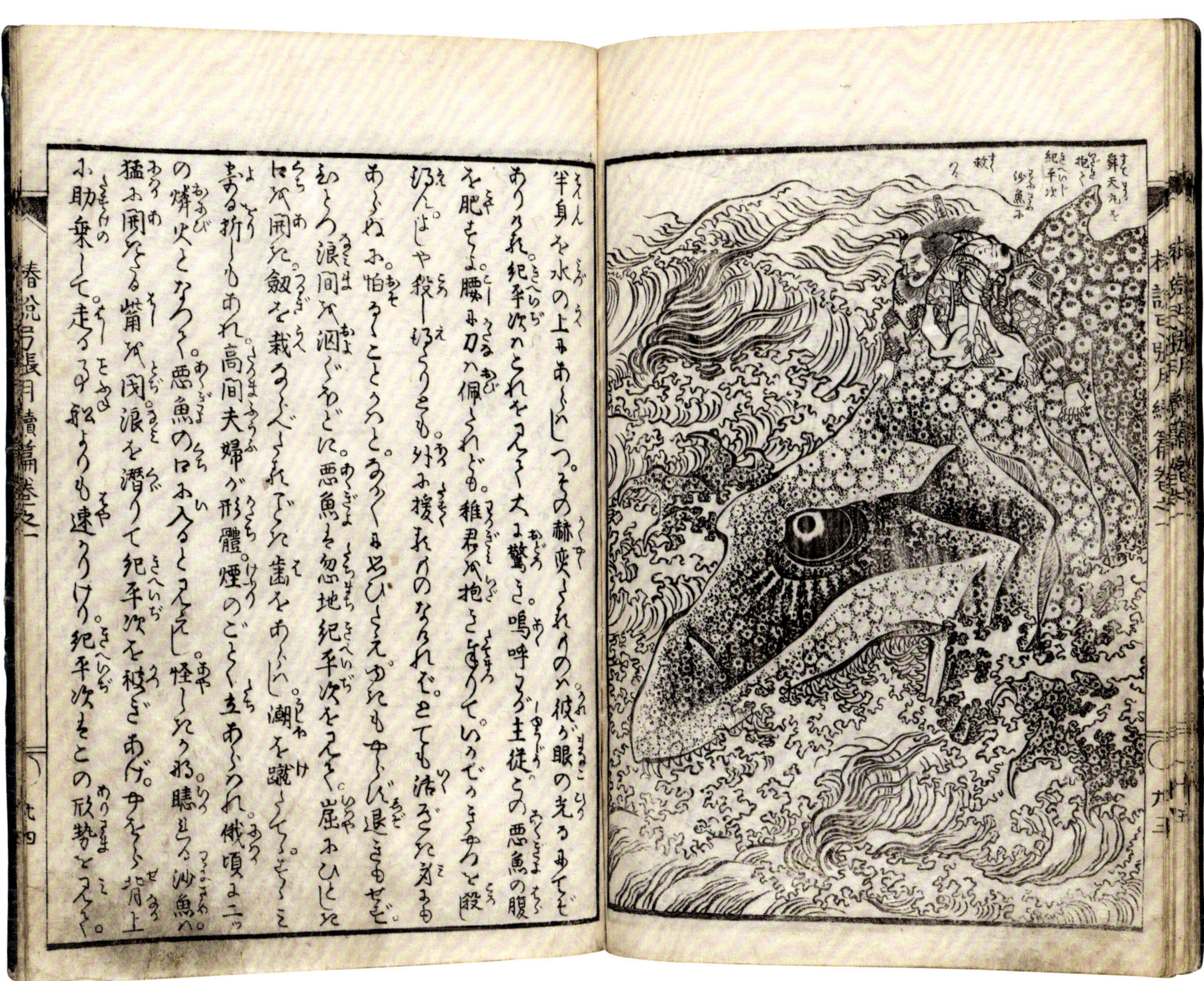

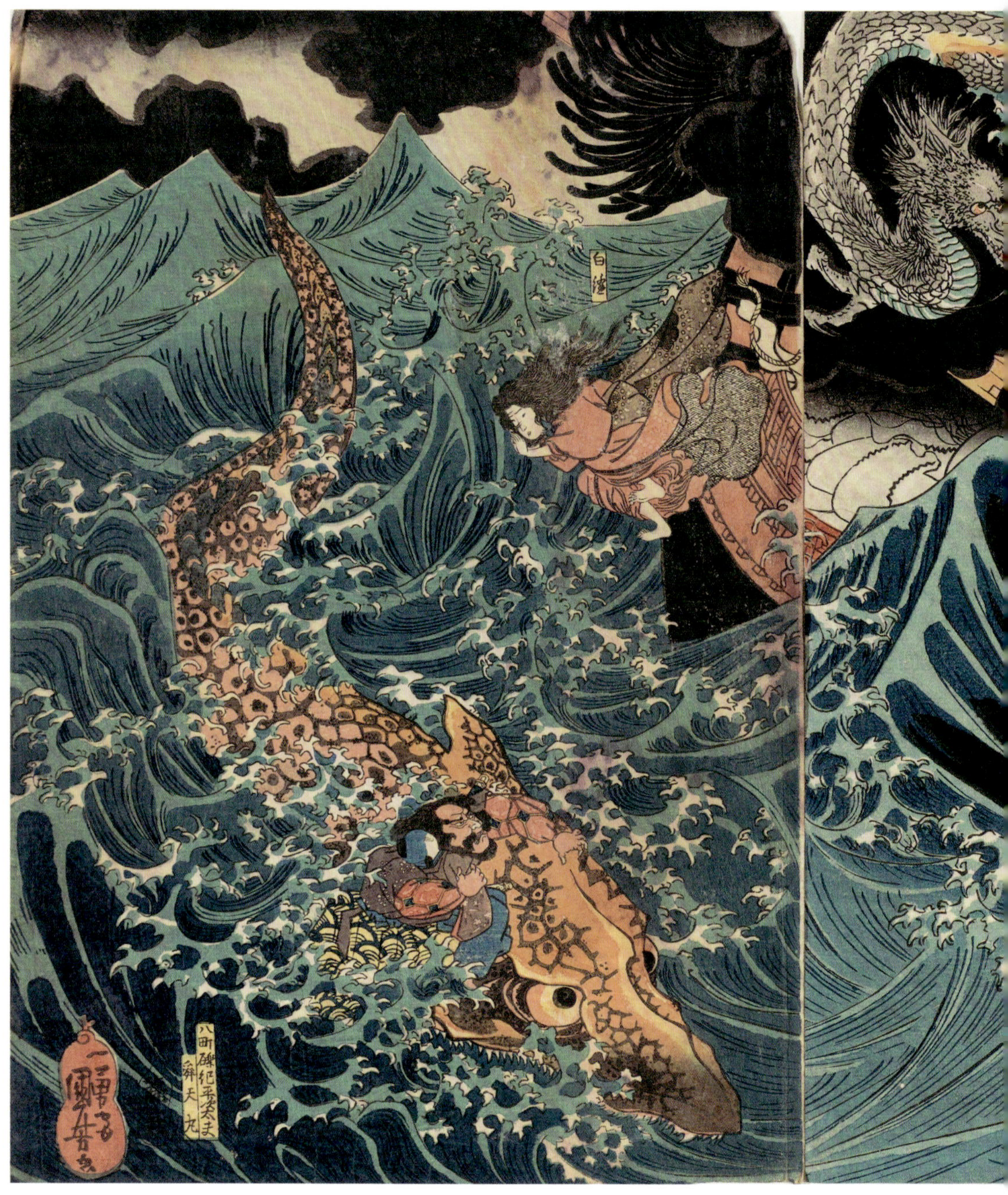

51

KUNIYOSHI

*On the Sea at Mizumata
in Hogo Province,
Tametomo Encounters
a Storm*, about 1836.
Color woodblock print
36.7 x 72.9 cm
(14½ x 28¾ in.)

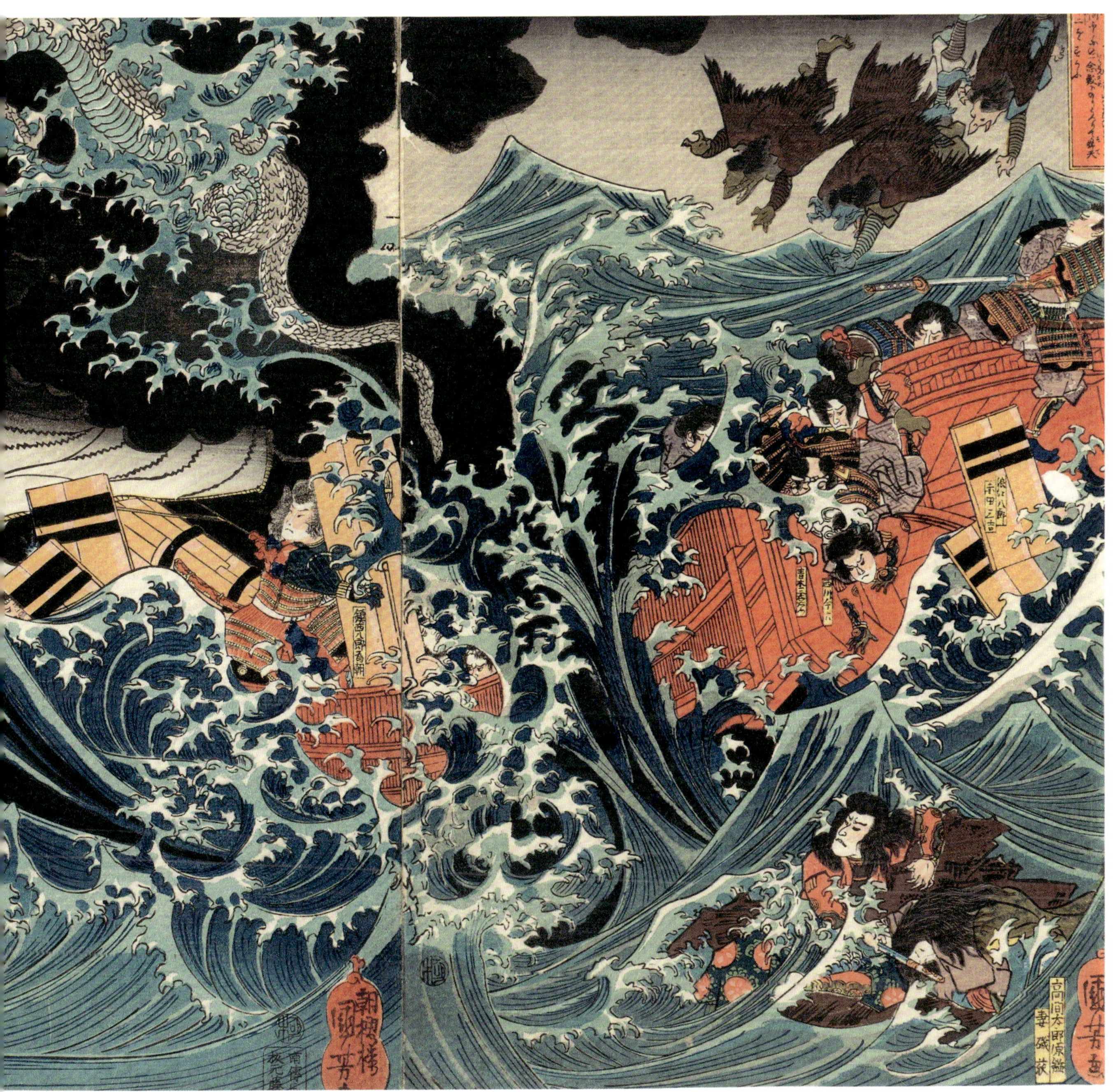

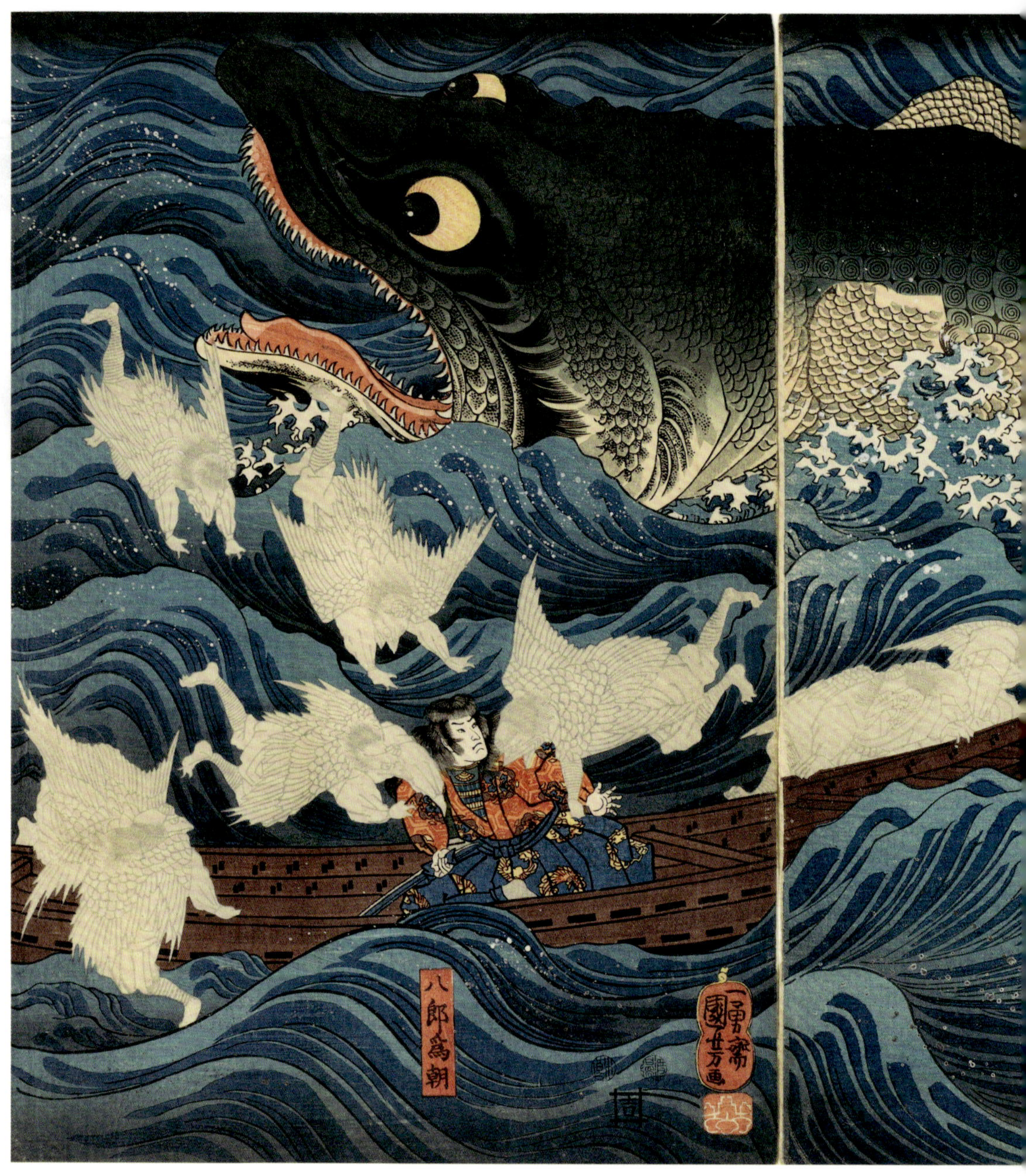

52

KUNIYOSHI
*The Former Emperor
[Sutoku] from Sanuki
Sends His Retainers
to Rescue Tametomo*,
about 1851–52.
Color woodblock print
36 x 76 cm
(14⅛ x 29⅞ in.)

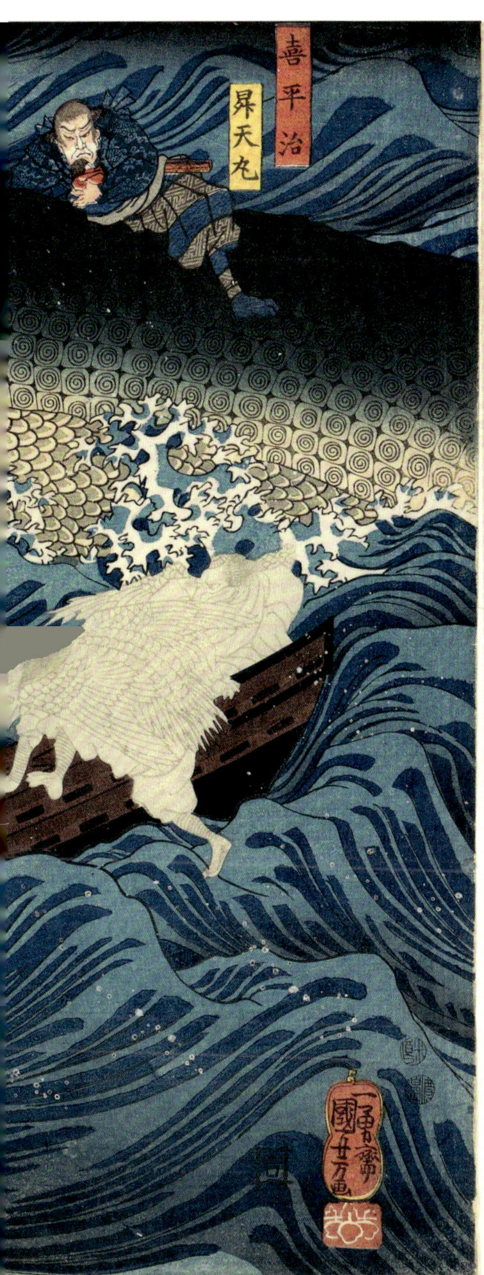
讃岐院眷属をして為朝をすくふ図
喜平治
昇天丸
白ぬん姫
一勇斎國芳画
一勇斎國芳画

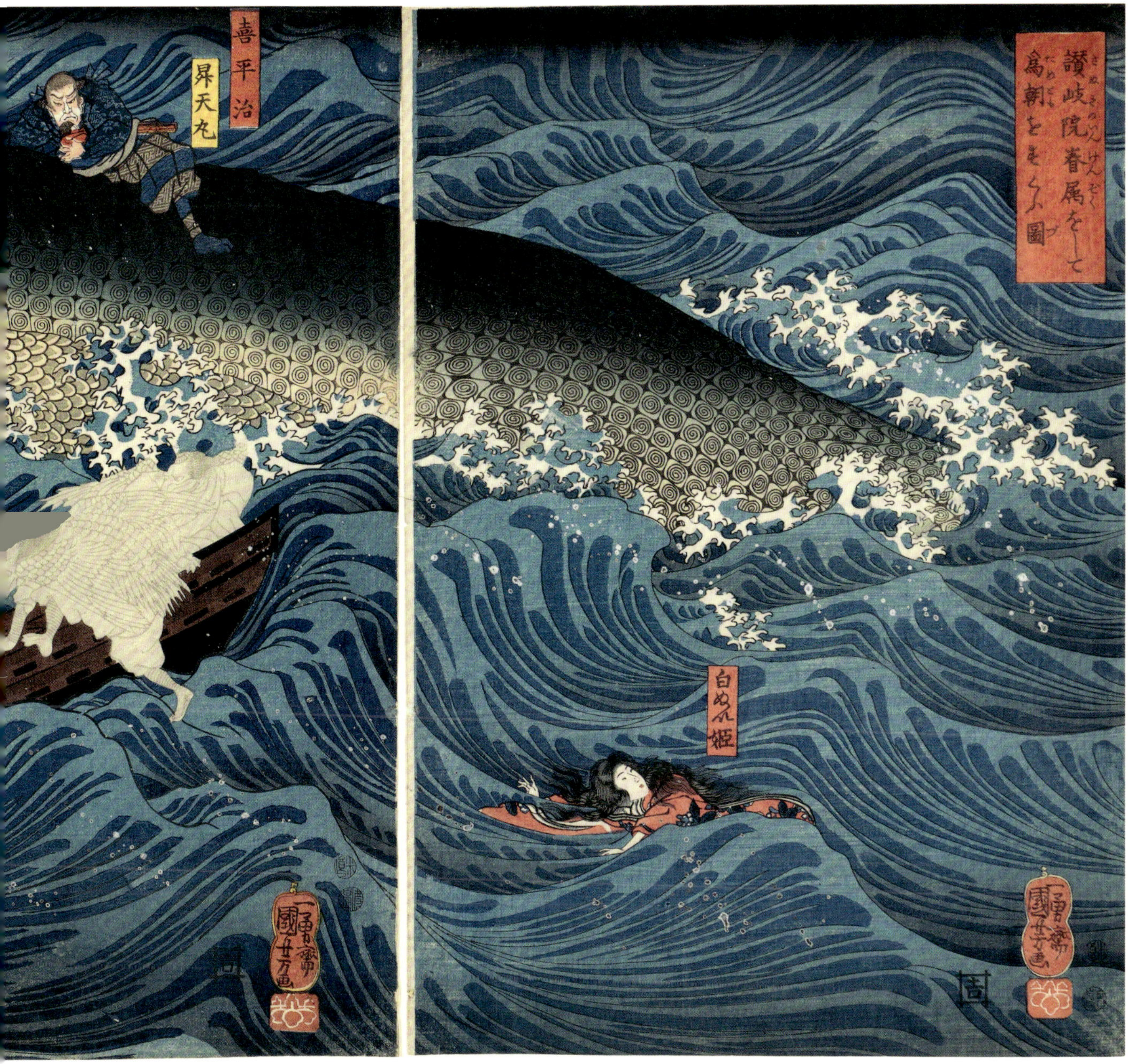

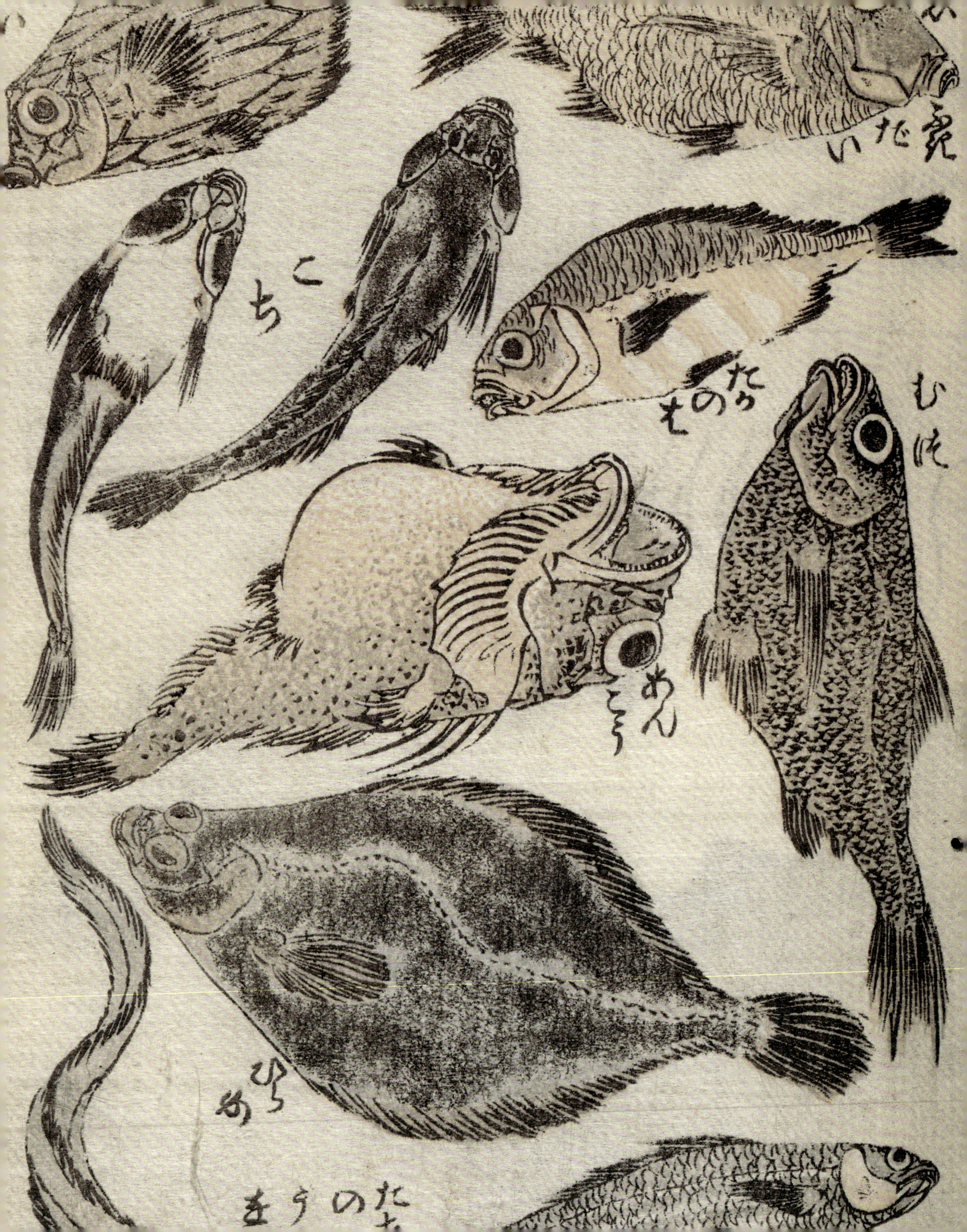

い亀
いた
こ
ち
ものた
むに
めんこう
ひらめ
たうのき

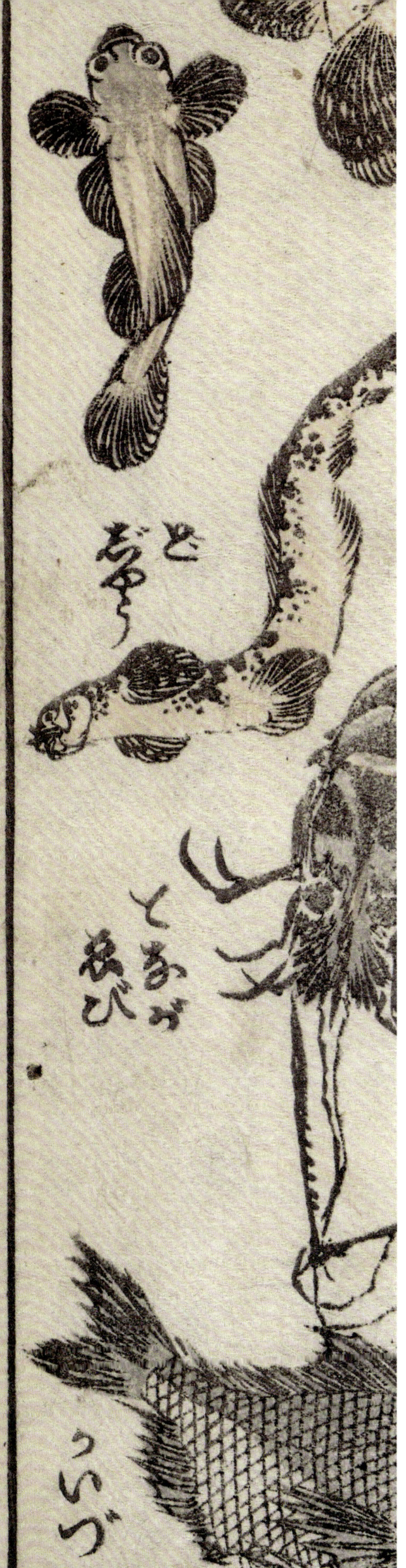

Hokusai's Global Influence

WITHIN A DECADE of Hokusai's death in 1849, his work had come to the attention of artists in Europe. In 1854 the shogunate's policy of near-isolation was ended, and points of contact with the outside world once again extended beyond Nagasaki. In 1858 Japan signed treaties of commerce with five Western powers, including the United States, Britain, France, and Russia, as well as their previous sole European trading partner, the Netherlands; and in 1859 the newly built port of Yokohama opened for foreign trade.

Some examples of work by Hokusai and other ukiyo-e artists had already left Japan, collected by Europeans as ethnographic curiosities rather than fine art. Japanese woodblock prints were in the collection of the Bibliothèque nationale in Paris as early as the 1790s. In 1822 the head of the Dutch East India Company in Japan commissioned Hokusai's studio to make fifty-four color paintings showing scenes of Japanese life, using a Europeanized style on Dutch paper provided for the purpose. The paintings were completed in 1826 and taken to Europe shortly afterward. They are thought to have been done primarily by Hokusai himself, with the aid of various pupils including his daughter Ōi.

In 1830 Philipp Franz von Siebold, a German physician working for the Dutch East India Company, returned from Japan with a large array of materials and settled in Leiden, where he opened the collection to

the public in 1831. His "Museum Japonicum" housed many botanical
specimens along with everyday objects, including woodblock prints and
printed books, some of which became the basis for illustrations in a
series of books on Japan that he began to publish in 1832.

Although Japanese prints and other artworks were present in
Europe in the first half of the nineteenth century, they do not seem to
have attracted the interest of European artists until the 1850s. The craze
for Japanese art in Europe is said to have begun with the arrival of a
small Japanese printed picture book, probably a volume of the *Hokusai
Sketchbooks*, in 1856. The printer Auguste Delatre, who worked with
many artists in Paris, had ordered a porcelain tea service from French
traders in Japan. When the crate arrived, inside was a small paper-bound
book that had apparently been tucked in as a wedge to hold the straw-
wrapped ceramics. This episode is likely the origin of the often repeated
but unverified claim that ukiyo-e prints were used to wrap ceramics
shipped to Europe.

When the young printmaker and designer Félix Bracquemond (1833–
1914) visited Delatre, who did printing for him, he saw the little book and
fell in love with its many charming illustrations. He prevailed on Delatre
to part with it and proudly showed it to his artist friends, sparking their
interest in Japanese art. Because trade with France was not officially
sanctioned until the signing of the treaty in late 1858, there is some
question about the 1856 date, though of course it is possible that unoffi-
cial trading was already going on. By 1859 Japanese books were certainly
known in Delatre's artistic circle, when he printed *Recueil des dessins
pour l'art et l'industrie* (Collection of Drawings for Art and Industry), a
large volume of etchings by Eugene Collinot and Adalbert de Beaumont
that presented an assortment of inspirational designs from various cultures and included several pages of motifs copied from books by Hokusai
and other Japanese artists.

The earliest traces of Japonisme in France, as seen in examples such
as the 1859 *Recueil des dessins*, were part of a new interest in pictorial
traditions of non-European cultures that soon focused on Japanese art.
Ukiyo-e prints were especially approachable for mid-nineteenth-century
Europeans: the figure prints showed a hedonistic urban society that
had much in common with their own, while the landscapes and images
from nature were done in a style that had already incorporated signifi-
cant influences from Western art, such as vanishing-point perspective.
The prints were also relatively inexpensive, even after they had been
imported into Europe, and widely available. Precisely because Japan had
been isolated and little-known for so long, it was of special interest now.

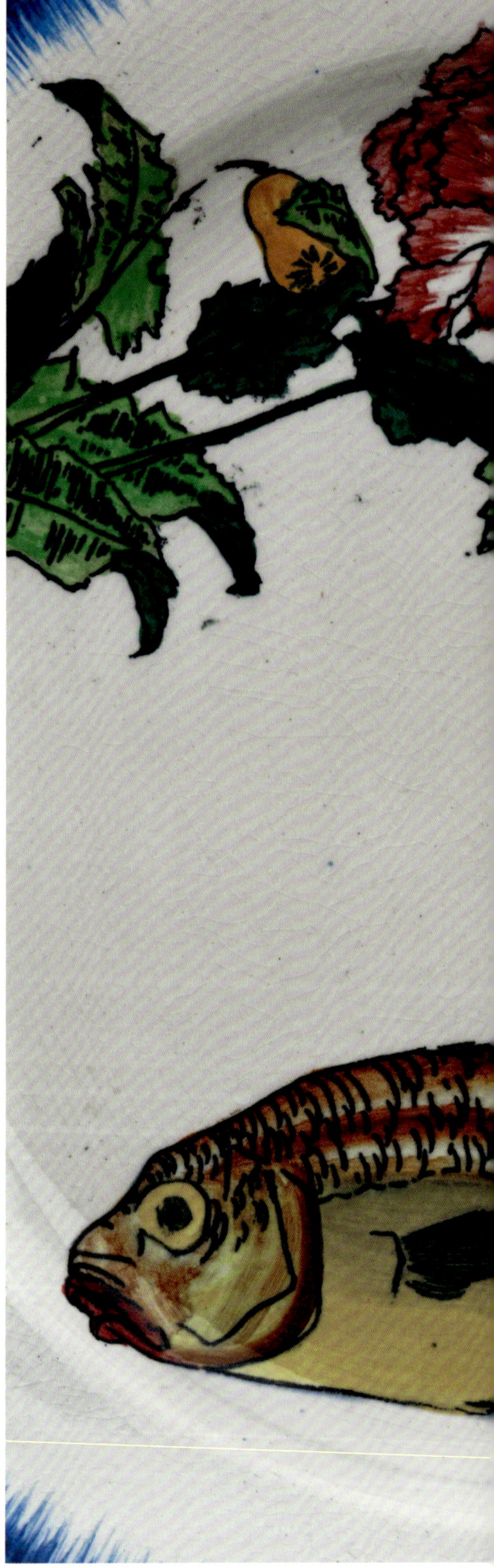

ROUSSEAU SERVICE PLATE (DETAIL, NO. 55)

By the early 1860s, ukiyo-e prints were available at a number of shops in Paris and were becoming a craze among French literary and artistic figures. In 1861 the poet Charles Baudelaire mentioned in a letter that he had purchased some as gifts for friends. The bestselling novelist brothers Jules and Edmond de Goncourt referred to their interest in Japanese art as early as 1862, and in 1866 they devoted a chapter of one of their novels to the hero's musings on his Japanese print collection, no doubt based on their own. A group of French artists and critics formed a secret club that met for monthly dinner parties to discuss Japanese art and other topics of interest, the Société du Jing-lar — named not for anything Asian but for the delicious local wine that they consumed at their meetings.

Information about Japan and Japanese art was spread by the great international expositions also known as world's fairs, which began in London in 1851. The Exposition Universelle in Paris in 1867 included, for the first time, an official exhibition sent by the Japanese government. In 1876 the Japanese pavilion at the Centennial Exposition in Philadelphia was instrumental in introducing Japanese culture to Americans. The trend continued at expositions in Paris in 1878, 1889, and 1900, and at the World's Columbian Exposition in Chicago in 1893.

One of the first examples in European art of clear influence from Hokusai and other Japanese artists is a ceramic table service designed by none other than Félix Bracquemond, first produced in 1866 and exhibited at the Exposition Universelle in 1867. Known as the Rousseau Service, it includes designs of fish, birds, insects, and plants copied from sources including the *Hokusai Sketchbooks* and other Japanese books. An early work to depict actual Japanese prints within the composition is James Abbott McNeill Whistler's *Caprice in Purple and Gold* of 1864, in which the female subject, dressed in a kimono and seated on the floor in front of a Japanese folding screen, views landscape prints by Hiroshige. Ukiyo-e prints are also depicted in the backgrounds of such works as Édouard Manet's *Portrait of Émile Zola* (1868), Claude Monet's Japonisme-inspired fantasy *La Japonaise* (1876), and Vincent van Gogh's *Portrait of Père Tanguy* (1887). Van Gogh also made direct copies in oils of two of Hiroshige's most striking designs from the *One Hundred Views of Edo* series. Other prominent European and American painters of the late nineteenth century whose compositions and choice of subject matter show a strong Japanese influence include Edgar Degas, Paul Gauguin, Henri de Toulouse-Lautrec, and Mary Cassatt. Printmaking, by these and other artists, was especially strongly affected by the influx of Japanese works.

What were the special features of the woodblock prints by Hokusai and other Japanese artists that Europeans admired and sought to emulate? One source of appeal was surely the prints' brilliant colors, an aspect that has been obscured because surviving works from the collections of Impressionist and Post-Impressionist artists are now often very faded due to light exposure. Another intriguing characteristic is the way flat areas of color—the natural result of the woodblock printing process—are assembled to build up the visual illusion of a three-dimensional landscape scene. European discussions of the Japanese prints emphasize their relative flatness, although one reason that European artists were able to respond emotionally to the Japanese landscapes was that Hokusai and his colleagues were using a version of European vanishing-point perspective.

The Japanese prints also strongly emphasize composition, which was becoming increasingly important in European pictorial art as the traditional goal of realistic representation was taken over by the new medium of photography. (Indeed, the claim of photography itself to the status of an art form also had much to do with the images' skillful composition). Hokusai's landscapes created striking effects by juxtaposing the underlying geometric shapes of natural and manmade phenomena, and Hiroshige went even further than Hokusai in exploring unusual or exaggerated viewpoints, directing the gaze of the viewer up from ground level, down in a bird's-eye view, around or even through foreground objects to a distant scene. In the late nineteenth century, Japanese-inspired compositions that juxtapose a highly detailed, close-up view in the foreground with a distant landscape in the background became widespread in European paintings and prints and may even have influenced the development of early French cinema in the 1890s.

Hokusai often populated his landscape prints with lively figures of people going about their daily business, working or relaxing. These small genre scenes embedded in landscapes had great appeal in nineteenth-century Europe because they resonated with the resurgence of interest in contemporary everyday life as opposed to the classical past. Also much admired and emulated in Europe were ukiyo-e prints with images of women modeling elegant kimono or playing with children; in this area the most influential artists were Utamaro and Kiyonaga rather than Hokusai, but figures from his printed picture books, such as the *Hokusai Sketchbooks*, also contributed. In addition, Hokusai was part of a long tradition in Japanese art of vividly imagined ghosts and monsters. Although he did not originate this theme, his bizarre supernatural images appealed to the fin-de-siècle European taste for

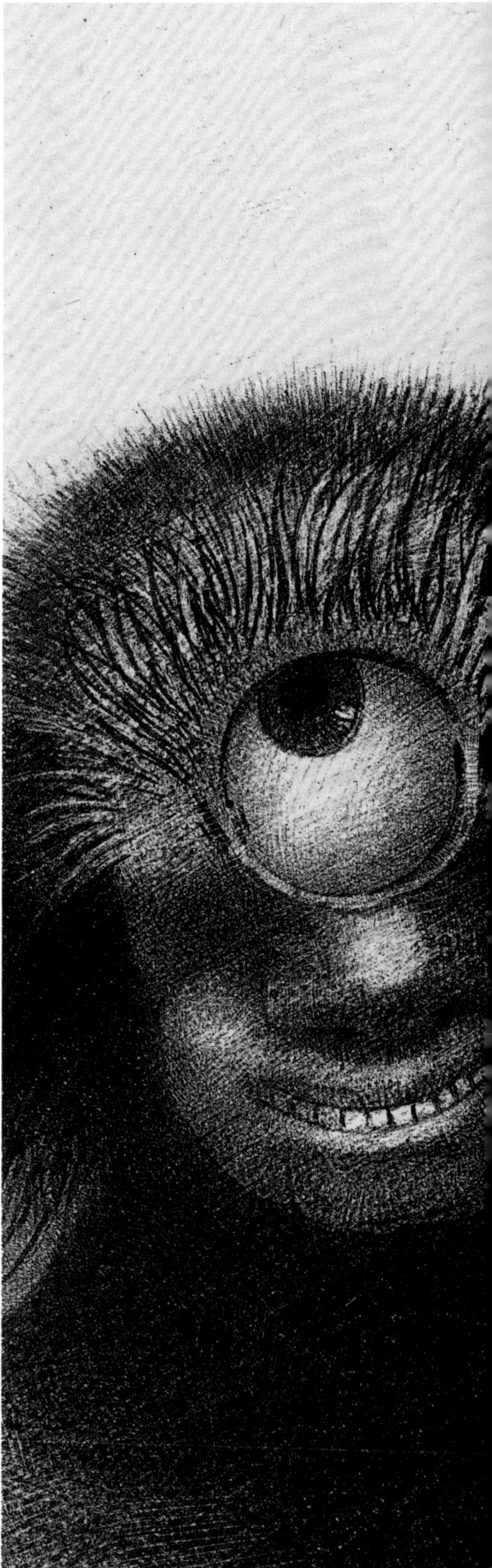

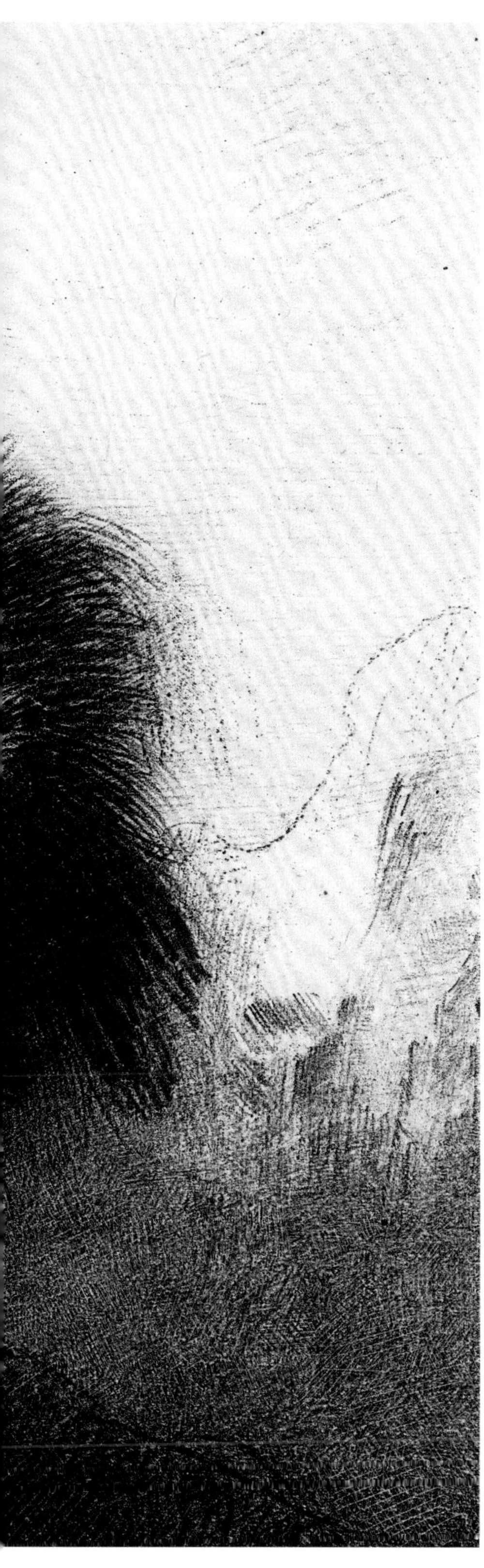

the grotesque. Their lingering influence can be traced in present-day Japanese *manga* comics.

Hokusai's studies of flora and fauna, especially flowering plants, inspired designs in decorative arts both in Japan and abroad, from Bracquemond's Rousseau Service to the Art Nouveau designs in various media that became popular in the late nineteenth century. Heavily influenced by Japanese art, the Art Nouveau movement — known by different names in different countries — sought to blur the distinction between fine arts and decorative arts. A key figure in its development was Siegfried Bing (1838–1905), a naturalized French citizen of German origin, who from 1888 to 1891 published a monthly journal known as *Le Japon Artistique* or *Artistic Japan* in its English edition (there was also a German edition), with copious illustrations in both monochrome and color that were copied by European artists. In 1895 Bing opened a famous gallery in Paris called Maison de l'Art Nouveau ("House of the New Art") that carried both Japanese prints and works by contemporary European artists who were influenced by them, and in 1900 he arranged a major exhibition of ukiyo-e prints in Paris.

In the United States, interest in Japan and its arts was sparked by the Centennial Exposition of 1876 and carried forward by recently established museums. At the Museum of Fine Arts, Boston, founded in 1870, an extraordinary and extensive collection of Japanese art was built by four scholars over the next four decades. In 1877 Edward Sylvester Morse — whose attention had been drawn to Japan by the Centennial Exhibition — traveled there for scientific research on marine life and began to collect Japanese ceramics. The next year, he was joined by Ernest Fenollosa, a professor at the Imperial University in Tokyo, who subsequently worked with his former student Okakura Kakuzō to make a serious scholarly study of Japanese art based on the work of Japanese connoisseurs. Both Fenollosa and Okakura later headed the department of Japanese art at the MFA. The fourth member of this group was William Sturgis Bigelow, who lived in Japan from 1882 to 1889 and amassed an enormous collection of Japanese art of all kinds that he eventually donated to the Museum in 1911. Bigelow's earlier experiences in France, when the Japonisme movement was taking off, were no doubt responsible for his love of ukiyo-e prints, even though Fenollosa and Okakura followed the lead of Japanese intellectuals of the time in regarding the prints as vulgar, lower-class art unworthy of serious attention. Fenollosa did eventually acknowledge Hokusai's great popularity by choosing him as the subject of the first scholarly exhibition of Japanese art at an American museum.

The Bostonian artist Arthur Wesley Dow (1857–1922) helped expand interest in ukiyo-e prints from the world of collectors and museums to the world of practicing artists. A painter, printmaker, and photographer who is best known for his work in art education, he was introduced to Japanese paintings and prints by Fenollosa. Dow was especially interested in compositional principles, a main source of the appeal of Japanese prints to Western artists. In his 1899 book *Composition: A Series of Exercises in Art Structure for the Use of Students and Teachers*, Dow stated that the primary goal of artists is not to copy nature but to create new works of art, using the compositional methods he described. The book was very influential, contributing significantly to the incorporation of lessons learned from Hokusai and other ukiyo-e artists into the processes of modern artists around the world.

The turn of the twentieth century also was when one design from Hokusai's Fuji series came to be singled out as an emblem of Japanese art in the eyes of the world. This is of course the famous *Under the Wave off Kanagawa*, better known today by its nickname "The Great Wave" (34). The print was described with special enthusiasm by Edmond de Goncourt in his 1896 biography of Hokusai (based on research for the 1893 Japanese biography by Iijima Kyoshin, originally commissioned by Siegfried Bing). It was Goncourt who renamed the print *La Vague*, removing the Japanese place name from the original title to give it a greater sense of universality. The Wave image was brought to the attention of an even larger audience by a remarkable example of Hokusai's influence in a field outside the visual arts, namely music. The French composer Claude Debussy's symphonic tone poem *La mer*, which debuted in 1905, is believed to have been inspired by Hokusai's print; the composer had an impression of it hanging in his living room and specifically requested that it be used on the cover of the published score, which was widely distributed, and the music itself incorporated Japanese-inflected harmonies.

By the early twentieth century, Hokusai had been canonized as a major world artist, one whose work would be at least somewhat familiar to anyone anywhere working in the arts. It becomes more difficult to identify visual quotations or influence in later abstract and modernist works, although elements derived from Japanese prints can be clearly seen in fields where representation remained important, such as book illustration and cartooning. The basic technique of outlined shapes that could be filled with color, as in ukiyo-e woodblock prints, was applicable to other kinds of inexpensive printing. Compositions with unusual viewpoints and angles, features that nineteenth-century European artists

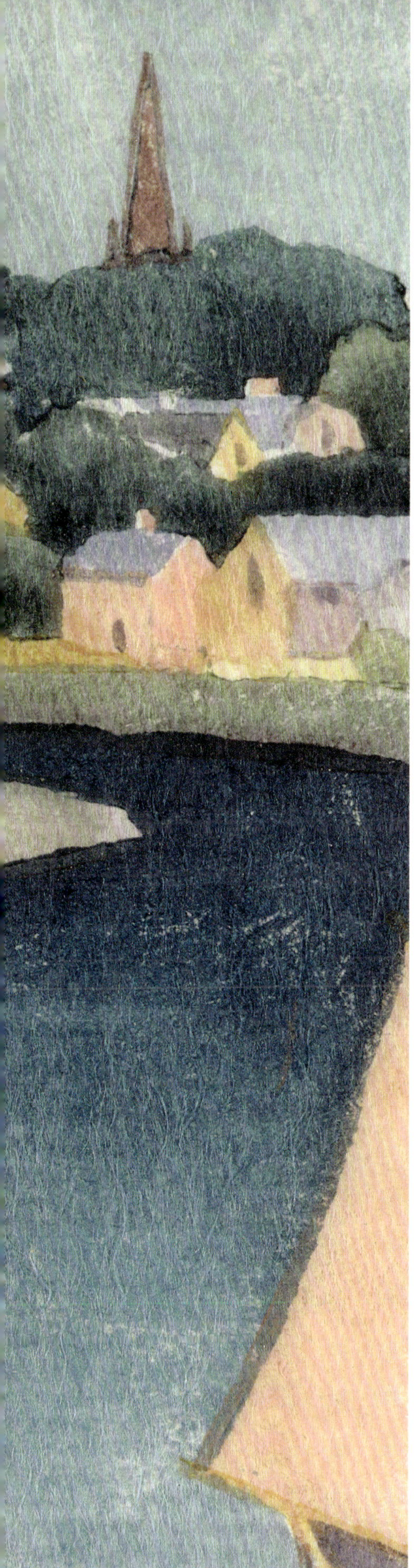

had found especially intriguing in the Japanese prints, were taken even further in twentieth-century narrative illustration. Future scholarship may make it possible to trace connections between ukiyo-e prints, early European cinema, twentieth-century book illustrations, mid-century American comics, and Japanese and Japanese-inspired manga and animation.

During the first half of the twentieth century, the worldwide spread of Japanese influence on the arts extended into new areas such as Latin America and Eastern Europe, where artists working to establish national styles of their own were seeking inspiration outside the French-dominated mainstream. An earlier understanding of Japonisme focused on its origins in France and its spread to Western Europe and North America, but more recently it has become clear that the movement became a global phenomenon by the middle of the twentieth century.

In China, the word *manhua*, written with the same characters as the Japanese word *manga*, became a common term in 1925, when the artist Feng Zikai (1898–1975), who had studied briefly in Japan, published a satirical cartoon series under the title *Zikai manhua* (*Zikai's Sketches* or *Sketches by Zikai*), a direct reference to the *Hokusai manga*. The Shanghai Manhua Society was founded in 1927 by a group including Zhang Guangyu (1900–1965), who contributed to the cartoon magazine *Shanghai manhua* in 1928–30 and later went into animation. There is much still to be discovered about the interaction of the traditions of cartooning in East Asia — manga, manhua, Korean manhwa — with each other and with their Western counterparts.

In postmodern art of the late twentieth and early twenty-first century, explicit references to Hokusai and other ukiyo-e artists have reappeared in the form of ironic appropriations that recast earlier works in a modern context; one prominent example is *A Sudden Gust of Wind (after Hokusai)*, a large color photograph transparency created in 1993 by the Canadian photographer Jeff Wall (born in 1946), who restaged *Ejiri in Suruga Province* from the *Thirty-Six Views of Mount Fuji* (32) as a scene on the outskirts of his hometown, Vancouver. Mount Fuji itself, as a visually impressive natural phenomenon, continues to be depicted frequently in Japanese art; Hokusai's so-called "Red Fuji" (30) is the best known example, but there are many more, some referring to Hokusai's work and some completely independent. An illustration of a diving woman with two octopuses, from Hokusai's erotic book *Kinoe no Komatsu* (literally *Pine Seedlings for New Year,* often translated *Pining for Love*) of about 1814, has become very famous under the invented title "The Dream of the Fisherman's Wife," and has spawned a large number

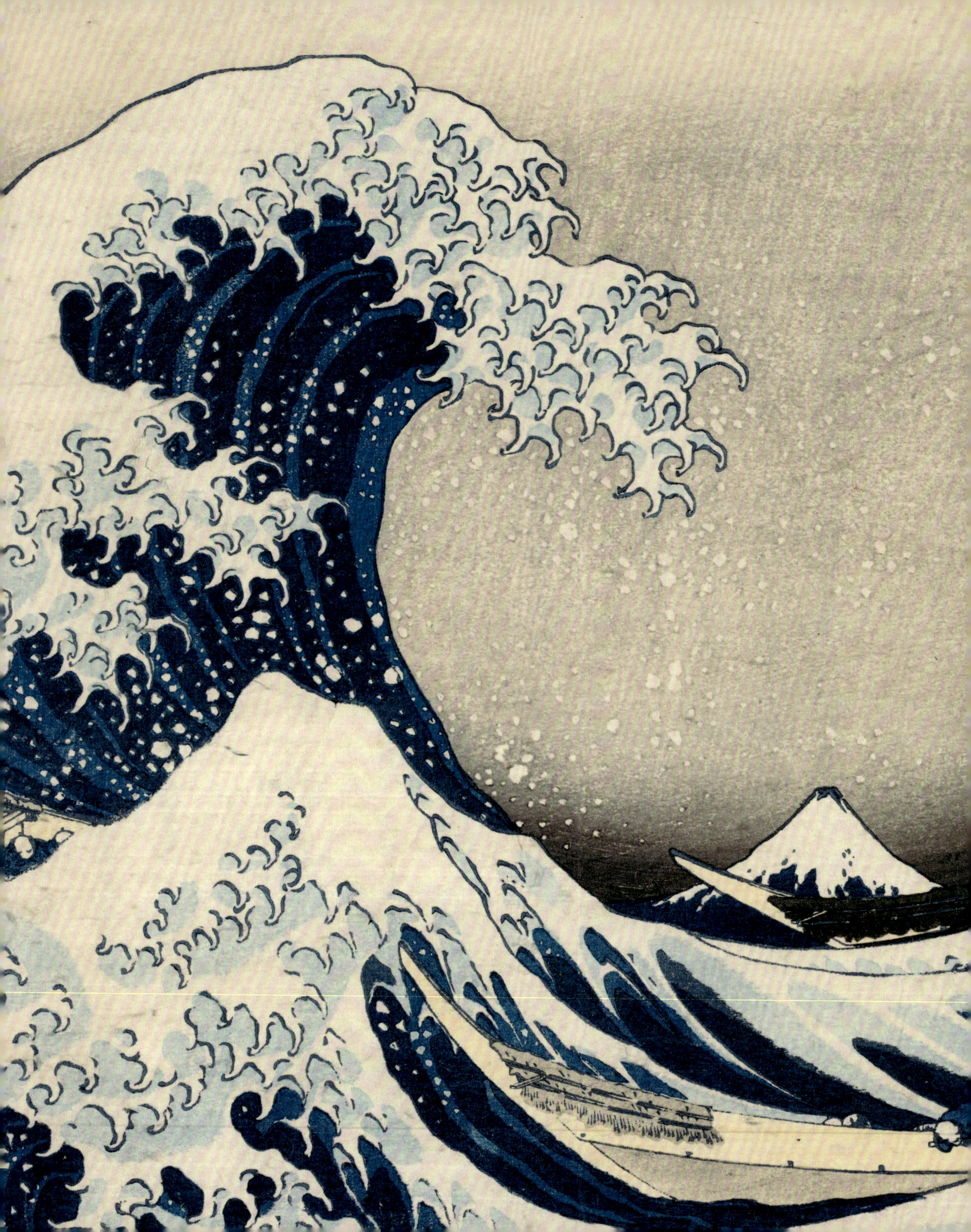

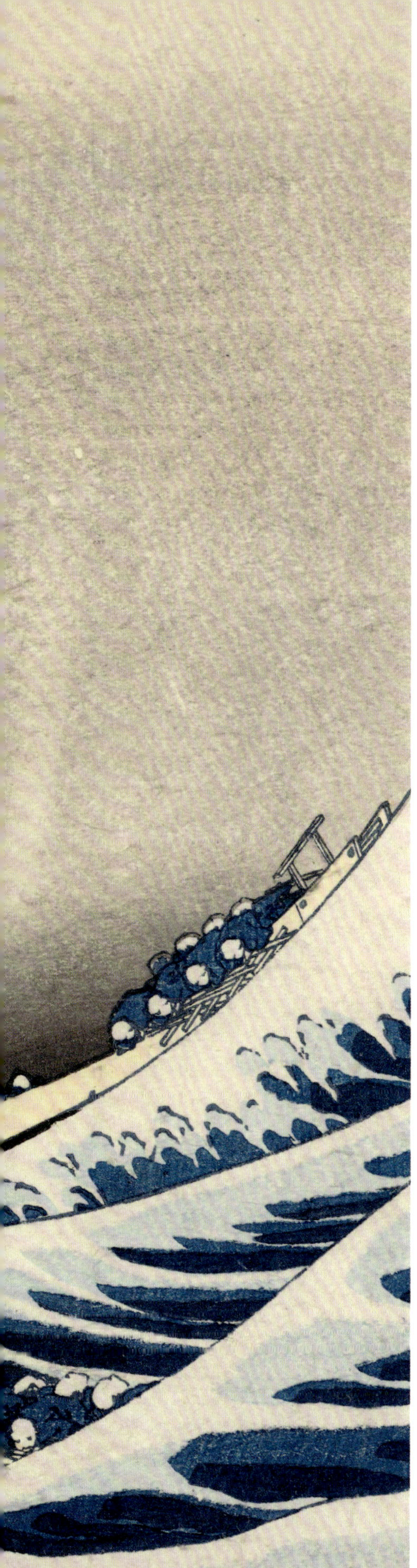

of visual references ranging from an entire Internet genre of tentacle erotica to serious works, often by women artists, that explore the embrace of the octopus as a metaphor for female sexuality.

By far the most often cited work by Hokusai in contemporary visual culture is of course the Great Wave, by now perhaps second only to the Mona Lisa as a thoroughly familiar and frequently parodied image. The briefest Internet search brings up dozens of images with the Wave rendered in an assortment of colors, expressed as a surge of cats or rabbits, combined with famous buildings or movie monsters, and on and on. Hokusai's original version has been rendered in media ranging from mural paintings on building walls, to neon signs, to fingernail art. On a more serious level, contemporary artists have used the powerful image to address issues such as the pollution of the oceans and the threat of tsunami and other natural disasters that are increasing as a result of anthropogenic climate change. As an expression of human emotion, the Wave can become a powerful metaphor for feelings of being overwhelmed — but remember that Hokusai's version also included Mount Fuji as a symbol of hope in the distance. In Hokusai's time, when Japanese were strictly forbidden to travel overseas, the ocean surrounding the islands was both a protective barrier against a possible foreign invasion and a symbol of the alluring, distant lands beyond. For the many people in the present-day world who move between countries and cultures, oceanic images can still suggest simultaneous apprehension of, and attraction to, the foreign.

As with all of Hokusai's prints, drawings, and paintings, each viewer responds with an individual interpretation, and those with especially strong creative urges may be moved to reproduce these interpretations in their own work. Hokusai's art continues to be a rich source of inspiration.

HOKUSAI (DETAIL, NO. 34)

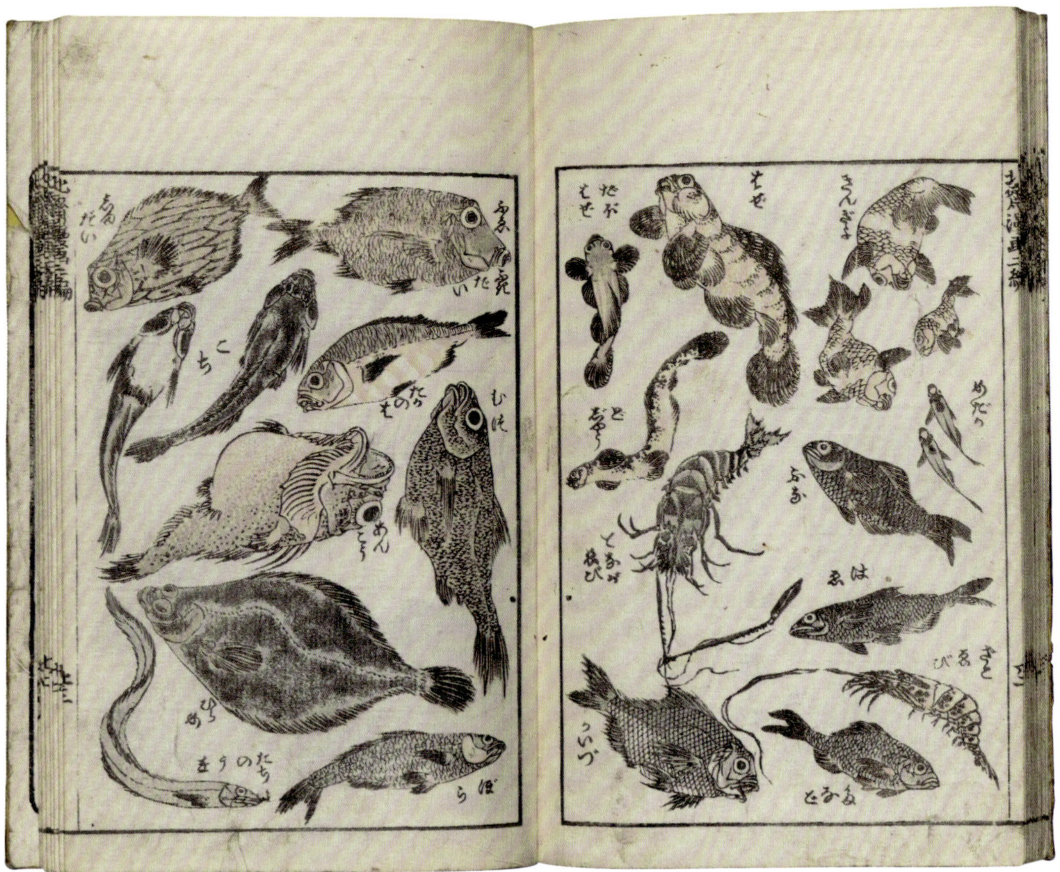

53

HOKUSAI
Fish, from *Hokusai Sketchbooks*, after 1815.
Woodblock printed book
22.6 x 15.6 cm
(8⅞ x 6⅛ in.)

54

FÉLIX BRACQUEMOND
Fish Patterns for the Rousseau Service, 1866.
Etching
53 x 33 cm
(20⅞ x 13 in.)

The *Hokusai Sketchbooks*, with their many charming drawings of a wide variety of subjects, not only made the artist a household name throughout Japan, but also became the first of his works to be widely appreciated overseas. A key figure in the origins of the movement that came to be known as Japonisme was the young French printmaker and designer Félix Bracquemond, who in about 1856 became fascinated by a small printed picture book, most likely a volume of the *Hokusai Sketchbooks*, that had been included in the crate with a tea service shipped from Japan to one of his friends (the book may have been used to wedge the straw-wrapped ceramics securely into the crate). Bracquemond later acquired the book and showed it to fellow artists, who were also intrigued by it, and he began to use Japanese motifs in his own designs.

One of the earliest examples of the influence of Japanese art on European art is an elegant set of dinnerware known as the Rousseau Service (55). It was designed by Bracquemond on behalf of François-Eugène Rousseau, the owner of a shop selling glass and ceramics who did some designs himself as well as commissioning them from other artists. Exhibited at the Universal Exposition in Paris in 1867, the Rousseau Service was a success both critically and commercially and was reissued in several editions over the years. In contrast to more traditional European tableware, with geometric or floral motifs arranged symmetrically, it featured images of fish and birds copied from Japanese book illustrations and placed asymmetrically against a white background for a look that would have been very modern at the time.

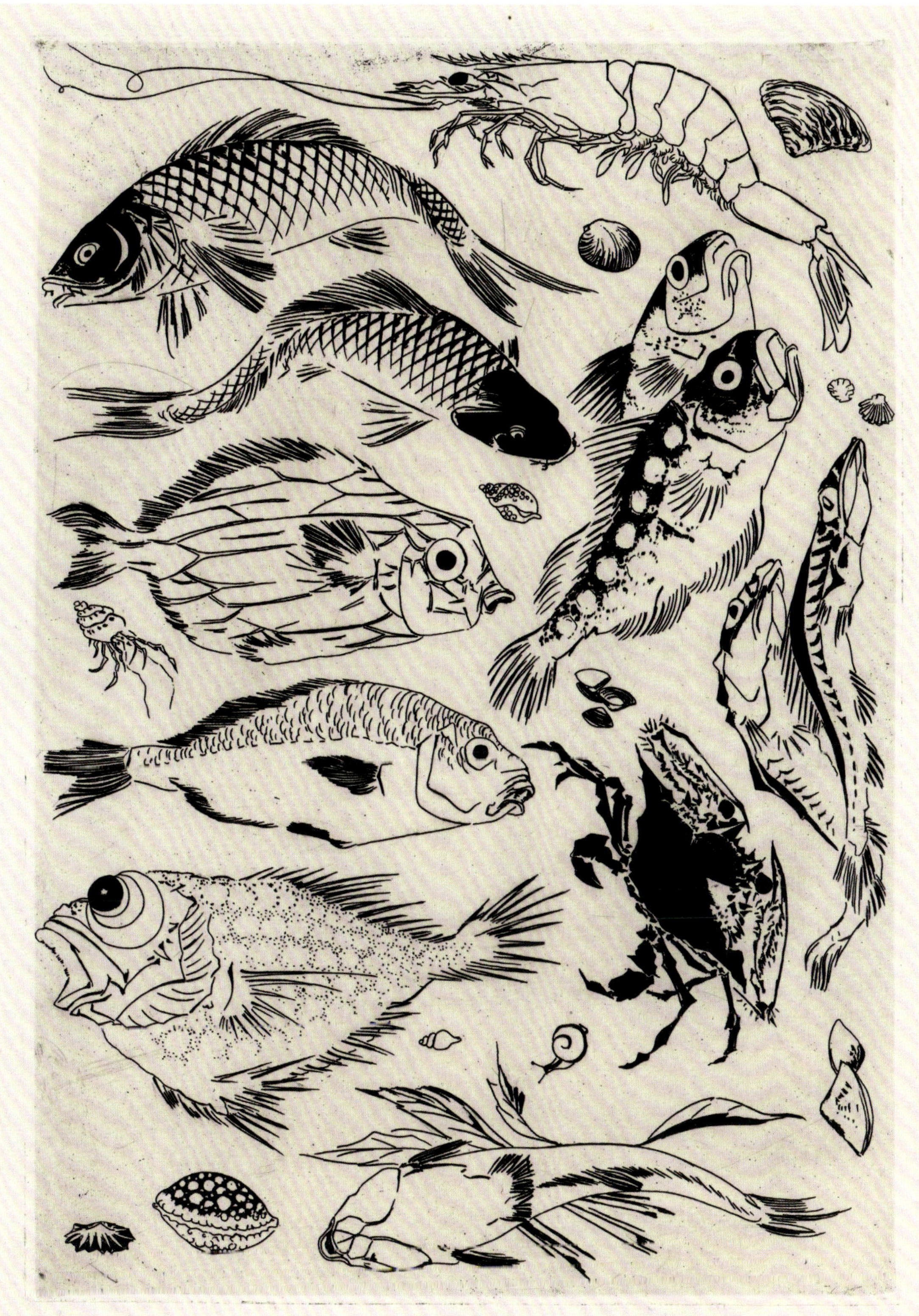

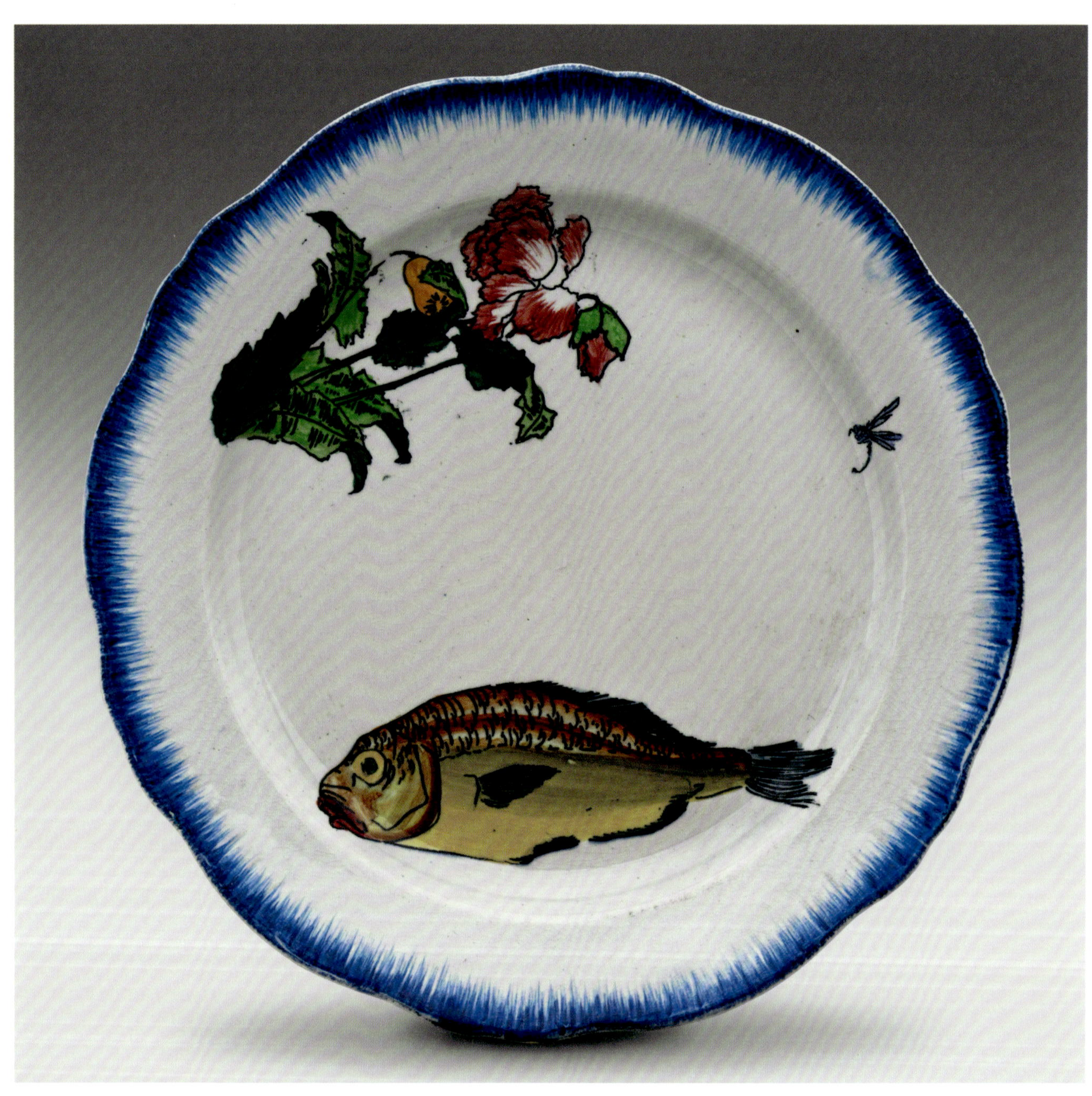

55
Plate from the Rousseau
Service, designed by Félix
Bracquemond, 1876–84.
Glazed earthenware
with colored enamels
Diameter: 25 cm
(9⅞ in.)

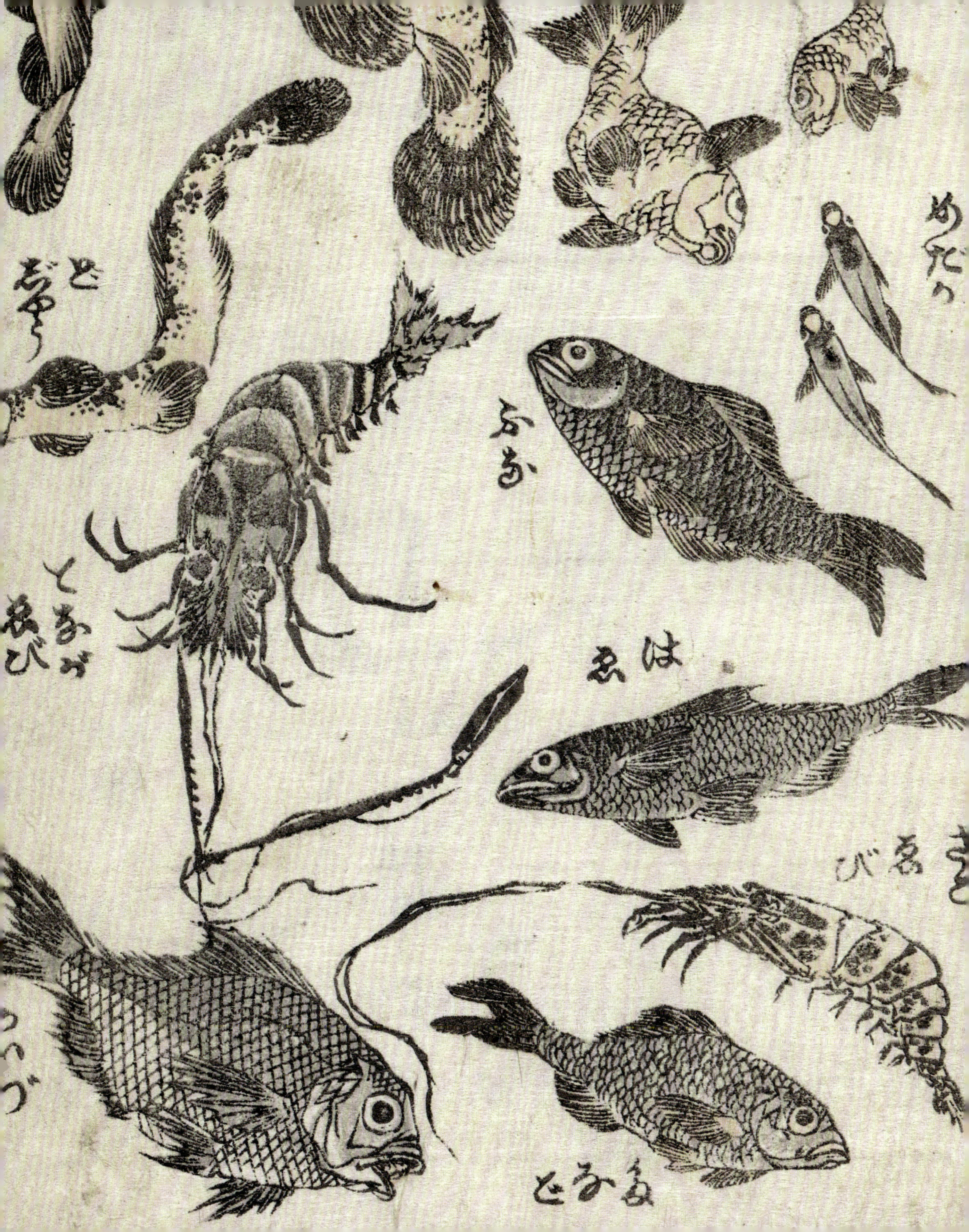

This silver inkstand, which can be separated into several smaller component parts, is lavishly decorated with cloisonné enamels in many colors, featuring a wide variety of Japanese motifs. The overall form of the inkstand resembles nothing in Japanese or other Asian art, but some of the components have been designed to suggest Asian elements: the central inkwell is in the shape of an ancient Chinese bronze vessel, and the nested cups that flank it look like stacks of porcelain bowls.

The magnificent desk accessory, exquisitely attuned to the taste of its time, was commissioned by Marie Louise Mackay, the wife of one of the wealthiest men in America — who had, appropriately enough, made his fortune in silver — from the prominent Paris jeweler Frédéric Boucheron. (His Maison Boucheron, founded in 1858, is still in business today.) The work was most likely designed by Paul Legrand, Boucheron's top designer, and executed by the firm of Crossville and Glachant. The collaborative production of the piece is somewhat reminiscent of the method used for ukiyo-e prints, but in this case the resulting object is a luxurious commission for a patron at the far end of the social scale from the humble Edo commoners who were the original audience for the mass-produced prints.

One likely source of the Japanese scenes that decorate the piece is a print by Hokusai from the Fuji series, showing men fishing from an embankment with Mount Fuji in the background (57). A curved fishing pole, juxtaposed with the familiar shape of the great mountain, can be seen on the central bowl shape in the stack at the right, against an azure-blue enameled background.

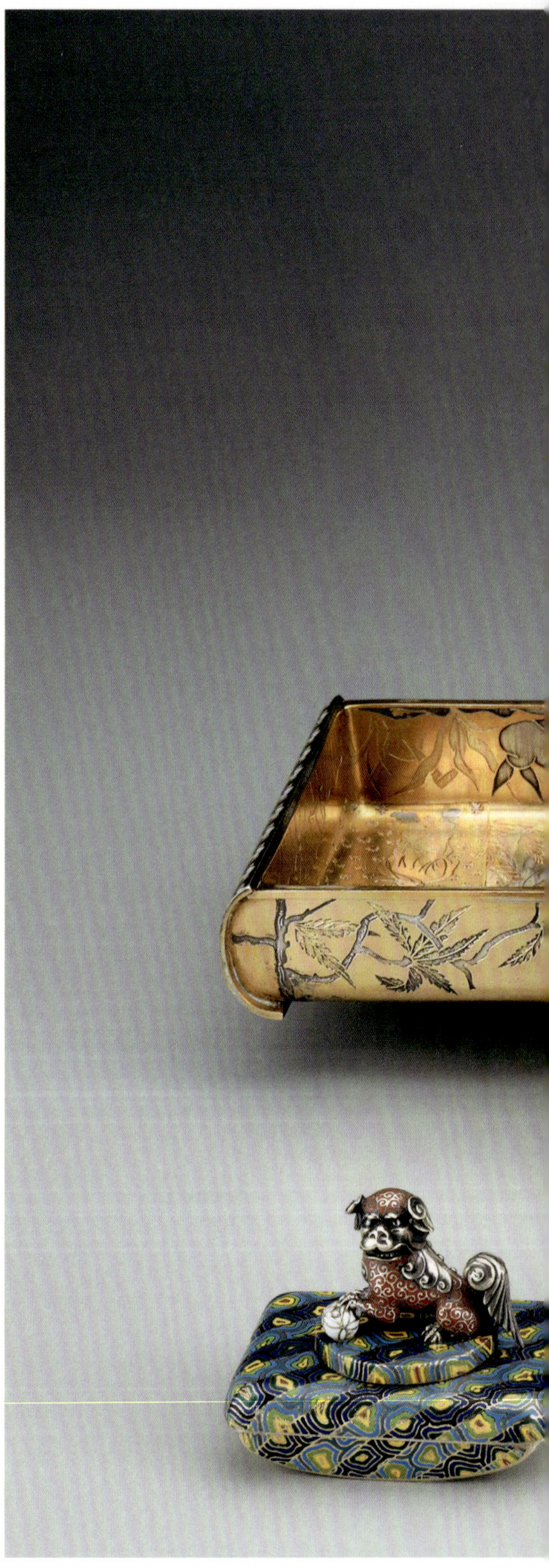

56
After **PAUL LEGRAND**
Inkstand, 1876.
Silver, partial gilt, champlevé, basse-taille, cloisonné enamels.
23.4 x 33.6 cm
(9¼ x 13¼ in.)

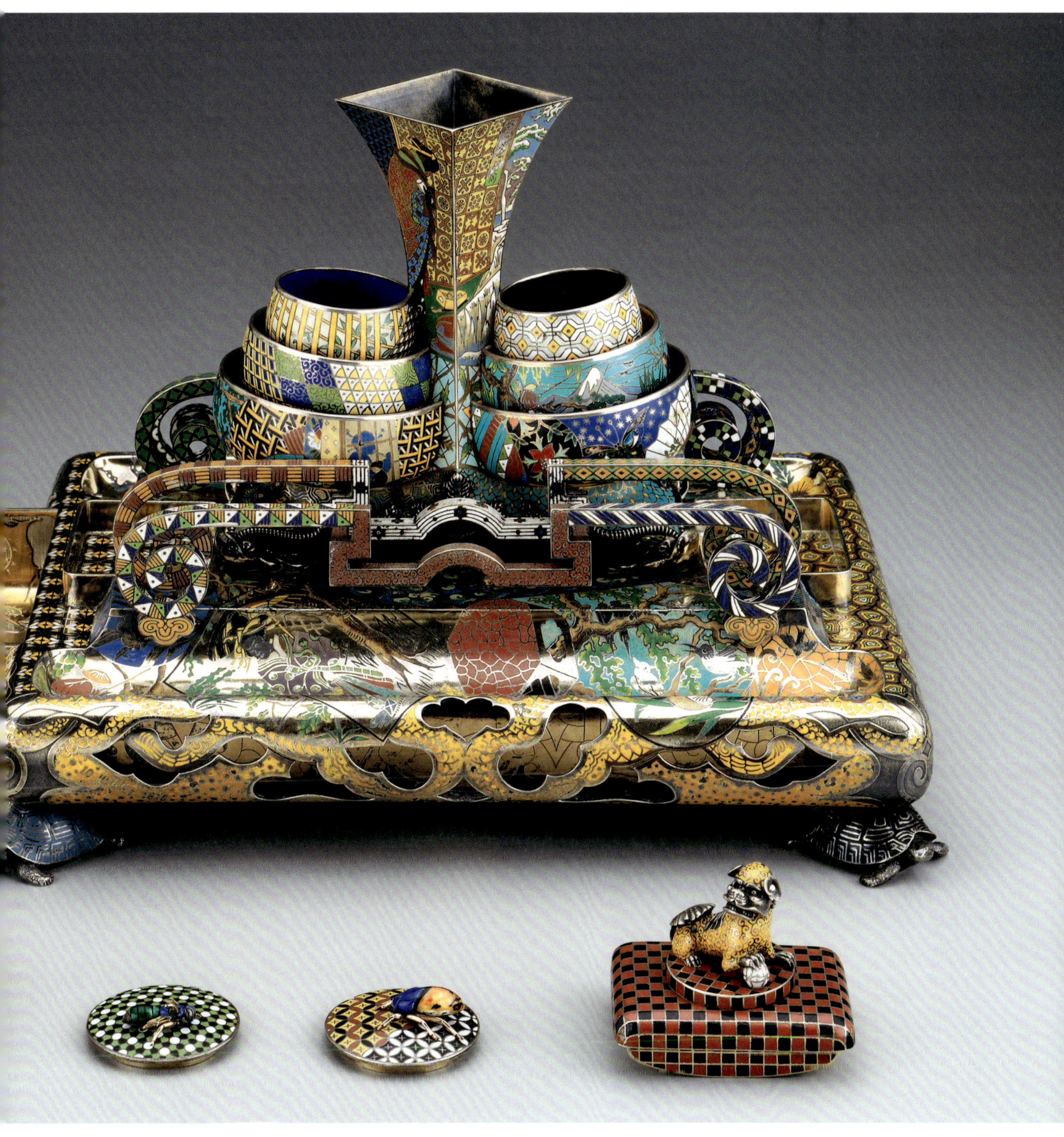

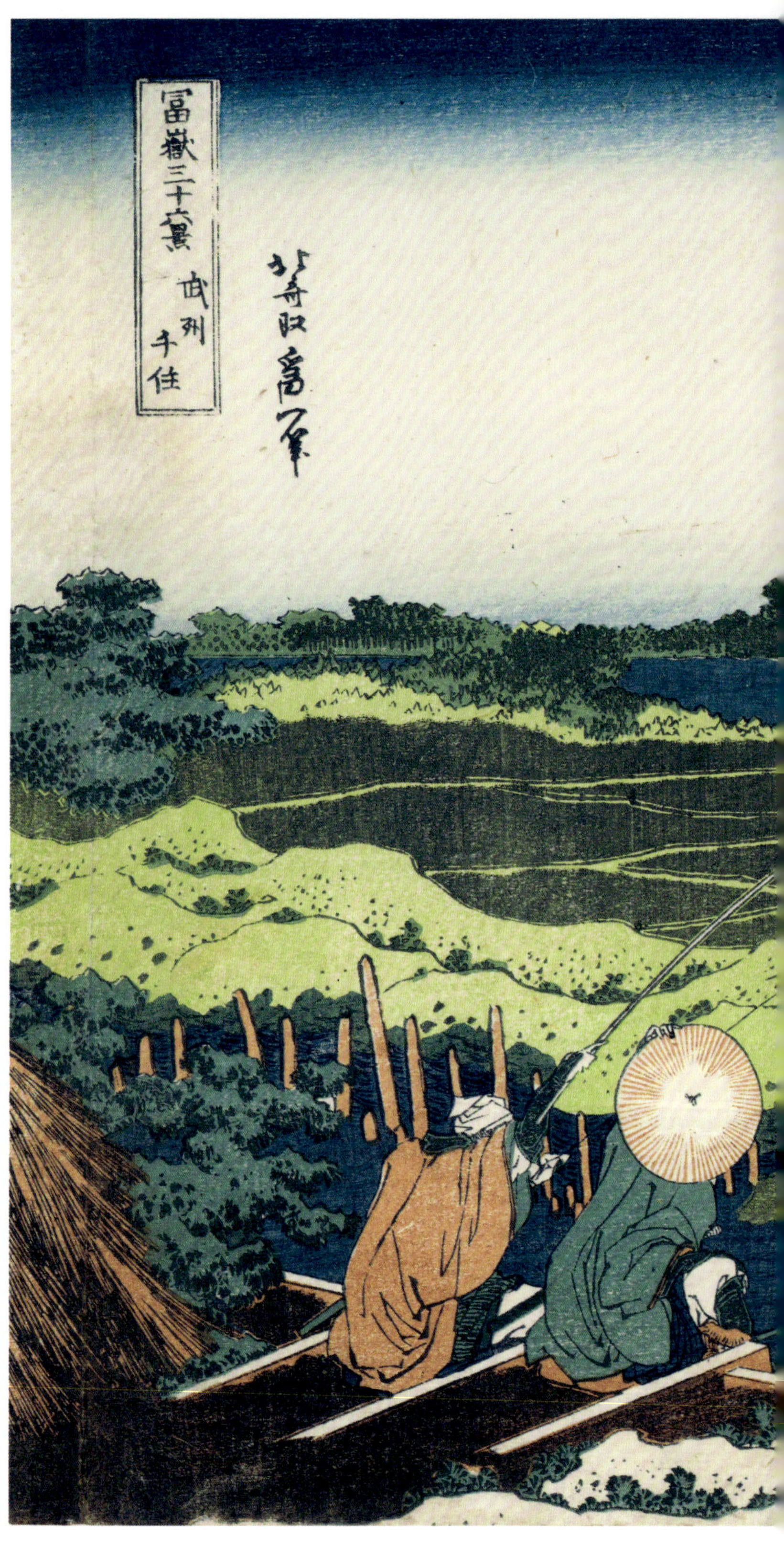

57
HOKUSAI
Senju in Musashi Province, about 1830–31.
Color woodblock print
24.5 x 37.3 cm
(9⅝ x 14⅝ in.)

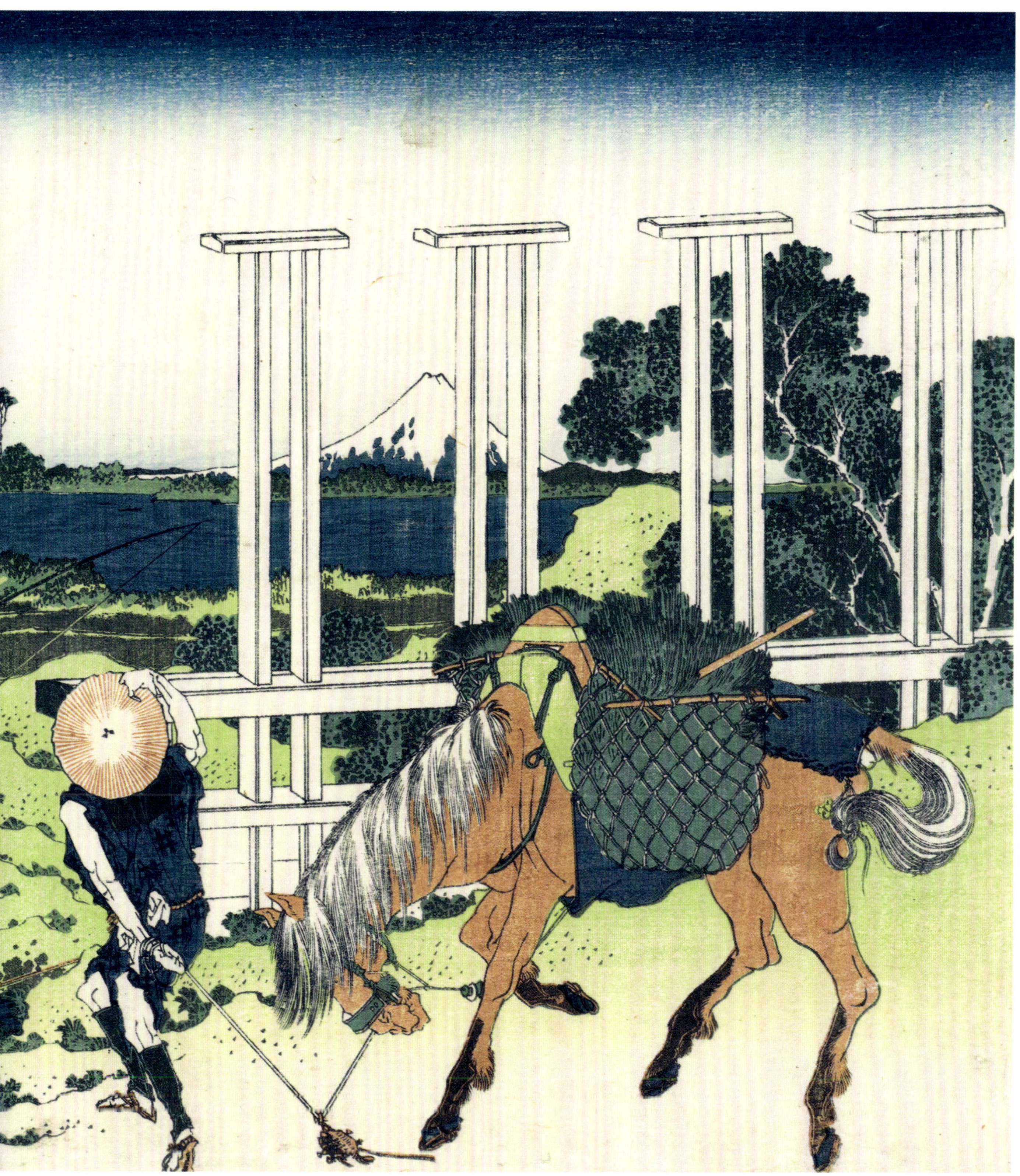

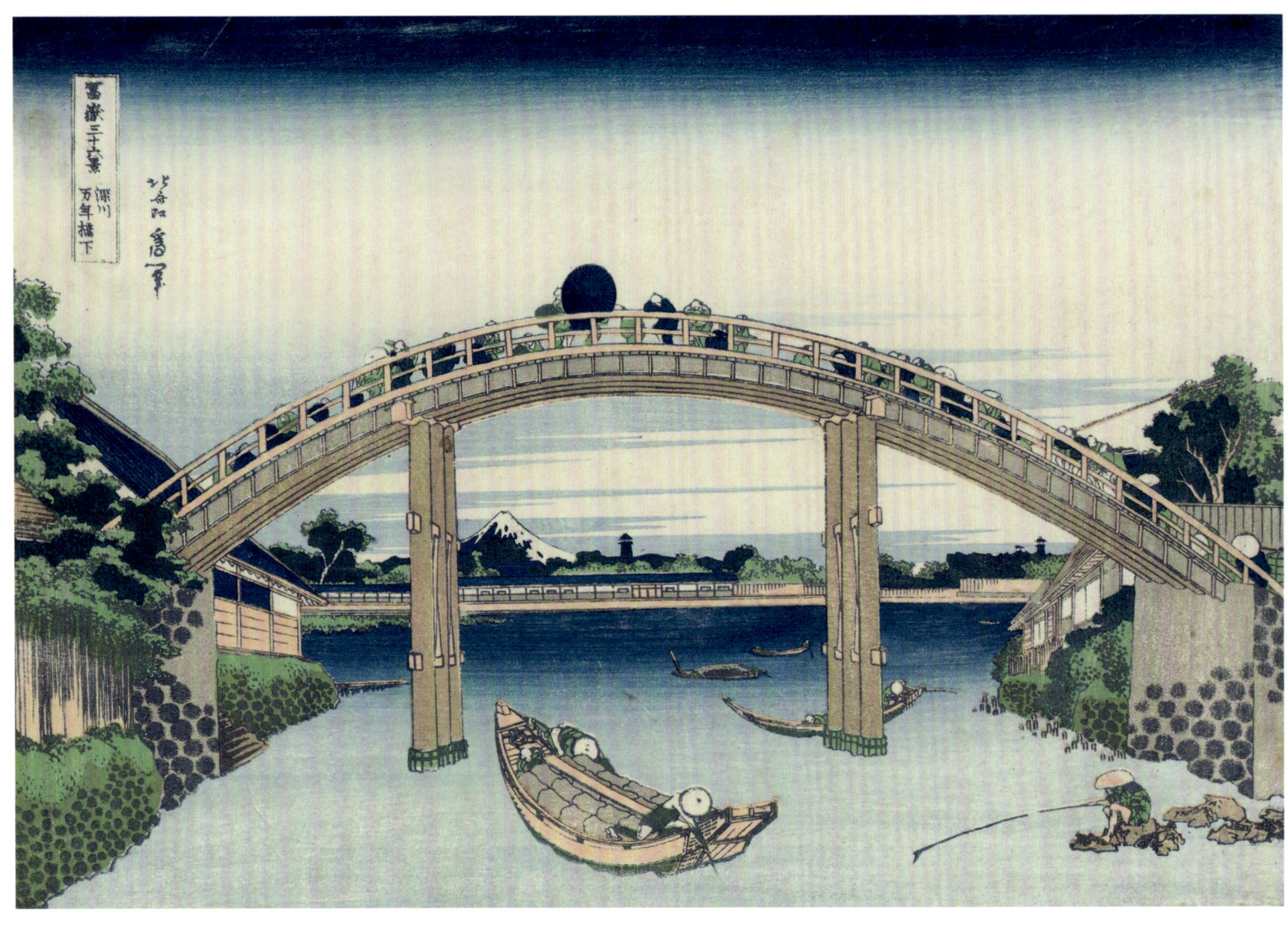

58

HOKUSAI
Under Mannen Bridge at Fukagawa, about 1830–31.
Color woodblock print
26.2 x 38.7 cm
(10³⁄₈ x 15¹⁄₄ in.)

Nineteenth-century Edo was a city of rivers and canals, with many bridges that often featured in cityscape prints. Ukiyo-e artists frequently showed the bridges from the viewpoint of water level, looking up at the underside of the bridge as if from an approaching boat, and this novel viewpoint was one of the compositional devices that caught the attention of Western artists.

Although many of the waterways of Edo are now buried beneath the streets of modern Tokyo, the canal spanned by Hokusai's Mannen Bridge still

exists, with a bridge of the same name in the same location. Hokusai uses the bridge as a framing device for the distant view of Mount Fuji, while in his view of a different location Hiroshige contrasts the curving arcs of a series of bridges with the strong verticality of upright bamboo poles for use in construction, stored in a lumberyard beside the river after being shipped in as rafts.

Whistler, an American who spent most of his life abroad, is credited with introducing ukiyo-e prints to the English-speaking art world when he

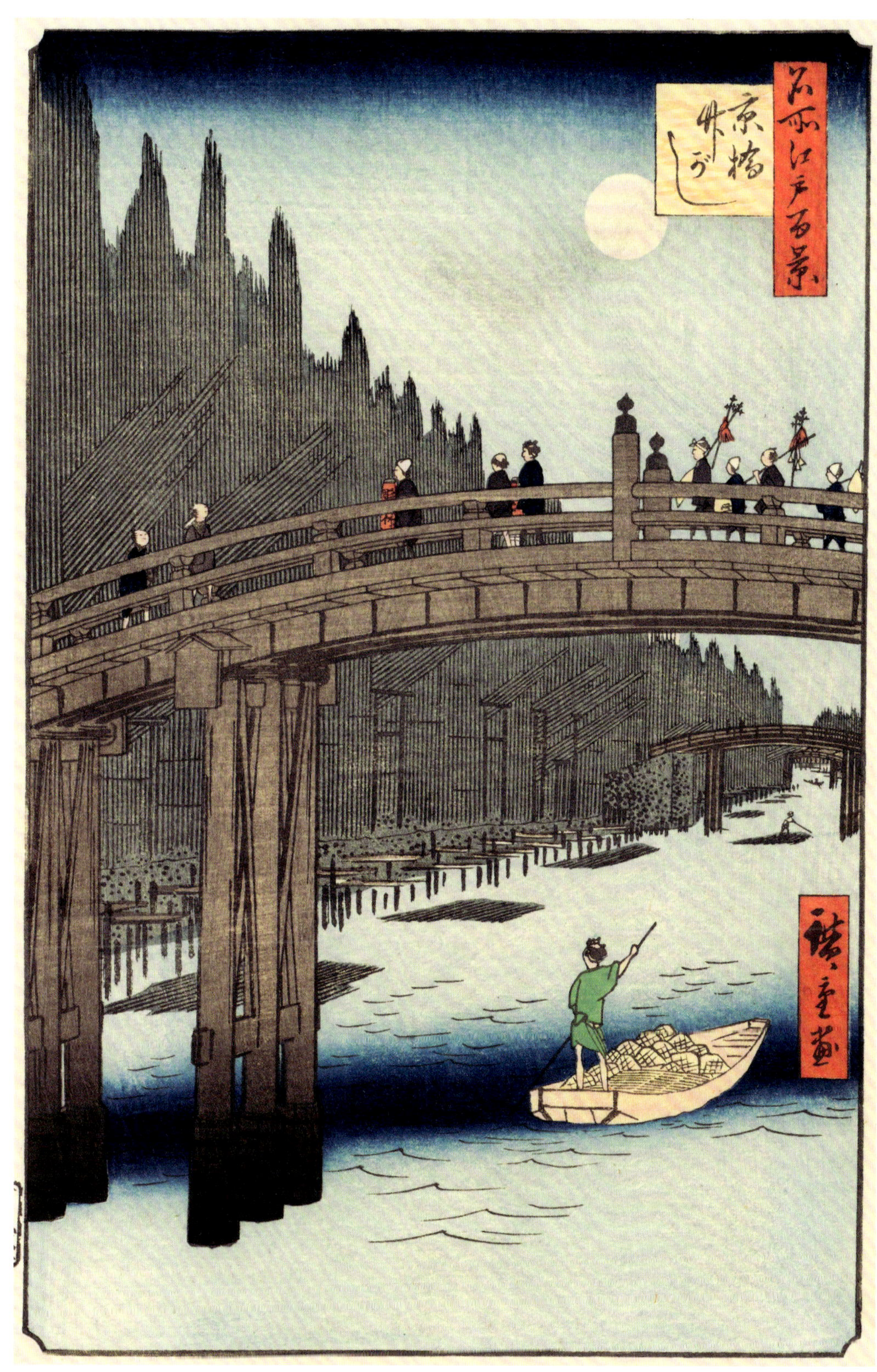

59

HIROSHIGE
Bamboo Yards, Kyōbashi Bridge, 1857.
Color woodblock print
36.2 x 23.7 cm
(14¼ x 9⅜ in.)

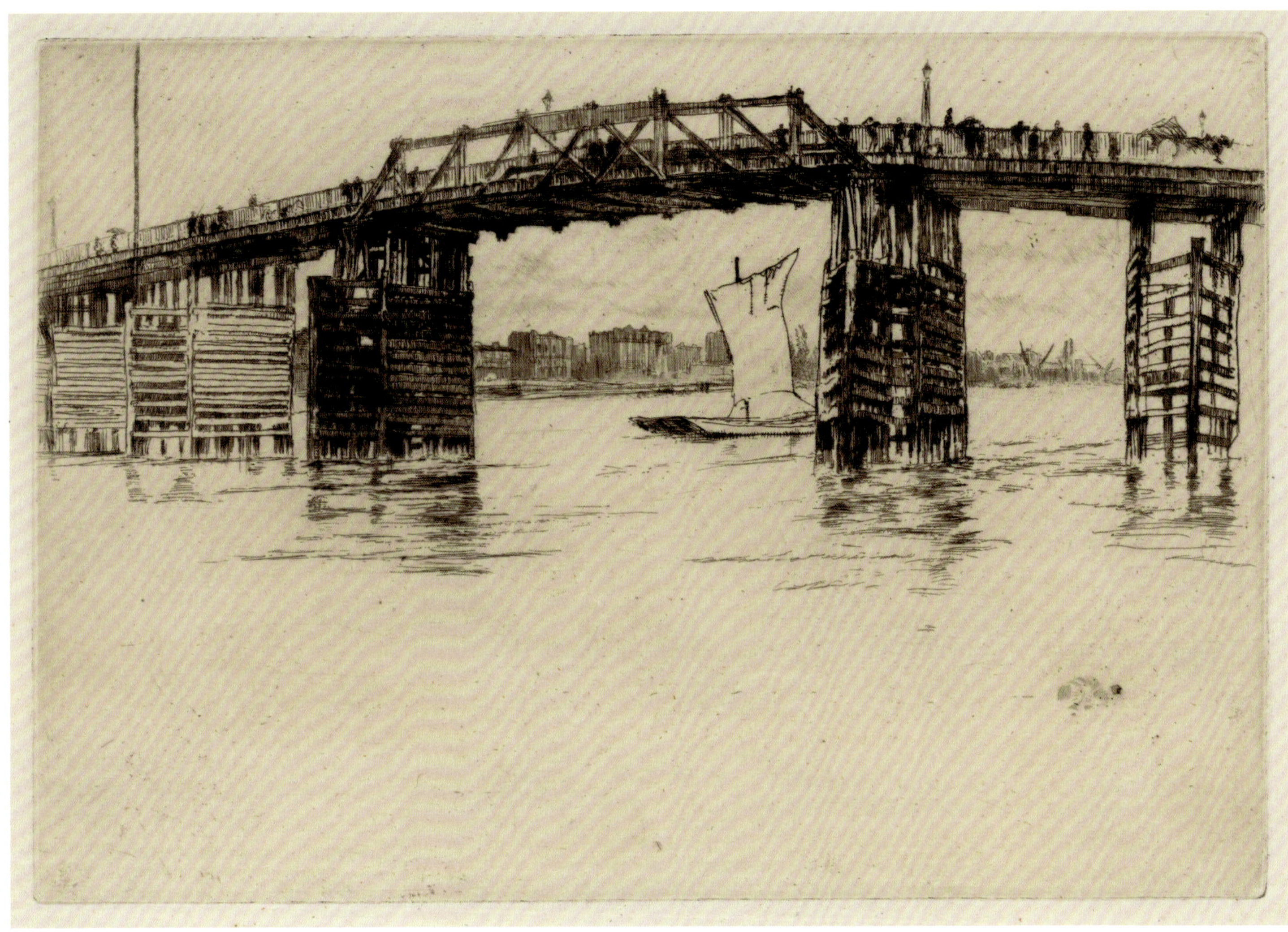

returned to London after visiting Paris in the late 1850s. He began to show actual prints in the backgrounds of some of his paintings, and gradually incorporated ideas from them into his own work. In the 1870s he produced a number of paintings that he described as "Nocturnes," showing night views of London clearly influenced by ukiyo-e prints, with the moonlit River Thames taking the place of the Sumida River. His prints of London bridges, especially an etching of the Old Battersea Bridge seen from the water, demonstrate the absorption of Japanese influences into his own style.

The artistic interchange worked in both directions: as Western artists were learning from Japanese art, Japanese artists were becoming familiar with Western art and responding to it in their own work, often creating patterns that come full circle. The printmaker, watercolorist, and sculptor Tobari Kogan, who studied in the United States in 1901–6, was one of the artists who promoted woodblock printing as a creative art form in Japan in the 1910s, after the role of ukiyo-e prints in the popular culture had been taken over by other media. His view of a Tokyo bridge suggests both Hiroshige and Whistler, with a factory smokestack in the background indicating this is a modern scene of the new industrial Japan.

60

JAMES ABBOTT MCNEILL WHISTLER
Old Battersea Bridge, 1879. Etching
25.9 x 40.5 cm
(10¼ x 16 in.)

61

TOBARI KOGAN
The Great Bridge at Senju, 1913.
Color woodblock print
48.8 x 35.8 cm
(19¼ x 14⅛ in.)

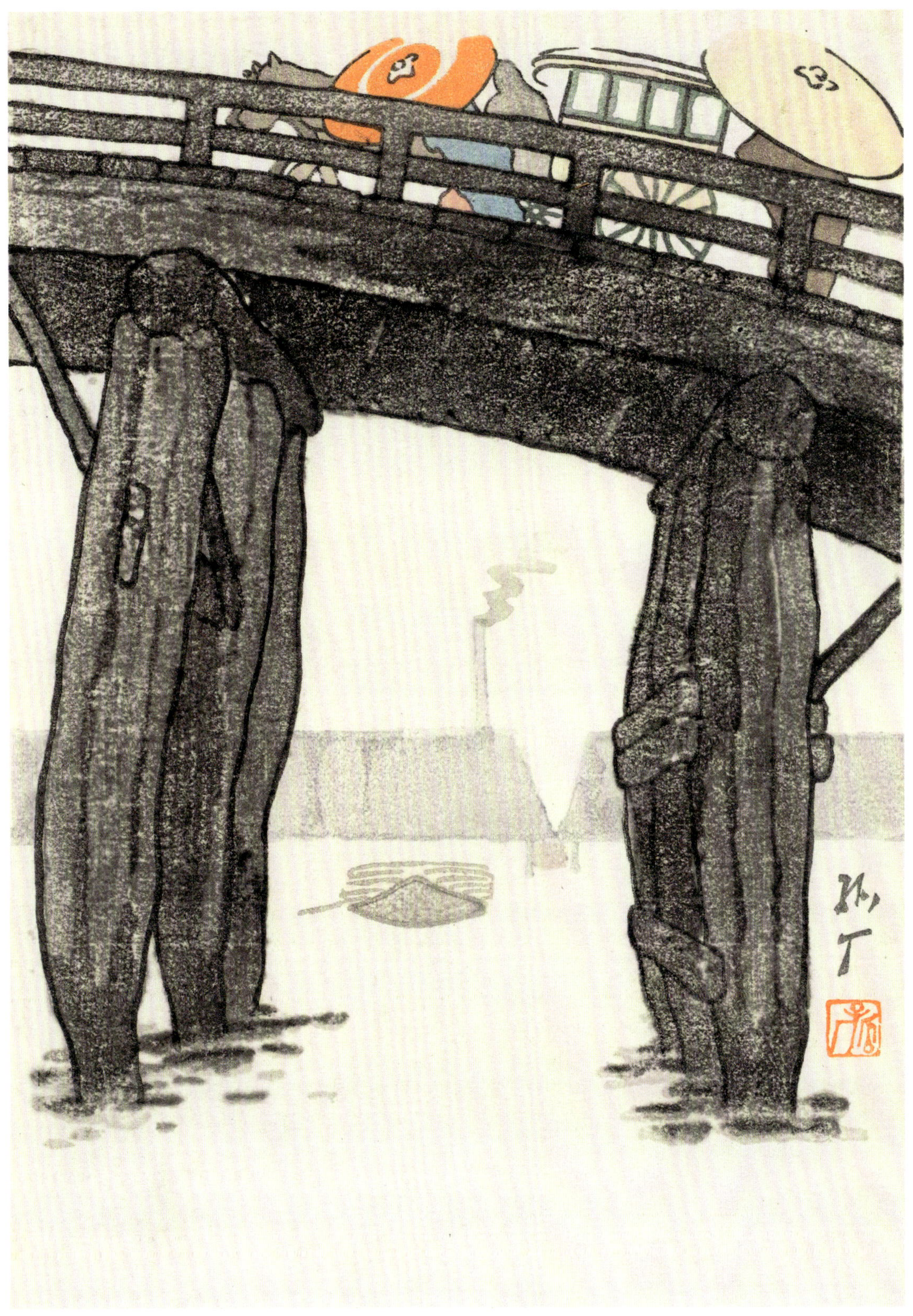

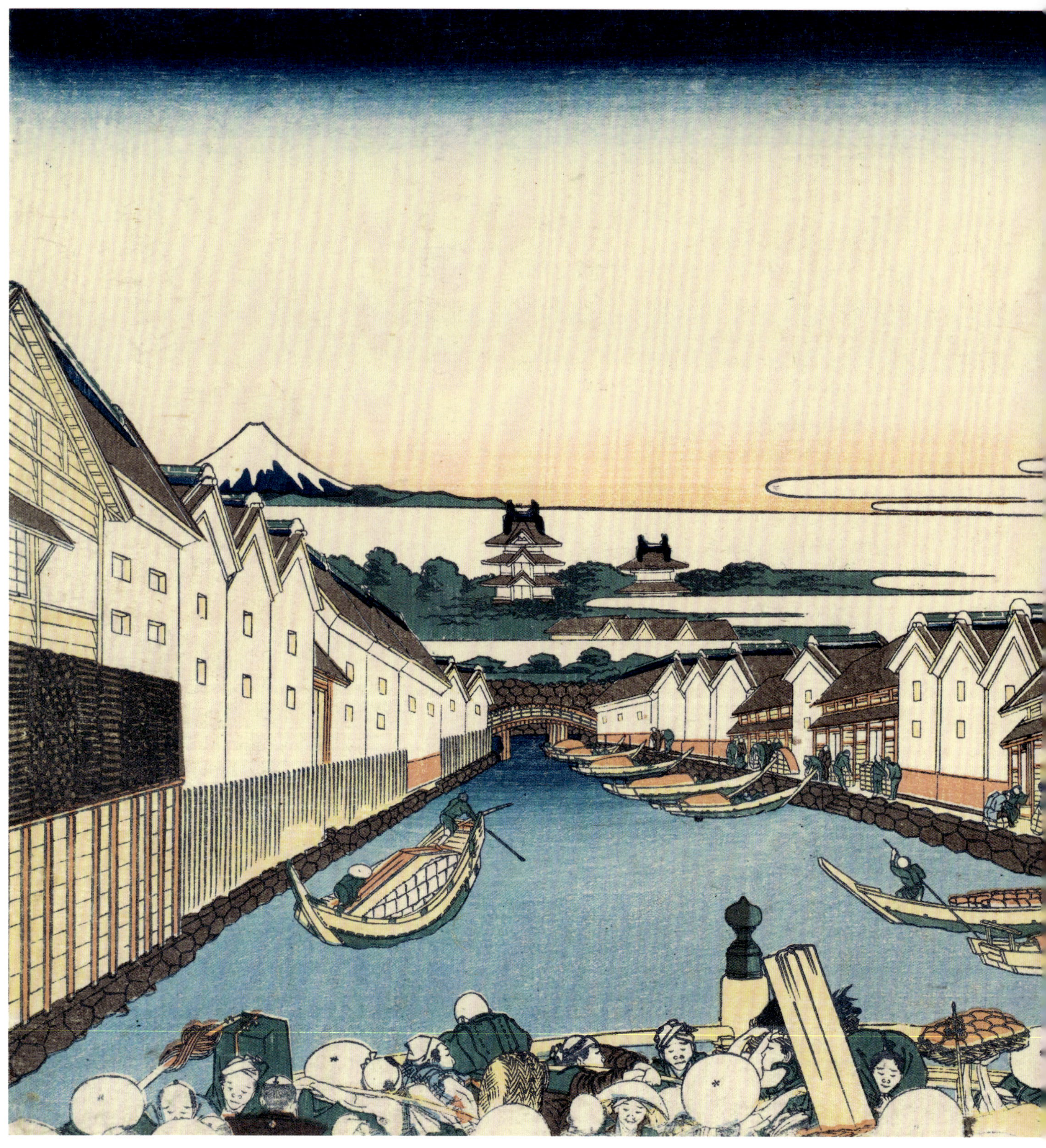

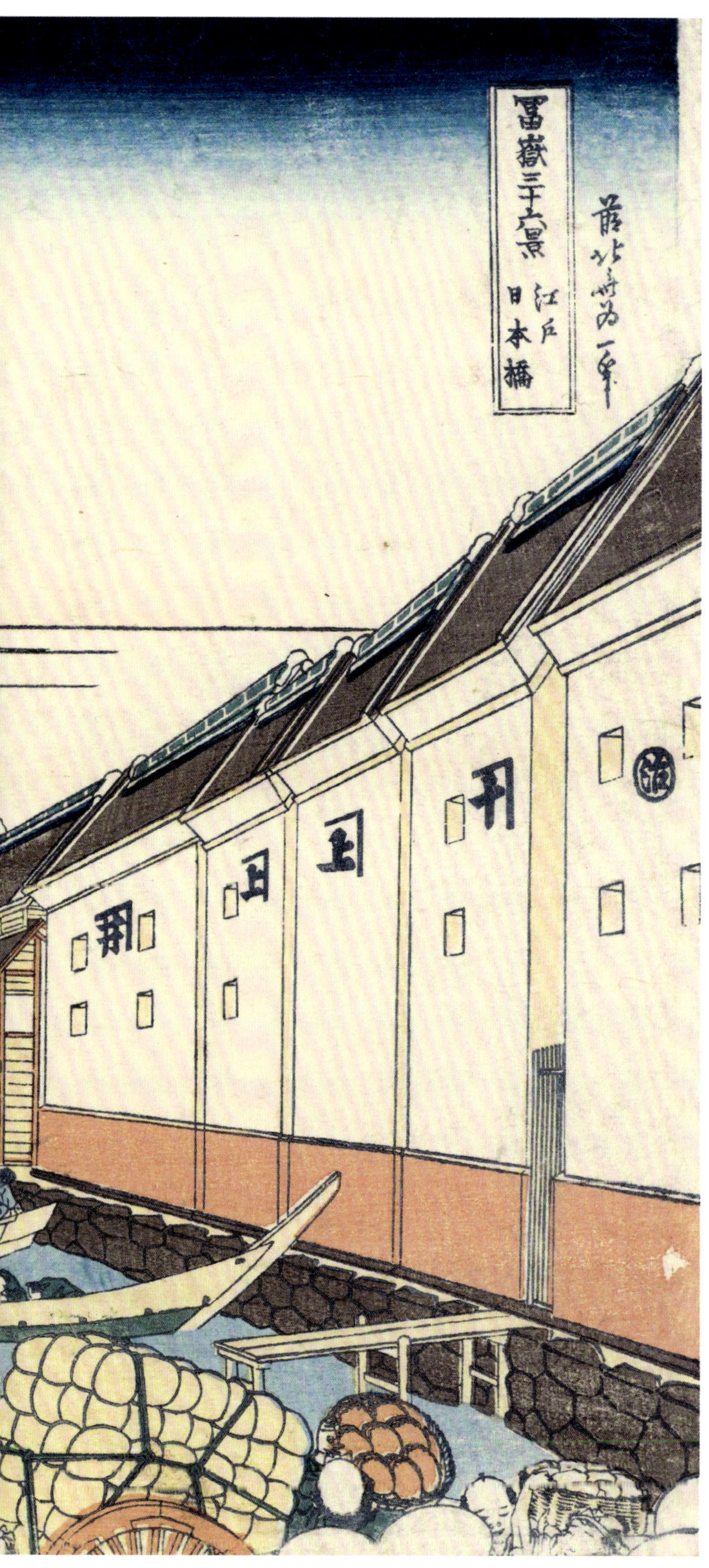

For European artists in the late nineteenth century, ukiyo-e prints were an intriguing combination of the familiar and the unfamiliar. The bustling metropolis of Edo had a general similarity to great European cities such as Paris, even if the styles of the clothing and buildings were very different. Landscapes and cityscapes by artists such as Hokusai were visually understandable to them because of the use of vanishing-point perspective that had begun in Japan in the eighteenth century; yet their renditions of three-dimensional scenes were constructed using flat areas of color produced by the color woodblock printing process. This Japanese-inspired use of flat color was taken up by the group of young French artists known as the Nabis, active in the 1890s, among them the painter and printmaker Édouard Vuillard.

Hokusai and his rival Hiroshige employed a variety of unusual compositional devices that surprised and delighted their original Japanese audiences, and later an overseas public as well. In Hokusai's view of Nihonbashi Bridge in the center of Edo, the viewer looks down on the heads of the crowd on the bridge; in other designs, the gaze is drawn upward, or even through or around a foreground object. The concept of a series of related images with a unified theme — Mount Fuji, the Tōkaidō highway — also appealed to European artists. An especially charming example is the series of color lithographs by Henri Rivière, *Thirty-Six Views of the Eiffel Tower*, based on drawings that he began in 1888 when the tower was under construction and continued after the completion of Paris's great landmark in 1889. Just as in Hokusai's series, he shows his subject from many different locations and viewpoints, in many different circumstances such as this snowy scene (64).

62

HOKUSAI
Nihonbashi Bridge in Edo, about 1830–31.
Color woodblock print
25.9 x 38.3 cm
(10⅛ x 15 in.)

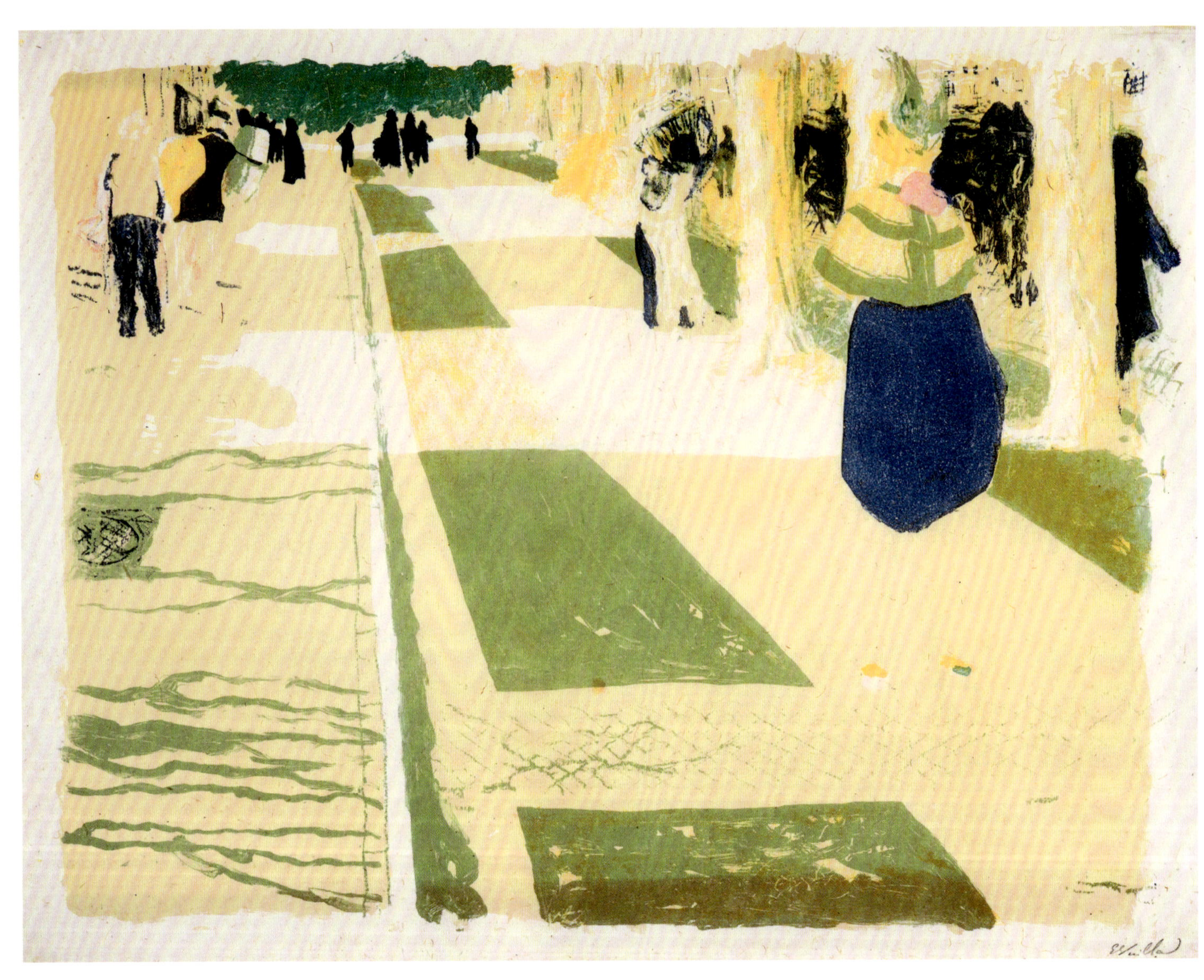

63

ÉDOUARD VUILLARD
The Avenue, 1899. Color
lithograph on china paper
33.4 x 45 cm
(13⅛ x 17⅝ in.)

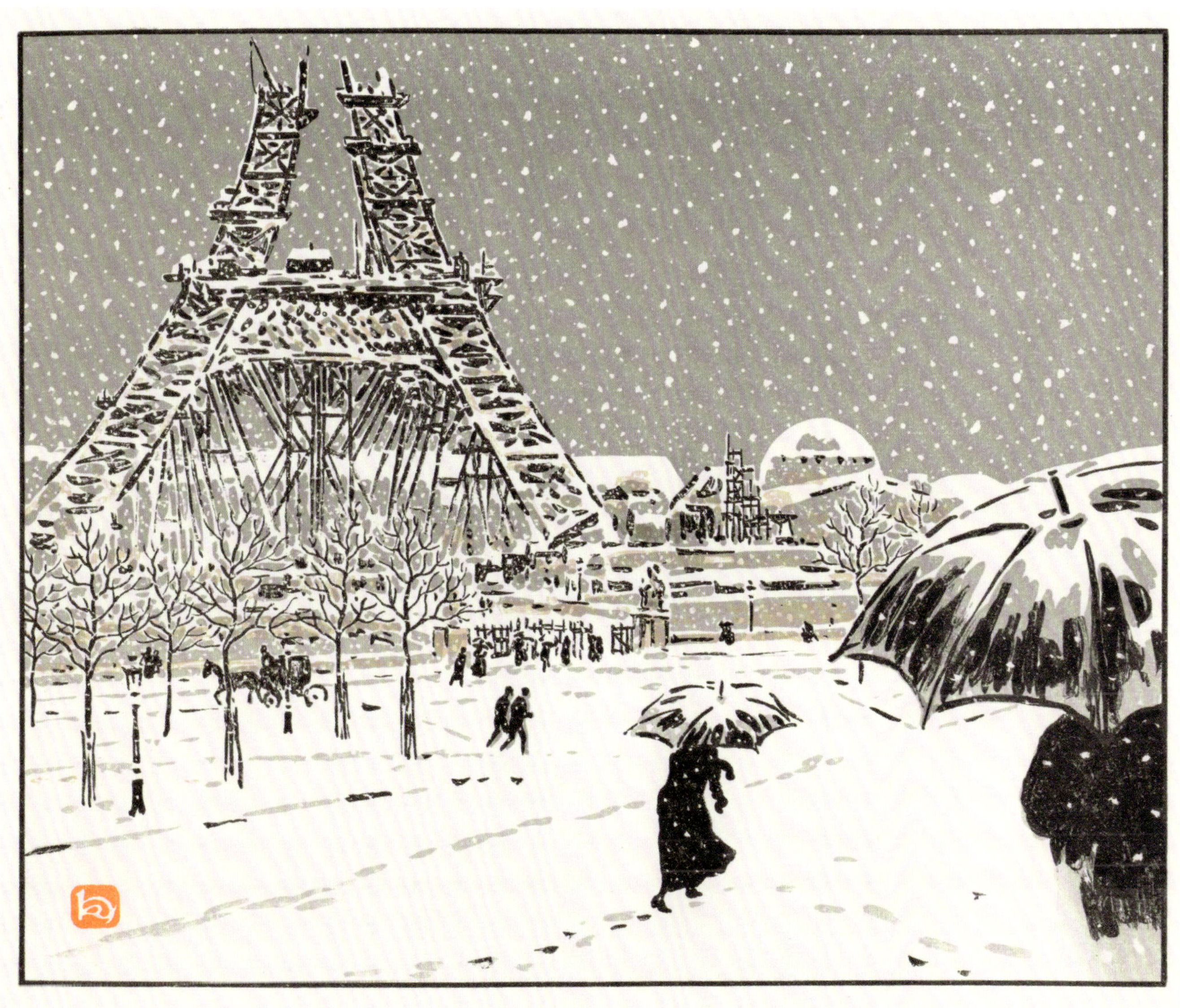

64

HENRI RIVIÈRE
The Eiffel Tower in Winter,
1902. Color lithograph
22.5 x 27 cm
(8⅞ x 10⅝ in.)

65

HOKUSAI
*Ushibori in Hitachi
Province*, about 1830–31.
Color woodblock print
25.2 x 37.4 cm
(9⅞ x 14¾ in.)

66

ARTHUR WESLEY DOW
Dory, about 1904.
Photograph, cyanotype
16.2 x 21.5 cm
(6⅜ x 8⅜ in.)

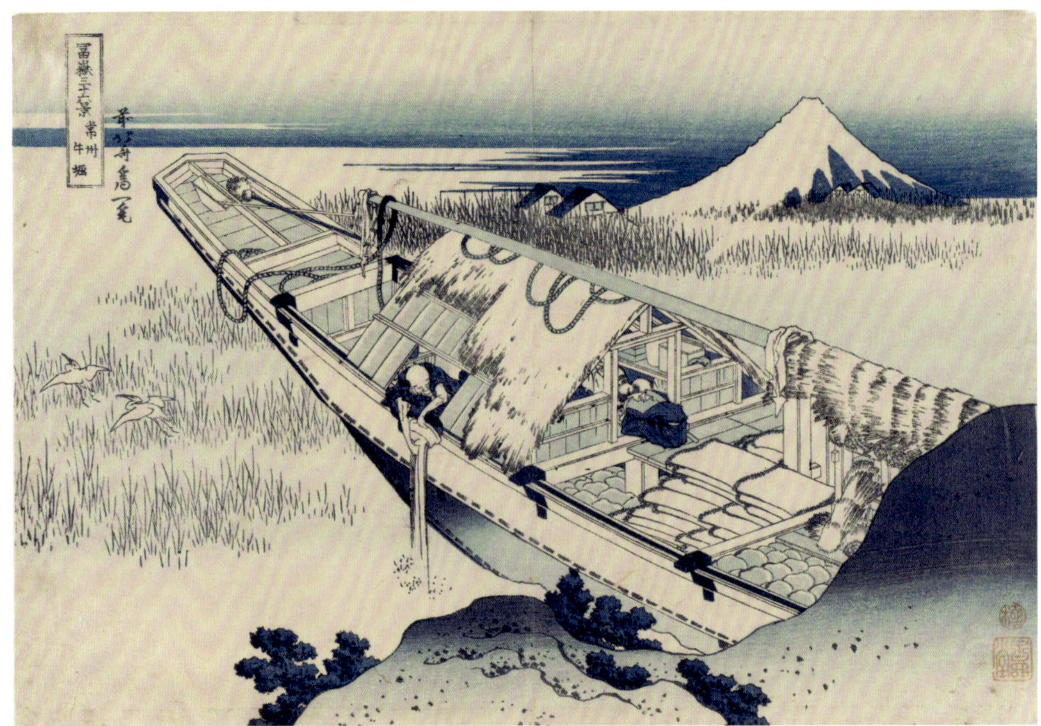

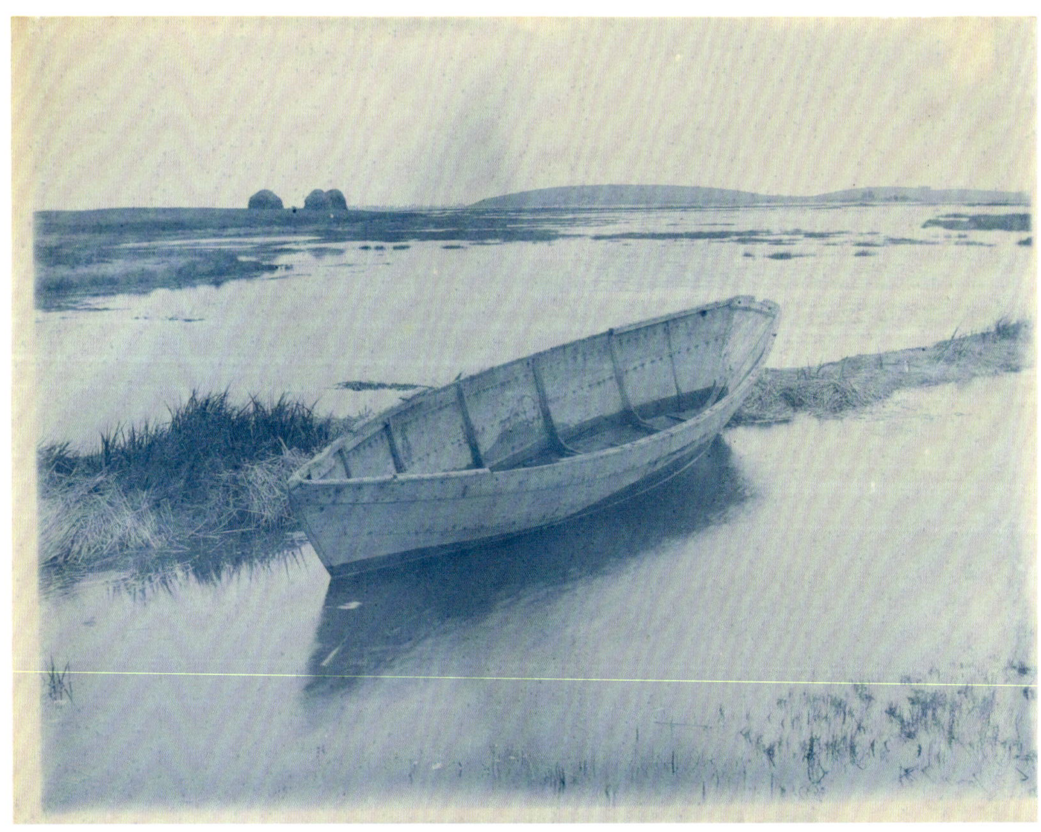

One factor in the new popularity of landscape prints in the 1830s was the introduction of a novel, imported European synthetic pigment into the ukiyo-e printmakers' color palette. Known as Prussian blue in English and Berlin blue in Japanese, the new color was much more resistant to fading than earlier blues, so that printed sky and sea colors retained their hues over time. Various ukiyo-e artists produced works colored almost entirely in tones of blue, including ten works in Hokusai's series *Thirty-Six Views of Mount Fuji* that are thought to be the first designs in the series to be published.

The blue Japanese prints may have been on Arthur Wesley Dow's mind when he decided to print photographs using the cyanotype process. As a printmaker, painter, photographer, and above all an art educator, Dow was an important force in bringing ukiyo-e prints into American art. Born in Ipswich, Massachusetts, Dow studied art in Boston and in Paris before returning to Boston, where in 1893 he became an assistant curator at the MFA working under Ernest Fenollosa. With Fenollosa's guidance, Dow made an extensive study of Japanese works in the collection that greatly affected his own ideas about art. His woodcut prints, such as this view of his hometown Ipswich, borrow heavily from the Japanese prints in terms of medium and color scheme, as well as compositional devices like the narrow format, truncated sides, and zigzag recession of the river.

Later he moved to New York City, where he taught first at the Art Students League and then at Teachers College, the graduate school of education at Columbia University. Dow's influential book *Composition: A Series of Exercises in Art Structure for the Use of Students and Teachers* was first published in 1899 and went through many subsequent editions. Dow strongly opposed the traditional distinction between fine arts and decorative arts and believed that the study of composition, rather than the imitation of either nature or old masters, should be the fundamental basis of art education.

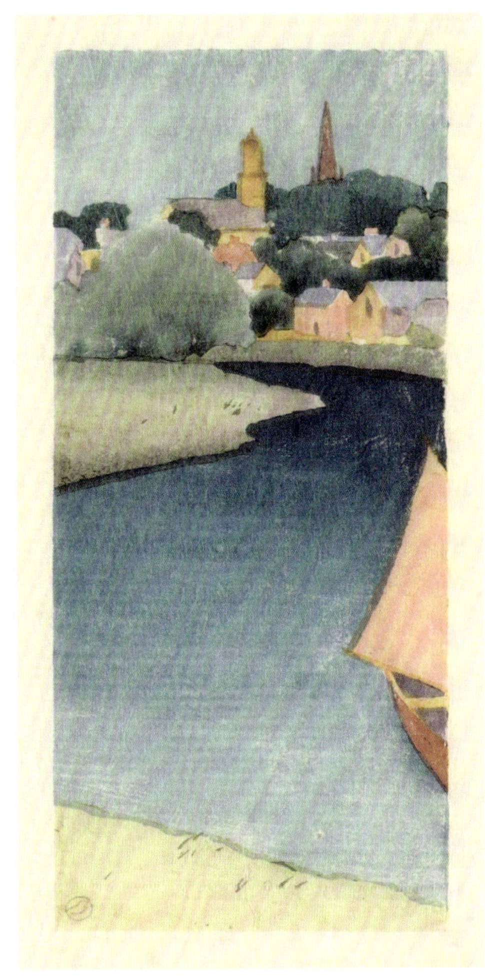

67
ARTHUR WESLEY DOW
View of Ipswich, 1895.
Color woodcut
12.7 x 5.9 cm
(5 x 2⅜ in.)

n the late 1860s in Europe, artists began depicting stormy seas or waves breaking on rocky coasts more frequently, very likely under the influence of Japanese prints. Gustave Courbet (1819–77) was especially admired for the wave paintings that he made from about 1867 to 1872, and Courbet's friend Whistler also painted notable waves. Winslow Homer, who spent a year in Paris in 1867–68, would certainly have seen Japanese prints at that time, as well as later in the United States, especially after the Centennial Exposition in Philadelphia in 1876 aroused American interest in Japanese art. Though Homer's seascapes, like Courbet's, were painted from life, he too may have been influenced by Hokusai and other ukiyo-e artists in his choice of subject matter and his way of approaching it, for example choosing to show a single large wave.

In France, the enthusiasm for Japanese culture continued through the 1890s, reinforced by the Art Nouveau style with its marked Japanese influence. The caricaturist Henri Gustave Jossot satirized the trend in a lithograph showing a man in a boat tossed head-over-heels by the impact of a wave clearly based on Hokusai's, with an artist's easel flying into the water (69). In Belgium, where the Art Nouveau style in architecture and interior design first became popular, the versatile artist Gisbert Combaz applied his talents as a designer and printmaker to a new format, the picture postcard. A set of twelve cards entitled *La Mer* (The Sea), inspired by Hokusai, displays the sinuous lines and clear, bright colors typical of Art Nouveau (70).

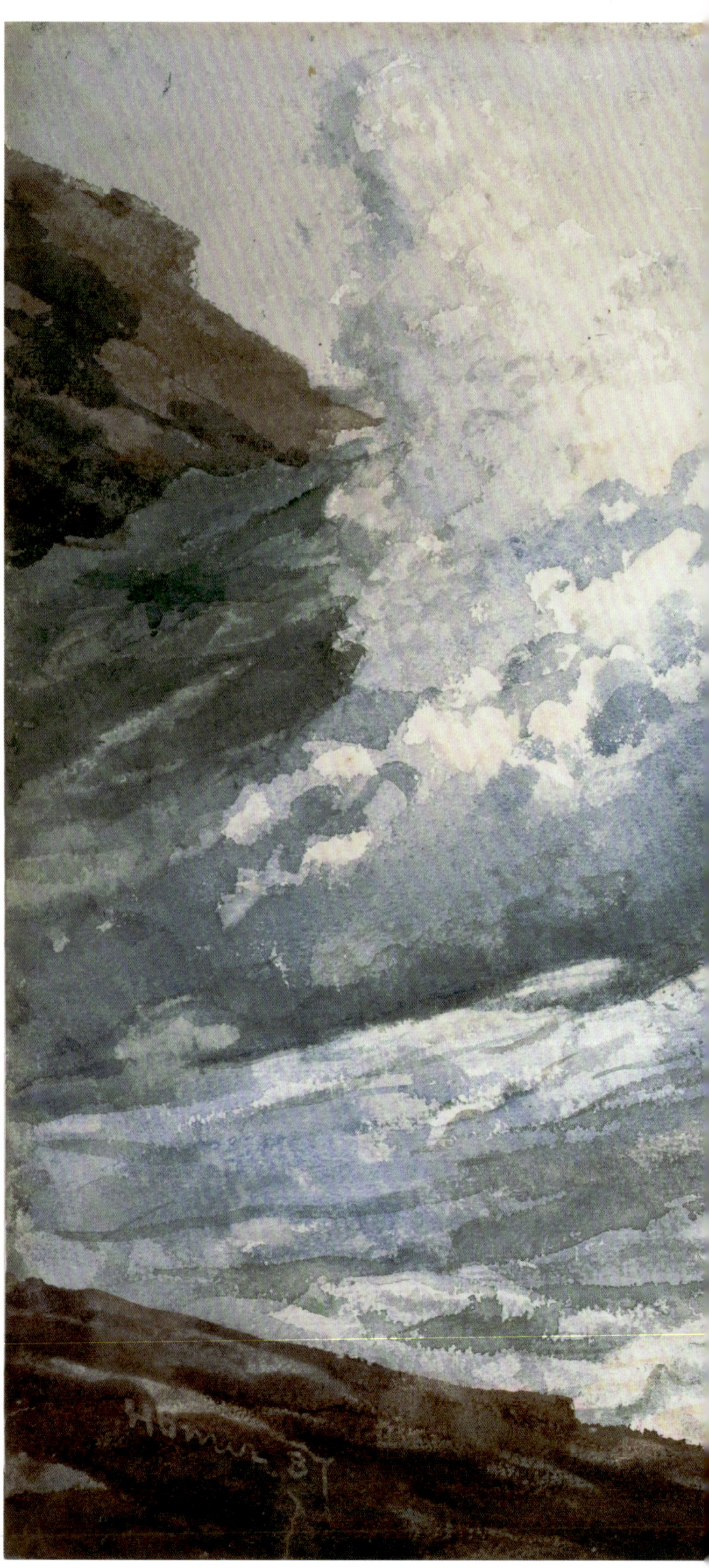

68

WINSLOW HOMER
Breaking Wave (Prout's Neck), 1887. Watercolor over graphite pencil on paper
38.7 x 54.6 cm
(15¼ x 21½ in.)

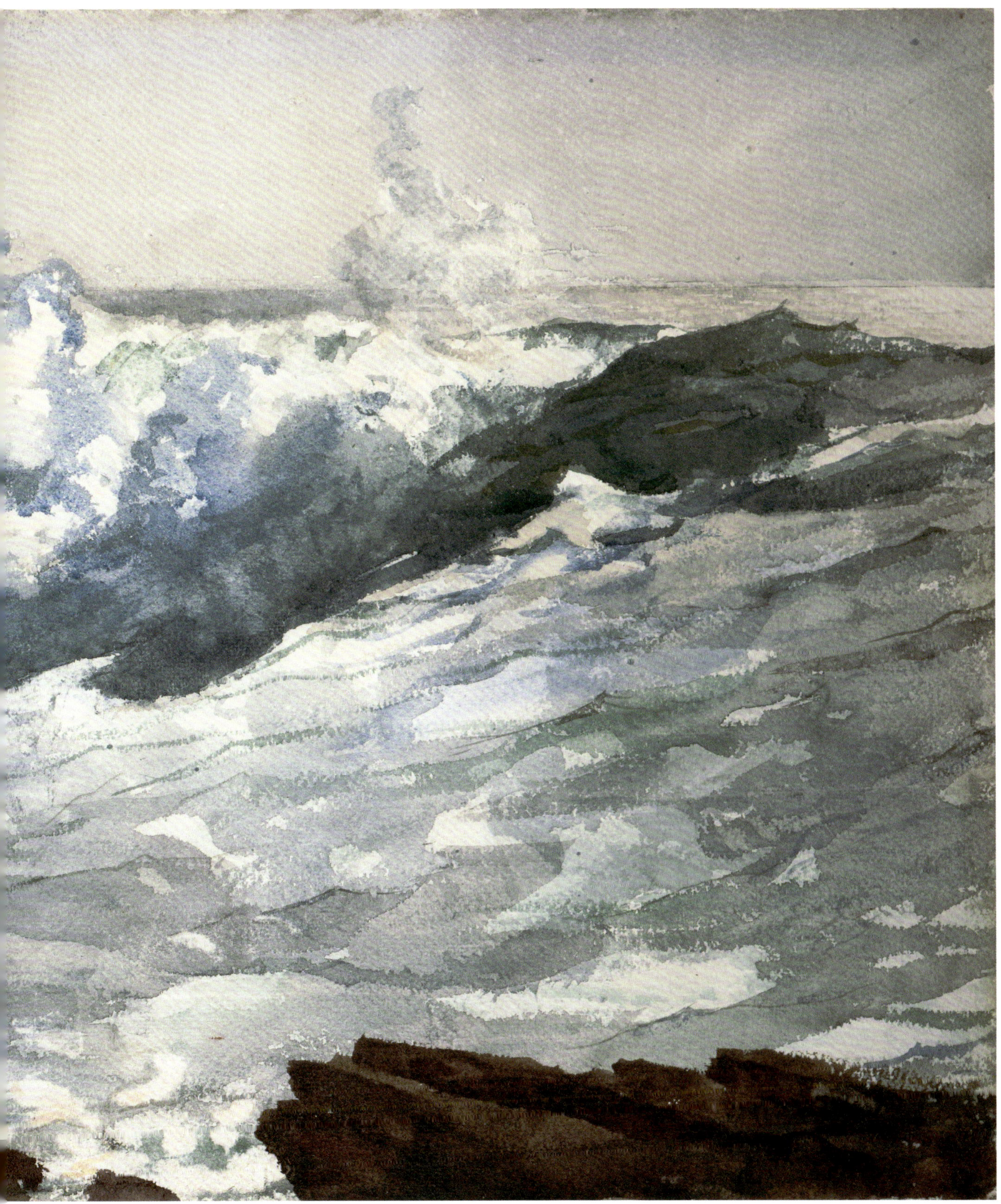

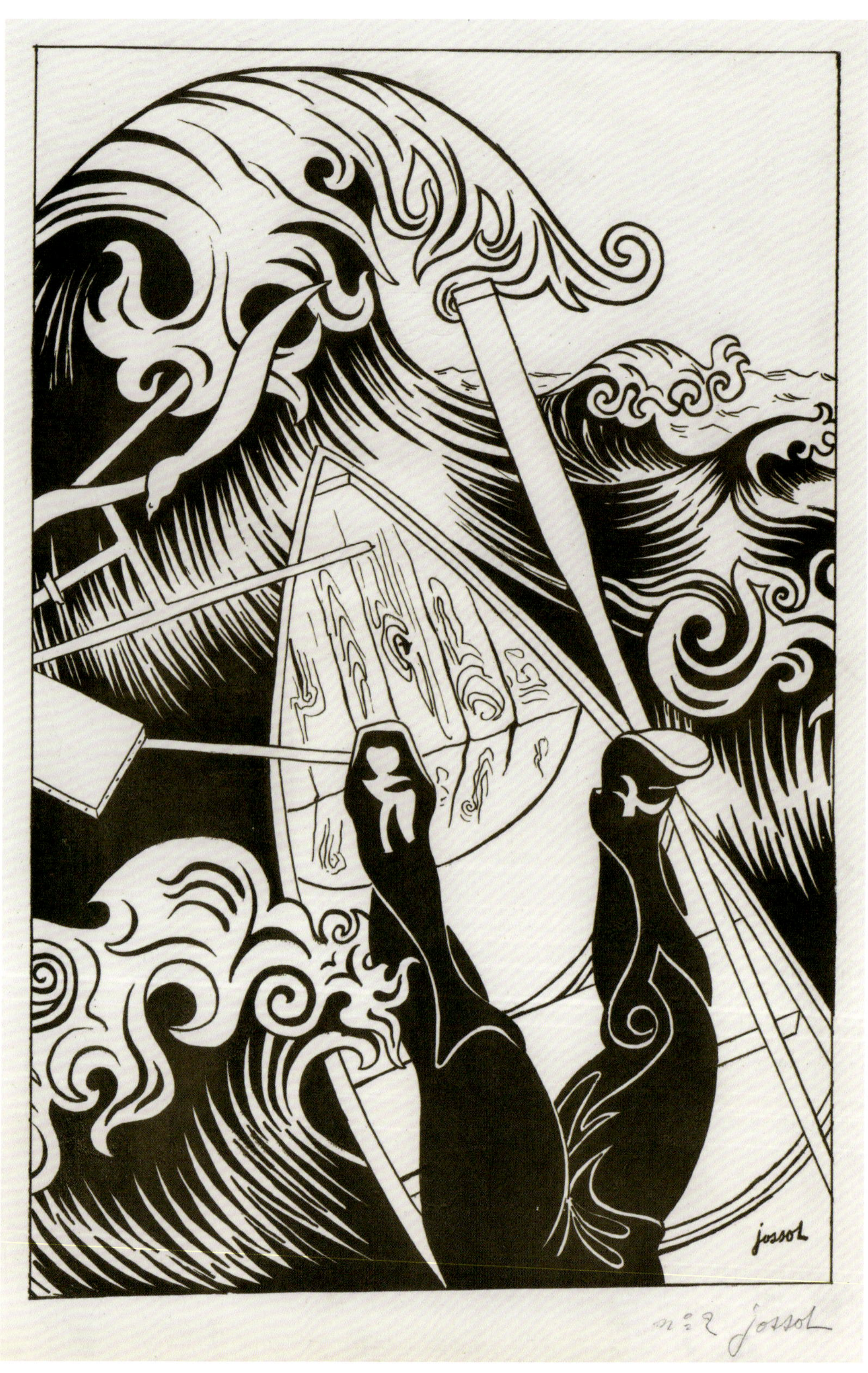

69
HENRI GUSTAVE JOSSOT
The Wave, 1894.
Lithograph
60.5 x 42.7 cm
(23⅞ x 16¾ in.)

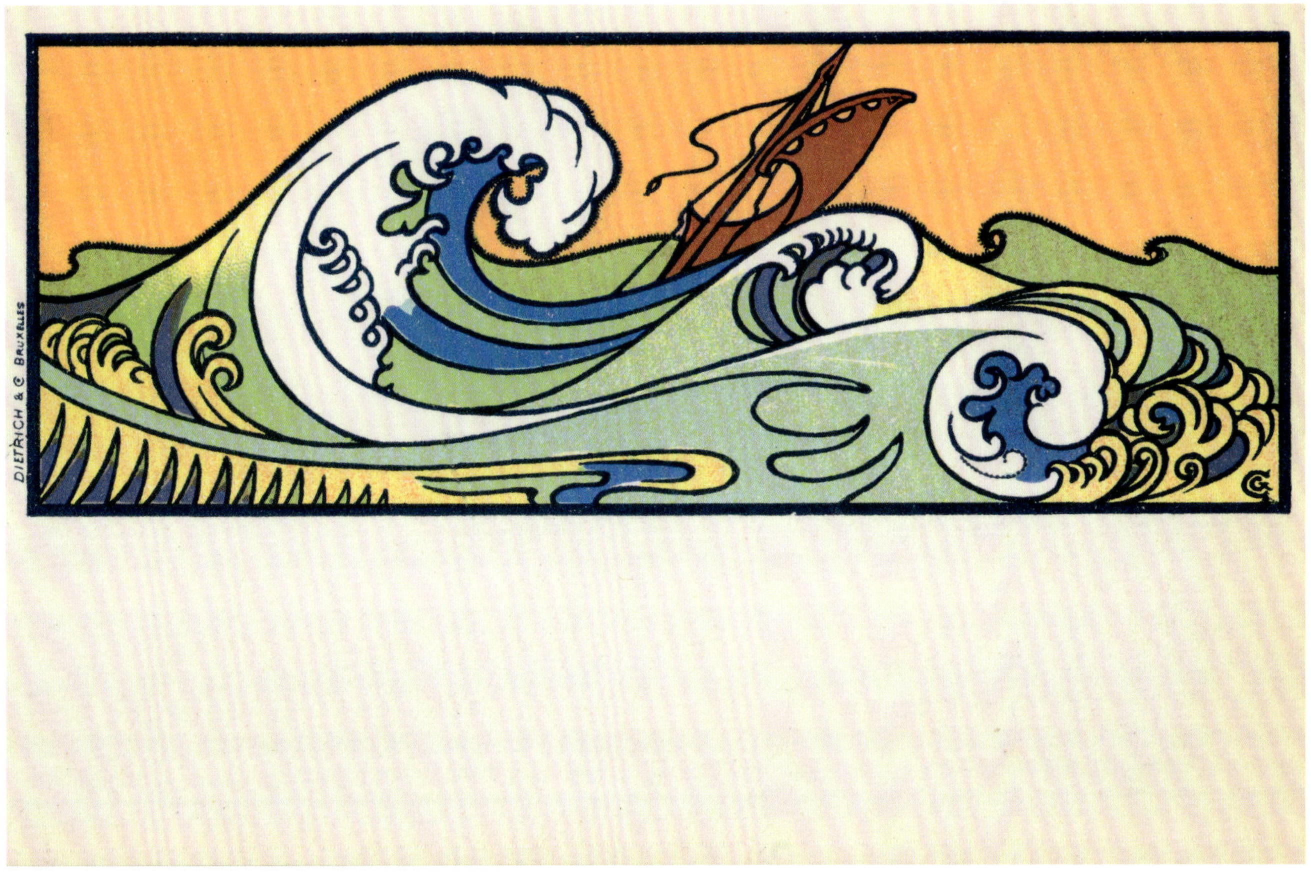

70

GISBERT COMBAZ
A Boat in the Waves,
1899. Color lithograph
postcard
8.9 x 14 cm
(3½ x 5½ in.)

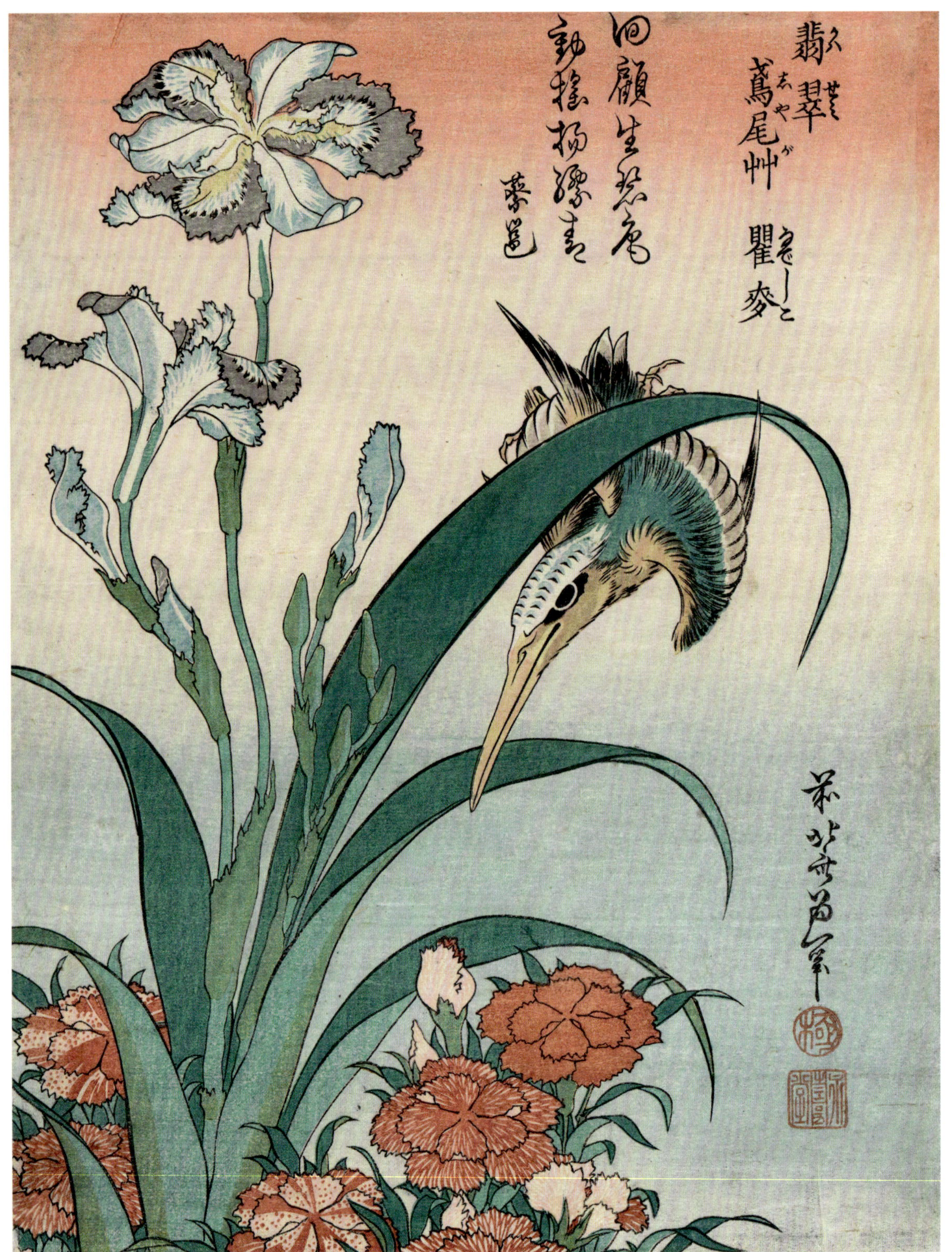

71

HOKUSAI
Kingfisher with Iris and Wild Pinks, about 1834.
Color woodblock print
24.1 x 18.8 cm
(9½ x 7⅜ in.)

72

Vase painted by Samuel
Wilson and made by
Doulton Manufactory,
1886–1902.
Glazed earthenware
45.7 x 20.3 cm
(18 x 8 in.)

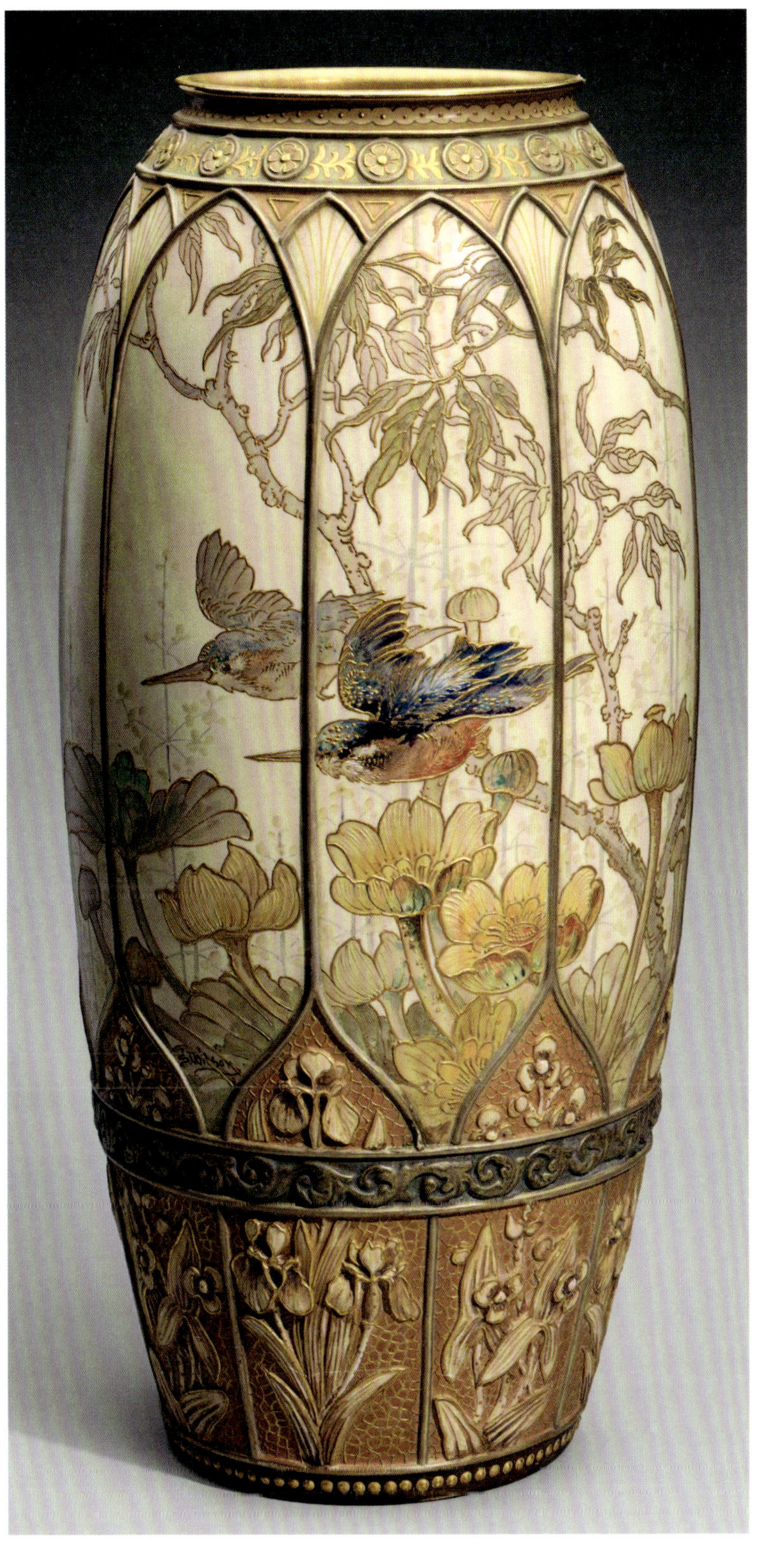

Following the great success of the untitled bird-and-flower series known as the "Large Flowers" (see 42), Hokusai designed a series of prints nicknamed "Small Flowers," which also show their subjects in vivid, close-up detail. The Large Flowers prints have no inscriptions other than the artist's signature, while the Small Flowers include lines of poetry in both Japanese and classical Chinese, a nod to the ancient East Asian tradition of combining poetry, calligraphy, and painting, and a testimony to Hokusai's excellent education. The couplet quoted here is from a poem by the Chinese poet Cai Yong (132–192 CE), a scholar and calligrapher of the Eastern Han dynasty, describing the brilliant feathers of the kingfisher: "Turning, a brilliant azure hue; / in motion, a delicate blue."

The common kingfisher is found all across the Eurasian continent. It is more often represented in art in Asia than in Europe, but there are some fine examples in Western art as well, such as this vase showing brightly colored kingfishers darting among assorted flowers in a scene very similar to Hokusai's print. Made by the company now known as Royal Doulton in the final decades of the nineteenth century, the vase reflects the ideals of the Arts and Crafts movement and the Aesthetic movement in Britain, closely related to the Art Nouveau movement in France. Known by different names in different countries, this international movement sought to blur the distinction between fine arts and decorative arts, emphasize the importance of handcraft, and create beautiful objects for use in the homes of ordinary people. The works produced by Doulton in the 1880s and 1890s combine mass-production techniques with hand-painted decorations, in this case signed by the artist. The designs are strongly influenced by Japanese prints and decorative arts, with special interest in gracefully curving, intricate plant forms.

Carp appear frequently in East Asian pictorial art as a symbol of courage and tenacity because in the wild, like salmon, they swim upstream to spawn. According to a Chinese legend, carp that could swim up the rapids at Longmen (literally "Dragon Gate") on the Yellow River would be transformed into dragons; hence, a painting of a carp was a suitable gift for a young man taking the civil service examinations to become an official. Japan did not use the examination system, but the message of perseverance leading to success was appropriate in many circumstances. In China, Korea, and Japan, carp have also been kept as decorative fish in garden ponds, and they can be tasty eating as well.

A large print by Hokusai whose vertical format suggests a hanging scroll painting shows two carp in a waterfall, barely visible in the rushing water (74). One swims bravely up the falls, while the other seems to be turning away. Does this fish represent a rejection of worldly success in favor of some other path in life? Or is it merely circling around to wait its own turn at the falls? As he often does, Hokusai implies a story that the viewer is left to imagine.

More straightforward depictions of ornamental carp are very common in prints by Hokusai, his students such as Hokkei, and other ukiyo-e artists (75). In the late nineteenth century, when the taste for things Japanese was at its height in both Europe and America, the motif was a popular one in Asian-inspired decorative arts. One of the most spectacular examples is a fine silver punchbowl, whose ornate decoration attested to the great wealth and fashionable taste of its original owner. Sea creatures and plants of many kinds adorn both the bowl and its matching ladle, with a carp-like fish as the main motif on one side and a dragon-like sea monster on the other. It's unlikely that the American designers knew of the legend of carp changing into dragons; most likely they were simply attracted to Asian-style aquatic images that they could combine into this masterful presentation.

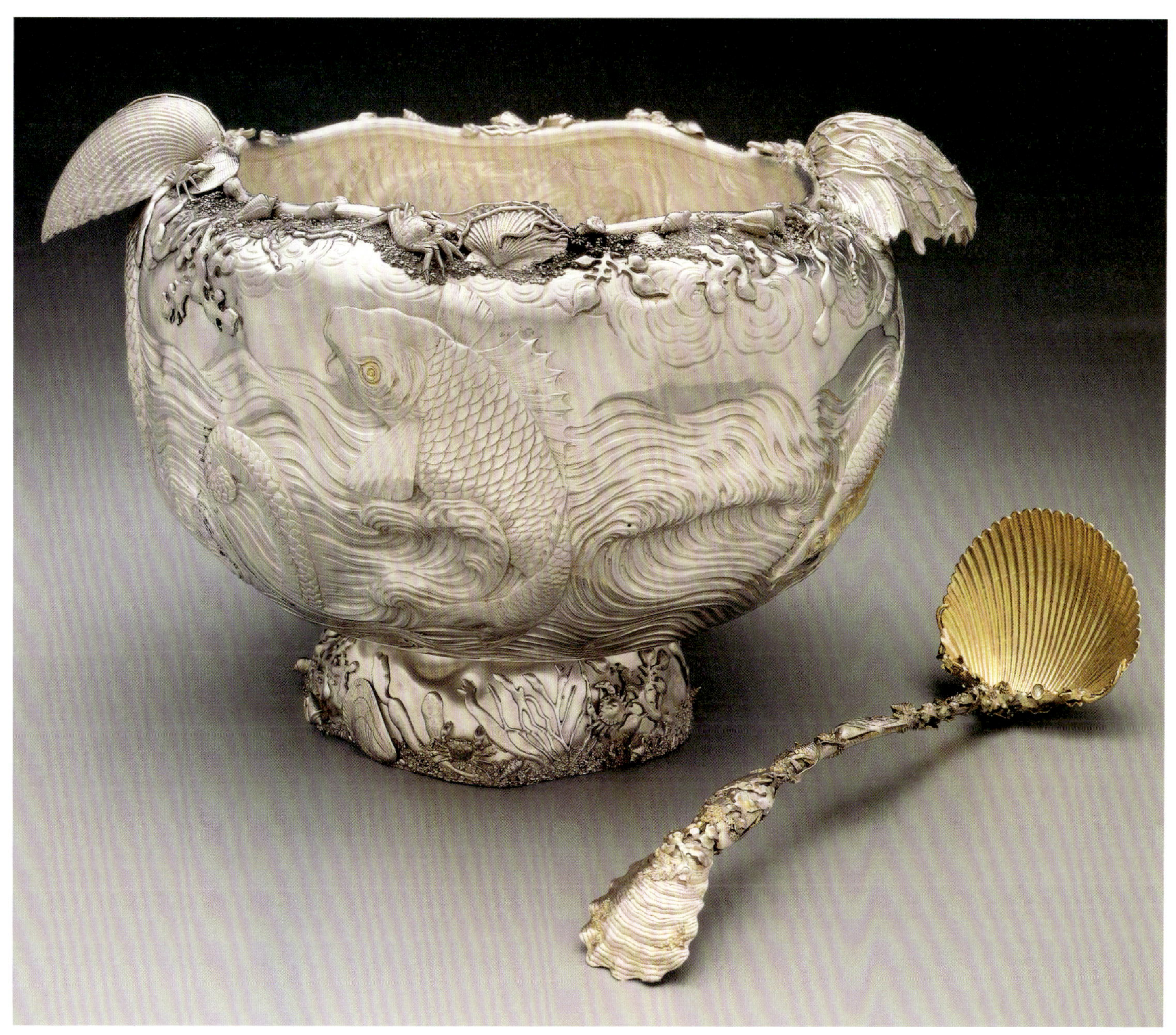

73
Punch bowl and ladle
made by Gorham
Manufacturing Company,
1885. Silver, gilding
Dowl.
25.7 x 38.7 x 17.8 x 23.5 cm
(10⅛ x 15¼ x / x 9¼ In.)

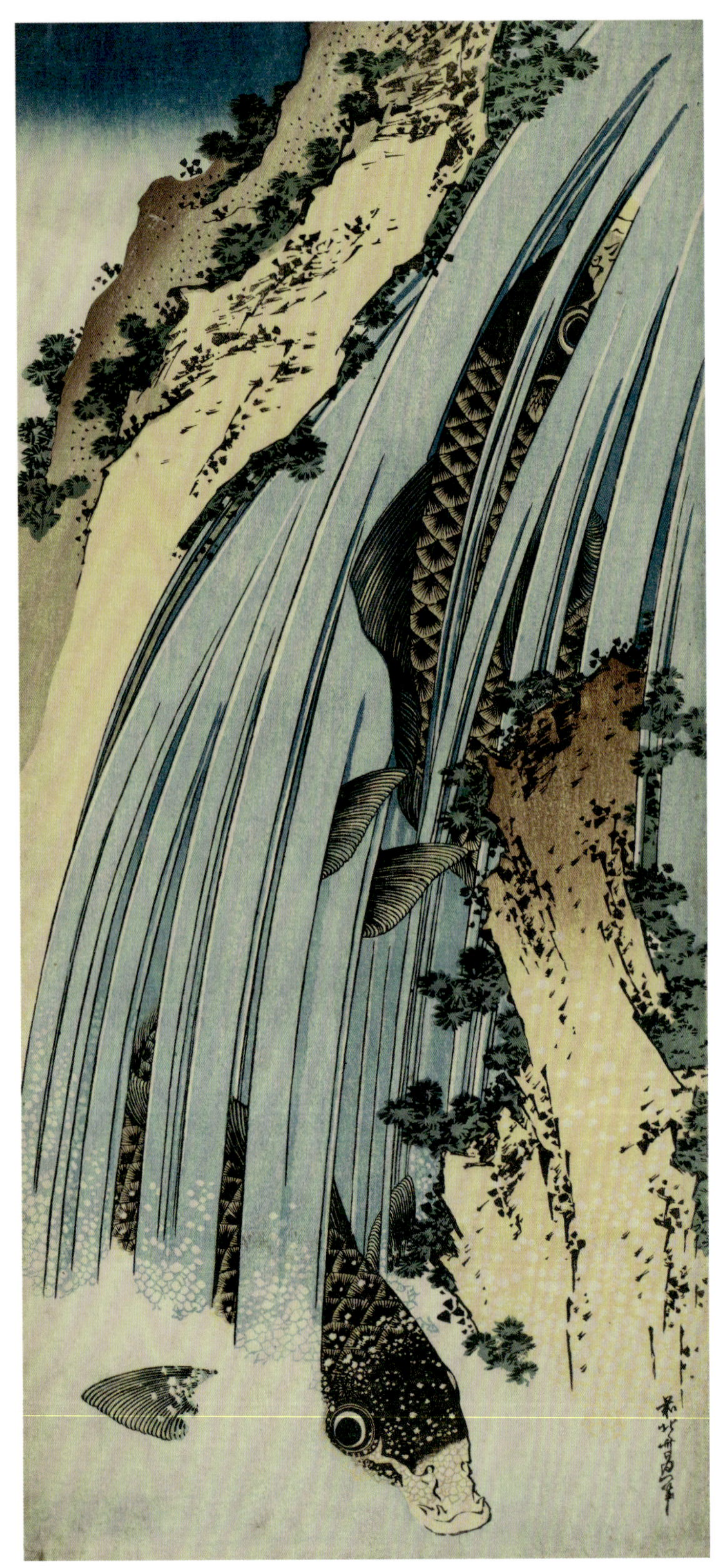

74
HOKUSAI
Two Carp in Waterfall,
about 1834.
Color woodblock print
52 x 23.7 cm
(20½ x 9⅜ in.)

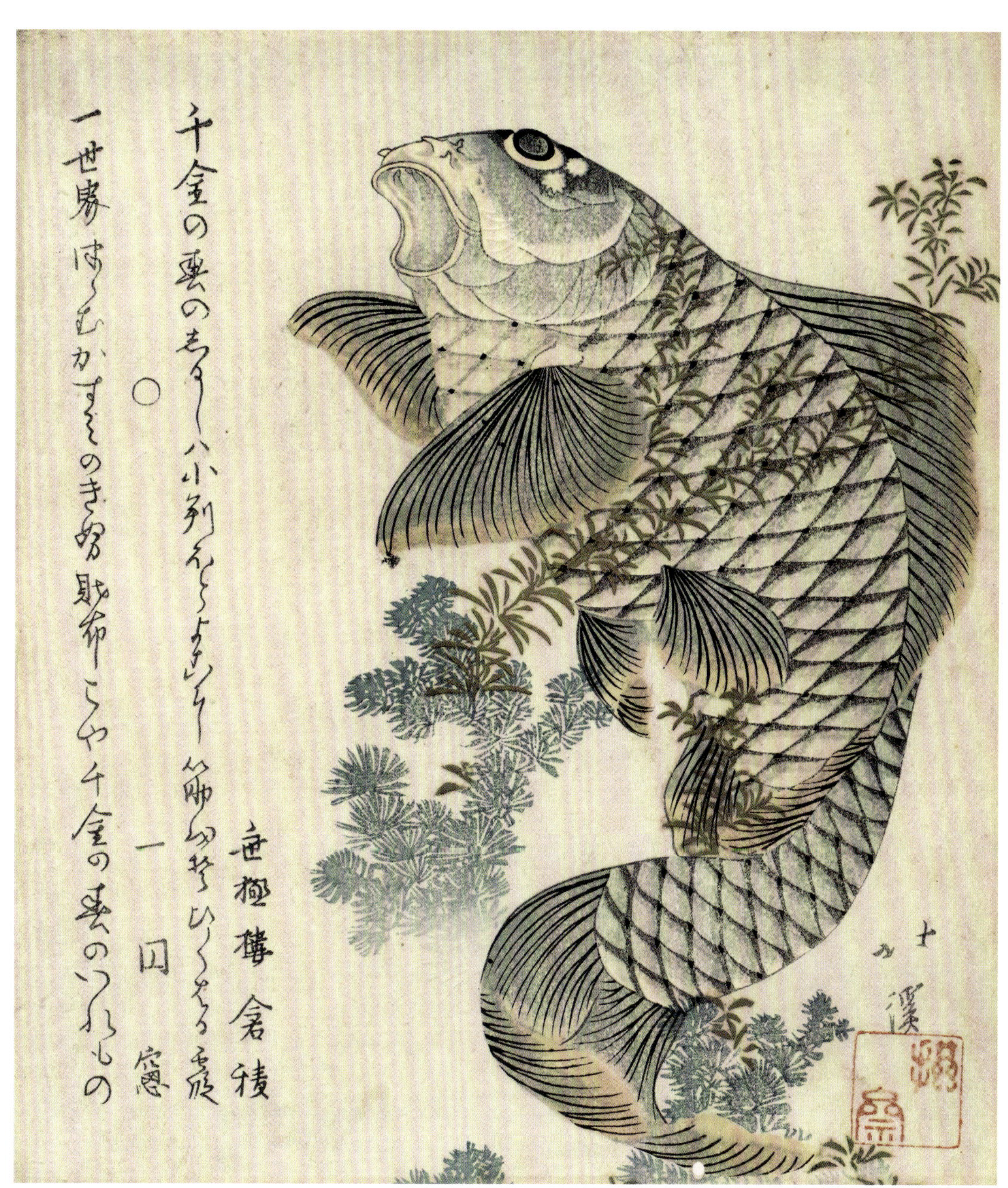

75

HOKKEI
Carp and Seaweed,
late 1810s. Color wood-
block print (surimono)
20.5 x 18.2 cm
(8⅛ x 7⅛ in.)

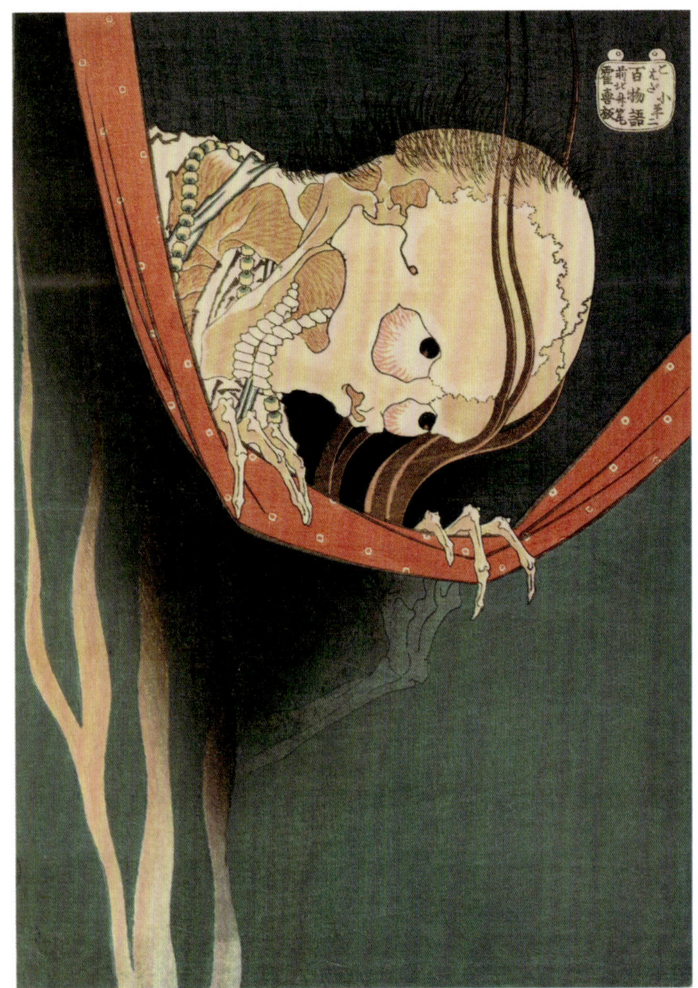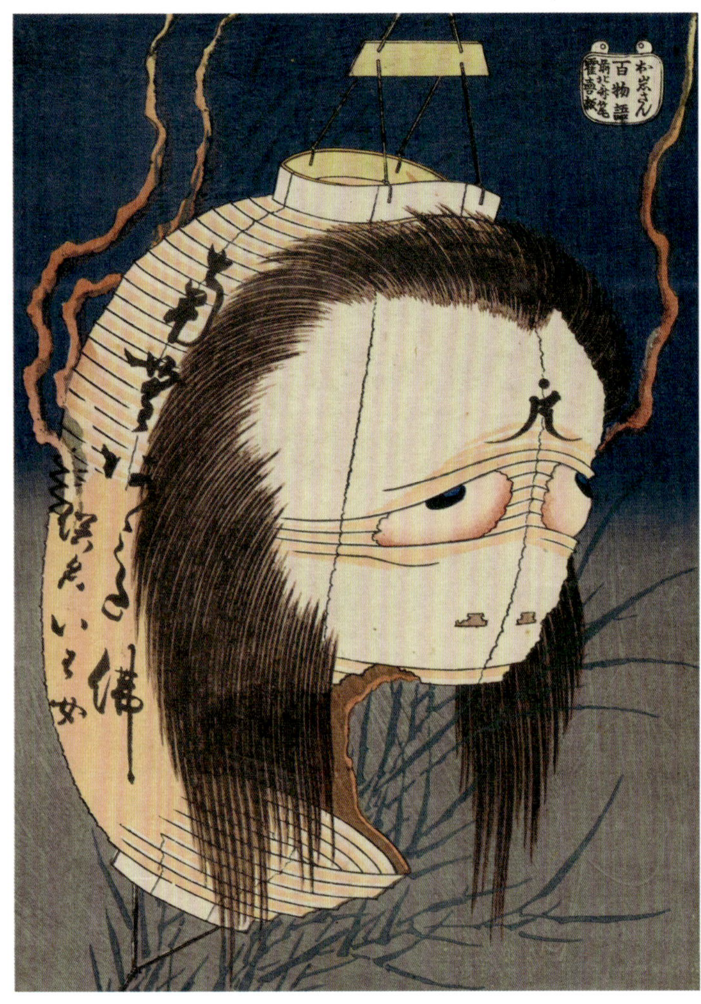

Among Hokusai's many imaginative depictions of ghosts and monsters, the most spectacular are brilliantly colored prints from a series named for the popular storytelling game called "One Hundred Ghost Stories," although only five designs are known. The two ghosts shown here are wronged spouses seeking vengeance beyond the grave. On a steamy summer night, the rotting corpse of Kohada Koheiji, who was murdered by his wife and her lover, claws down the mosquito netting over the bed to glare balefully at the guilty couple. The most famous ghost story of all, *A Strange Tale of Yotsuya*, tells of a man who killed his wife, Oiwa, in order to marry the rich girl next door, using a poison that caused poor Oiwa to become disfigured before she died. Her ghost returned to torment the killer by possessing everyday objects, such as the lantern that takes on the distorted shape of her dying face. Kabuki plays based on the story showcased

76

HOKUSAI
*The Ghost of Kohada
Koheiji*, about 1831–32.
Color woodblock print
26.5 x 19 cm
(10³⁄₈ x 7¹⁄₂ in.)

77

HOKUSAI
The Ghost of Oiwa,
about 1831–32.
Color woodblock print
25.8 x 18.9 cm
(10¹⁄₈ x 7¹⁄₂ in.)

78

ODILON REDON
"The misshapen polyp
floated on the shores,
a sort of smiling and
hideous Cyclops," 1883.
Lithograph
32.2 x 26.5 cm
(12³⁄₄ x 10³⁄₈ in.)

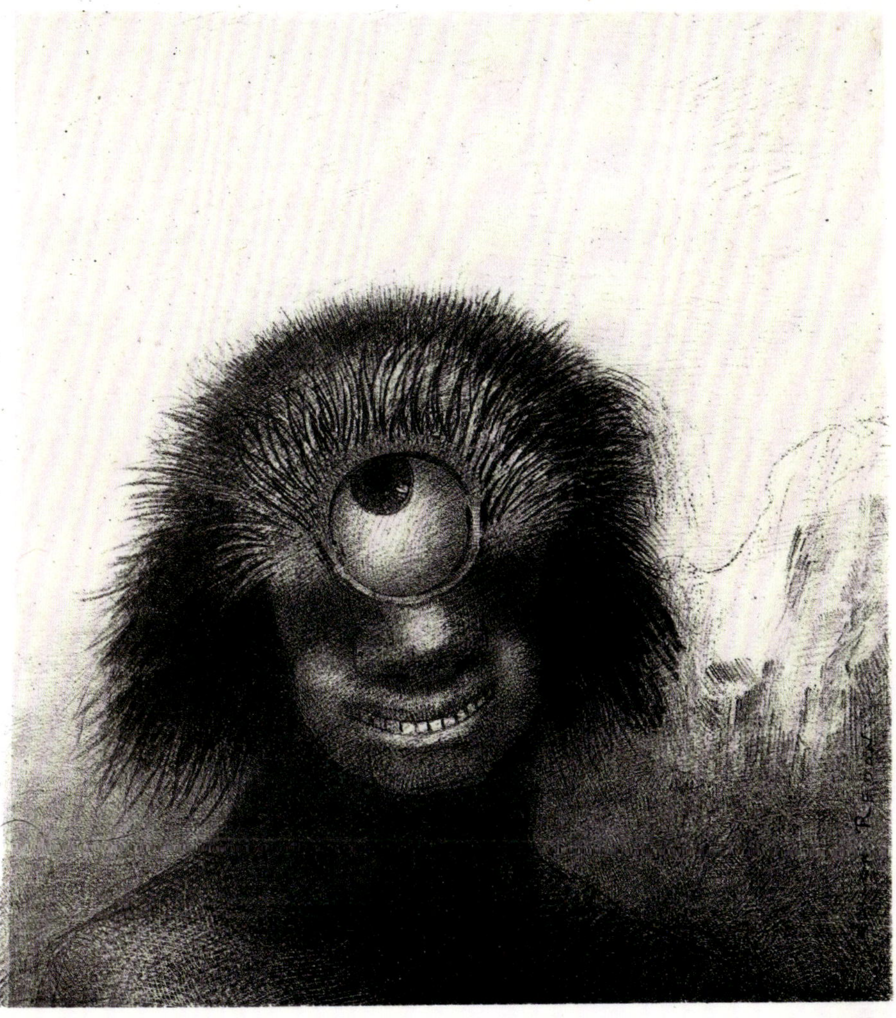

the talents of actors, makeup artists, and special-effects technicians.

In the nineteenth century, a taste for the macabre was common to both Japan and Europe, and by the final decades of the century, European artists had become interested in the Japanese tradition of the grotesque. Such imagery was especially appealing to Symbolist artists such as the painter and printmaker Odilon Redon, whose dreamlike — or nightmarish — visions of gigantic heads and staring eyeballs evoke the same mix of fear and pity as Hokusai's ghosts.

A more recent, and more humorous, take on traditional Japanese ghosts — with occasional nods to Hokusai and Kuniyoshi — can be found in the work of the late, much-loved manga artist Mizuki Shigeru (1922–2015), whose hit series *GeGeGe no Kitarō*, originally published in the 1960s, relates the adventures of a little one-eyed ghost boy growing up in a graveyard among fellow ghosts.

We seldom think of Hokusai in connection with the Harlem Renaissance, but here is visual evidence suggesting that at least one major artist associated with that movement was fond of his work. Loïs Mailou Jones created this clever repeat design for fabric when she was only twenty years old, studying at the School of the Museum of Fine Arts in Boston and making frequent visits to Harlem. In her mature career as a painter, from about 1930 on, she was primarily inspired by Africa and the African diaspora, but clearly she was aware of other non-European traditions as well. The bright colors and strong design sense of Hokusai's prints may have made them especially appealing.

This watercolor design for a fabric pattern is based on two of Hokusai's prints from the Waterfalls series, his second major landscape series and the only one in a vertical format. The waterfall where the great twelfth-century general Minamoto Yoshitsune is said to have washed his horse — known today as Takataki and one of the features of a popular hiking trail in Yoshino-Kumano National Park — has an interesting double cascade in a zigzag flow that probably sparked the idea for a repeating pattern, with the falls repeated in mirror images both vertically and horizontally (80). In place of Hokusai's humorous depiction of two commoners washing their horse where the famous general once did, Jones substitutes more sedate figures taken from another print in the series, showing a group of travelers admiring the falls (81). The result is a harmonious composition that would have made a very attractive printed fabric, although as far as we know it was never actually produced.

79
LOÏS MAILOU JONES
Japanese Waterfall,
1925. Opaque watercolor
on board
51 x 48 cm
(20⅛ x 18⅞ in.)

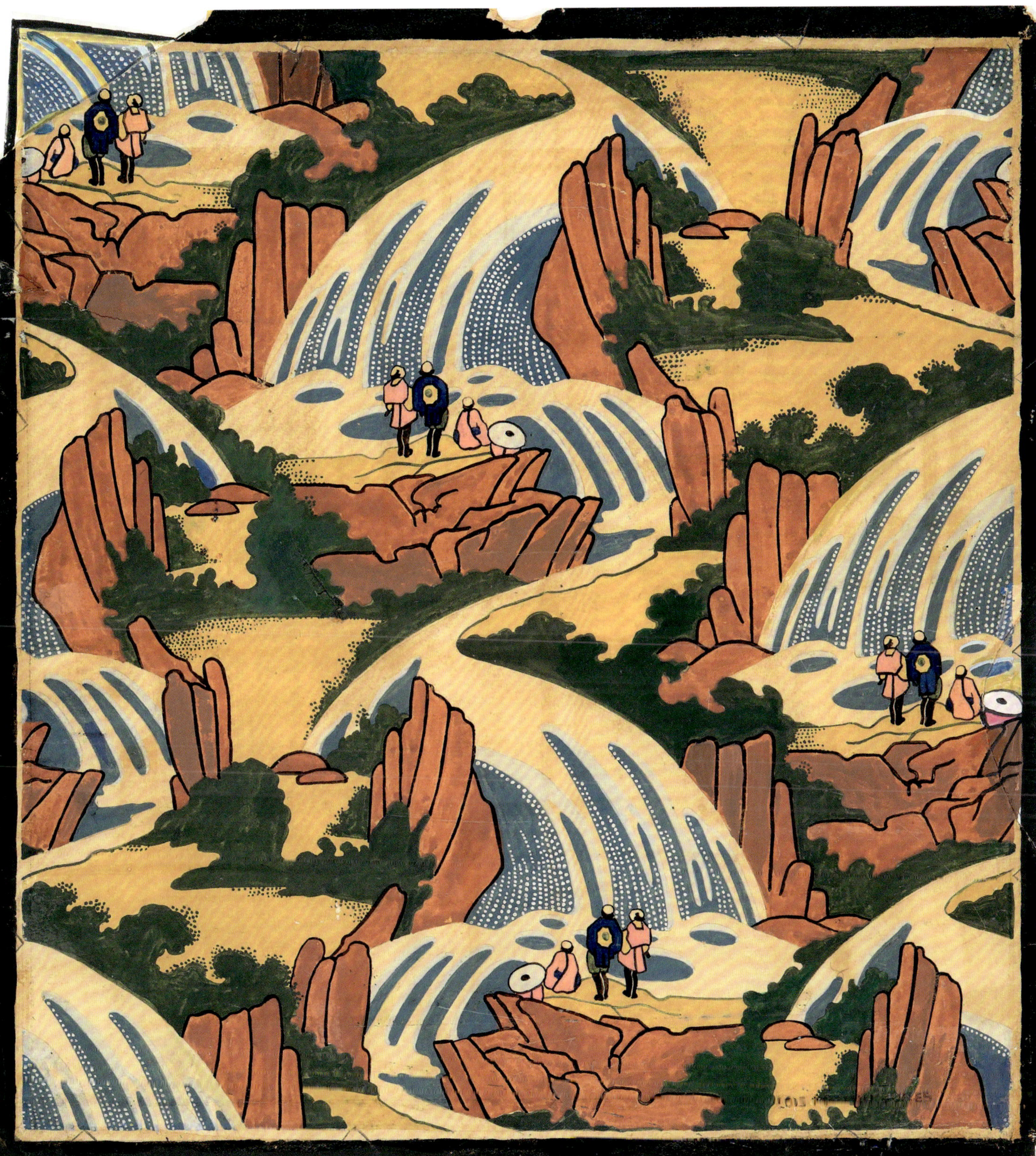
LOIS

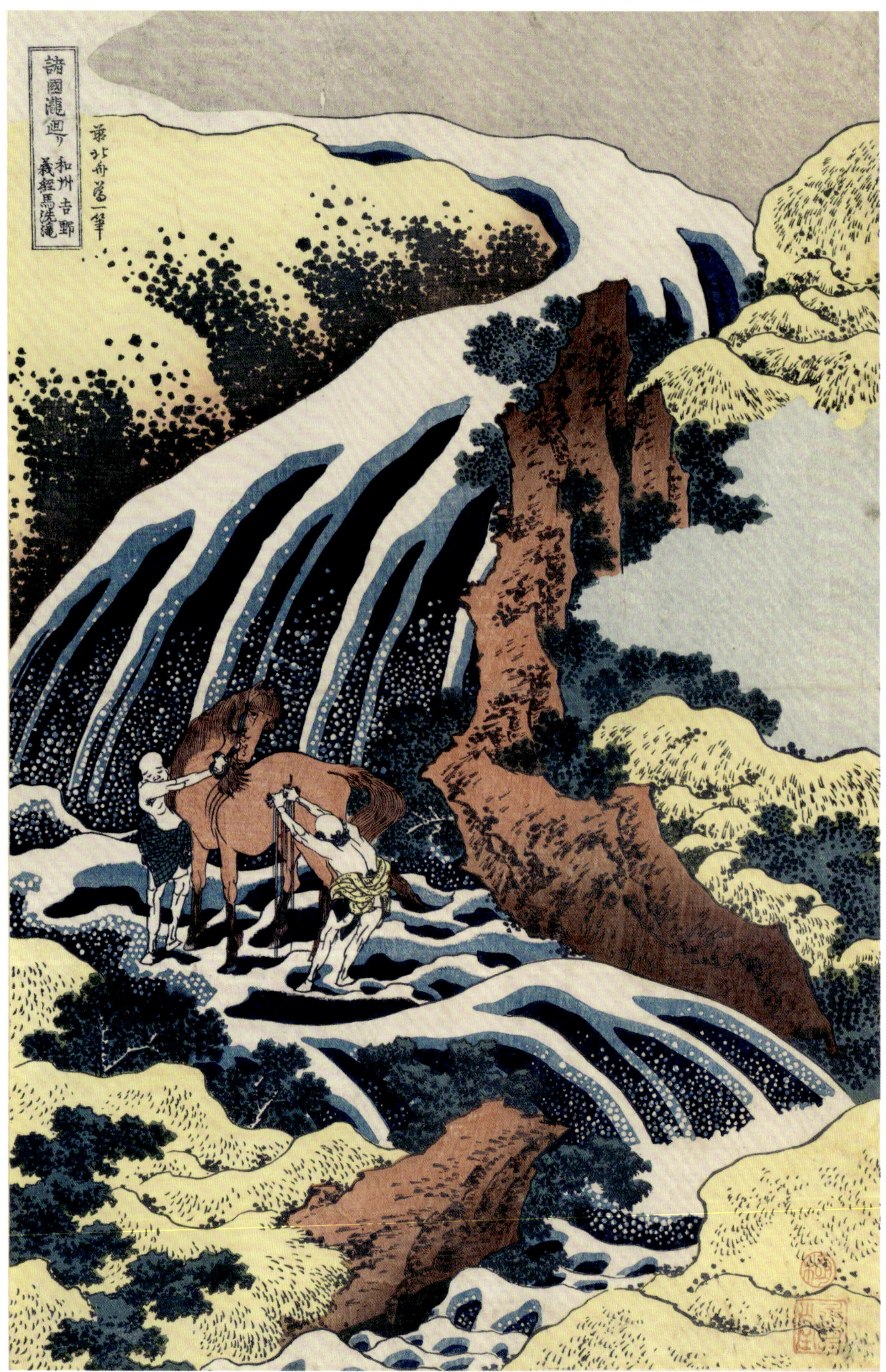

80
HOKUSAI
*Yoshitsune's Horse-
Washing Falls at Yoshino
in Yamato Province*,
about 1832.
Color woodblock print
37 x 24.5 cm
(14⅝ x 9⅝ in.)

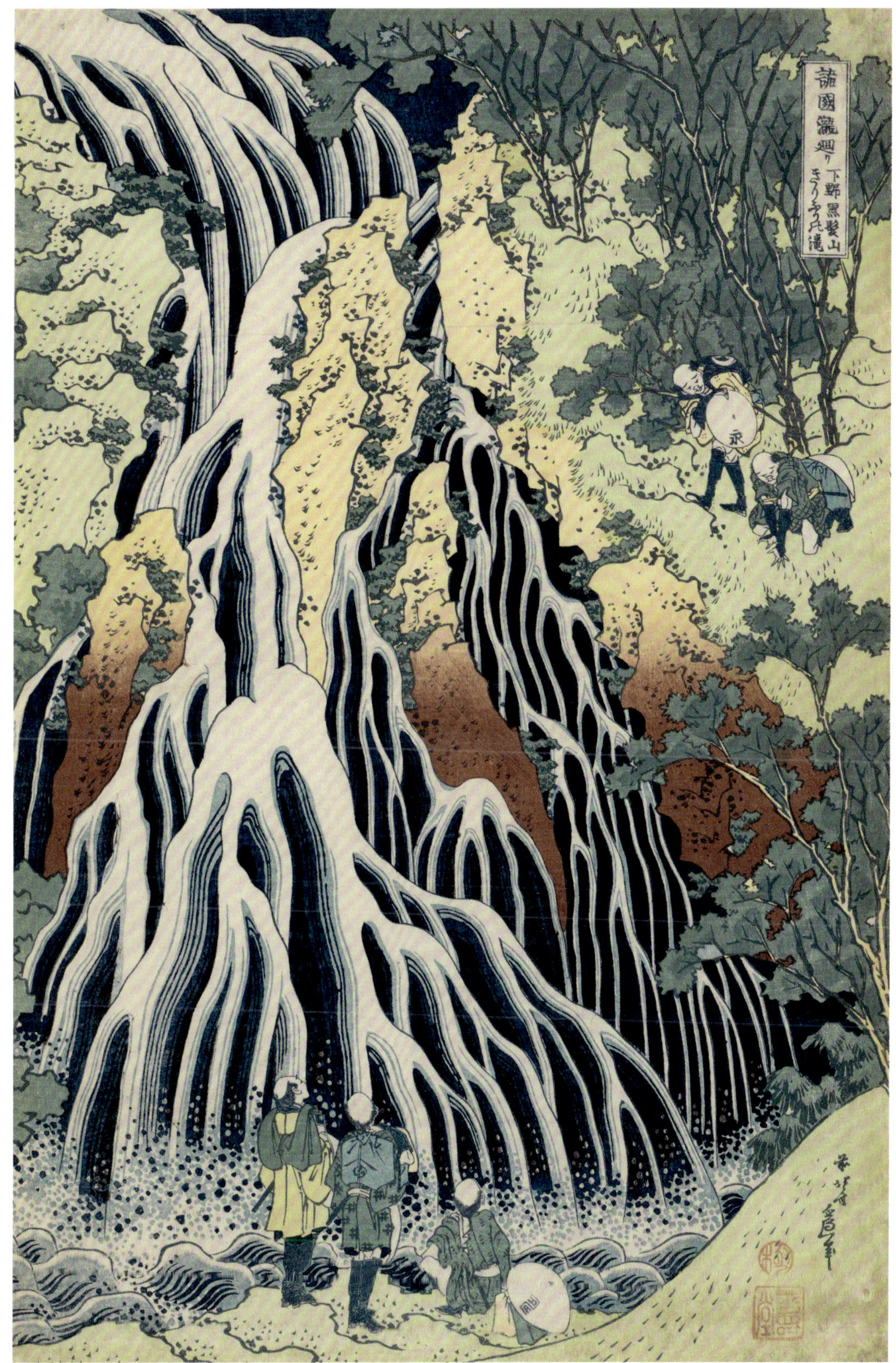

81

HOKUSAI
*Falling Mist Waterfall
at Mount Kurokami in
Shimotsuke Province*,
about 1832–33.
Color woodblock print
38 x 25.7 cm
(15 x 10⅛ in.)

The many contemporary works inspired by Hokusai's iconic Great Wave include not only prints, paintings, and digital images, but three-dimensional creations as well.

The California sculptor John Cederquist assembles carefully shaped pieces of wood into imaginative constructions, often based on functional furniture, and paints them with cartoon-like *trompe l'oeil* motifs that deliberately blur the distinction between two dimensions and three. His strong preference for imagery based on Hokusai's Wave may be related to his past experience as a surfer: while most people who encountered a gigantic wave in real life would find it terrifying, surfing aficionados would be drawn to the challenge of riding it. In this piece, five different waves seem to burst through the wooden surface of what is actually a usable chest of drawers. The title of the work is a humorous tribute to *How to Wrap Five Eggs*, a well-known book on traditional Japanese packaging first published in 1975 as the catalogue of an exhibition at the Japan Society in New York City, which made a splash in the American design world at the time.

Annabeth Rosen also creates large assemblages made up of smaller components, but in the medium of glazed ceramics. Her *Wave* plays on the nature of her chosen medium, with heavy, brittle ceramic components coming together in a graceful curve that suggests the fluidity of water (83). The grouping of many smaller forms implies a moving and even animated surface. Each of the small pieces wired together to form the massive wave has a power of its own, with vase-like shapes decorated in a cobalt-blue glaze that is not only appropriate to the water symbolism but also a reference to the artist's interest in the long history of blue-glazed wares, from Tang-dynasty China to the present day.

82

JOHN CEDERQUIST
How to Wrap Five Waves, 1994–95. Baltic birch plywood, poplar, maple, Sitka spruce, pine, epoxy resin inlay, oil-based lithography inks, metal hardware
188 x 124.5 x 35.6 cm (74 x 49 x 14 in.)

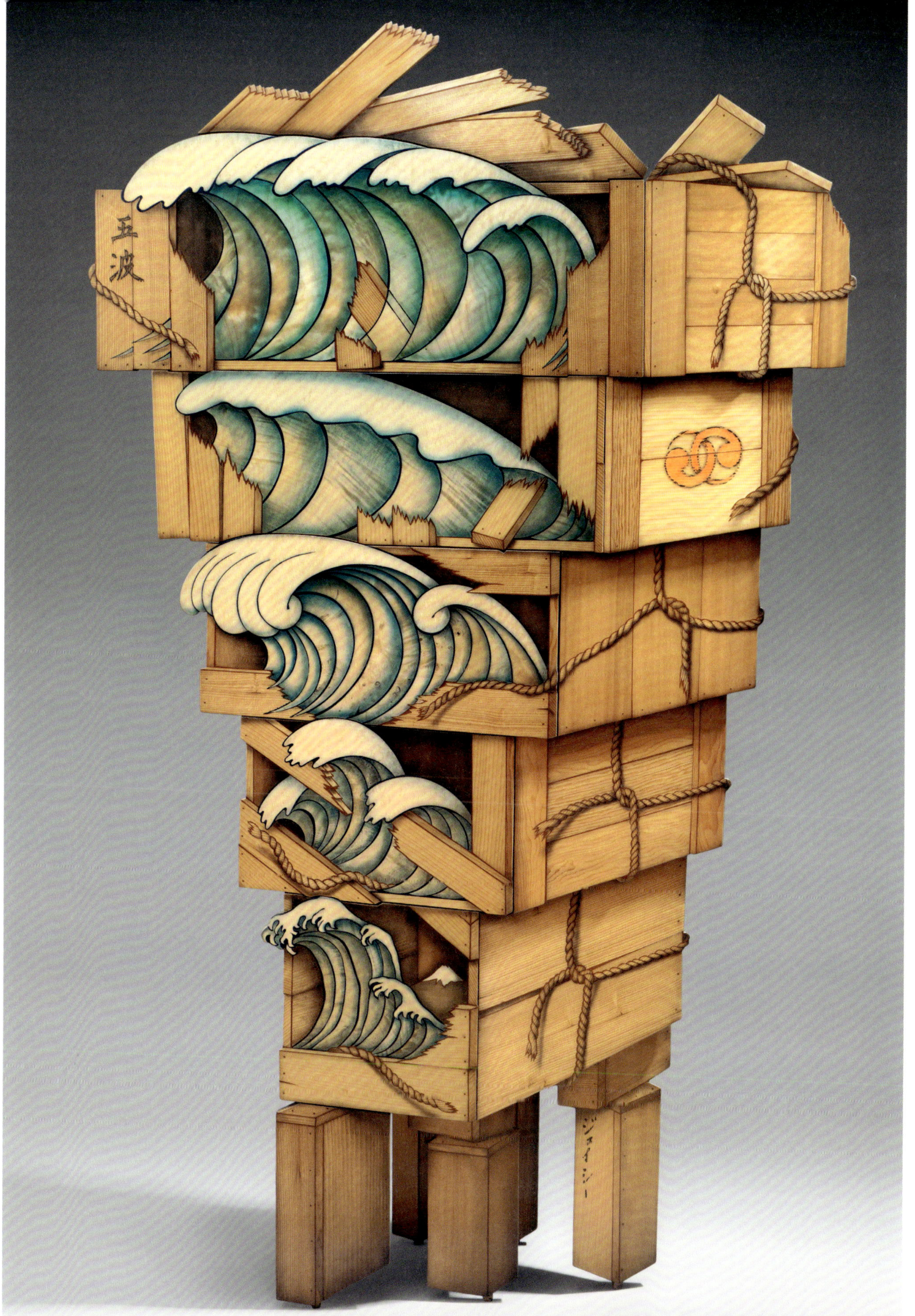

五波
ジョイシー

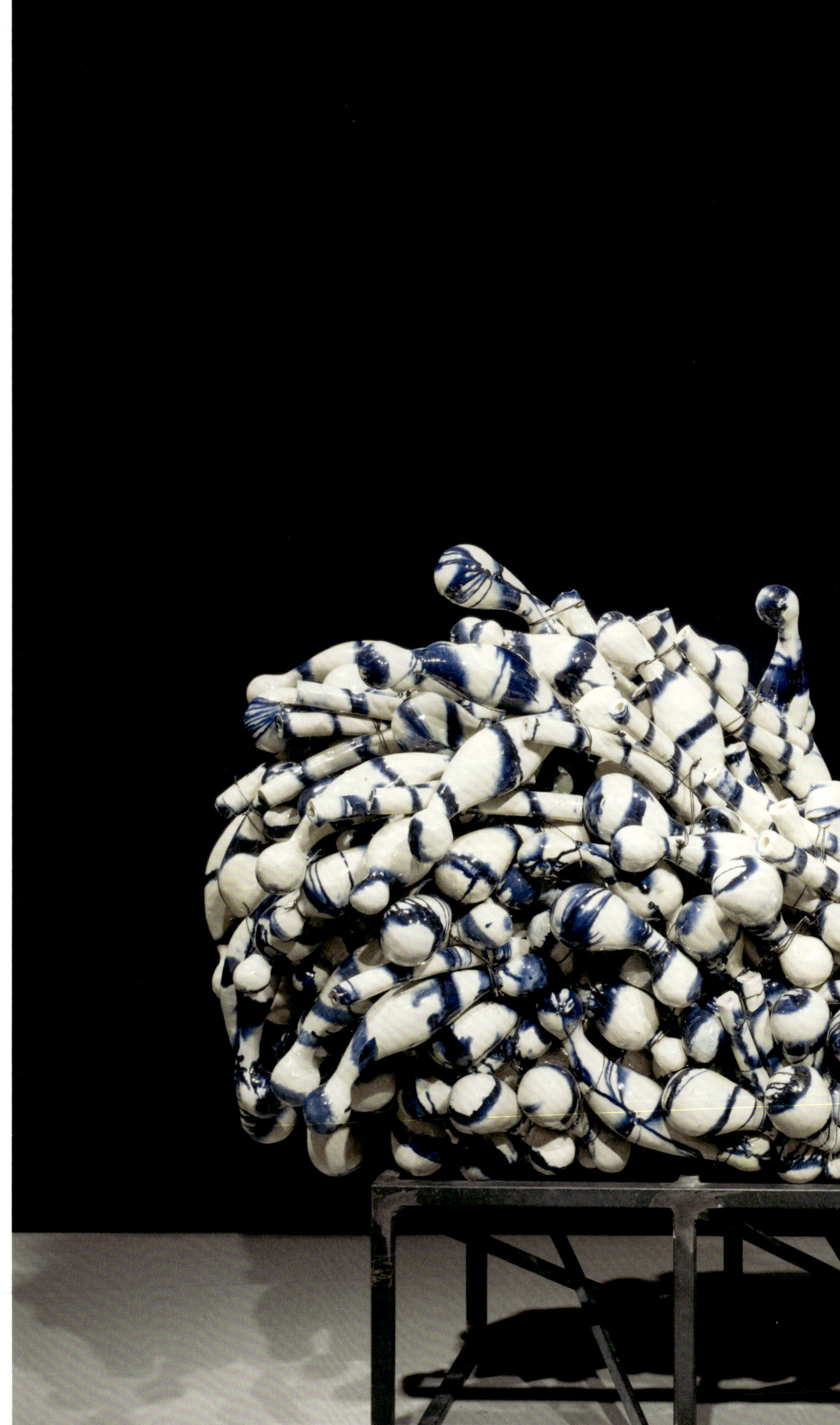

83

ANNABETH ROSEN
Wave, 2012.
Glazed earthenware,
steel wire, steel
183 x 208 x 86 cm
(72 x 82 x 34 in.)

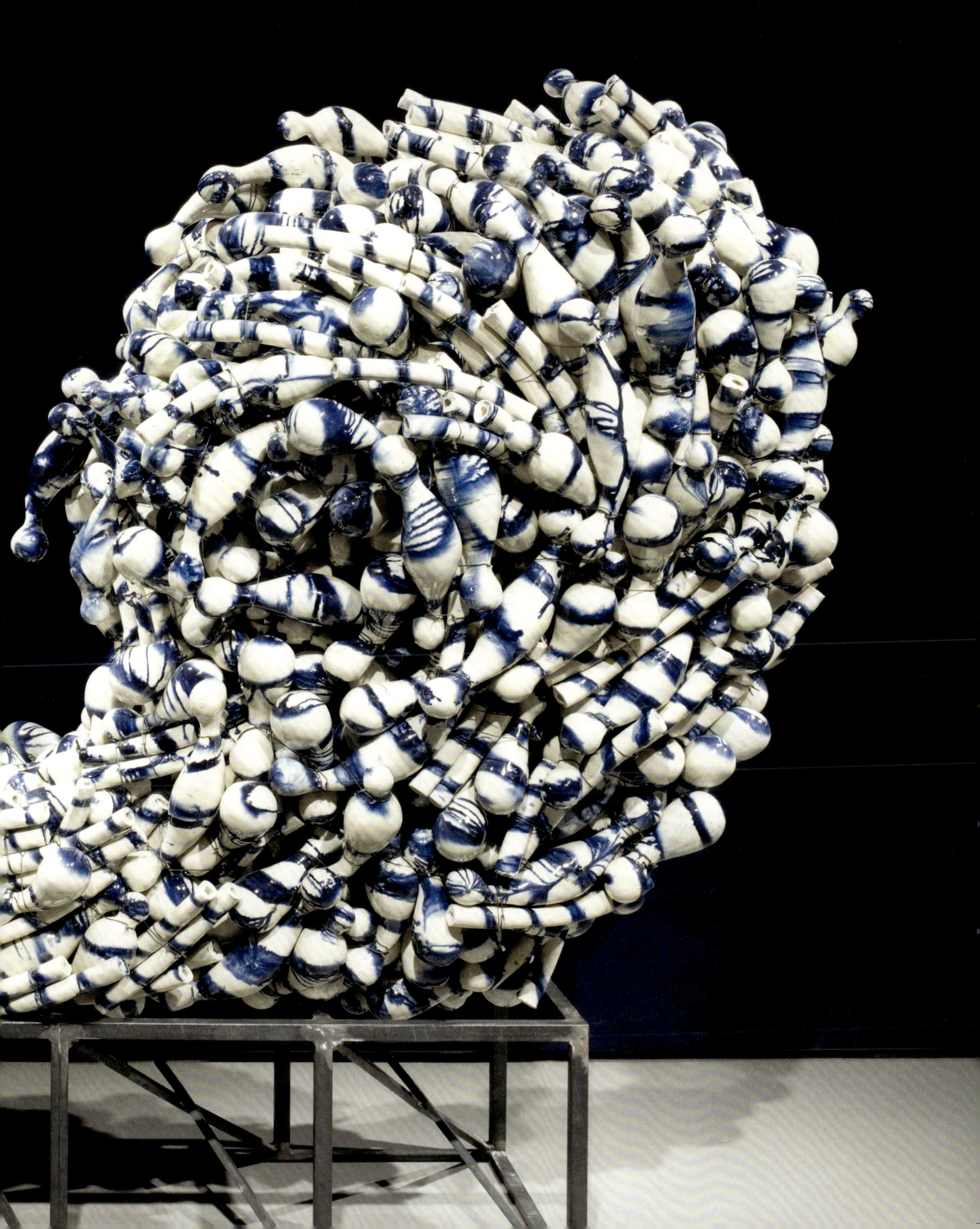

Bibliography

Asano Shūgō. "Hokusai in Old Age — His Ideas, His Way." In Clark, ed., *Hokusai: Beyond the Great Wave*, 40–47.

Barmé, Geremie. *An Artistic Exile: A Life of Feng Zikai (1898–1975)*. Berkeley: University of California Press, 2002.

Bouillon, Jean Paul, et al. *Art, industrie et japonisme: le service "Rousseau."* Exhibition catalogue, Musée d'Orsay. Paris: Éditions de la Réunion des musée nationaux, 1988.

Burnham, Helen, with Sarah E. Thompson and Jane E. Braun. *Looking East: Western Artists and the Allure of Japan*. Boston: MFA Publications, 2014.

Calza, Gian Carlo, ed. *Hokusai*. London: Phaidon, 2003.

———, with John T. Carpenter, eds. *Hokusai Paintings: Selected Essays*. Venice: International Hokusai Research Centre, 1994.

Carpenter, John T., ed. *Hokusai and His Age: Ukiyo-e Painting, Printmaking and Book Illustration in Late Edo Japan*. Amsterdam: Hotei Publishing, 2005.

Chiba City Museum of Art. *Japonisumu — Sekai o miryō shita ukiyo-e* (Ukiyo-e Viewed through Japonisme). Exhibition catalogue. Chiba: Chiba City Museum of Art, 2022.

Clark, Timothy, ed. *Hokusai: Beyond the Great Wave*. Exhibition catalogue, British Museum. London: Thames & Hudson, 2017.

———. *Hokusai: The Great Picture Book of Everything*. London: British Museum, 2021.

———. *Hokusai's Great Wave*. London: British Museum, 2011.

———. "Katsukawa Shunshō: Ukiyo-e Paintings for the Samurai Elite." In Meech and Oliver, eds., *Designed for Pleasure*, 100–113.

Coman, Sonia. "The Bracquemond-Rousseau Table Service of 1866." *Journal of Japonisme* 1, no. 1 (2016): 17–40.

Eidelberg, Martin. "Braquemond, Delatre and the Discovery of Japanese Prints." *The Burlington Magazine* 123, no. 937 (April 1981): 220–27.

Fenollosa, Ernest. *Hokusai and His School*. Exhibition catalogue, Museum of Fine Arts, Boston. Boston: Alfred Mudge & Son, 1893.

Forrer, Matthi, with texts by Edmond de Goncourt. *Hokusai*. New York: Rizzoli, 1988.

———. *Hokusai: Bridging East and West*. Exhibition catalogue. Nagano: Nagano Prefectural Shinano Art Museum, 1998.

———. *Hokusai: Prints and Drawings*. Exhibition catalogue, Royal Academy of Arts. Munich: Prestel, 1991.

Guth, Christine M. E. "Hokusai's Geometry." *Review of Japanese Culture and Society* 20 (December 2008): 120–32.

———. *Hokusai's Great Wave: Biography of a Global Icon*. Honolulu: University of Hawaii Press, 2015.

———. "Hokusai's Great Waves and the Maritime Turn in Japanese Visual Culture." *The Art Bulletin* 93, no. 4 (December 2011): 468–85.

Hillier, Jack. *The Art of Hokusai in Book Illustration*. Berkeley: University of California Press, 1980.

Iijima Kyoshin. *Katsushika Hokusai den* (A Biography of Katsushika Hokusai). First edition, Tokyo: Kobayashi Bunshichi, 1893. Unpublished English translation by Yasuhara Akio.

Itabashi Art Museum. *Hokusai ichimon nikuhitsuga kessaku sen — Hokusai DNA no yukue* (The Future of Hokusai's DNA: Selection of Hokusai School Hand-Drawn Masterpieces). Nihon bunka series no. 24 (Edo Culture Series No. 24). Tokyo: Itabashi Kuritsu Bijutsukan, 2008.

Ives, Colta Feller. *The Great Wave: The Influence of Japanese Woodcuts on French Prints*. New York: Metropolitan Museum of Art, 1974.

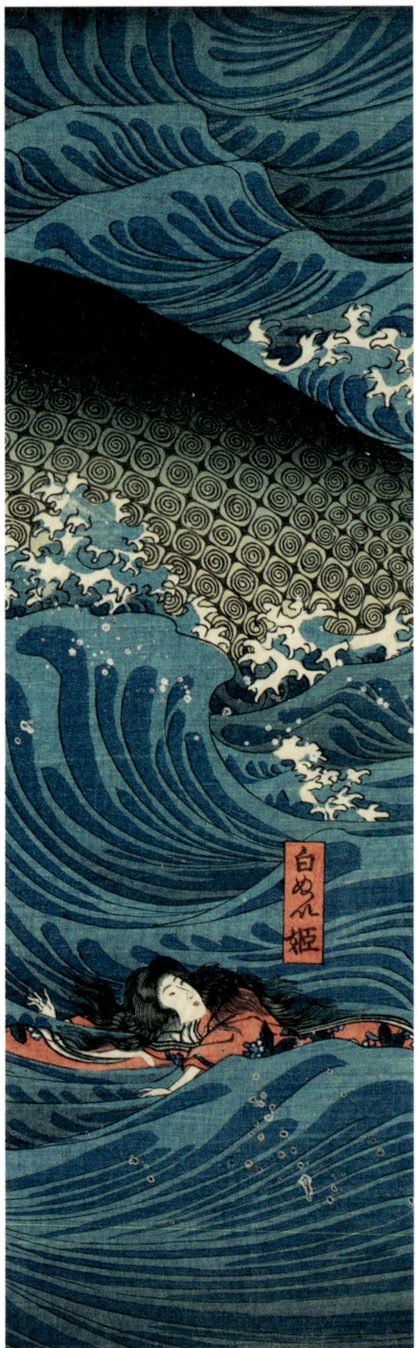

Jordan, Branda G., and Victoria Weston, eds. *Copying the Master and Stealing His Secrets: Talent and Training in Japanese Painting*. Honolulu: University of Hawaii Press, 2003.

Keyes, Roger. "'My Master Is Creation': Prints by Hokusai Sōri (1795–1798)." *Impressions* 20 (1998): 38–51.

Lambourne, Lionel. *Japonisme: Cultural Crossings between Japan and the West*. London: Phaidon, 2005.

Meech, Julia, and Gabriel P. Weisberg. *Japonisme Comes to America: The Japanese Impact on the Graphic Arts, 1876–1925*. New York: Abrams, 1990.

Meech, Julia, and Jane Oliver, eds. *Designed for Pleasure: The World of Edo Japan in Prints and Paintings, 1680–1860*. Exhibition catalogue, Asia Society and Japanese Art Society of America. Seattle: University of Washington Press, 2008.

Menegazzo, Rosella, ed. *Hokusai: The Master's Legacy*. Exhibition catalogue, Museo dell'Ara Pacis, Rome. Milan: Skira, 2018.

Miyao, Daisuke. *Japonisme and the Birth of Cinema*. Durham, NC: Duke University Press, 2020.

Morse, Anne Nishimura, et al. *Drama and Desire: Japanese Paintings from the Floating World, 1690–1850*. Exhibition catalogue. Boston: MFA Publications, 2006.

Morse, Peter. *Hokusai: One Hundred Poets*. New York: George Braziller, 1989.

Museum of Modern Art, Shiga. *Katsushika Hokusai ten: Konna ni tanoshii! Hokusai waarudo* (Katsushika Hokusai Exhibition: So Much Fun! The World of Hokusai). Exhibition catalogue. Shiga kenritsu kindai bijutsukan and Kyoto shinbunsha, 2008.

Nagata Seiji. "Hokusai's Artistic Career and Topics for Research." In Yonemura et al., *Hokusai*, 1–7.

———. *Hokusai: Genius of the Japanese Ukiyo-e*, translated by John Bester. Tokyo: Kodansha International, 1995.

———. "Katsushika-ha monjinroku (miteikō)/ List of Katsushika Pupils (Unfinished Manuscript)." *Ukiyo-e geijutsu/Ukiyo-e Art* 68 (1980): 3–32.

———, with Kobayashi Tadashi and Asano Shūgō. *Hokusai*. Exhibition catalogue, Tokyo National Museum. Tokyo: Nihon Keizai Shimbun, 2005.

———, Sarah E. Thompson, et al. *Hokusai from the Museum of Fine Arts, Boston*. Exhibition catalogue, Nagoya/Boston Museum of Fine Arts. Tokyo: Nihon Keizai Shimbun, 2013.

———, Iwakiri Yuriko, et al. *Shin Hokusai ten/ Hokusai Updated*. Exhibition catalogue, Mori Arts Center Gallery. Tokyo: Nikkei Inc., NHK, and NHK Promotions, 2019.

Smith, Henry D., II. "Hokusai and the Blue Revolution in Edo Prints." In Carpenter, ed., *Hokusai and His Age*, 234–61.

———. *Hokusai: One Hundred Views of Mount Fuji*. New York: George Braziller, 1988.

Spawski, Piotr. *Japonisme in Polish Pictorial Arts (1885–1939)*. PhD thesis, University of the Arts London, 2013.

Thompson, Sarah E. *Hokusai*. Boston: MFA Publications, 2015.

———. *Hokusai's Landscapes: The Complete Series*. Boston: MFA Publications, 2019.

———. *Hokusai's Lost Manga*. Boston: MFA Publications, 2016.

Tsuji Nobuo. *Bosuton bijutsukan nikuhitsu ukiyo-e* (Ukiyo-e Paintings, Museum of Fine Arts, Boston) III. Tokyo: Kodansha, 2000.

———. "The Impact of Western Book Illustrations on the Designs of Hokusai— The Key to His Originality." In Carpenter, ed., *Hokusai and His Age*, 340–51.

Tsurumi, Shunsuke. "Edo Period in Contemporary Popular Culture." *Modern Asian Studies* 18, no. 4 (1984): 747–55.

Watanabe, Toshio. *High Victorian Japonisme*. Volume 10 of *Schweizer Asiatische Studien: Studienhefte*. Bern: Peter Lang, 1991.

Weisberg, Gabriel P. *Japonisme: Japanese Influence on French Art 1854–1910*. Exhibition catalogue. Cleveland Museum of Art, Rutgers University Art Gallery and Walters Art Gallery, 1975.

Yonemura, Ann, et al. *Hokusai*. Exhibition catalogue. Washington, DC: Freer Gallery of Art and Arthur M. Sackler Gallery, Smithsonian Institution, 2006.

List of Illustrations

13

SAKAI HŌITSU (1761–1828)
After Ogata Kōrin (1658–1716)
Waves, from the picture book *Kōrin hyakuzu*
(*One Hundred Pictures by Kōrin*)
1826 (Bunsei 9)
Woodblock printed book; ink on paper
Overall: 26.1 x 18.2 cm (10¼ x 7⅛ in.)
Gift of the Estate of Henry Adams, 2022.1749.2

14

HOKUSAI
*Women Imitating the Story of Narihira
at Yatsuhashi*
Late 1790s
Woodblock print (surimono); ink and color
on paper
Ebangire; 19.2 x 51.9 cm (7½ x 20⅜ in.)
William Sturgis Bigelow Collection, 11.20161

15

HISHIKAWA SŌRI (active about 1789–1818)
Courtesan with Child Attendants
About 1798–1810s (Kansei 10–mid-Bunka era)
Hanging scroll; ink and color on silk
85.5 x 33.2 cm (33⅝ x 13⅛ in.)
William Sturgis Bigelow Collection, 11.7445

16

KATSUSHIKA ŌI (active about 1818–after 1854)
Three Women Playing Musical Instruments
1820s–1830s (Bunsei–Tenpō eras)
Hanging scroll; ink and color on silk
46.5 x 67.5 cm (18¼ x 26⅝ in.)
William Sturgis Bigelow Collection, 11.7689

17

ŌI
Types of Women, frontispiece to Takai Ranzan,
Onna chōhōki (*A Woman's Treasury*)
1847 (Kōka 4)
Publisher: Suharaya Mohei (Senshōbō)
Woodblock printed book; ink and color
on paper
25.3 x 17.9 cm (10 x 7 in.)
Gift of Mrs. Jared K. Morse in memory of
Charles J. Morse, 1997.425

18

Attributed to **MANJIRŌ HOKUGA**
How to Paint a Tiger, from an album of
color sketches
1856 (Ansei 3), 11th month
Ink and color on paper
32.4 × 23.9 cm (12¾ × 9⅜ in.)
William Sturgis Bigelow Collection, 11.46042

19

MANJIRŌ HOKUGA (died in 1856?)
Tiger in a Thunderstorm
Late 1840s–mid-1850s (Kōka–Ansei eras)
Hanging scroll; ink and color on flax
53.8 x 34.2 cm (21⅛ x 13½ in.)
William Sturgis Bigelow Collection, 11.7405

20

YANAGAWA SHIGENOBU I (1787–1832) and
SHUNKŌSAI HOKUSHŪ (active 1810–1832)
*Memorial Portrait of Actor Arashi Kitsusaburō I
(Rikan) as Yorimasa*
1821 (Bunsei 4), 9th month
Woodblock print; ink and color on paper
Vertical ōban; 37.7 x 26 cm (14⅞ x 10¼ in.)
William Sturgis Bigelow Collection, 11.25824

21

NUMATA GESSAI (1787–1864)
The Female Captain of the Boat
About 1818–30 (Bunsei era)
Hanging scroll; ink and color on silk
91.9 x 33 cm (36⅛ x 13 in.)
William Sturgis Bigelow Collection, 11.7340

22

HOKUSAI
Sumo Wrestlers Doing Chores, from *Hokusai
Sketchbooks*, vol. 9
1819 (Bunsei 2)
Publisher of this edition: Kadomaruya Jinsuke
(Shūseikaku)
Woodblock printed book; ink on paper
Each page: about 23.5 x 16 cm (9¼ x 6¼ in.)
Source unidentified, 1997.860

23

HOKUSAI
Deities of the Planets, from vol. 2 of an album
of drawings for a three-volume picture book,
possibly *The Great Picture Book of Everything*
1820s–40s
Ink on paper
Each page: 13.8 x 20.4 cm (5⅜ x 8 in.)
Source unidentified, 1998.670.1-3

24

HOKUSAI (and unidentified artists)
Decorative designs from an album of
miscellaneous sketches
1830s (Tenpō era)
Ink on paper
Each page: 33.2 × 24.2 cm (13⅛ × 9½ in.)
William Sturgis Bigelow Collection, 11.46044

25

HOKKEI
Painted Horse Escaping from Ema
1834 (Tenpō 5)
Woodblock print (surimono); ink and color
on paper
Shikishiban; 20.3 x 18.1 cm (8 x 7⅛ in.)
William Sturgis Bigelow Collection, 11.25469

26

TOTOYA HOKKEI (1780–1850)
The Hall of Immortality
1831 (Tenpō 2)
Woodblock print (surimono); ink and color
on paper
Shikishiban, upright diptych; 42.6 x 18 cm
(16¾ x 7⅛ in.)
William Sturgis Bigelow Collection, 11.19634

27

HOKUSAI
*Komagata-dō Temple, Onmaya Embankment,
and the Hitching Stone* (right to left), from the
series *A Set of Horses*
1822 (Bunsei 5)
Woodblock print (surimono); ink and color
on paper

Shikishiban triptych; 21 x 55.1 cm
(8¼ x 21¾ in.)
Museum of Fine Arts, Boston — Worcester Art
Museum exchange, made possible through
the Special Korean Pottery Fund, Museum
purchase with funds donated by contribution,
and Smithsonian Institution — Chinese
Expedition, 1923–24, 54.259-61

28
HOKKEI
Mount Fuji, from an untitled series of
Three Lucky Dreams
1820s (Bunsei era)
Woodblock print (surimono); ink and color
on paper
Shikishiban; 20.8 x 18.7 cm (8¼ x 7⅜ in.)
Gift of Dr. G. S. Amsden, 52.1406

29
SHŌTEI HOKUJU (1763–1824)
True Depiction of the Fuji River, from the series
The Tōkaidō Road
About 1804–24 (Bunka 1–Bunsei 7)
Publisher: Yamamotoya Heikichi (Eikyūdō)
Woodblock print; ink and color on paper
Horizontal ōban; 23.3 x 36 cm (9⅛ x 14⅛ in.)
Denman Waldo Ross Collection, 06.1359

30
HOKUSAI
Fine Wind, Clear Weather, also known as
"Red Fuji," from the series *Thirty-Six Views of
Mount Fuji*
About 1830–31 (Tenpō 1–2)
Publisher: Nishimuraya Yohachi (Eijudō)
Woodblock print; ink and color on paper
Horizontal ōban; 23.9 x 36.5 cm (9⅜ x 14⅜ in.)
Nellie Parney Carter Collection — Bequest of
Nellie Parney Carter, 34.314

31
UTAGAWA HIROSHIGE I (1797–1858)
Kanbara: Night Snow, from the series
Fifty-Three Stations of the Tōkaidō Road,
also known as the "First Tōkaidō" or
"Great Tōkaidō"
About 1833–34 (Tenpō 4–5)
Publisher: Takenouchi Magohachi (Hoeidō)
Woodblock print; ink and color on paper
Horizontal ōban; 24 x 36 cm (9½ x 14⅛ in.)
William Sturgis Bigelow Collection, 11.25156

32
HOKUSAI
Ejiri in Suruga Province, from the series
Thirty-Six Views of Mount Fuji
About 1830–31 (Tenpō 1–2)
Publisher: Nishimuraya Yohachi (Eijudō)
Woodblock print; ink and color on paper
Horizontal ōban; 25 x 37.7 cm (9⅞ x 14⅞ in.)
William Sturgis Bigelow Collection, 11.17662

33
HIROSHIGE
Yokkaichi: Mie River, from the series *Fifty-Three
Stations of the Tōkaidō Road*, also known as
the "First Tōkaidō" or "Great Tōkaidō"
About 1833–34 (Tenpō 4–5)
Publisher: Takenouchi Magohachi (Hoeidō)
Woodblock print; ink and color on paper
Horizontal ōban; 22 x 34.6 cm (8⅝ x 13⅝ in.)
Source unidentified, 2009.2411.44

34
HOKUSAI
Under the Wave off Kanagawa, also known as
"The Great Wave," from the series *Thirty-Six
Views of Mount Fuji*
About 1830–31 (Tenpō 1–2)
Publisher: Nishimuraya Yohachi (Eijudō)
Woodblock print; ink and color on paper
Horizontal ōban; 25.2 x 37.7 cm (9⅞ x 14⅞ in.)
William Sturgis Bigelow Collection, 11.17652

35
HIROSHIGE
The Sea off Satta in Suruga Province, from the
series *Thirty-Six Views of Mount Fuji*
1858 (Ansei 5), 4th month
Publisher: Tsutaya Kichizō (Kōeidō)
Woodblock print; ink and color on paper
Vertical ōban; 35.8 × 24.7 cm (14⅛ × 9¾ in.)
William Sturgis Bigelow Collection, 11.39213

36
HOKUSAI
Fuji at Sea, from vol. 2 of the picture book
Fugaku hyakkei (*One Hundred Views of
Mount Fuji*)
1835 (Tenpō 6)
Publisher: Eirakuya Tōshirō (Tōhekidō)
Woodblock printed book; ink and color
on paper
Each page: 22.6 x 15.7 cm (8⅞ x 6⅛ in.)
Source unidentified, 1997.816.1-3

37
HOKUSAI
Fuji View Plain in Owari Province, from the
series *Thirty-Six Views of Mount Fuji*
About 1830–31 (Tenpō 1–2)
Publisher: Nishimuraya Yohachi (Eijudō)
Woodblock print; ink and color on paper
Horizontal ōban; 25.2 x 37.7 cm (9⅞ x 14⅞ in.)
William Sturgis Bigelow Collection, 11.17649

38
HIROSHIGE
*Barrel-Maker; Copied from a Picture by Old
Master Katsushika*
1836 (Tenpō 7)
Publisher: Tsujiya Yasube
Woodblock print; ink and color on paper
Uchiwa-e on horizontal aiban sheet;
21.1 x 28.2 cm (8¼ x 11⅛ in.)
William S. and John T. Spaulding Collection,
21.10102

39
HIROSHIGE
Plum Estate, Kameido, from the series
One Hundred Famous Views of Edo
1857 (Ansei 4), 11th month
Publisher: Uoya Eikichi
Woodblock print; ink and color on paper
Vertical ōban; 37 x 25.7 cm (14⅝ x 10⅛ in.)
William Sturgis Bigelow Collection, 11.45649

40
HOKUSAI
The Care-of-the-Aged Falls in Mino Province,
from the series *A Tour of Waterfalls in Various
Provinces*
About 1832 (Tenpō 3)
Publisher: Nishimuraya Yohachi (Eijudō)
Woodblock print; ink and color on paper
Vertical ōban; 36.7 x 24.3 cm (14½ x 9⅝ in.)
William Sturgis Bigelow Collection, 11.25226

41
KEISAI EISEN (1790–1848)
*Backward-Viewing Falls, One of the Three
Waterfalls*, from the series *Famous Scenic
Spots in the Mountains of Nikkō*
1843–47 (Tenpō 14–Kōka 4)
Publisher: Yamamotoya Heikichi (Eikyūdō)
Woodblock print; ink and color on paper
Vertical ōban; 35.5 x 24.4 cm (14 x 9⅝ in.)
William Sturgis Bigelow Collection, 11.23156

42
HOKUSAI
Peonies and Butterfly, from an untitled series
known as "Large Flowers"
About 1833–34 (Tenpō 4–5)
Publisher: Nishimuraya Yohachi (Eijudō)
Woodblock print; ink and color on paper
Horizontal ōban; 26.3 x 39 cm (10³⁄₈ x 15³⁄₈ in.)
William Sturgis Bigelow Collection, 11.17593

43
HIROSHIGE
Hibiscus
1843–47 (Tenpō 14–Kōka 4)
Woodblock print; ink and color on paper
Chūtanzaku; 33.5 x 11.3 cm (13¼ x 4½ in.)
William Sturgis Bigelow Collection, 11.21131

44
HIROSHIGE
Mallard Ducks and Snow-Covered Reeds
About 1836 (Tenpō 7)
Publisher: Sanoya Kihei (Kikakudō)
Woodblock print; ink and color on paper
Ōtanzaku; 37.6 x 17.2 cm (14¾ x 6¾ in.)
Denman Waldo Ross Collection, 11.2140

45
HOKUSAI
Illustrations from Kyokutei Bakin, *Shinpen
suiko gaden (An Illustrated New Edition of
"The Water Margin")*
Reprint, after 1838; 1st edition 1805–7
(Bunka 2–4)
Publishers: Kawachiya Mohei (Gungyokudō) et al.
Woodblock printed book; ink on paper
Each page: 22.3 x 15.5 cm (8¾ x 6⅛ in.)
Source unidentified, 1997.691.1-10

46
UTAGAWA KUNIYOSHI (1797–1861)
*Huang Xin, Guardian of Three Mountains,
from the series One Hundred and Eight Heroes
of the Popular Shuihuzhuan*
About 1827–30 (Bunsei 10–Tenpō 1)
Publisher: Kagaya Kichiemon (Kichibei)
Woodblock print; ink and color on paper
Vertical ōban; 36.3 x 25.3 cm (14¼ x 10 in.)
Bequest of Maxim Karolik, 64.808

47
KUNIYOSHI
Saginoike Heikurō, from the series *Eight
Hundred Heroes of the Japanese Shuihuzhuan*
About 1834–35 (Tenpō 4–5)
Woodblock print; ink and color on paper
Publisher: Kagaya Kichiemon (Kichibei)
Vertical ōban; 36.3 x 25.3 cm (14¼ x 10 in.)
Bequest of Maxim Karolik, 64.850

48
HOKUSAI
*Watanabe no Gengo Tsuna and Inokuma
Nyūdō Raiun*, from an untitled series of
warriors in combat
About 1833–35 (Tenpō 4–6)
Publisher: Yamamotoya Heikichi (Eikyūdō)
Woodblock print; ink and color on paper
Vertical ōban; 37.4 x 26.5 cm (14¾ x 10⅜ in.)
William Sturgis Bigelow Collection, 11.17552

49
KUNIYOSHI
Hokusai and Bakin, with historical figures;
illustration from Hanaga Bunkyō, *Nihon kijin
den (Extraordinary Persons of Japan)*
1845 (Kōka 2)
Publishers: Katsumura Jiemon et al.
Woodblock printed book; ink on paper
Overall: 22.6 x 14.2 cm (8⅞ x 5⅝ in.)
Source unidentified, 1997.957

50
HOKUSAI
Tametomo's Shipwreck; illustrations
from Bakin, *Chinsetsu yumiharizuki
(The Crescent Moon Bow)*
1807–8 (Bunka 4–5)
Woodblock printed book; ink on paper
22.9 x 16.1 cm (9 x 6⅜ in.)
Source unidentified, 2011.1589.1-17

51
KUNIYOSHI
*On the Sea at Mizumata in Hogo Province,
Tametomo Encounters a Storm*
About 1836 (Tenpō 7)
Publisher: Fujiokaya Hikotarō (Shōgendō)
Woodblock print; ink and color on paper
Vertical ōban triptych; 36.7 x 72.9 cm
(14½ x 28¾ in.)
William Sturgis Bigelow Collection, 11.16461a-c

52
KUNIYOSHI
*The Former Emperor [Sutoku] from Sanuki
Sends His Retainers to Rescue Tametomo*
About 1851–52 (Kaei 4–5)
Publisher: Sumiyoshiya Masagorō
Woodblock print; ink and color on paper
Vertical ōban triptych; 36 x 76 cm
(14⅛ x 29⅞ in.)
William Sturgis Bigelow Collection,
11.26999-7001

53
HOKUSAI
Fish, from *Hokusai Sketchbooks*, vol. 2
Undated later edition; 1st edition 1815
(Bunka 12)
Publisher: Eirakuya Tōshirō (Tōhekidō)
Woodblock printed book; ink on paper
22.6 x 15.6 cm (8⅞ x 6⅛ in.)
Source unidentified, 1997.837

54
FÉLIX BRACQUEMOND (French, 1833–1914)
Fish Patterns for the Rousseau Service, 1866
Etching
Sheet: 53 × 33 cm (20⅞ × 13 in.)
Lee M. Friedman Fund, 1993.100

55
Plate from the Rousseau Service, 1876–84
(first edition, 1866–75)
Designed by **FÉLIX BRACQUEMOND**
Made for François-Eugène Rousseau
(French, 1827–1891)
Made by Barulet et Cie (France)
Glazed earthenware with colored enamels
Diameter: 25 cm (9⅞ in.)
H. E. Bolles Fund, 2021.1064

56
Inkstand, 1876
After **PAUL LEGRAND** (French, 1840–1910)
Possibly made by Crossville and Glachant
(Paris, founded in 1861)
Silver, partial gilt, champlevé, basse-taille,
cloisonné enamels
23.4 x 33.6 cm (9¼ x 13¼ in.)
Museum purchase with funds bequeathed by
Genevieve Gray Young in memory of Patience
Young and Patience Gray Young, Frederick
Brown Fund, William E. Nickerson Fund, Otis

Norcross Fund, Arthur Tracy Cabot Fund, H. E.
Bolles Fund, Russell B. and Andrée Beauchamp
Stearns Fund, Ernest Kahn Fund, Helen B.
Sweeney Fund, and European Decorative Arts
Insurance, Deaccession and Deaccession
Income Funds, 2000.977-1-7

57

HOKUSAI
Senju in Musashi Province, from the series
Thirty-Six Views of Mount Fuji
About 1830–31 (Tenpō 1–2)
Publisher: Nishimuraya Yohachi (Eijudō)
Woodblock print; ink and color on paper
Horizontal ōban; 24.5 x 37.3 cm (9⅝ x 14⅝ in.)
Nellie Parney Carter Collection — Bequest of
Nellie Parney Carter, 34.310

58

HOKUSAI
Under Mannen Bridge at Fukagawa, from the
series *Thirty-Six Views of Mount Fuji*
About 1830–31 (Tenpō 1–2)
Publisher: Nishimuraya Yohachi (Eijudō)
Woodblock print; ink and color on paper
Horizontal ōban; 26.2 x 38.7 cm
(10⅜ x 15¼ in.)
William Sturgis Bigelow Collection, 11.17650

59

HIROSHIGE
Bamboo Yards, Kyōbashi Bridge, from the
series *One Hundred Famous Views of Edo*
1857 (Ansei 4), 12th month
Publisher: Uoya Eikichi
Woodblock print; ink and color on paper
Vertical ōban; 36.2 x 23.7 cm (14¼ x 9⅜ in.)
Gift of Dr. G. S. Amsden, 52.1424

60

JAMES ABBOTT MCNEILL WHISTLER
(American, active in England, 1834–1903)
Old Battersea Bridge, 1879
Etching
Sheet: 25.9 x 40.5 cm (10¼ x 16 in.)
Gift of Mrs. Walter Scott Fitz, M21275

61

TOBARI KOGAN (1882–1927)
The Great Bridge at Senju
1913 (Taishō 2)
Woodblock print; ink and color on paper
48.8 x 35.8 cm (19¼ x 14⅛ in.)
Gift of Paul Bernat, 54.1796

62

HOKUSAI
Nihonbashi Bridge in Edo, from the series
Thirty-Six Views of Mount Fuji
About 1830–31 (Tenpō 1–2)
Publisher: Nishimuraya Yohachi (Eijudō)
Woodblock print; ink and color on paper
Horizontal ōban; 25.9 x 38.3 cm (10⅛ x 15 in.)
William Sturgis Bigelow Collection, 11.17518

63

ÉDOUARD VUILLARD (French, 1868–1940)
The Avenue, from *Paysages et intérieurs: Douze
lithographies en couleurs*, 1899
Publisher: Ambroise Vollard (French, 1867–
1939)
Color lithograph on china paper
Sheet: 33.4 x 45 cm (13⅛ x 17⅝ in.)
Bequest of W. G. Russell Allen, 60.107

64

HENRI RIVIÈRE (French, 1864–1951)
The Eiffel Tower in Winter, from *Thirty-Six Views
of the Eiffel Tower*, 1902
Bound volume with 36 color lithographs
Sheet: 22.5 × 27 cm (8⅞ × 10⅝ in.); mounted:
23.5 × 29.2 cm (9¼ × 11½ in.)
Charles Amos Cummings Fund, 2021.1045
© 2022 Artist Rights Society (ARS), New York/
ADAGP, Paris

65

HOKUSAI
Ushibori in Hitachi Province, from the series
Thirty-Six Views of Mount Fuji
About 1830–31 (Tenpō 1–2)
Publisher: Nishimuraya Yohachi (Eijudō)
Woodblock print; ink and color on paper
Horizontal ōban; 25.2 x 37.4 cm (9⅞ x 14¾ in.)
Gift of C. Adrian Rübel, 46.1405

66

ARTHUR WESLEY DOW (American, 1857–1922)
Dory, about 1904
Photograph, cyanotype
Sheet: 16.2 x 21.5 cm (6⅜ x 8⅜ in.)
A. Shuman Collection — Abraham Shuman
Fund, 1983.187

67

ARTHUR WESLEY DOW
View of Ipswich, 1895
Color woodcut
12.7 x 5.9 cm (5 x 2⅜ in.)
Gift of Mrs. Ethelyn H. Putnam, 41.710

68

WINSLOW HOMER (American, 1836–1910)
Breaking Wave (Prout's Neck), 1887
Watercolor over graphite pencil on paper
Sheet: 38.7 x 54.6 cm (15¼ x 21½ in.)
William Sturgis Bigelow Collection, 26.788

69

HENRI GUSTAVE JOSSOT (French, 1866–1951)
The Wave, 1894
Lithograph
Sheet: 60.5 × 42.7 cm (23⅞ × 16¾ in.)
Irving W. and Charlotte F. Rabb Fund for the
Acquisition of Prints and Drawings, 2019.772

70

GISBERT COMBAZ (Belgian, 1869–1941)
A Boat in the Waves, from the series
The Sea (La Mer), 1899
Publisher: Dietrich et Cie.
Postcard; color lithograph on card stock
Overall: 8.9 x 14 cm (3½ x 5½ in.)
Leonard A. Lauder Postcard Archive —
Gift of Leonard A. Lauder, 2012.6920.4

71

HOKUSAI
Kingfisher with Iris and Wild Pinks, from an
untitled series known as "Small Flowers"
About 1834 (Tenpō 5)
Publisher: Nishimuraya Yohachi (Eijudō)
Woodblock print; ink and color on paper
Vertical chūban; 24.1 x 18.8 cm (9½ x 7⅜ in.)
William Sturgis Bigelow Collection, 11.21696

72

Vase, 1886–1902
Painted by **SAMUEL WILSON**
(English, active about 1880–1909)
Made by Doulton Manufactory
(England, established 1815)
Glazed earthenware
45.7 x 20.3 cm (18 x 8 in.)
Gift of Madeleine O'Mara in memory of Rosa
Dupius and Henry J. Robert, 2015.2921

73
Punch bowl and ladle, 1885
Made by Gorham Manufacturing Company
(United States, active 1865–1961)
Silver, gilding
Bowl: 25.7 x 38.7 x 17.8 x 23.5 cm
(10⅛ x 15¼ x 7 x 9¼ in.)
Edwin E. Jack Fund, 1980.383

74
HOKUSAI
Two Carp in Waterfall
About 1834 (Tenpō 5)
Woodblock print; ink and color on paper
Vertical nagaban; 52 x 23.7 cm (20½ x 9⅜ in.)
William Sturgis Bigelow Collection, 11.19647

75
HOKKEI
Carp and Seaweed
Late 1810s
Woodblock print (surimono); ink, color, and
metallic pigment on paper
Shikishiban; 20.5 x 18.2 cm (8⅛ x 7⅛ in.)
William Sturgis Bigelow Collection, 11.20596

76
HOKUSAI
The Ghost of Kohada Koheiji, from the series
One Hundred Ghost Stories
About 1831–32 (Tenpō 2–3)
Publisher: Tsuruya Kiemon (Senkakudō)
Woodblock print; ink and color on paper
Vertical chūban; 26.5 x 19 cm (10⅜ x 7½ in.)
William Sturgis Bigelow Collection, 11.20438

77
HOKUSAI
The Ghost of Oiwa, from the series
One Hundred Ghost Stories
About 1831–32 (Tenpō 2–3)
Publisher: Tsuruya Kiemon (Senkakudō)
Woodblock print; ink and color on paper
Vertical chūban; 25.8 x 18.9 cm (10⅛ x 7½ in.)
William Sturgis Bigelow Collection, 11.20457

78
ODILON REDON (French, 1840–1916)
"The misshapen polyp floated on the shores,
a sort of smiling and hideous Cyclops";
plate 3 from the set *The Origins*, 1883
Lithograph
Sheet: 32.2 x 26.5 cm (12¾ x 10⅜ in.)
Lee M. Friedman Fund, 67.276

79
LOÏS MAILOU JONES (American, 1905–1998)
Japanese Waterfall, 1925
Opaque watercolor on board
Sheet (irregular): 51 x 48 cm (20⅛ x 18⅞ in.)
Gift of the Loïs Mailou Jones Pierre-Noël Trust,
2005.342
© Loïs Mailou Jones Pierre-Noël Trust

80
HOKUSAI
*Yoshitsune's Horse-Washing Falls at Yoshino
in Yamato Province*, from the series *A Tour of
Waterfalls in Various Provinces*
About 1832 (Tenpō 3)
Publisher: Nishimuraya Yohachi (Eijudō)
Woodblock print; ink and color on paper
Vertical ōban; 37 x 24.5 cm (14⅝ x 9⅝ in.)
William Sturgis Bigelow Collection, 11.25224

81
HOKUSAI
*Falling Mist Waterfall at Mount Kurokami in
Shimotsuke Province*, from the series
A Tour of Waterfalls in Various Provinces
About 1832 (Tenpō 3)
Woodblock print; ink and color on paper
Vertical ōban; 38 x 25.7 cm (15 x 10⅛ in.)
William Sturgis Bigelow Collection, 11.19718

82
JOHN CEDERQUIST (American, born in 1946)
How to Wrap Five Waves, 1994–95
Baltic birch plywood, poplar, maple, Sitka
spruce, pine, epoxy resin inlay, oil-based
lithography inks, metal hardware
188 x 124.5 x 35.6 cm (74 x 49 x 14 in.)
The Daphne Farago Collection, 2017.4774
Reproduced with permission

83
ANNABETH ROSEN (American, born in 1957)
Wave, 2012
Glazed earthenware, steel wire, steel
183 x 208 x 86 cm (72 x 82 x 34 in.)
Museum purchase with funds donated by
Martin and Deborah Hale, 2013.1469
© Annabeth Rosen

List of Artists

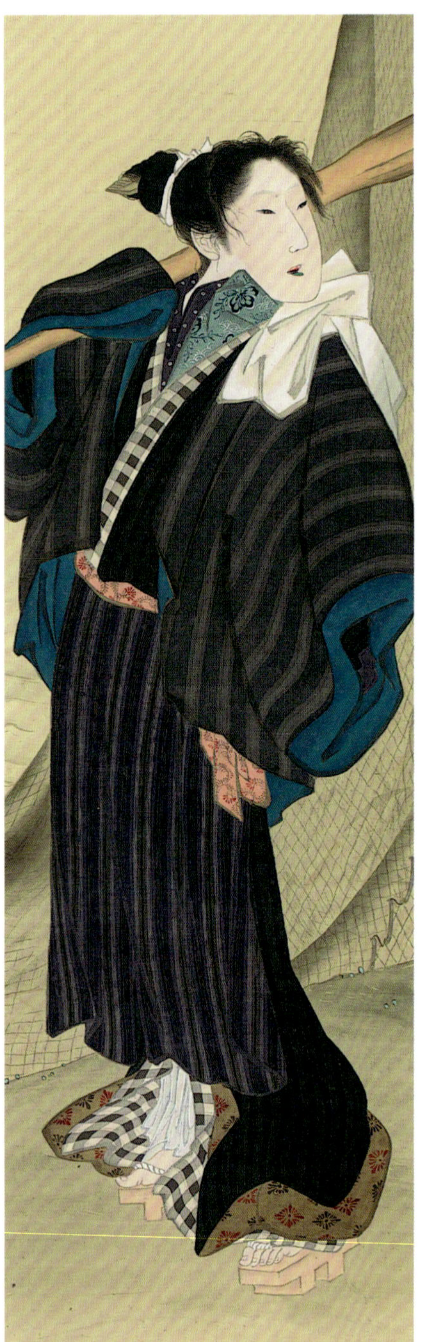

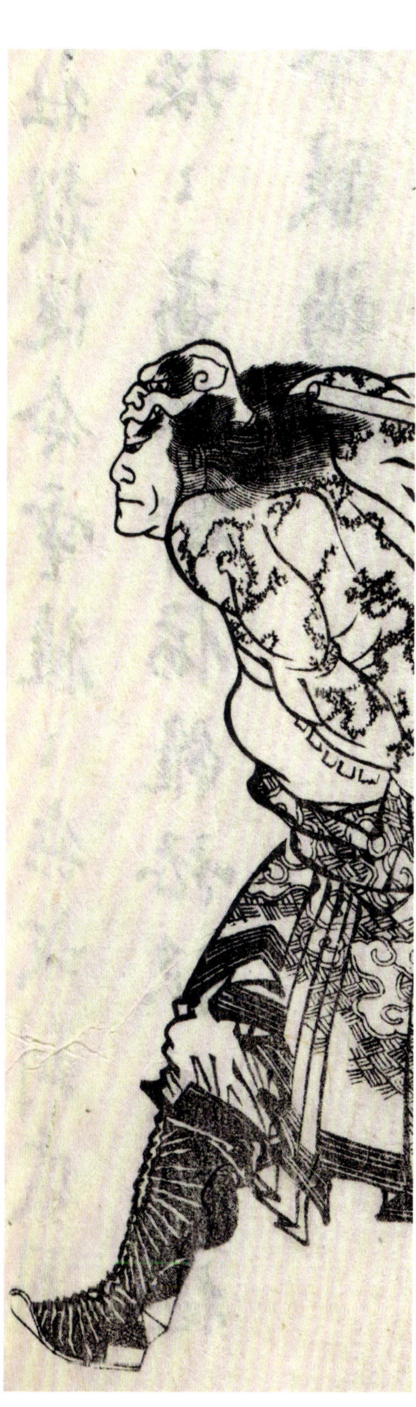

MFABoston

MFA Publications
Museum of Fine Arts, Boston
465 Huntington Avenue
Boston, Massachusetts 02115
www.mfa.org/publications

Published in conjunction with the exhibition
Hokusai: Inspiration and Influence,
organized by the Museum of Fine Arts, Boston,
from March 26 to July 16, 2023

Exhibition sponsored by UNIQLO USA, LLC

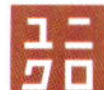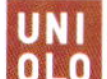

Additional support from the Jean S. and
Frederic A. Sharf Exhibition Fund, the Museum
Council Artist in Residency Program Fund, the
Dr. Terry Satsuki Milhaupt Fund for Japanese
Textiles, the MFA Associates/MFA Senior
Associates Exhibition Endowment Fund,
and the Patricia B. Jacoby Exhibition Fund

Generous support for this publication provided
by the Andrew W. Mellon Publications Fund

For a complete listing of MFA publications,
please contact the publisher at the above
address, or call 617 369 4233.

Illustrations in this book were photographed
by the Imaging Studios, Museum of Fine Arts,
Boston, except where otherwise noted.

Edited by Jennifer Snodgrass
Proofread by Kathryn Blatt
Designed by Susan Marsh
Production by Hope Stockton
Typeset in Meta Pro with Didot LT and Filosofia
by Matt Mayerchak
Printed on 150 gsm Gardapat Bianka
Printed and bound at Graphicom, Verona, Italy

Distributed by
ARTBOOK | D.A.P.
75 Broad Street, Suite 630
New York, New York 10004
www.artbook.com

SECOND EDITION

Printed and bound in Italy

This book was printed on acid-free paper.

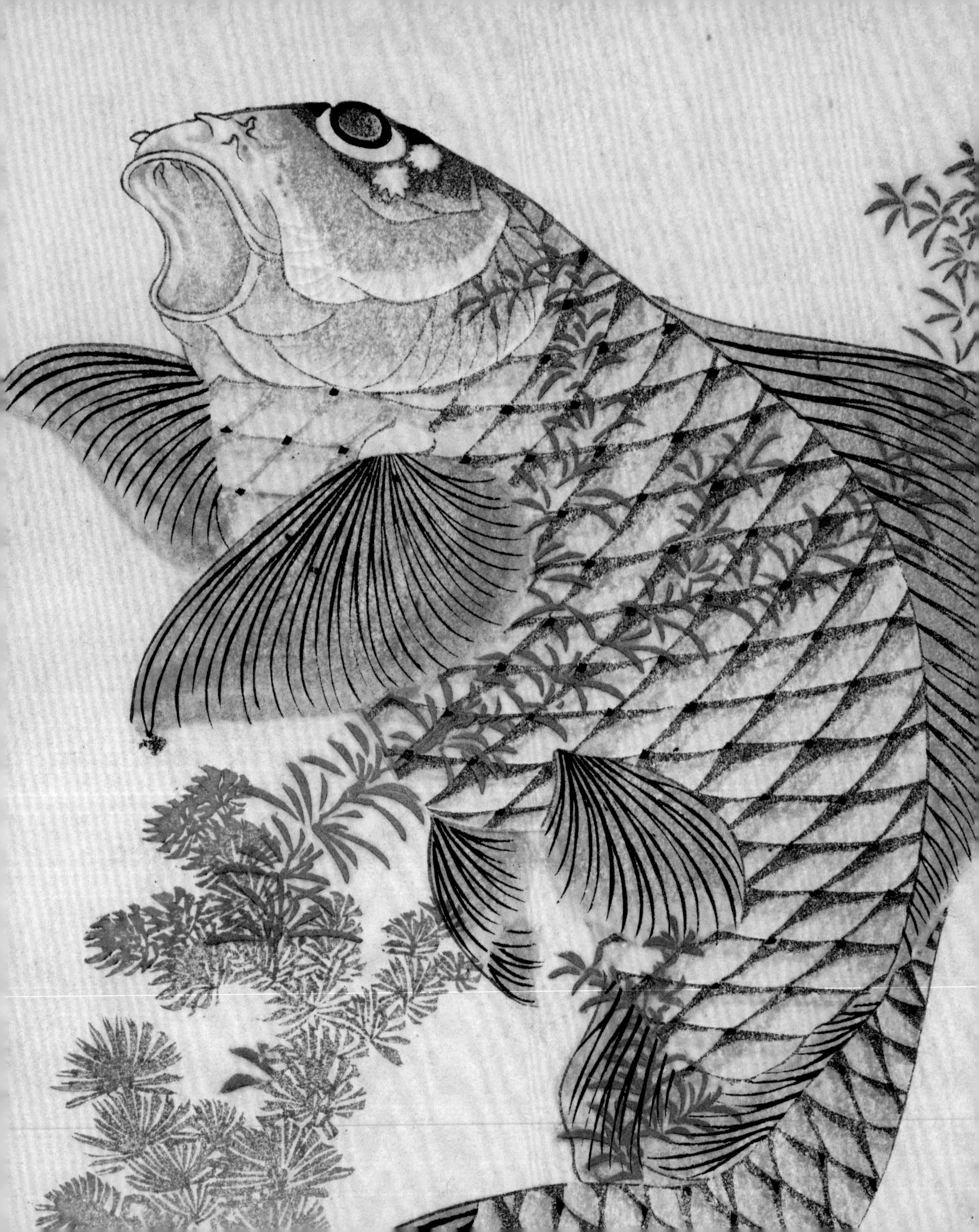